WHEN WE
VISIT JESUS
IN PRISON

A GUIDE FOR CATHOLIC MINISTRY

Chaplain Dale S. Recinella

WHEN WE VISIT JESUS IN PRISON
A Guide for Catholic Ministry
Chaplain Dale S. Recinella

Design by Patricia A. Lynch
Cover image © Inked Pixels, under license from Bigstock

Published by ACTA Publications, 4848 N. Clark St.,
Chicago, IL 60640, (800) 397-2282, actapublications.com

Nihil obstat: Deacon David Williams, Chancellor
            Censor Librorum July 21, 2016

Imprimatur: The Most Reverend Felipe J. Estévez, STD
            Bishop of St. Augustine July 21, 2016

Library of Congress Catalog Number: 2016949529
ISBN: 978-0-87946-576-6
Printed in the United States of America by Total Printing Systems
Year 30 29 28 27 26 25 24 23 22 21 20 19 18 17
Printing 12 11 10 9 8 7 6 5 4 3 2

♻ Text printed on 30% post-consumer recycled paper

*This book is dedicated to the thousands of men and women
God has allowed me to serve inside prisons and jails,
and to the hundreds of volunteers
God has allowed me to stand next to as we served them.*

This book was made possible by grants from:

The ACTA Foundation
Mundelein, Illinois

and

Art & Nancy Gase
St. Augustine, Florida

CONTENTS

PART IV: CONSTRAINTS THAT AFFECT RESTORATIVE JUSTICE

FOREWORD

Sign me up, *Brother* Dale!

I begin the honor of presenting this book to potential readers by admitting that, from the start, I never thought that I would ever find myself thinking about or highlighting the importance of the call to prison ministry. Quite frankly, I'm involved in many other things. In fact, the title selected for this book by "Brother" Dale (as Recinella is called by those involved with prisons in Florida), *When We Visit Jesus in Prison: A Guide for Catholic Ministry*, was at first a bit too much for me to absorb. My first thought was: Jesus is in prison? He can be found there?

Oh, yes, that's right, he's in the prison chapel when priests or ministers visit inmates. I would never argue—the good Catholic that I claim to be—that Jesus is not present in the Eucharist. I also would never argue that Jesus is not present in the many hardworking prison staff who, I submit, have one of the most difficult jobs in the world. That would include, I'm quite sure, the "correctional counselors" who make themselves available to help those inmates who genuinely show an interest in wanting to change their behavior. In taking on these seemingly near-impossible tasks, these committed agents are going above and beyond their call of duty and acting as instruments of good will in a place where little good is ever visibly present.

It is from that point of reference, then, that I reflect on the phrase "when we visit Jesus in prison." It causes me to pause and wonder why anyone would want to begin a book on prison ministry with such a title. Why not something more practical like, *A Catholic Layman's Guide to Volunteering in Prisons* or *What Every Catholic Volunteer Needs to Know about Prisons and Prison Ministry*? Maybe it's just me, but if I were thinking about volunteering in a prison, the thing that would grab my attention would be to know—and be forewarned about—what I would be getting myself into, lest I might become intimidated and scared or, worse, assaulted.

As I opened this book, however, expecting to begin reading about how I might need to cautiously prepare myself for prison ministry and about my need to heed the potential warnings from its author, who has spent the better part of his adult life in prison ministry, I was stunned. You see, I thought the focus of prison ministry preparation would be all about the one who was volunteering his or her time. I thought the focus would center on self-protection and Bible verse memorization. I thought I would learn about special techniques to counter arguments that God was not real and about how hard it is to find grace in a prison setting. With my thirty-plus years of law enforcement experience, along with the commensurate amount of accrued cynicism, I expected to read stories about how prison volunteers need to be keen to the tricks and not get "conned" by the cons. After all, in this kind of work, the time is short and we need to be well-prepared to meet the challenge to quickly convince prisoners to repent in order to save their souls.

I was wrong! As Dale Recinella points out, prison ministry is a faith walk, not a head trip. What he makes unmistakably clear is that the focus of this book is not about the volunteer. It's not about me, and it's not about you. It's not about anyone who thinks it would be a novel idea to volunteer in a prison because it would create good conversation at a cocktail party or that it would make a prison volunteer look good among their friends in church. It's not about self-protection or about learning any tricks of the trade at all. No, the focus is about something entirely different, and far more important. It's about discerning a call to make ourselves available in loving service by opening our own eyes and looking for Jesus in the eyes of those who are considered among the least in our society: the incarcerated. It's about visiting the Jesus who lives in each and every one of our brothers and sisters who have been locked away in prison and ostensibly forgotten about. It's about witnessing the suffering Jesus in inmates who are held captive for ransom—a ransom that they cannot pay—a ransom that they, like us, will never be able to pay.

The focus of this book is about reaching out to those who need to know and learn that there is One who has paid the ransom already. The fact that Jesus has paid the ransom for them is best illustrated by our witness that he has paid the ransom for us. That in itself is something to seriously ponder and reflect upon. We are sinners, too. Without that basic understanding and acceptance of our weak selves, we will never be able to reach out to those in prison who are in need. Brother Dale clearly explains that in order to be an agent of transformation, we must first be engaged in personal transformation ourselves, in and through our Catholic faith. That is what empowers us to be our brothers' and sisters' keeper.

To be sure, there are many who might read this book and never involve themselves in direct prison ministry. This kind of work is not for everyone, and certainly not for the faint of heart. But for those whose hearts have been set on fire to evangelize in a way consistent with what Pope Francis has declared over and over, this book is a challenge for us to awaken, to listen to Jesus calling us beyond our own limited ideas of mercy, and to see Jesus at the center of a movement to set the captives free. What perfect timing for this book to be released now, in the midst of so much national turmoil over criminal justice reform.

Let's make no mistake about what it means to set captives free; I am not suggesting that we open the doors to prisons and let everyone walk freely into society. Most inmates are not ready for that and, understandably, neither are we. What I am suggesting, though, is exactly what Dale Recinella is challenging us to do: to sense the importance of seeing Jesus in those who are held captive and to share with them the truths of our faith that, by Jesus' blood, we have all been set free. *Brother* Dale reveals to us how our suffering Lord lives in the hearts and minds of all those who are held captive—no matter what they have done—and how Jesus longs to reach out to them, with a love that only he can provide. They are, after all, God's children, no less than each one of us "free-people" are.

Many of us have been brought to our own knees in thanksgiving and gratitude for being set free—from ourselves and from sin. Through our own experience of sharing in Christ's death and resurrection, of coming to the end of ourselves and surrendering our own woundedness, we hold at our disposal the keys to God's kingdom. Because those keys are deep within our heart, we can share the "good news" with those who desperately need to be set free from their own suffering. In so doing, we become involved in alleviating the very suffering that Jesus endured for all of us. That is the powerful message of this book.

Weaving together the truths of our Trinitarian faith and themes developed through the many writings of our church forbearers and current leaders, Dale Recinella provides us with a road map to becoming an effective prison minister. I must reiterate that this book is not going to result in every reader becoming a prison minister. In fact, it might confirm to some readers that prison ministry is not how they are called to serve. But for those of us who are interested in prison ministry and how closely it is tied to the pastoral mission of the Church, this book will heighten our awareness and perhaps even encourage us to answer and pursue the call to prison ministry. Embedded in this complete and thorough manuscript are virtually all the resources available to become a Catholic prison minister; but these resources are secondary to the primary purpose of the book, which is to set our hearts on fire and assist us in understanding the nature of prison ministry in our Catholic faith. Being able to recognize the tools of a trade doesn't make anyone a natural for the task. It is only through sincere preparation and becoming aware of why the tools are important for the task that we can use them effectively.

With thirty-two-plus years of working in law enforcement under my belt, this book did exactly that for me. After reading it, I sensed more strongly than ever before that God was calling me to prison ministry. It is interesting to me, but I suppose not surprising after my many years of presenting violators of the law before judges and watching many of them be taken off to prison, that I now sense that my role—my calling—has evolved to one of accepting the challenge to reach out and to help "set the captives free." I hope and pray that, whatever the reason you have been led to read this book, some of you will sense that same calling and will be moved to engage, either directly or by becoming prayer warriors, in the ministry to "visit Jesus in prison."

Thank you, Brother Dale, for opening my eyes and for being the light of Christ for all who have been so enormously blessed to know you and your wife Susan.

George F. Kain, Ph.D.
Police Commissioner, Town of Ridgefield, Connecticut
Professor, Division of Justice and Law Administration,
Western Connecticut State University

Pope Francis washed the feet of a dozen inmates at a juvenile detention center in a Holy Thursday ritual that he celebrated for years as archbishop and is continuing now that he is pope.... "This is a symbol, it is a sign—washing your feet means I am at your service," Francis told the youngsters. "Help one another. This is what Jesus teaches us. This is what I do. And I do it with my heart. I do this with my heart because it is my duty, as a priest and bishop I must be at your service."[1]

INTRODUCTION

Imagine that you have been asked by your bishop or pastor to do volunteer ministry at a nearby jail or prison. With the assistance of your diocesan or parish ministry office, you have worked hard to obtain all the clearances necessary to enter the detention facility. You have learned all the rules about entering and leaving, signing in and signing out. You have learned which bathrooms you are allowed to use and when. You have learned which buildings and wings you are allowed to enter. You have learned how you will be searched and what you must never bring into the prison. You have learned the long list of things that you cannot even have in your locked car parked in the prison parking lot. You have memorized the internal phone number that you are to call in case of an emergency or if you are threatened or taken hostage in a locked or barricaded room or if an inmate under your responsibility suddenly has a seizure. And you have learned which phone you must use to make such calls.

You have accepted the indignities of being searched so thoroughly at the prison entrance station that the uniformed and gloved strangers who clear you know more about the moles and bumps on your backside than you do. You have tried (and are still trying) to get accustomed to razor wire and electric charged fences and to the gnawing feeling in your gut at being locked inside those fences, unable to leave—unable to even get to your car in the parking lot—unless somebody somewhere pushes a button that pops a door or a gate open for you. You have learned not to think about the fact that the someone who holds your freedom in the palm of his or her hand may be a person you do not even know, somebody you cannot even see, someone on the receiving end of a microphone or a camera embedded in the walls, someone who may not like you and may not like the fact that you are in this prison. You have learned not to think about the fact that you are totally at that stranger's mercy until you step outside the prison fence.

You knew this would not be easy. You have sought and received spiritual support and encouragement. Your friends at church have prayed with you for spiritual guidance and protection. Your bishop or pastor has prayed over you, commissioned you, perhaps even blessed and anointed you. Your spouse and family struggled with the idea of you serving in this way. But they have come to terms with it. Before you leave the house to head to the prison, they hug you and whisper, "Say hello to Jesus for me."

And now you are there, inside, standing in front of a chapel full of inmates in blue or grey or white or orange prison clothes. Or standing at cell front in a maximum security segregation wing looking at one man through the Plexiglas window in the solid steel door of his cell. Or sitting in a metal floor-bolted chair in a small circle of female inmates in a day room at a detention center. Or sitting in a molded plastic chair in front of a bulletproof glass wall holding a phone tight against your ear to hear the connection to the death row inmate on the other-side of the wall.

The inmate right in front of you stares so intently that you feel disrobed. Not just through your clothes, but as though he or she is peering through your very skin to your soul. His face does not register approval or amusement. She does not look hopeful or grateful.

WHEN WE VISIT JESUS IN PRISON

Instead you sense a kind of dismay, maybe even disbelief or disappointment. The words finally spoken without real interest or anticipation cut you like a knife.

"Why should I spend my time with you instead of watching the game on TV in the day room or pushing iron on the rec yard?"

"What the heck are you doing here?"

"What exactly do you hope to accomplish?"

In the moment of awkward silence that allows the blunt-force trauma of the inmate's lack of enthusiasm at your hard-earned availability to sink into consciousness, you realize those are darn good questions. They deserve darn good answers.

The purpose of this book is to provide the reader with answers to those questions. Not just any answers, but the answers based upon the mission and identity of the Catholic Church, although we hope some of what is here may be valuable to others of different faith, as well.

We will begin by drawing from the social justice teaching, the ecclesial framework and the catechetical practices of the Church to answer those questions. We will start from the social and economic conditions of the 1980s and 1990s, the period when many current inmates left society for the world inside the prison fences. When those inmates speak of the *world outside*, that is the society they are referencing. Our survey of that world will include the response of our Church to the needs and conditions of those times, a response that is not framed in isolation but rather is rooted in the broader mission of the Church. That will require us to wrestle with the purpose of punishment and criminal justice. We will also address the Catholic understanding of prison ministry as evangelization and how such ministry is to be conducted in a pluralistic setting, especially when there is hostility to Catholic teaching and beliefs.

Then we will look at the most human elements of Catholic prison ministry: first, addressing the needs of the prison ministry volunteers themselves. How does one live out their faith as a Catholic prison ministry volunteer without burnout, without losing their grip on the fundamentals of faith and Eucharistic community?

Next we address the humanity of the offender. Why do people

commit crime? Do those who have broken the law think differently than other people? Do prison ministry volunteers need to watch out for patterns of criminal behavior?

And what are the pastoral needs of people held in prison? What about the officers and staff who work inside the walls and fences? What are the pastoral needs of those affected by incarceration, such as the family and loved ones? Are there special pastoral needs for different types of inmates: the newly incarcerated, the seriously ill, the dying, or those held long-term in solitary confinement cells?

What are the pastoral needs of women held in prison? What about inmates with children on the outside? Do the mentally ill in prison have special needs?

Finally, we must address how Catholic restorative justice teaching challenges us to make changes to our criminal justice system. What are the economic constraints in our society that inhibit such changes? What are the religious constraints in our culture that push against improving our criminal justice system?

This book is intended to introduce the reader to a very broad picture of the facts and realities of Catholic prison ministry in our modern world, illuminated by Catholic teaching and traditions. Where additional resources can be helpful to the reader for deeper understanding, they will be identified.

When possible throughout this writing, I will illuminate and personalize various points by sharing some of my actual experiences from more than twenty-five years of prison ministry. Most often, this will be done through adaptations of various on-point articles I wrote that were first published in *The Florida Catholic*, the statewide newspaper of the Catholic bishops of Florida, or in the *I Was in Prison Online Ezine*. A dotted line before and after each article distinguishes it from the text.

One of the most respected scholars of our day on the subject of the Catholic Church and criminal justice is Professor Andrew Skotnicki of the religious studies department at Manhattan College in New York City. In his book *Criminal Justice and the Catholic Church*, he asserts: "I believe it is essential that Christians find Christ in the prisoner, or that Christ *be* the prisoner"[2] (emphasis in original).

Just out of sight, in the background of every principle set forth in this book on Catholic prison ministry, is my deep conviction that when we visit a man or woman in prison, we visit Jesus Christ coming to us in the face of the prisoner.

As Pope Francis spoke to the young inmates on Holy Thursday of 2013, he told them that it is his duty, as a priest and bishop, to be at the service of those in prison. For those of us who are Catholic but are not priests and bishops, we are offered the privilege of participating in this pastoral work of the Church. As a Catholic prison ministry volunteer, you are part of an ever-expanding army of workers who share in the pastoral ministry of our bishops and priests by bringing the Good News into the darkest and most isolated corners of western civilization: our prisons, jails, and detention centers. God bless your efforts with an abundant harvest and with abundant joy.

Dale S. Recinella
Catholic Correctional Chaplain
Florida Death Row

Christmas through a Looking Glass

It is Christmas Eve morning. Nothing could have prepared me for this.

I process through the guard station and collect my chapel keys.

Spirals of razor wire are heaped two-stories high on the three rows of electrified fence. The silver-gray teeth glisten like tinsel in the crisp morning air. A dozen inmates peer at me from the other side. They are huddling at the gate that separates the chapel from the prison compound.

"Merry Christmas," smiles the officer. My stomach tenses into a knot.

She hits the button that releases huge electric locks on the steel access doors. A loud bang echoes through the sally port. I step inside the prison. The knot in my belly tightens even more.

The inmates at the gate beat their arms, warming themselves against the

December chill. Small clouds of breath hang in front of their blue fatigues.

Why does this picture jar me? The specifics are no different than usual. It should be just another other day as a volunteer spiritual counselor at Florida's Appalachee Correctional Institution.

But this is not just another day. It is Christmas Eve.

In that moment, I am amazed that I have never wondered what Christmas is like behind bars.

Chapel appointments with volunteers are by "call-out," written requests processed through administration. We open the chapel. A clerk hands me the day's roster—19 call-outs. A normal morning is five.

I phone my wife, "I'll be here until 6:00."

I am wrong. We won't close the chapel until 9:30 Christmas Eve night.

But there's no way I could know that. It's my first time in prison on the morning before Christmas.

I dig in with coffee and my first inmate appointment at 8:30 am. We pray and I ask, "What's on your heart this morning?"

"Give me a reason to not go for the wall," he whispers.

We both know the term is prison slang for feigning an escape attempt in front of the guards, in the hope they will have to kill you.

Men are said to have done such things when they received a "Dear John" letter from their wife or learned of the death of a child. Is Christmas here that painful?

We talk, we cry, we pray. Man after man, blue shirt after blue shirt. Murderers. Rapists. Molesters. No one to call at Christmas. No one to write. No one to see. Their families too far away to visit. Their children severed and adopted by other fathers.

About 5:00 o'clock I tell the clerks we need more "prison Kleenex." The rolls of toilet paper we unwrapped that morning are all down to the cardboard.

My last call-out, an intelligent and verbal man, has met regularly with me all year.

"I'm not saying I shouldn't be here," tears tug at his eyes, "I did terrible things and don't even know why. I can understand why society wants me behind this fence. I'll be here the rest of my life. But I'm a human being. I still need friends and relationships with normal people. I'm a baptized, practicing

WHEN WE VISIT JESUS IN PRISON

Christian. Christmas is our day. Where are the Christians?"

My lame response about people confusing compassion toward wrong-doers with approval of their bad behavior only angers him.

"Jesus said that when his followers visit an inmate, they visit *him*!" he grips the tissue roll with both hands. "Jesus didn't say the inmate had to be innocent. Why isn't anybody visiting Jesus at Christmas?"

Looking away, I stammer, "I don't know."

Soon, it's time for us to end.

"What do you want to pray for?" I ask.

He leans back in his chair, as if he is talking through the ceiling to the heaven above, "What do I want God to give me for Christmas?"

"Sure," I reply.

"That every Christmas all the prisons in Florida will be busting at the seams from all the Christians trying to get in to visit Jesus."

"Brother," I caution, "that prayer could take a long time to answer."

He shrugs, "I'll be here."

PART I

THE FRAMEWORK
FOR MINISTRY

"[Tzedakah][1] which is linked with justice, was developed in Christianity in the Social Doctrine of the Church. It took quite some time to assimilate the concept of social justice, though now it is accepted everywhere."

Cardinal Jorge Mario Bergoglio,
now known as Pope Francis[2]

CHAPTER 1

The Social Justice Framework of Credible and Responsible Prison Ministry

In his discourses with Rabbi Abraham Skorka, then Cardinal Jorge Mario Bergoglio, now known as Pope Francis, describes how the deepest meanings of the concept from the Hebrew Scriptures of an affirmative duty to care for the poor—*tzedakah*—have been seeded into Christian understanding through the words of Jesus Christ. For example, with regard to those in prison, Catholics look to the description by Jesus of the Judgment of the Nations:

"When the Son of Man comes in his glory, and all the angels with him, he will sit upon his glorious throne, and all the nations will be assembled before him. And he will separate them one from another, as a shepherd separates the sheep from the goats. He will place the sheep on his right and the goats on his left. Then the king will say to those on his right, 'Come, you who are blessed by my Father. Inherit the kingdom prepared for you from the foundation of the world. For I was…in prison and you visited me.' Then the righteous will answer him and say, 'Lord, when did we see you…in prison and visit you?' And the king will say to them in reply, 'Amen, I say to you, whatever you did for one of these least brothers of mine, you did for me.'

Then he will say to those on his left, 'Depart from me, you accursed, into the eternal fire prepared for the devil and his angels. For I was…in prison, and you did not care for me.' Then they will answer and say, 'Lord, when did we see you…in prison and not minister to your needs?' He will answer them, 'Amen, I say to you, what you did not do for one of these least ones, you did not do for me.' And these will go off to eternal punishment, but the righteous to eternal life."[3]

Some commentators have summed-up the words of Jesus Christ in Matthew 25:34-40 as: radical evil is apathy in the face of relievable human suffering. This usage of *radical* is in its classic sense as "the root," in other words, the root of evil is apathy in the face of relievable human suffering. One rarely hears about social justice, our God-given duty to care for our fellow man, in popular descriptions of the Last Judgment. But in Jesus' description of the Last Judgment, it appears that our choices whether or not to extend ourselves to care for the suffering of others matter a great deal.

If despite Matthew 25:34-40 we still harbor doubt as to whether Jesus would really judge us for mere indifference (apathy) to the suffering of others, we need only look at his Gospel parable of Dives and Lazarus in Luke 16:19-31:

"There was a rich man who dressed in purple garments and fine linen and dined sumptuously each day. And lying at his door was a poor man named Lazarus, covered with sores, who would gladly have eaten his fill of the scraps that fell from the rich man's table. Dogs even used to come and lick his sores.

"When the poor man died, he was carried away by angels to the bosom of Abraham. The rich man also died and was

WHEN WE VISIT JESUS IN PRISON

buried, and from the netherworld, where he was in torment, he raised his eyes and saw Abraham far off and Lazarus at his side. And he cried out, 'Father Abraham, have pity on me. Send Lazarus to dip the tip of his finger in water and cool my tongue, for I am suffering torment in these flames.'

"Abraham replied, 'My child, remember that you received what was good during your lifetime while Lazarus likewise received what was bad; but now he is comforted here, whereas you are tormented. Moreover, between us and you a great chasm is established to prevent anyone from crossing who might wish to go from our side to yours or from your side to ours.'

"He said, 'Then I beg you, father, send him to my father's house, for I have five brothers, so that he may warn them, lest they too come to this place of torment.'

"But Abraham replied, 'They have Moses and the prophets. Let them listen to them.'

"He said, 'Oh no, father Abraham, but if someone from the dead goes to them, they will repent.'

"Then Abraham said, 'If they will not listen to Moses and the prophets, neither will they be persuaded if someone should rise from the dead.'"[4]

Lord, Send Us Your Spirit

In my twenty-some years of practicing law, I was never in court as a lawyer. Never filed a complaint. Never argued a motion. My arenas were conference rooms and closing tables. Now, here I am in court.

I have been subpoenaed to testify in the lawsuit about the summer heat on Florida's death row. Not too many people walk around back there. Who else can they call to provide onsite experience of the grueling effects of incessant Florida summer heat and moisture on the human constitution?

While waiting my turn in the last row of the courtroom's wooden pews, I imagine the questions that might be asked. "Probably they will start with:

How hot is it?"

"Sounds like the lead in for a bad joke on the old *Tonight Show*," I chuckle to myself. "The answer might sound like a bad punch line."

Is it okay to say "as hot as I thought hell would be, but with higher humidity" on the witness stand in a federal court? Probably not. But I cannot give temperatures. I am not allowed to carry a thermometer around the prison.

Maybe I should describe how, in all the towns surrounding that prison, cows are dropping dead on the farms in droves. Outside temperatures have been hitting a hundred or higher with humidity in the high 90s.

It is a lot hotter than the **tourist temperature**. That is what everyone calls the official temperature from Jacksonville, which seems geared to convincing northern tourists that it is safe to come on down to Florida. Those readings do not appear related at all to the physical environment in a concrete and steel box—with no air conditioning, shade or air movement—in the middle of a former cow pasture in rural Florida.

My mental gymnastics are curtailed by the jolting testimony of a death row inmate who has taken the stand. He is 50-ish and has been asked to describe the physical effects of the heat. He testifies that he has been filing grievances about the summer heat for almost ten years. He is required to take psychotropic medications that have instructions to avoid excessive heat. He describes dizziness. Disorientation. Confusion. Palpitations. Nausea. Vomiting. Blood pressure irregularities. Breathing difficulties. Heat and stress induced sleep disorders. He has passed out and split his head open against the metal sink in his cell.

Can we believe our ears? Is anybody listening? I look around the room. How are people responding to this?

To my right is a group of escort officers from the death row prison, listening attentively and solemnly. They have probably been in those wings in July and August. They know what it is like to be in that heat for just thirty or forty minutes, let alone to live in it.

Suddenly a pert young woman seated about three rows in front of them stands up and turns her back to the witness stand. Her crisp blue suit and badge give her away as a government agent of some kind. She has obviously heard enough. Her meticulously coifed blonde hair swirls to catch up with the rotation of her perfectly exercised body, as she gestures towards the

WHEN WE VISIT JESUS IN PRISON

officers. Sneering sharply, with eyes rolling and nostrils flaring in a snort, she sarcastically signifies her dehumanization of the man on the witness stand.

The officers try to act as though they did not see her. I saw her. I am aghast.

This is our response to human agony?

This is our spirit in the face of relievable human suffering created by us, our man-made torment for those controlled and dominated by us?

Lord, save us from our hearts of stone. Cast out from us this dark spirit and give us hearts of flesh.

Lord, please, send us your Spirit.

The social justice teaching of the Catholic Church does have political implications, but it is far more than simply political. The foundational notion of *solidarity* recognizes that we are all responsible for each other as members of the human family. This is closely linked with *subsidiarity*, which focuses our problem solving efforts on the most basic community level possible. These principles of Catholic social justice teaching introduce a *relational* aspect to our understanding of our duty to those who are suffering. Relationship implies commitment. Reflecting upon Jesus' description of the Last Judgment, then Cardinal Jorge Mario Bergoglio, now known as Pope Francis, emphasizes this aspect of Jesus' teaching:

> In Christianity, the attitude we must have toward the poor is, in its essence, that of true commitment. And [Jesus] added something else: this commitment must be person to person, in the flesh. It is not enough to mediate this commitment through institutions.... They do not excuse us from our obligation of establishing personal contact with the needy.... Those in prison must be visited.... It is terribly difficult for me to go to a prison because of the harshness of life there. But I go anyway, because the Lord wants me to be there in the flesh, alongside those in need, in poverty, in pain.... We cannot accept the underlying idea that we who are doing well give something to those who

are doing badly, but they should stay that way, far away from us. That is not Christian.[5]

Our touchstone for the social justice framework for credible and responsible prison ministry is the year 2000 Statement of the Catholic Bishops of the United States, *Responsibility, Rehabilitation and Restoration: A Catholic Perspective on Crime and Criminal Justice*.[6] The statement challenges us to break out of political paradigms that offer only false or extreme solutions and, instead, to see that crime demands not only punishment and accountability but also rehabilitation and restoration. Crime victims deserve our best efforts toward healing and restoration. And our communities deserve preservation of the common good and restoration of the harm done.

> [A] Catholic approach does not give up on those who violate these laws. We believe that both victims and offenders are children of God. Despite their very different claims on society, their lives and dignity should be protected and respected. We seek justice, not vengeance. We believe punishment must have clear purposes; protecting society and rehabilitating those who violate the law.[7]

As Catholics, we are mindful that the Jesus Christ of Scripture allowed himself to be incarcerated as an inmate. In Jesus' description of the Great Judgment, he told us that when we visit the least of our brethren in prison, we visit him. The Good Samaritan in the Gospel (Luke 10:25-37) chose compassionately to inconvenience himself and spend his own money in order to bring healing and restoration to a victim of crime. And the Gospel story of the Prodigal Son (Luke 15:11-32) reminds us all that we are to rejoice and celebrate the repentance and reformation of the evildoer, rather than stand in resentment like the elder brother that Jesus described. This comprehensive understanding of the problems of crime and justice in our society is rooted in the mission of the Church. It also requires us to squarely face a fundamental question: are prisoners human beings?

Are Prisoners Human Beings?

We have already synthesized a foundational moral principle: Apathy in the face of relievable human suffering is radical evil.

That maxim begs a deeper question: Are prisoners human beings?

If prisoners are not human beings, then apathy in the face of their suffering may be morally permissible. Put differently, the question may be asked: Does one lose his or her status as a human being by virtue of incarceration? The Bible teaches that every human being is made in the image and likeness of God.[8]

> Then God said: Let us make human beings in our image,
> after our likeness.... God created mankind in his image; in the
> image of God he created them; male and female he created them.
> Genesis 1:26-27

It is clear, therefore, for people of biblical faith (and the Catholic faith is profoundly biblical) that every inmate started out in the image and likeness of God. In other words, each inmate began as a human being.

Thus, we may refine our question as follows: Do felons lose their status as human beings by virtue of their conviction and incarceration?

We can look for guidance in our answer to the words of Pope Paul VI given in his address at Boy's Town in Rome, January 1, 1972:[9]

> And there is another justice which concerns man's nature itself:
> the justice that wants every man to be treated as a man.... Every
> man has his dignity, an inviolable dignity: woe betide anyone who
> touches it! It matters not whether he is little or great, poor or rich,
> white or black. Every man has his rights and duties, because of
> which he deserves to be treated as a person. Indeed, we Christians
> say that every man is our brother. He must be treated as a brother:
> that means he must be loved.... The smaller, the poorer, the more
> suffering, the more defenseless, even the lower a man has fallen,
> the more he deserves to be assisted, raised up, cared for, and hon-
> ored. We learn this from the Gospel.... This is justice![10]

Could this dignity of the human person of which Pope Paul VI is speaking even reside with those who have committed horrible crimes?

It certainly seems so, especially based upon the words of Pope John Paul II:

> A sign of hope is the increasing recognition that the dignity of human life must never be taken away, even in the case of someone who has done great evil.[11]

This is the second step in our effort to determine the moral parameters for punishment of prisoners: Inmates in prisons are human beings and retain their right to be treated with the dignity of a human person, made in the image and likeness of God.

....

The principle that every human being is made in the image and likeness of God found in Genesis 1:26-27 is referred to as the *imago Dei* (image of God). The Catholic understanding of human dignity simply recognizes the *imago Dei* as a reality that must be incorporated into our choices and our policies.

Given the facts that prisoners are human beings and justice requires that we are to love them, what is our response to the suffering of those who are incarcerated?

....

As I Have Loved You

To address the moral nature of punishment, its purposes and limitations in our first-world American society: *First*, we synthesized a foundational moral principle: Apathy in the face of relievable human suffering is radical evil.

Next, we determined that prisoners are human beings, made in the image and likeness of God and that such human dignity must never be taken away from them, even in the case of someone who has done great evil.

And, through the words of Pope Paul VI, we understand the practical ramification that prisoners, even those who have fallen to the depths, must

WHEN WE VISIT JESUS IN PRISON

be loved, and that doing so is justice.

The next step in our inquiry is obvious: it is the basic question "what is love?"

Our attempt to fashion an answer from Scripture faces an immediate dilemma. There are three root words for love in the Greek: *erōs, philia,* and *agapē.*[12]

We commonly think of *erōs* as being sexual in nature, as meant in the word erotic. Some scholars, however, point out that the essence of *erōs* is its conditional nature: I only give if I get. The object of this love is a thing used for my gratification. Thus, I can *erōs* (love) pasta or *erōs* (love) my girlfriend. When either ceases to gratify me, I do not love it or her anymore. It is by nature conditional and self-interested.

Philia also has a commonly understood meaning: brotherly or sisterly love. That is the root of the name Philadelphia, the city of brotherly love. *Philia* is most like friendship.

The term *agapē* is much tougher to pin down. We usually start by distinguishing it from the other two, by describing what it is *not*.[13] It is a love that is not conditional and is much broader and deeper in scope than the solidarity among brothers and sisters in the same boat. The word *agapē* is even used to describe the nature of God's love for us. Sometimes the word "charity" is used to translate *agapē,* especially when the Scriptures are talking about giving alms or caring for the poor. But charity, in our way of thinking, is a vastly different love than the kind I have for my children, church members, or next-door neighbors.

The essence of *agapē* seems to be the lack of any requirement for reciprocity. This love is love just because it is.[14]

All three Greek words are translated into English as love. Which kind of love is the love that every person deserves, even those who have fallen into the depths? Which kind of love is the love of justice? What is the love we Christians are called to live out with our fellow man, including prisoners?

Erōs does not appear in the Greek New Testament. Not even once. Out of the over 300 times that the words for love appear in the Greek New Testament, the word *philia* is used less than 30 times. The other times, the word for love is *agapē.*[15]

In the critical passages from the Gospel of John, where the teaching of

Jesus becomes so revolutionary as to use himself, his life, and his deeds as the definition for love. The Savior commands us to love one another as he has loved us.[16] The word used for love in the Greek text of John's Gospel below is *agapē*:

> I give you a new commandment: Love one another. As I have loved you, so you also should love one another. This is how all will know that you are my disciples, if you have love for one another.
> John 13:34-35

Moreover, this Christian disinterested love precludes retaliation for offenses.[17] It has been said that based upon the life and teachings of Jesus Christ, the best definition of *agapē* is the willingness to suffer without the desire to get even; the willingness to serve without the desire for anything in return, not even gratitude.[18]

We are honing in on the core issue, the difference between love and revenge. The New Testament Scriptures forbid one and command the other. We better know the difference between the two.

What is the difference between love and vengeance?

In the *Compendium of the Social Doctrine of the Church* we are reminded that "God, in Christ, redeems not only the individual person but also the social relations existing between men." [¶52][19] The *Compendium* further explains that the Church's mission of redemption extends to every aspect of the social plane, transforming all human relationships. [¶53] The very model of Trinitarian love becomes "the basis of the meaning and value of the person, of social relations, of human activity in the world." [¶54] And this mission of transformation is a not just a historical need, but is a "fundamental requirement of our time, as well." [¶55] The promised justice of the new earth that fills Christian hope is the ultimate restoration in and through Jesus Christ of our social relations.[20]

WHEN WE VISIT JESUS IN PRISON

The good things—such as human dignity, brotherhood and free-
dom, all the good fruits of nature and of human enterprise—that
in the Lord's Spirit and according to his command have spread
throughout the earth, having been purified of every stain, illumi-
nated and transfigured, belong to the Kingdom of truth and life,
of holiness and grace, of justice, of love, and of peace that Christ
will present to the Father, and it is there that we shall once again
find them. The words of Christ in their solemn truth will then
resound for all people: "Come, O blessed of my Father, inherit
the kingdom prepared for you from the foundation of the world;
for I was hungry and you gave me food, I was thirsty and you
gave me drink, I was a stranger and you welcomed me, I was
naked and you clothed me, I was sick and you visited me, I was
in prison and you came to me…. As you did it to one of the least
of my brethren, you did it to me" (Matthew 25:34-36,40). [¶57]

Prominent in the social justice and catechetical traditions of the
Catholic Church is the role of personal relationships in mediating this
fulfillment of the human person.

Being conformed to Christ and contemplating his face instill in
Christians an irrepressible longing for a foretaste in this world,
in the context of human relationships, of what will be a reality
in the definitive world to come; thus Christians strive to give
food, drink, clothing, shelter, care, a welcome and company to
the Lord who knocks at the door (cf. Matthew 25:35-37). [¶58]

Consequently, for the Catholic prison ministry volunteer, the
mission is always much broader and much deeper than what is simply apparent in the moment. He or she is in fact always embarked
upon a mission of evangelization that enfleshes the Gospel in every
corner of society and in every circumstance. As the *Compendium of
the Social Doctrine of the Church* relates, this means "infusing into the
human heart the power of meaning and freedom found in the Gospel in order to promote a society befitting mankind because it befits

Christ: It means building a city of man that is more human because it is in greater conformity with the Kingdom of God." [¶63]

There is no problem of mission creep in this deep understanding of evangelization. Moreover, the elevation of our natural human and social relationships to the higher plane of the supernatural is simply the faithful living out of that mission.

Every time Catholic volunteers enter the close of a prison or detention facility, they do so in order to overcome the sin-laden futility of the fallen world, to deliver the Good News of the Incarnation to those subject to incarceration, to proclaim to them that God's love is all-present and all-powerful here and now, even for those inside the barbed wire fences:

> Man is touched by this love in the fullness of his being: a being that is corporeal and spiritual, that is in a solidary relationship with others. The whole man—not a detached soul or a being closed within its own individuality, but a person and a society of persons—is involved in the salvific economy of the Gospel. [¶65]

In *Christifideles Laici*, Pope John Paul II emphasizes the significance of this aspect of the Church's mission:

> To rediscover and make others rediscover the inviolable dignity of every human person makes up an essential task, in a certain sense, the central and unifying task of the service which the Church, and lay faithful in her, are called to render to the human family.[21]

This key principle in Catholic social doctrine is the God-given dignity of human life.

> The fundamental starting point for all of Catholic social teaching is the defense of human life and dignity: Every human person is created in the image and likeness of God and has an inviolable dignity, value, and worth.... Therefore, both the

WHEN WE VISIT JESUS IN PRISON

most wounded victim and the most callous criminal retain their humanity.[22]

Vengeance Is Not Ours

In developing our inquiry into the moral nature of punishment, its purposes and limitations in our first world American society, we have addressed several critical issues:

+ Apathy in the face of relievable human suffering is radical evil.
+ Popes Paul VI and John Paul II tell us that prisoners are human beings, made in the image and likeness of God.
+ Such human dignity must never be taken away, even in the case of someone who has done great evil.
+ Even those who have fallen to the depths must be loved, and doing so is justice.
+ Jesus defines love for us by commanding us to love one another as He loved us.

How does punishment fit into this template? Are there to be no consequences for wrongs committed against society and its members? Can punishment be loving?

We begin our search for answers to such questions with paragraph 2266 of *The Catechism of the Catholic Church*. The text tells us that the state's duty to safeguard the common good of society includes its efforts "to curb the spread of behavior harmful to people's rights and to the basic rules of civil society." Therefore, government has the right and duty to inflict appropriate punishment. Such punishment must be proportionate to the offense committed.

There are no surprises here, except perhaps the shock of how grossly disproportionate some of our punishments are. Poor nonviolent offenders, especially minorities with addictions, can face prison terms of ten, twenty, or more years. Meanwhile, some corporate executives and their high paid professional advisors who have devised schemes to defraud the public, bankrupting the pensions of their own employees and of untold tens of thousands of investors, receive a slap on the wrist. In some cases, we are told that even though billions of dollars have disappeared, no one can find any law that has been broken.

Mercy for the rich, with the guillotine for the poor, cannot stand in the face of Scripture or Christian Tradition. A system of punishments that are not proportional does not meet the requirements of our faith.

Paragraph 2266 of *The Catechism of the Catholic Church* also tells us that the primary purpose of punishment is "redressing the disorder introduced by the offense." Based on *Webster's* definitions, redress means setting things right, compensating for an injury, removing the cause of a grievance or complaint, or avenging a loss or injury by paying retribution. When a crime has been committed, society and the victim have suffered a disorder. The graver the crime, the greater the disorder.

Punishment, therefore, must attempt to set right this disorder—for the victim, society, and perpetrator. This "setting right" can take place through restitution or some other means: e.g., the removal of the perpetrator, the cause of the grievance, from society by confinement in jail or prison.

Retribution can also be part of this concept. The word literally means "to pay back." Ideally retribution should mean a punishment that compensates society and the victim for their loss. In its current popular usage, however, the word **retribution** has come to mean "revenge," that is, the vengeance that seeks an eye for an eye and a tooth for a tooth. Such retribution is antithetical to Scripture. "Vengeance is mine, I will repay, says the Lord." Romans 12:19 [23] This position is also unsupported by *The Catechism of the Catholic Church*, which provides at paragraph 2302:

> To desire vengeance in order to do evil to someone who should be punished is illicit, but it is praiseworthy to impose restitution "to correct vices and maintain justice."

The term used to describe punishment that seeks not revenge but rather seeks to redress the disorder through restitution to and restoration of the community, the victims, and the offender, is *restorative justice*.

Restorative justice is loving punishment.

In our efforts to respond to crime in accordance with the teaching of our Catholic Church, the U.S. Conference of Catholic Bishops suggest that the four elements of the sacrament of Penance (also known as the Sacrament of Confession or Reconciliation) in our sacramental heritage provide a poignant model for our social response to crime and the offender:[24]

+ **Contrition:** Genuine sorrow, regret, or grief over one's wrongs and a serious resolution not to repeat the wrong.
+ **Confession:** Clear acknowledgment and true acceptance of responsibility for the hurtful behavior.
+ **Satisfaction:** The external sign of one's desire to amend one's life. [e.g., restitution].
+ **Absolution:** After someone has shown contrition, acknowledged his or her sin and offered satisfaction, then Jesus, through the ministry of the priest and in the company of the church community, forgives the sin and welcomes the person back into "communion." (Bracketed language added.)

It is important not to confuse these elements with expectations of an emotional, dewy-eyed, Hollywood-style expression of remorse. Such displays are highly overrated. As will be discussed in *Chapter 8: Characteristics of Criminal Thinking*, any well-practiced psychopath can deliver an academy-award-worthy performance of remorse that means absolutely nothing. Nor is remorse meant to describe the off-handed whimsical gesture that passes culturally as "I'm sorry." The bishops' model requires a "sorrow of the soul and detestation for sin committed, together with the resolution not to sin again."[25]

Based upon my own experience, the proof of the pudding is in the eating. True remorse, true contrition, is made manifest in the present lived life—not in the way the incarcerated say they will live on the outside someday if they get out of prison. That is wishful thinking. The proof of their change of heart is in the lived life today, while still in prison.

Sometimes the men or women in a prison will tell a volunteer, "You think you know certain prisoners, but day in and day out they are not at all like the way they are in front of you." No prison ministry volunteer wants to hear that about one of their charges. *Chapter 9: Pastoral Needs of Inmates* deals with the different ways one can respond to such information.

But a prison ministry volunteer will also hear the hoped for reports from the community inside the fence. "That guy who has been coming to your RCIA class has really changed. We all know it. I want what he has. Can I start, too?" Such changes in the choices of a man or woman's lived life, here and now in prison, is usually a reliable indicator of true contrition.

An integral component of this model is the act of forgiveness. Forgiveness is not a new or recent concept in our Christian response to human injury. In the *Our Father* or *Lord's Prayer* that Jesus taught his disciples, we pray "forgive us our trespasses as we forgive those who trespass against us." Such a biblical response to human injury based on the teachings of the Christian Scriptures does not allow for human vengeance.

This truth was fully incorporated into the *Catechism of the Council of Trent* (1566) which provides as follows in the teachings concerning murder and the Fifth Commandment:[26]

> **Forgiveness of Injuries Commanded:** But the most important duty of all, and that which is the fullest expression of charity, and to the practice of which we should most habituate ourselves, is to pardon and forgive from the heart the injuries which we may have received from others. The Sacred Scriptures, as we have already observed, frequently admonish and exhort us to a full compliance with this duty. Not only do they pronounce *blessed* those who do this, but they also declare that God grants pardon to those who really fulfill this duty, while he refuses to pardon those who neglect it, or refuse to obey it.

How to Persuade Men to Forgive Injuries: As the desire of revenge is almost natural to man, it becomes necessary for the pastor to exert his utmost diligence not only to instruct but also earnestly to persuade the faithful that a Christian should forgive and forget injuries; and as this is a duty frequently inculcated by sacred writers, [the priest] should consult them on the subject in order to be able to subdue the pertinacity [perverse stubbornness] of those whose minds are obstinately bent on revenge, and he should have ready the forcible and appropriate arguments which those Fathers piously employed.

Trent's four-hundred-fifty-year-old model does not support punishment and the suffering of incarceration for their own sake, for mere vengeance. Punishment and the suffering of imprisonment must serve a purpose consistent with the principles discussed above, which is why Catholic bishops still teach:[27]

Punishment by civil authorities for criminal activity should serve three principal purposes:

1. the preservation and protection of the common good of society,
2. the restoration of public order, and
3. the restoration and conversion of the offender.

Pope John Paul II Sets the Stage

The issue of prisons and punishment is among the most burning of our day. For many of the currently imprisoned men and women who came to prison in the 1990s and the 2000s, the society they experienced before incarceration is still their reality for life on the outside. That reality is abysmal.

According to the U.S. Justice Department for 2005, our country's inmate population exceeded two million. One out of every seventy-five men in the

U.S. was behind bars. The national incarceration rate of 715 prisoners for every 100,000 in population was the highest in the world, far surpassing the incarceration rates in England (143), Canada (116), Mexico (169) and even Russia (584).

If we broaden our vision to include Americans who are on probation or parole, the 2005 total was a staggering 6.9 million people.

One out of every thirty-two Americans was under the supervision of a state or federal correctional system.

In the year 2004 alone, 630,000 formerly incarcerated Americans were returned to their home communities. Most had almost no assistance in restarting their lives. Almost all of them were replaced by new admissions to prisons and jails. The implications of this churning cycle affect every corner of our society.

Our democratic institutions are affected. In 48 out of 50 states, inmates found guilty of felonies were prohibited from voting. While some states return the right to vote automatically when one's debt to society has been repaid, as of 2005 an estimated 1.7 million Americans had not regained their right to vote.

Despite this disenfranchisement of the incarcerated, prisoners are included in the census numbers that determine voting districts. In effect, millions of people have been moved from their home voting districts (frequently urban areas) to alien districts (frequently rural areas), shifting political power to those whose interests may be directly adversarial to the inmates' home base.

Also of concern are the hundreds of thousands of inmates nationwide who are in jails awaiting trial or serving time for misdemeanors. These Americans retain their constitutional right to vote. Almost no one, however, can find any system that has been established to facilitate their voting in any election: local, state, or federal.

Our veterans are affected. As of 2005 at least a quarter-million American veterans were currently incarcerated.

Our economic and political institutions are affected. This effect goes far beyond creating a dependency by local economies upon high incarceration rates in order to maintain jobs and essential services.

Prison privatization and the use of prison labor by private enterprise are of growing concern nationally, especially in the South. One study of the year 2000 elections established that prison companies made over $1.1 million in political contributions in the 14 southern states, targeting state officials involved in criminal justice decisions. American prisons are threatening to become big business. As recent criminal justice experience nationwide evidences, mixing prisons and profit can create a huge potential for conflicts of interest.

Our communities are affected. Most prisoners are from disadvantaged minority communities. That is where they return upon release. The burden of supporting millions of politically and economically disenfranchised Americans falls squarely and unfairly upon the communities with the least resources. While this is a pervasive reality for our inner-city communities, it is no less true with respect to our Native American populations and the horrendous conditions in the jails run by the Bureau of Indian Affairs.

As American Catholics, we must respond to this crisis.

Pope John Paul II leads our way:

> Measures that are simply repressive or punitive…are inadequate for reaching the objective of an authentic recuperation of inmates. Therefore, it is necessary to rethink the situation in prisons in its very foundation and ends…. The dutiful application of justice to defend citizens and public order must not contrast with the due attention to the rights of prisoners and to rehabilitating them.[28]

The prison ministry volunteer must be aware that the abject reality described by these numbers is the society that still exists in the memories and attitudes of men and women who came to prison ten or more years ago. Unfortunately, the current statistics, which are presented in the next chapter, are not much better. In some cases they are worse.

With its broad, encompassing social justice framework in the background, Catholic prison ministry volunteers must take a deep breath and step across the threshold from the "free" world into the island police state known as a prison or jail. In our next chapter, we will look at the ecclesial and catechetical practices that our Church provides to equip us for this work.

"Now the Church, although scattered over the whole civilized world to the end of the earth, received from the apostles and their disciples its faith…. Having received this preaching and this faith, the Church carefully preserves it, as if living in one house…. The real Church has one and the same faith everywhere in the world."

St. Irenaeus (second-century Bishop of Lyons and a Father of the Church)[1]

CHAPTER 2

The Ecclesial Framework and Catechetical Practices of Credible and Responsible Prison Ministry

Many aspects of Catholic prison ministry can be quite different from those of other Christian ministries. Such differences can be evident in the way ministry is done (e.g., relational), in the focus of the ministry activity (e.g., Eucharist, other sacraments and magesterial teaching), and in the very means of teaching the faith (e.g., catechetical practices). Another significant difference in Catholic prison ministry is the framework of authority that grants the volunteer the privilege of participating in prison ministry on behalf of the Church.

Authority is a critical threshold issue. If a volunteer does not get the authority issue right, the volunteer's status in Catholic prison ministry will experience a failure to launch. In other words, there are only two options. On the one hand, the volunteer enters the prison as a participant in the Church's pastoral service to prisoners. Or, on the other hand, the volunteer is solely on their own without any authority to use the name "Catholic" or claim to be part of the Church's activities. There are no "free agents" or "loose cannons" in Catholic prison ministry.

The key question I ask when meeting a *Catholic* prison ministry volunteer is: "Who is your pastoral authority?" This is not a management question. This is not a bureaucratic question. This is an essential question, because in the Catholic Church there is no such thing as pastoral ministry except that which is vested through Holy Orders in bishops and priests. The ministry of Deacons has a distinct sacramental basis that flows from their Sacrament of Orders. All pastoral ministry performed by Catholic volunteers is a participation in the pastoral ministry vested in a bishops or priest.

So, the question "Who is your pastoral authority," does not ask "Who do you work for?" Rather, this question asks, "In whose pastoral ministry do you participate and by what authority are you granted the privilege to do so?" That is, the relationship between pastoral ministry and the Sacrament of Holy Orders is at the core of the ecclesial framework which forms the lattice for Catholic volunteer ministry. The metaphor that I use to explain this concept in presentations for groups of Catholic volunteers is as follows:

> Grace is our participation in the life of God.[2] But participation in the life of God does not make us into gods. Likewise, our volunteer service in prison ministry is our participation in the pastoral ministry of our bishop or priest. But participation in the pastoral ministry of their priesthood does not make us into bishops or priests.

We need not delve here into the deeper theological discussions that explain this concept. Suffice it to say that the basis is apostolic succession and the ecclesial role of bishop and priest. In 1997, Pope John Paul II promulgated a definitive statement in this regard called *Ecclesiae de Mysterio*.[3] It deals with all facets of Church activity in which the non-ordained faithful collaborate in the sacred ministry of Catholic priests. The document clarifies the distinction between the "common priesthood" of the faithful through Baptism and the "ministerial or ordained priesthood" through Holy Orders. One of the key principles set out in this document is the difference between *collaboration* and *substitution*:

> The hierarchy entrusts the laity with certain charges more closely connected with the duties of pastors [for example, teaching Christian doctrine]. Since these tasks are most closely linked to the duties of pastors (which office requires reception of the sacrament of Orders), it is necessary that all who are in any way involved in this collaboration exercise particular care to safeguard the nature and mission of sacred ministry and the vocation and secular character of the lay faithful. *It must be remembered that "collaboration with" does not, in fact, mean "substitution for"* (pp. 12-13, bracketed language and italics added).

Although lay Catholic prison ministry volunteers are never a "substitute" for the presence of a priest, their proper role does not in any way negate their participation in the common priesthood of the faithful through Baptism (p. 19). In fact, the crucial distinction is between the ministerial priesthood through Holy Orders and the common priesthood of the faithful. The ministerial priesthood of the priest differs in its essence because the Sacrament of Holy Orders "confers a sacred power for the service of the faithful" (p. 19).[4]

This principle is not up for discussion. "To base the foundations of the ordained ministry on apostolic succession…is an essential point of Catholic ecclesiological doctrine" (p. 20). This distinction has nothing to do with whether or not the lay faithful are called to be as holy as the ordained. All of the faithful—lay, religious, and ordained—are called to holiness (p. 18). Rather, lay prison ministry recognizes a difference in the *mode of participation* in the priesthood of Christ.

It is an understandable mistake for modern westerners to transmute the mechanics of our corporate and bureaucratic worlds onto the ministerial roles of the priests and the lay faithful as though we are divvying up job descriptions on an organization chart. That is to misunderstand both the nature of ministerial priesthood and the nature of collaboration in it by the lay faithful. The duties and functions of the ministerial priesthood cannot be subdivided and parceled out as though they are simply tasks to be accomplished for assessing corporate performance in meeting goals and objectives. The functions of the priest, taken as a whole, constitute a single, "indivisible unity and cannot be understood if separated one from the other" (p. 21). The instruction continues:

> Only in some of these functions, and to a limited degree, may the non-ordained faithful cooperate with their pastors should they be called to do so by lawful authority and in accordance with the prescribed manner.... *The exercise of such tasks does not make pastors of the lay faithful,* in fact, a person is not a minister simply in performing a task, but through sacramental ordination.... The task exercised [by the lay faithful] takes its legitimacy formally and immediately from the official deputation given by pastors, as well as its concrete exercise under the guidance of ecclesiastical authority" (p. 21, italics in original; bracketed language added).

In other words, every Catholic prison ministry volunteer should be formally commissioned for their work by the pastor who is responsible for that work under Church law. But that is not all. The actual conduct of that volunteer's work, the sites where they serve, the nature of the service they provide in the name of the Church, even the specifics of how their service is conducted must all be under the guidance of Church authority. All Catholic prison ministry volunteers need to know the name and title of the ordained minister (i.e., priest or bishop) who has authorized them to carry out the activities they perform in prison. This bottom line bears repeating: There is no place for "free agents" or "loose cannons" in Catholic volunteer prison ministry.

These foundational principles point to some additional truths that must be borne in mind. First of all, Catholic prison ministry volunteers must always be aware that the ability to minister in jails and prisons is a privilege with respect to the Catholic Church. Under Church law, there is no right to enter a prison or jail as a Catholic prison ministry volunteer. That right is housed in the pastor through Holy Orders, and the duty imposed upon that pastor to exercise that right within a specific area is based in Church law. Most long-term Catholic prison chaplains can share stories of well-meaning and deeply-motivated Catholic prison ministry volunteers who wrongly believed they had accrued the right to serve the Church in prisons and jails, through years of service, or training and preparation, or the like. There is no such right for the lay faithful.

Where there is no right, then, there is only a privilege; and the privilege can be revoked at any time. A new bishop or pastor has the full authority under Church law to determine who among the lay faithful will be participants in his pastoral ministry. The existing bishop or pastor can decide at any time to make a change in the lay faithful who will participate in his pastoral ministry. The bishop or priest need not enumerate reasons or justifications. He need not prove that the volunteer did anything wrong. The ministry is not the ministry of the lay volunteer; it is the pastoral ministry of the bishop and priest.

Secondly, the very use of the term *ministry* must not be appropriated by Catholic prison ministry volunteers as a term that describes something which belongs to the volunteer. One cannot appropriate what one has no right to own. The word *ministry* must always be carefully used as reference to participation in the pastoral ministry of the priest and bishop who share in the one priesthood of Christ.

> Only with constant reference to the one source, the "ministry of Christ,"...may the term *ministry* be applied to a certain extent and without ambiguity to the lay faithful: that is, without it being perceived and lived as an undue aspiration to the *ordained ministry* or as a progressive erosion of its specific nature (p. 28).

It is no surprise that perhaps the greatest risks of confusion as to the distinction between volunteer lay ministry and ordained ministry arise in the context of the Eucharist. A mainstay of Catholic volunteer prison ministry is the service of bringing the Eucharist to our brothers and sisters confined in prisons, jails, and detention facilities. This can be done with multiple recipients in chapel settings or one-on-one at cell-front in confinement or at bedside in prison hospitals and prison hospices. The awesome honor of serving as an Extraordinary Minister of the Eucharist, to bear the Body of Christ to our confined brothers and sisters, is more than mere words can describe. The risks of confusion to the faithful are great. Accordingly, it is incumbent upon the prison ministry volunteer who serves as an Extraordinary Minister of the Eucharist to affirmatively exercise great caution and discipline in avoiding any words, any manner of speech or ritual, or any manner of dress that might engender confusion in the faithful.

Supplemental to the teaching of *Ecclesiae de Mysterio*, the Catholic bishops in the United States have issued a document to provide direction to all the lay faithful involved in participation in the pastoral ministry of their pastor and bishop: *Co-Workers in the Vineyard of the Lord: A Resource for Guiding the Development of Lay Ecclesial Ministry*.[5] This document acknowledges the growing role of the lay faithful in performing Church ministries (p. 5) and contextualizes this role within the universal call to holiness[6] (pp. 5-6) and the Church's embarking upon the Third Millennium.

> Therefore the Church of the Third Millennium will need to encourage all the baptized and confirmed to be aware of their active responsibilities in the Church's life. Together with the ordained ministry, other ministries, whether formally instituted or simply recognized, can flourish for the good of the whole community, sustaining it in all its many needs: from catechesis to liturgy, from education of the young to the widest array of charitable works[7] (p. 10).

The document then defines a lay ecclesial minister:

> The ministry is *lay* because it is service done by lay persons.... The ministry is *ecclesial* because it has a place within the com-

WHEN WE VISIT JESUS IN PRISON

munity of the Church.... Finally, it is *ministry* because it is a participation in the threefold ministry of Christ (pp. 11-12).

The American bishops then touch upon our highly individualistic culture by recognizing the commonly described sense of "being called" to lay ministry:

> These lay ecclesial ministers often express a sense of being called. This sense motivates what they are doing, guiding and shaping a major life choice and commitment to Church ministry. At the same time, they know that a self-discerned call by the individual is not sufficient. Their call must also become one that is discerned within the Church and authenticated by the bishop, or his delegate, who alone is able to authorize someone to serve in ecclesial ministry (pp. 11-12).

A lay ecclesial minister could well fill a compensated position for full or part-time work at the parish, diocesan or provincial level. In reality, however, there are few Church-compensated positions in Catholic prison ministry (other than perhaps a staff position coordinating or supervising those who go into the prisons and jails), so it is reasonable to address the points of this book in terms of Catholic *volunteer* prison ministry. The following are some of the particularly poignant points made by the U.S. bishops in *Co-Workers* that certainly apply to Catholic volunteers in prison ministry (pp. 17-20):

+ All ministry finds its place within the communion of the Church and serves the mission of Christ in the Spirit.
+ The one true God is fundamentally relational: a loving communion of persons.
+ Pope John Paul II has described the Church as "a mystery of Trinitarian communion in missionary tension." In other words, the reality of the Church is the communion of each Christian with the Triune God and, by means of it, the communion of all Christians with one another in Christ.

+ Holiness is nothing other than the gift of loving union with God and the sharing of this love in right relationship with others.
+ Such love becomes mission because holiness involves a dynamic openness and movement toward others.

The bishops then describe the different roles in the ecclesial relationships that form the community which is the local Church (pp. 21-24):

+ The bishop is the center of communion in the local Church and the link of hierarchical communion with the universal Church. The bishop is given the duty of oversight to order these new ministerial relationships and to affirm and guide the use of gifts that the lay ministers bring; to test everything and retain what is good (pp. 22-23).
+ The priest makes present the bishop to the local community and sacramentally represents Christ, the head of the Church, and so serves to guide the Body of Christ in its mission of salvation and transformation of the world.
+ Lay ecclesial ministry flows from an explicit faith commitment, is animated by love of God and neighbor, and entails an explicit relationship of mutual accountability to and collaboration with the Church hierarchy.

The bishops then set forth a very profound description of the general minimum requirements one should meet to be in lay ecclesial ministry. They must be persons (pp. 25-26):

1. Who are known for a genuine love of the whole Catholic Church.
2. Who exist in full communion of heart and mind with the Pope as successor of Peter.
3. Whose ecclesial identity is shaped by obedience to the bishop of the diocese and to the universal magisterium.
4. Whose ecclesial identity is expressed by generous collaboration with ordained and other lay ecclesial ministers alike.
5. Who do not foster an elitism that places them above or outside the laity.
6. Who use their gifts and leadership roles always for the good of the Church.

This comprehensive document by the American bishops also contains extensive discussion of preparation and formation of individuals who are considering lay ecclesial ministry. We will be referring to those portions of *Co-Workers* in *Chapter 6: The Spiritual, Communal and Individual Practices for Catholic Prison Ministers to Avoid Burnout*.

Suffice it to say that one of the most critical requirements for serving as a Catholic prison ministry volunteer is commitment. I am frequently asked: "What is the most important thing about prison ministry?" My answer is very simple and very basic: "You have to show up. Nothing can happen if you do not show up."

No Excuses

As young boy scouts, my friends and I memorized the virtues that should shape our life. We all liked bravery. Every issue of our scouting magazine, *Boys' Life,* carried at least one hair-raising true story of courage in the face of imminent peril. A young man pulling a family from a burning car. A teenager belly-crawling across thin ice to rescue a child in frigid waters. We imagined ourselves in the picture, leaping to the heroic. Courage was popular.

The virtue called "trustworthiness" was not as big a hit. Trustworthy was tougher to visualize. We knew we should not lie or steal. But it is hard to picture a negative. Our young minds tended to skew trustworthiness towards loyalty, especially to our country. The fifties and sixties were Cold War years. Our culture was immersed in spy drama: books, television, movies—as well as the real ones on the news. It was not hard to imagine trustworthiness as refusing cooperation with the enemy at all costs. That sounded exciting. Like bravery.

But our troop leader, Mr. Pelligrino, would not have it. "It means doing what you said you are going to do!" he insisted. Mr. Pelligrino harped on a definition of trustworthiness that sounded dull and boring to us. "It means being where you should be when you are supposed to be there," he said. "It means people can rely on you." His emphasis would increase in proportion to our waning attention.

That was forty years ago. But based on his description, we may be living in an age that needs trustworthiness more than it needs bravery. I have seen enough "No Fear" decals to last me a lifetime. I am ready for some that say, "No Excuses." My brothers who live in prison must feel that way, too. I know the guys at Union Correctional do. They have heard it all:

+ Promises to write. No letters.
+ Promises to visit. No call outs.
+ Promises…promises…promises.

"A pocket full of mumbles," as Simon and Garfunkel called them. In prison when someone does what he or she promises to do, it is not soon forgotten. That may be why one of the best-known and most respected people on the entire compound at Union Correctional was a short elderly man from outside. He was pegged with the unlikely moniker, "Big John." Big John always promised to come back. He always did.

Kairos is a *Cursillo*-type weekend that has been adapted to the prison environment. The weekend is given by free-people from parishes and churches near the prison. Inmates apply to participate in the weekend and are screened for faith readiness. The program is now nationwide. I have been told that it started at Union Correctional in Florida in the 1970s.

Big John showed up for the sixth Kairos weekend at Union in 1980. He made about 50 more of the weekends after that, only missing three over twenty years. Moreover, he and his wife, Julia, were regulars at the Sunday Catholic services at Florida State Prison and Union Correctional for over eighteen years. Big John passed away in 2003 at age 94. His wife Julia continued to come to weekly Mass at the prisons for many years after he passed, until she also went home to the Lord at age 94 in 2011. It is not hard to come up with good excuses for not being able to share the Mass or Communion service with our Catholic brothers in blue every Sunday. Big John was a man with no excuses. Big John showed up. As his slight frame eased into the prison grounds each week, cane in one hand and a fistful of jokes in the other, virtually every officer, every inmate, every guest, knew that the shadow of a really Big Man had crossed their path.

As Catholic prison ministry volunteers exercising the privilege of participation in the pastoral ministry of our priests and bishops, it is incumbent upon us to make ourselves aware of the Church's teaching about prisons and criminal justice in our society. Thanks to the Internet, that is easier today than it used to be.

A key element of our Church's social teaching is the fundamental option for the poor and vulnerable. This teaching recognizes that every public policy must be assessed by how it will affect the poorest and most vulnerable people in our society. That is not always a politically popular position. But the Catholic prison ministry volunteer bears the burden of holding forth the Church's social justice teaching not because it is popular but simply because it is the Church's social justice teaching. Political popularity polls and focus group results in the media have no bearing on the truth taught by the Church.

Many Catholic prison ministry volunteers are being called into this service at a point in their life that coincides with retirement and a sudden increase in discretionary time. The blessing of such timing is that they bring a wealth of secular skills and life experience to their participation in the Church's prison ministry. This is exactly what the Church envisions as the blessing of putting those gifts peculiar to the vocation of the laity at the service of our brothers and sisters inside prisons and jails. On the other hand, no one should be surprised that many volunteers coming to prison ministry in their golden years have life experiences which may not have included many actual encounters with the poor and vulnerable. The prisons, jails, and detention centers rarely house the rich and powerful.[8] The decision to become a Catholic prison ministry volunteer is a decision to immerse oneself in the life stories and broken dreams of some of the poorest and most vulnerable adults in our society.

Where does a new Catholic prison ministry volunteer start in trying to get a handle on this "other world" of incarceration that has been hidden in plain sight for most of his or her life? Because of the ecclesial lattice provided as a support for Catholic volunteer prison ministry, there is a wealth of information and teaching available from our bishops. For example, we have seen in Chapter 1 that the U.S. Conference of Catholic Bishops (USCCB) issued a document on the national level on this subject, *Responsibility, Rehabilitation, and Restoration: A Catholic Perspective on Crime and Criminal Justice.*

We also have the benefit of regional teaching from our bishops. For example, the Catholic bishops of the South issued a series of pastoral letters on the subject of crime and punishment in the southern region of our country. The social and economic conditions described by the statistics cited in the bishops' letters prevailed in the 1980s and 1990s, the period when many current inmates left society for the world inside the prison fences. The Catholic prison ministry volunteer needs to be familiar with the world outside that those inmates left behind.

In the first letter in that series, *Challenges for the Criminal Justice Process in the South,*[9] they acknowledge the national document of the USCCB and then proceed to address the Catholics in the southern region of the country, saying:

+ Our Catholic approach begins with the recognition that our belief in the dignity of each human person applies to both victim and offender.
+ As Catholics, we are convinced that our tradition and our faith offer better alternatives than the slogans and policy clichés of conservatives and liberals.

This means that the Catholic prison ministry volunteer does not walk into the prisons quoting the self-serving platitudes that are touted by the vested interests at either end of the political spectrum. Catholic teaching is on a completely different plane. My experience is that the Southern bishops are exactly right: authentic Catholic teaching on criminal justice in our society causes extreme discomfort to both political poles.

The bishops then address the plight of the victims of crime, noting that the criminal justice system must do more to be supportive of them and to be effective in reducing crime. They touch upon the fact that, while the U.S. at large has more people incarcerated per capita than any other country in the world,[10] the southern region of the U.S. exceeds the national average. "All seven of the states with the highest incarceration rates in the nation are in the South," they note.[11]

Updating the 2001 statistics relied upon by the bishops of the U.S. South reveals that very little has changed. Based upon the numbers from 2013,[12] the U.S. per capita rate of adult incarceration stood at 623 per 100,000 in population, but the southern region of the country exceeded the national average. Moreover, of the nine states with the highest incarceration rates, all but one (Arizona) are in the South: Louisiana (1,114), Mississippi (918), Oklahoma (873), Alabama (840), Texas (819), Arizona (775), Arkansas (760), Georgia (710) and Florida (659).

Even more startling are the rates of incarceration of adult males. Nationally that rate in 2013 was 904 per 100,000 – that is a hair's breadth from 1%. Again, the southern region of our country holds prominence, well exceeding the national average with Louisiana above 1.5% of adult incarceration (1,633), and with Mississippi (1,328), Alabama (1,225), Oklahoma (1,191), Texas (1,120), Arkansas (1,087), Arizona (1,077), and Georgia (1,020) all exceeding 1% of their adult male population incarcerated.

When local jails and facilities for juvenile incarceration are added to these numbers, the U.S. per capita rate of incarceration at the end of 2013 stands at 737 per 100,000 in population. This number far exceeds any other country in the world, even Russia which is at 615. The midpoint rate worldwide is between 140 and 150, which is also where the United Kingdom falls.[13]

Supervised populations include those who are not in prison or jail but are under federal, state, or local supervision, such as those on probation or parole. When this group is added to those in prisons and jails, the total adults in the U.S. under the control of correctional authorities is 6,899,700. At year end 2013, almost 3% of adults in the U.S. (1 in every 35) were under some form of correctional supervision; approximately 1 in every 51 adults in the U.S. was supervised in the community on probation or parole; and about 1 in every 110 adults was incarcerated.[14] At least with the number of adults on probation and parole having been reduced somewhat since 2004, the number of adults under some form of correctional supervision has dropped from 1 in 32 to one in 34. (Not exactly a precipitous drop!)

A significant number of the adults incarcerated or under supervision on probation and parole are actually moving through the system and will, at some point, move out of that status. Most states disenfranchise anyone convicted of a felony, taking away major civil rights, like voting, during the time that they are in prison. Many states do not restore those rights so long as the felon remains on probation or parole. In some states, those rights are not even automatically reinstated after the man or woman has paid their debt to society and is completely off any state or federal supervision. This process, called *felony disenfranchisement*, results in the disenfranchising of a large segment of the population. Almost 5.85 million Americans today are disenfranchised from voting because of felony convictions.[15]

Since 1997, there has been some progress in addressing this issue. With the disparity in incarceration rates based on race, it is not surprising that disenfranchisement disproportionately affects African Americans. According to *The Sentencing Project:*[16]

+ The percentage of African American adults incarcerated is 5.6 times the percentage of white adults incarcerated.
+ The percentage of white adults under felony disenfranchisement is 2.5%
+ The percentage of African American adults under felony disenfranchisement is 7.7%, more than 3 times the rate for whites.

In several states, the percentage of adult African Americans under felony disenfranchisement is much higher than the national average:[17]

+ Florida: 23.3%
+ Kentucky: 22.3%
+ Virginia: 20.4%
+ Tennessee: 18.9%
+ Wyoming: 18.3%
+ Alabama: 15.0%
+ Mississippi: 13.9%
+ Nevada: 12.6%
+ Arizona: 11.2%

Bias in Black and White

In their pastoral letter, *Challenges for the Criminal Justice Process in the South,* the Southern bishops raise the issue of racial bias in incarceration rates, saying:

> There is evidence of racism in the criminal justice system. In the age group 25-29, just over 1% of white males are in state or federal prison, compared to 3% of Hispanic males and 10% of African American males. Racial profiling of African Americans remains a

troubling practice in too many areas of law enforcement.... There are now more black men in jail or prison than there are in colleges or universities.

The racial disparities exist across gender lines as well. A 2004 report by *The Sentencing Project* indicates that "one of every 18 black females born today can expect to go to prison...six times the rate for white women."[18] The statistics bear out such racial disparities across all age groups and across all states, including the South.

When it comes to capital punishment, the discrepancies based on race can be nothing short of phenomenal. Although only 12 percent of Floridians are black, African Americans make up over 38% of Florida's death row. Yet, the real racial bias inherent in the U.S. death penalty is primarily based on the race of the victim of the crime. In Florida, a defendant is more than three times more likely to receive the death penalty for killing a white than for killing a black. In Georgia the ratio is more than seven times. And a black who kills a white in Georgia is nearly twenty-two times more likely to receive the death penalty than a black who kills a black. Scholars tell us that in Florida's history with the death penalty, dating back to 1769, no white person has ever been executed for killing a black person.

Some of this can be explained by history. The modern American death penalty is historically rooted in the death penalty of slavery.[19] Some can be attributed to outright racially discriminatory practices. These can be as blatant as racial profiling or the deliberate use of legal tactics to eliminate African Americans from juries, as occurred in a recent Texas case that went to the U.S. Supreme Court. Some is attributable to unintended consequences of politically popular laws. For example, crack cocaine is a derivative of powder cocaine. Yet, until very recently, Federal drug laws provided much harsher sentences for crack cocaine (known as the *poor black drug*) than for powder cocaine (known as the *rich white drug*). Selling just 5 grams of crack carried the same sentence as selling 500 grams of powder. And enforcement can be selective. Even though two-thirds of users are white, 83% of crack defendants were black. These racial disparities are destructive to communities and families. On any given day, one out of every 14 black American children has a parent in prison or jail.

WHEN WE VISIT JESUS IN PRISON

The teaching of our Catholic Church is quite clear. As stated in paragraph 1935 of *The Catechism of the Catholic Church*:

Every form of social or cultural discrimination in fundamental personal rights on the grounds of sex, race, color, social conditions, language, or religion must be curbed and eradicated as incompatible with God's design.

The Catholic Bishops of the South are simply calling us to put our faith into action by eradicating racial bias in our criminal justice system.

As noted above, the decision to become a Catholic prison ministry volunteer is a decision to immerse oneself in the life stories of people who have literally been disenfranchised from society and the life experiences which many of us have taken for granted. Some of them are angry and depressed about their place in the world. Some of them have tough questions for us. Some are envious and resentful of our "privileged" lives. Most will challenge us to explain why we have come to prison and what it is that we have to offer them. The way we explain and teach the faith that we have come inside the prison to share with them is called *catechesis*. In the section titled "Handing on the Faith: Catechesis," the *Catechism* describes catechesis as follows:

Quite early on, the name catechesis was given to the totality of the Church's efforts to make disciples, to help men believe that Jesus is the Son of God so that believing they might have life in his name, and to educate and instruct them in this life, thus building up the body of Christ....[20]

Catechesis is built on a certain number of elements of the Church's pastoral mission which have a catechetical aspect, that prepare for catechesis or spring from it. They are: the initial proclamation of the Gospel or missionary preaching to arouse faith; examination of the reasons for belief; experience of Christian living; celebration of the sacraments; integration into the ecclesial community; and apostolic and missionary witness.[21]

For Catholic prison ministry volunteers, *catechesis* is the word that describes the process of transmitting the Gospel, as the Christian community has received it, understands it, celebrates it, lives it, and communicates it. In the preceding chapter, I said that every time Catholic volunteers enter the "close" of a prison or detention facility, they are to deliver the Good News of the Incarnation to those subject to incarceration. This sounds pretty straightforward, but it can actually be complex. The reason for this is that the individual inmates and the prison culture can be quite complex. These are special situations that require special approaches.

Rarely does a Catholic prison ministry volunteer start the process of getting to know the inmates by giving a speech about the Gospels. Many of the seasoned inmates have heard a hundred such speeches, but they have experienced little or nothing that would inspire them to believe the words they are hearing. In most prison or jail situations, the effective volunteer must first earn the right to be trusted, earn credibility. In prison slang, one would say that the volunteer must "walk the walk before they talk the talk." In short, the inmates are not just listening to every word, but are also watching every attitude, reaction, tone of voice, facial expression, even body language to determine if this *newbie free person*, this *green guy* or *green girl*, is for real. The primary lubricant to grease the gears of catechesis in prison is authenticity:

> Since catechesis always occurs within a social and cultural context, catechists must carefully consider both the integrity of the Christian message they announce and the particular circumstances in which they announce it.[22]

So, inside a prison, the authenticity of the volunteer is crucial to receptivity of the message. This will be dealt with in greater detail in *Chapter 5: Catholic Prison Ministry as Evangelization.*

Assuming that the inmates have accepted the volunteer as a person who can be trusted to speak the truth, the *National Directory for Catechesis* can be extremely helpful to the volunteer in planning his or her presentations of the faith. For example, the "Catechesis for the Sacrament of Penance and Reconciliation" is a road map for reassessment of one's life and conversion to the Gospel.[23] This rich outline for the sacrament, which is also called the sacrament of Conversion or of Forgiveness, touches upon many key elements crucial to the spiritual needs of inmates. Its use need not be limited to Catholic inmates. With appropriate and sensitive adjustments in wording, it can be very effective with trans-denominational groups where repentance is the focus. But even among the willing in spirit, repentance is predicated upon knowledge of God's law.

I have been amazed at the number of inmates encountered who do not know the Decalogue. The Decalogue is the formal name for the Ten Commandments from the Hebrew Scriptures, the commands given by God to Moses on Mt. Sinai. The Decalogue provides the threshold basis for revealed Christian morality: love of God and love of neighbor. The stress upon learning the Ten Commandments as part of the learning of the faith goes back at least to the time of St. Augustine.[24]

In this regard as well, the *National Directory for Catechesis* can be extremely helpful to volunteers in planning their presentations of the Ten Commandments. The "Catechesis on the Decalogue" fills out the full depth and meaning of the commands which are to guide and govern the Christian life (see pp. 173-184). For example:

+ Catechesis on the First Commandment awakens belief in God.
+ Catechesis on the Second Commandment encourages a sense of the sacred in life.
+ Catechesis on the Third Commandment recognizes that creatures owe their Creator worship and praise.
+ Catechesis on the Fourth Commandment understands the family in light of Trinitarian love.
+ Catechesis on the Fifth Commandment fosters respect for human life.

- Catechesis on the Sixth and Ninth Commandments impart the Christian understanding of the gift of human sexuality.
- Catechesis on the Seventh and Tenth Commandments focus upon social and economic justice.
- Catechesis on the Eight Commandment teaches that God is the source of all truth, which is fully revealed in the person of Jesus Christ.

Finally, the *National Directory for Catechesis* integrates the "Decalogue and the Spirit of the Beatitudes," describing the path that leads to the Kingdom of God. Every Catholic prison ministry volunteer should have a command of the subjects and explanations of this "Catechesis on the Decalogue." Effective evangelization about the Good News of the Christian Scriptures cannot be meaningfully understood until the Decalogue has been imparted to an inmate.

Do the Math

The huge metal door from E-corridor slams behind me as I push the Catholic literature cart onto H-Wing. The corridor sergeant bolts the door shut from outside as the wing officer bolts it from inside.

"What you peddling today?" laughs the inside sergeant.

"Same as always: Good News. And it is free."

"Hope you have got some takers," he opens the barred door to the mezzanine level of the three-story cell tier. The cart's wheels duel with the corrugated metal of the catwalk, thundering like car tires against the rumble strips on a freeway shoulder. The barred door and lock clang shut. I am locked in and ready to work.

This wing houses men who have advanced beyond the solitary cells with solid steel doors in the behavior modification program. Their doors are only barred. With continued improvement in behavior, they will be returned to general population in other prisons.

The energy on this wing is refreshing after the depression and hopelessness in the long-term solitary wings. Sensory deprivation makes a man's eyes hollow and his face empty. Long term solitary makes him sullen and unresponsive. The men on this wing are getting their spunk back.

"Hey, preach!" yells a voice near the front of the wing. "Don't waste our time. Tell us what you've got to say in ten words or less."

The corrugated floors of the catwalk are perforated. The guys downstairs and upstairs are all listening. It is show time. I respond loudly.

"Life is short. Eternity is long. You do the math."

A downstairs protagonist cuts a teaser: "Is that ten words or eleven?"

All three levels explode in raucous discussion of the word count. I ease on down to the far end of the wing and hawk my wares: "*Florida Catholic, Word Among Us,* prayer cards...."

"Hey, Brother Ragu," an intense, middle-aged man barks out my prison name, motioning me to a stop. "Why are you always writing against the death penalty? Don't you know God's Book says those guys deserve it?"

I park the cart against the barred wall between him and me and pull out the Bible. "Do you remember the time when the woman caught in adultery was brought before Jesus for stoning?"

"Yeah, course I do."

"That was our Gospel reading the other day at Church. Jesus asked a different question than you are asking. Maybe that is why he came up with a different answer."

"What are you talking about?"

"You are asking if the person about to be stoned deserves death. Jesus asked if the people doing the stoning deserved death."

"Yeah, man, but you can't work from that. We all deserve death because of sin. That's why Jesus came to save us. What about the crime? What about the victims?"

"When Jesus told the crowd, 'Let he who is without sin cast the first stone,' was he approving of adultery?"

"No, Jesus doesn't approve of adultery."

"Was Jesus saying he did not care about the victims of adultery, the spouse of the woman or of the man she slept with?"

"No, Jesus hates sin! He proved that. He told her to go and sin no more."

"He also did not argue about whether or not she deserved death, did he?"

The man pauses, gripping the bars of His cell door. "No, he didn't."

"Listen, brother, I think Jesus knows something very troubling about our fallen human nature. I think he knows that we all have a tendency to make ourselves feel better about our own sins by killing someone else for their sin. If we ask the question Jesus asked, every one of us is on the execution block but none of us would dare to be the executioner."

In the next chapter we will begin to address the world inside the fences. Whom will we meet there? What is their life like inside prison? How will we ourselves be affected by spending time inside prison with them?

"We are sons of eternal damnation who deserve the pains of hell, and every day we increase the vengeful flames by our horrible crimes. And we do not know whether we will be able to obtain mercy from God for the crimes we have committed…. Let's go to St. Francis and, if he gives us hope that we can obtain mercy from God for our great sins, let's do whatever he commands us to do so that we may free our souls from the punishment of hell."

The Three Murderous Robbers
converted by St. Francis of Assisi[1]

CHAPTER 3
The Pastoral Framework
of Credible and Responsible Prison Ministry

The first two chapters of this book dealt extensively with Church teaching in doctrinal areas. In this chapter we shift gears toward the interpersonal dynamics of ministry in prisons and jails. In order to be effective and credible in prison ministry, we must first shed our own world and enter into the world of those in prison. For a free person who is preparing to serve in a prison or jail as a Catholic volunteer, the very attempt to mentally and emotionally move from a freedom consciousness to a prison consciousness can trigger a brain freeze. Most citizens of the free world have never experienced a police state. Yet in its essence, prison is a police state located inside a fence. How does a person who has only lived free come to understand the consciousness necessary for inmates to survive inside barbed wire fences? What is life like, day in and day out, for an inmate in prison?

An exercise of imagination can be helpful in preparing ourselves for the journey inside the fence. Imagine that you were arrested and charged with a crime. Have you ever considered what it means to be arrested? The arrest is the moment when the police take you into custody. The police will decide where to arrest you. You can imagine the different places in your normal daily routine that could be the scene for such an arrest. What would it mean if you were arrested in front of your home with your spouse, children, and neighbors watching? Or were taken into custody at work in front of your co-workers? Or at school? Or even in your church in the middle of the Sunday service? What if your arrest were broadcast on television or splashed across the pages of the local newspapers? Imagine the thoughts that would be streaming through your mind immediately after such an arrest as you sit in the mesh cage in the back of the patrol car on the way to the police station for booking.

After being booked, you would be escorted by officers to a holding cell. The booking process is much more than just being entered into the jail log with identification and fingerprints. All your personal property is taken from you: keys, rings, watch, wallet—even your comb. If you do not voluntarily empty your pockets or turn over your purse, your personal items will be forcibly removed from you. What do you imagine you would feel as you surrender your house and car keys, your wallet and your cell phone—all to the hands of a stranger in uniform?

Once you have been photographed for the infamous "mug shot" which will be spoon fed to the media to portray you to the community as less than human, you would be marched to a holding cell. How would your body physically react to the sensation of people grasping you by the arms and shoulders and forcibly putting you in a locked space? What thoughts and emotions would run through you as the barred door to the holding cell slams shut, locked from the outside? You could size up the other people locked in the holding cell with you, wondering what crimes they are charged with. You might worry whether you will be able to protect yourself from those in the cell who are physically much bigger and stronger than you. What would it be like to be suddenly transported from your normal life in the world of civility and law into the world of physical domination and intimidation that rules inside the barbed wire fences?

After being arraigned, the suspect is usually held in the jail until the trial. It is true that for the few fortunate ones who can post a bail bond it is possible to stay home until the trial. But most of the inmates a volunteer will encounter in prison did not have either the celebrity or the money to post bond. Most of the inmates you will meet sit in jail waiting for their day in court. Imagine it was you cooling your heels in that jail. What thoughts and emotions might course through you sitting in the jail for months or even years waiting for trial, all the while knowing that you are legally innocent until proven guilty—at least in theory? Can you imagine it?

You would be absolutely without a voice. Everyone speaks *at* you, and no one listens *to* you. You would have no say in the temperature of the place, or about who shares your cell, or even whether your cell-mate or the staff avert their eyes instead of staring at you when you do your toilet. No one would ask what you want to eat or when you want to eat it. The lights would be turned on and off without anyone asking your opinion. You would not be at liberty to pick what you wear or how often your clothes and bedding are laundered. There may be rumors that the last three jail mates who slept on your mattress all died from a fatal flesh eating bacteria. You would have no right to swap out that mattress. And the option of sleeping on the cell floor would put your face in kissing distance of the base of the toilet. When you are outside the cell, you would march carefully between the yellow painted lines on the floor, following behind the jail mate in front of you, making eye contact with no one, speaking to no one.

The jail staff is not there to listen to your sad story. The officers are not there to be emotionally supportive or hear your tale of woe. Even your lawyer, whether private or court appointed, does not seem to have the time to listen—only time to tell you what to do and why you should cut a deal for a plea bargain, even if you did not commit the crime. And of course your attorney would warn you not to talk to anyone, especially cellmates and other jail mates who can succor a better deal from the prosecutors for themselves by testifying that you confessed to them. If the jail's security videotapes show you talking to any other inmate, even though all you said was "Good morning," you would be shocked to find out that your polite greeting has been recast as an impulsive confession. In such cases the audio always seems to be muffled. It would be your word against the other inmate's word. The state would claim you are lying, even though the jailhouse snitch is being given a free ride out of prison for saying you confessed. Your lawyer would also warn you to be especially paranoid of speaking to any psychological staff or prison ministers. Too often they can show up at trial as witnesses for the state, claiming that you "kind of seemed like you might have done it."

Your family might try to visit at the jail, but finally both you and they would give up. In the portion of the visiting park that is for contact visits, other jail mates would always be sitting nearby, ogling your sister and your wife and leaning in your direction, hoping to catch some valuable information whenever you speak. In the non-contact visiting park, you and your family might be alone but separated by a wall of bulletproof glass. All your conversations would be made over a phone which is monitored and recorded. Every word you say, every inflection or lack of it, could and most likely will be used against you by the state in your trial.

Can you imagine how hard it would be to hold on to the belief that the system really maintains you are innocent until proven guilty?

By the time of the actual trial, you could feel as though you have forgotten how to use your voice box. Everything outside your wing of the jail feels surreal and artificial. Every place is unsafe to speak or to show feelings. Your entire world has become a 60-square foot concrete space with a stainless steel bunk, a ¼-inch mattress, and a toilet in everyone's plain sight. Then, finally, it is time for the trial. Imagine the moment, sitting in open court with your family and loved ones in the audience, that you are found guilty and sentenced to prison, called "hard time" for a reason.

What would it be like to sit in shackles and black-box handcuffs in the cage of a prison transport vehicle as the state moves you hundreds of miles from the jail near your home to the prison that is to be your new "home"? Imagine how you would handle the "perp revue" or "beauty pageant," as it is called, which is the morning lineup and escort of all the new arrivals from the transport vehicle to the inside of the prison. Watching closely would be the meanest and strongest inmates in that prison, raucously calling out dibs by serial number on which of the new inmates' bodies they each claim to own. What terrors would grip you as strangers boisterously announce their right to use and sell your body without your consent?

This new home is a state prison. Imagine what it would be like to live in that prison. As you do so, how do you picture the living arrangements? You could be in a huge open bay dorm with bunk beds and 70 other convicts. If so, would you be sleeping with one eye open to make sure that no one saunters by in the middle of the night and clobbers you with a rock or lock swung in a sock, smashing your skull while you sleep because you refuse to be pimped by the strongman who claims to "own" you from the perp revue?

Or you'd be in a two-man cell sleeping all night behind a locked steel door in shared space with a prison cellmate. What would that be like? Your new cellmate could seem severely deranged and brag about having killed people inside and outside of prison, or could be much larger than you physically and demand that you provide sexual favors or else. Would you count yourself truly blessed if the worst problems with your new cellmate are horrendous personal hygiene and constant flatulence?

What would happen to your relationship with your family? In the visiting park of the state prison, there would be almost three hundred people in the room on visiting day. Signs warn you against kissing your wife or hugging your children for longer than ten seconds. Holding hands with your wife or your daughter could get you thrown in disciplinary confinement, a solitary confinement cell that is called "going to jail" inside the prison. Microphones in the ceiling record every word you say in the visiting park. Can you imagine relaxing and relating as a family in such an environment?

Moreover, you and your family would be surrounded by other inmates having their visits. What if inmates who are rumored to have molested children are staring at your kids in the visiting park? Would you worry whether those inmates have friends in that particular crime on the outside? What if your wife starts getting phone calls late at night at home from strangers who say they heard from a friend of a friend that she is lonely or might be able to use some extra money in exchange for a few favors? Would you be obsessed with finding out who in the prison is selling her name and phone number? Could it be other inmates? Other visitors? Guards? Staff members? Would you finally tell your wife and children to stop visiting for their own protection?

The phone calls to your family are outrageously expensive, at least three times more expensive per minute than for normal people on the outside. All calls from inmates must be made collect. Even worse, all your family phone calls are taped. Imagine what you and your wife and children, your mom and dad, your brothers and sisters, would talk about on a phone call that you know is being taped by the state. Could you ever talk about anything meaningful? Would you stop making calls to your wife and children and your extended family to spare them the exorbitant expense for calls that seem pointless?

Most free people, those who have lived their whole life outside prison, would find it hard to imagine these scenarios. The reality is that on a regular basis the prison ministry volunteer will encounter inmates who have had such experiences, and perhaps much worse. What effect does living this way have on any human being?

Imagine that you are a prison inmate for five years, ten years, twenty years, or more. As the years go by, you are talked at twenty-four hours a day, seven days a week, three hundred and sixty-five days a year. You are told when to sit, when to stand, when to stoop, when to dress, when to shave, and when to strip. You never exercise a single choice about anything, except the choice to do what you are told right now or pay the consequences. Even asking a question of staff in the face of an order is insubordination. You never talk to anyone, staff or inmate, about anything except professional and college sports and the rotten prison food.

Now imagine that after several years of such a life, the prison administration puts out a memo that a Catholic volunteer is coming to the prison chapel to minister to interested inmates. As that inmate, when you think about maybe going to the chapel to meet this man or woman, what would you need from him or her the most?

In this chapter, we will learn how a Catholic prison ministry volunteer can make a difference in such an inmate's life. We begin with the grand Christian event marking the 2000-year anniversary of the Incarnation.

In his Apostolic Letter for the Jubilee Year 2000, As the *Third Millennium Draws Near* (*Tertio Millennio Adveniente*), Pope John Paul II finds great joy in marking this milestone of God's intervention in human history. He also takes great moment from this event as an impetus to launch a new evangelization. He considers this milestone so significant in Christian history that he models our preparation, commemoration, and celebration regarding the start of the third Millennium after Christ upon the Great Year of Jubilee of the Hebrew Scriptures.[2] He also instructs us specifically, in his *Papal Bull of Indiction of the Great Jubilee of the Year 2000* (*Incarnationis Mysterium*), about the meaning of the Jubilee as an outpouring of grace and Divine Mercy:[3]

> The coming of the Third Millennium prompts the Christian community to lift its eyes of faith to embrace new horizons in proclaiming the Kingdom of God. It is imperative therefore at this special time to return more faithfully than ever to the teaching of the Second Vatican Council, which shed new light upon *the missionary task of the Church* in view of the demands of evangelization today (italics in original, ¶2)....

> For us believers, the Jubilee Year will highlight the Redemption accomplished by Christ in his Death and Resurrection. After this Death, no one can be separated from the love of God (cf. Rm 8:21-39), except through their own fault. The grace of mercy is offered to everyone, so that all who have been reconciled may also be "saved by his life" Romans 5:10 (¶6)....

> Let no one in this Jubilee year wish to exclude [himself or herself] from the Father's embrace. Let no one behave like the

elder brother in the Gospel parable who refuses to enter the house to celebrate (cf. Luke 15:25-30). May the joy of forgiveness be stronger and greater than any resentment.... The merciful Father takes no account of the sins for which we are truly sorry (cf. Isaiah 38:17). He is now doing something new, and in the love which forgives he anticipates the new heavens and the new earth (¶11).

Perhaps our Holy Father understood that in our weakness, contorted by the culture of death to thirst after vengeance, we might hear these words and think they only apply to the people who are valued and esteemed by the world. Perhaps he knew that in our mistaken sense of self-righteousness, we might only imagine a Jubilee for people we wrongfully consider to be as "worthy" of mercy as ourselves. Perhaps our esteemed pope considered how hard it would be for the outcast children of God, sitting in prisons and jails, the darkest places of the world, to believe that even they are granted the grace of a Jubilee in God's Plan of Divine Mercy. Perhaps he knew that all of us—God's children, inside and outside of the prison fences—might fail to question ourselves as to how anyone could ever be *worthy* of mercy which, by definition, is doled out as a gift, grace to those who cannot possibly merit it. Regardless of his intention, John Paul II anticipated our need for more specific direction in order to see that the Jubilee is even for those who have erred so badly that they are housed in our prisons and jails. So he states it plainly and clearly in the *Message of His Holiness John Paul II for the Jubilee in Prisons.*[4]

WHEN WE VISIT JESUS IN PRISON

Jubilee Breaks Out In Florida Prison

It is something you do not see every day: a bishop in prison.

But he comes every year. And he does not just say Mass in the chapel. He also goes "in the back," making cell front rounds in the solitary confinement section and on death row. For decades he has faithfully come to the men who cannot come to him, the men behind bars at Florida State Prison and Union Correctional Institution, the prisons that house Florida's highest security cells.

Even so, this year's visit is special. Pope John Paul II has declared that the Year of Jubilee is for prisoners too:

> In the framework of this Holy Year of 2000 it was unthinkable that there should not be a Day of Jubilee for prisoners. Prison gates cannot exclude from the benefits of this great event those who find themselves spending part of their lives behind them (¶1).

We begin at the solitary confinement building that houses inmates under protective management (PMs). PMs are in solitary confinement for their own protection. For whatever the reason, the administration has determined that their lives are in danger inside the prison. They must live in prison inside prison for their own protection.

The Catholic volunteers have a Communion service with the Catholic PMs once a month. Sometimes we have used a small side room. Sometimes we have celebrated the service standing in a storage room. Once we held it standing in the hall next to the laundry carts. Today Bishop Snyder is coming. The staff has moved the service to the PM dining room.

The first batch of men has been escorted to the dining hall. They take their places around the table. The escort officer is seated nearby. Bishop Snyder and his assistant begin the service. As I step out to retrieve two more men, I hear his words to them over my shoulder, "You are so important to us. I pray for you and your families every day."

Finally, I return with the last straggler, a tall good-looking young man. There was a delay in securing his permission to attend because he was at a work assignment. Originally condemned to death row, he is now a PM. This fellow practices his faith fervently and never misses an opportunity to receive the sacraments. He has a gentle, almost bashful, way of speaking and a warm, sincere gaze. If I had met him on the outside, he is the kind of person I would want as a friend.

"You know," he confides as we approach the hall where the service is underway, "Bishop Snyder confirmed me."

We enter and join the others around the table. My seat is on the corner. I can see everyone at once.

As my bishop shares words of encouragement and hope with the circle of my brothers dressed in prison blue, I find myself remembering each of their stories. Some attended Catholic school. Some were altar boys. Some served Mass in Latin before Vatican II. Some were not born until well after that Council.

Now, all of them are leaning forward, devouring their bishop's every word. I sense a brief return of their youthful innocence. For a moment, it seems they are all younger, less scourged by harsh lives and faulty choices. Less tired. Perhaps even somewhat restored. I can picture them as young boys eager to help, to serve, to learn.

It occurs to me that I am experiencing the Jubilee. This just might be what Pope John Paul II meant when he expressed these thoughts:

> The hope that the Risen Lord, who entered the Upper Room
> through closed doors, will enter all the prisons of the world and
> find a welcome in the hearts of those within, bringing peace and
> serenity to everyone.[5]

In "The Impossible Dream," the song made famous by the Broadway musical *Man of La Mancha*, the hero professes that he is "willing to march into hell for a heavenly cause." That may seem to be pushing the limits of rationality, or even worse, proposing wasted energy by courting an ineffective result. But in the *Message of His Holiness John Paul II for the Jubilee in Prisons,* our pontiff asks us to pursue a mission more difficult to imagine than even that. We are to march into the man-made hell of the jails and prisons to proclaim to the people trapped inside that the Kingdom of God is already here, with them, in that hell; that the Kingdom of Heaven is already at hand for them, even in the midst of their prison world; that the gates of eternal hell cannot prevent heaven from reaching them; and that the isolation of their prison life cannot keep Jesus Christ and the power of the Holy Spirit away from them. The pope continues:

In this Jubilee, the Church celebrates in a special way the mystery of the Incarnation of our Lord Jesus Christ. Two thousand years have passed since the Son of God was made man and came to dwell among us. Today, as then, the salvation brought by Christ is continually being offered to us so that it may bear abundant fruits of goodness in keeping with the plan of God, who wishes to save all his children, especially those who have gone away from him and are looking for the way back. The Good Shepherd is always going in search of the lost sheep, and when he finds them he puts them on his shoulders and brings them back to the flock. *Christ is in search of every human being, whatever the situation!*

This is because Jesus wants to save each one. And with a salvation which is *offered, not imposed.* What Christ is looking for is trusting acceptance, an attitude which opens the mind to generous decisions aimed at rectifying the evil done and fostering what is good. Sometimes this involves a long journey, but always a stimulating one, for it is a journey not made alone but in the company of Christ himself and with his support. Jesus is a patient travelling companion, who respects the seasons and rhythms of the human heart. He never tires of encouraging each person along the path to salvation[6] (emphasis in original).

This is a transformative message indeed. Jesus does not tire in seeking the lost, does not grow weary of our constant mistakes and backsliding, does not give up on any of us, and does not turn away or cut us off...even if our entire city, our entire country, our entire world has condemned us, has judged us to be refuse and despises us as worse than dung. Jesus seeks our acceptance of his invitation to travel with him on the road of redemption and sanctification.

Long before tailoring the Jubilee message to the needs of the incarcerated, Pope John Paul II identified in the core concept of the biblical Jubilee a reality that is fulcrum to the consciousness of every jail and prison inmate in the world: *time*.

> *In Christianity time has a fundamental importance.* Within the dimension of time the world was created; within it the history of salvation unfolds, finding its culmination in the "fullness of time" of the Incarnation and its goal in the glorious return of the Son of God at the end of time. *In Jesus Christ, the Word made flesh, time becomes a dimension of God,* who is himself eternal. With the coming of Christ there begin "the last days" (cf. Hebrews 1:2), the "last hour" (cf. 1 John 2:18), and the time of the Church, which will last until the Parousia.
>
> From this relationship of God with time there arises *the duty to sanctify time.* This is done, for example, when individual times, days, or weeks, are dedicated to God, as once happened in the religion of the Old Covenant and as happens still, though in a new way, in Christianity[7] (emphasis in original).

As a Catholic prison ministry volunteer, part of your pastoral mission is to provide the men and women in jails and prisons with the means to redeem their time in prison, to redeem and sanctify the time spent isolated from society, even if that time will stretch for the rest of their life. The Church offers the means for this through the liturgical year:

> *Christ is the Lord of time;* he is its beginning and its end; every year, every day and every moment are embraced by his Incarnation and Resurrection, and thus become part of the "fullness of time." For this reason, the Church too lives and celebrates the liturgy in the span of a year. *The solar year is thus permeated by the liturgical year,* which in a certain way reproduces the whole mystery of the Incarnation and Redemption, beginning

from the First Sunday of Advent and ending on the Solemnity of Christ the King, Lord of the Universe and Lord of History. Every Sunday commemorates the day of the Lord's Resurrection[8] (emphasis in original).

Tangible materials can greatly enhance the mission of equipping prisoners with the means to achieve this transformation. Monthly devotionals such as *The Word Among Us®*, *Magnificat®*, *Living Faith Catholic Devotionals®*, and others can be very helpful. Catholic calendars with religious pictures for each month and with the relevant information about the feasts and liturgical cycles stated for each day of the year are also important. This author has personally experienced the redemptive power such calendars exert on the prison environment as they hang in control rooms, movement control stations, and wing quarter decks, as well as in the cells of inmates.

Yet, it is fair to ask whether this message of redemption and sanctification of a prisoner's time is really for everyone in every prison. Is there anywhere that is so desperate, so isolated, so forlorn, that this message is not really true?

....

How Can We Not

Loudly discordant, like mismatched cymbals clashing. That is the feeling that goes with passing out tracts of Pope John Paul II's Jubilee message to prisoners on Q-Wing in July. Q-Wing is the State of Florida's highest security wing.

Q-Wing used to be called X-Wing. The name was changed last year. And one of the cells was sealed-off. The red security tape went up on the door one year ago this month. The door is sealed and will remain sealed until conclusion of the criminal cases against suspected staff. I do not stop anymore to give Communion to the man who used to be in that cell. His name was Frank Valdez.[9]

This is the month in which the Holy Father has declared the year of Jubilee for prisoners. It is also the one-year anniversary of Frank's death.

I work my way from cell-to-cell on Q-Wing offering our pope's powerful words of encouragement and hope to the men on the most severely restricted wing in the state's prison system. Our Holy Father says the Jubilee includes men in prison, even in the worst parts of a prison:

> The Jubilee reminds us that time belongs to God. Even time in prison does not escape God's dominion. Public authorities…are not masters of the prisoners' time. In the same way, those who are in detention must not live as if their time in prison had been taken from them completely: even time in prison is God's time.[10]

The essence of prison is time. Doing time. The Jubilee is about redeeming time. John Paul II weaves this common fiber into a redemptive cloth:

> At times prison life runs the risk of depersonalizing individuals, because it deprives them of so many opportunities for self-expression. But they must remember that before God this is not so. The Jubilee is time for the person, when each one is himself before God, in his image and likeness. And each one is called to move more quickly towards salvation and to advance in the gradual discovery of the truth about himself.[11]

This was happening in Frank. Perhaps I could see it better than he because of my privileged vantage point. Holding a man's hands in prayer. Placing the Eucharist on his tongue. Seeing a man as he is in the presence of his Creator.

I am told that Francis of Assisi genuflected in front of a notorious criminal, saying, "I kneel before the presence of God in you." The man was transformed. What man would not be changed to his core—no matter how terrible his mistakes—if he could see the presence of God in himself? How will he ever see it, if we who claim to believe it, do not see it first?

I believe Frank was starting to see it, beginning to see himself through the eyes of his heavenly Father. The last time I was with him, I sensed a new awareness of the value of his life before God. We prayed. He received the Eucharist. I left on vacation. When I returned, he was dead.

It is usually hot on Q-Wing. In July, it is beyond hot. The poor officers who must endure hellish heat for hours at a time politely escort me through the wing. I greet the men who are sweltering in their cells. Yet, even in the heat and the sweat, I find myself remembering Frank and the words of the Vicar of Christ:

> To celebrate the Jubilee means to strive to find new paths of redemption in every personal and social situation, even if the situation seems desperate. This is even more obvious with regard to prison life: not to promote the interests of prisoners would be to make imprisonment a mere act of vengeance on the part of society, provoking only hatred in the prisoners themselves.[12]

I have heard bishops and even a few cardinals share stories of the anger and outrage expressed by the "free-world" (that is, those not in prison) members of their flock because a bishop or cardinal visited men and women in prison. One cardinal, killing time with me as we waited for our airport shuttle after a conference, shakes his head sadly. "People were furious when I visited our state's death row. They said they had been loyal faithful Catholics all their life, tithing and supporting the Church, putting their children through Catholic schools, but never once did I come to their house to visit them. They were outraged that I would now go to prison to visit murderers!"

He and I both resist the temptation to analogize that reaction to the stance of the elder brother in the parable of the Prodigal Son. While not condemning him, Jesus' story makes it clear that the elder brother misses out on the banquet because he will not accept the redemption and restoration of his wayward brother. The point the cardinal and I discuss is that a fact even more obvious than that is being ignored.

The people in the free-world can come to their parish church. They can come to see their priest at the parish or their bishop or their cardinal at the cathedral at Mass and at major liturgical events. But those who are institutionalized, whether through illness or incarceration, cannot come to the Church. The Church must come to them. It is sad to me to see Catholics and other Christians who adamantly stand in the posture of the Prodigal Son's elder brother miss out on the Jubilee banquet.

Pope John Paul II goes so far as to claim that the Jubilee year must be used "to right injustices committed, to mitigate excesses, and to recover what might otherwise be lost." He points out that this "is especially true of the experience of prison, where life is particularly difficult." So, it behooves all of us "to strive to find new paths of redemption in every personal and social situation, even if the situation seems desperate."[13] In short, his message calls us to redemption, restoration, and re-evaluation.

The Three Rs of Jubillee

The scene is a prayer meeting with new ex-cons. After the closing Benediction, a young man heads my way. "Hey, you one of those guys that follows the pope?"

"I am Catholic," I admit proudly.

"Yeah. Sure. Whatever," he punctuates each syllable with emphatic street gestures. "I was a runaround in the hole." That means he was a trusted inmate assigned work in solitary confinement. Everything for each solitary cell must be brought in and out to cell front: food, toothpaste, laundry, medicines, toilet paper—everything. The work in the halls of the confinement wings never seems to stop.

And boy does it get hot. Especially on summer nights, right after the showers. It is bad enough catching Florida sun all day in a building that is just a concrete and steel box. But every night at least 40 of the 100 men in each wing must be escorted to the shower cell. By the time steam from 40 showers has filled each wing, the thermal index is off the charts.

You have no idea how hard it is to be a corrections officer at a solitary confinement or maximum security facility until you have experienced the summer heat and humidity in the wings. When I make rounds in the summers, after just a few minutes I am drenched with sweat. The officers pull full shifts on those same wings.

The young fellow addressing me used to work as an inmate in those wings; he continues, "So what is with all this Jubilee in prison stuff? Is the

WHEN WE VISIT JESUS IN PRISON

Pope for real?"

I do my best to summarize the Old Testament basis for the Jubilee.

He shrugs it by, "Yeah. But we are talking prison, man!"

"Well, it boils down to three Rs: Redemption, Restoration, and Re-evaluation."

He grimaces, waiving his hand into a fan-like web. I smile and continue. "*Redemption* is bringing Christ into the prisons. We Christians must do that by physically going in there. And we must ensure that our government never impedes that. Then, *Restoration* is the process of restoring the community and the offender by allowing Christ to mediate the Reconciliation of the Cross here and now. We have to embrace it. We have to reject revenge and choose Christ's healing."

"Sure. Great. And so what is with that last thing you said, re-whatever?"

"*Re-evaluation*. That is not the word the Pope used. It is my word to summarize the third point of his message. Basically, he said that all of us involved with criminal justice, including government officials, must reevaluate whether or not what we are doing accomplishes those first two things. Our justice system must be accountable to Gospel morality."

"Gimme a fer instance."

As I stroke my chin, a memory flames up. My wife and I stuck with our five children in the August heat in a van with a broken air-conditioner. We have great kids. But in the unbearable heat, they all turned into their evil twins. My wife is generally acknowledged to be a saint. (Everyone agrees that three miracles would be child's play compared to decades of marriage to me.) She had no patience whatsoever that day. I was unspeakable. The memory provides an example.

"Well, take for instance, reducing violent behavior in prison. We Floridians are spending untold millions of dollars on security enhancements and behavior modification. But the most common sense thing in the world to improve everybody's behavior and increase their patience is air-conditioning. None of us is on our best behavior under extreme heat and humidity. As a security concern, air-conditioning should be our top priority, but it's not even on the list."

"So, that last point is about when what we should be doing—and what we are doing—do not add up?"

"That is it. And the Pope is saying that when we hold ourselves accountable to what Jesus said we should be doing, that is the Jubilee."

Even when the message of God's love is simple and clear, the actual mechanics of bringing that message into the prisons and jails can be complex. Catholic prison ministry volunteers must deal with the human realities of their service as well. One of the most critical aspects of volunteer prison ministry is *boundaries*. Just as the old real estate adage claims that the three most important factors in valuing a piece of land are location, location, and location, so too the three most important practical aspects of volunteer prison ministry are boundaries, boundaries, and boundaries. I break the subject of boundaries into three categories:

+ Physical Boundaries
+ Emotional Boundaries
+ Spiritual Boundaries

A boundary defines where one thing ends and another starts. It also can delineate acceptable and unacceptable behavior. All these meanings apply in prison. Almost by definition, prison is about boundaries.

Physical boundaries. Physical boundaries, at the most basic level, are about safety. Every time prison ministry volunteers walk into a room, a corridor, or a space, whether indoors or outside, they should be consciously aware of where they are, where the inmates are, where the officers are, and where the exits and entrances are. They should also be aware of every single thing within that space that could be used as a weapon or to threaten them. There is no such thing as an innocuous item inside the prison fence. I have seen lethal weapons made from ballpoint pens and discarded food items. The free-world consciousness of the volunteer must be checked at the prison gate. Looking at routine household items inside prison with the same eyes as one does

WHEN WE VISIT JESUS IN PRISON

at home could get a volunteer or someone else killed.

In assessing physical boundaries, the first level of scrutiny is what volunteers carry on their person. For example, purses or bags with long straps can be fatal. Anything that is long enough to wrap around a human neck and leave room for a strong grip on each end can be used to strangle someone.

Long zippers can be used to slice a person open. So can strong filaments of string. Laminated cards, like holy cards, can have their edges sharpened to the point of a razor. A chicken bone in a bag lunch brought from home can become a murderous shiv. No volunteer should ever bring anything that is metal or sufficiently hard enough to be filed to a point and long enough to puncture the human body inside the prison fence. (There are exceptions, of course, for liturgical items to be used at the chapels, and such exceptions are dealt with by prison security.)

The next level of scrutiny is the space within which volunteers will provide their services: the group room, the sanctuary at the chapel, the prayer room for one-on-one counseling, etc. In group rooms, the volunteer should always be aware of the closest exit to either an officer supervised area or to the outside of the building. That exit should always be in the volunteer's direct line of sight and no inmate should be allowed to position themselves between the volunteer and that exit.

This level of scrutiny can be fairly easy to achieve in a large group setting in the chapel or a multipurpose room. It can be much more difficult in a one-on-one situation. In either case, the volunteer must always be aware that inside prison, furniture is a weapon. Are the chairs and tables bolted to the floor? If not, is the room small enough that no one could swing either one over their head to establish the momentum to harm the other person in the room? As a volunteer starts to see their prison surroundings with physical boundaries in mind, matters that seemed annoying or dumb, like uncomfortably small rooms and floor mounted furniture, start to make sense.

The next level of physical boundaries is the safety that comes in numbers. People tend to control their strong impulses in a room full of witnesses. Also, the presence of officers helps. The savvy volunteer will always be conscious that any combination of factors that results in being alone with an inmate could be a setup for harm. For a religious volunteer, this is an occupational hazard.

In the milieu of inmates that cross the path of a regular prison ministry volunteer, the overwhelming majority will have good intentions and be seeking religious instruction and counsel for the right reasons. Some will even be protective of the volunteer, helping him or her navigate the unfamiliar terrain and warning them of pitfalls and dangerous characters. As with any human beings, the validity of such apparent virtues is proved out by consistency over time. This author has been spared from serious or lethal harm more than once by the protective instincts and actions of such good-hearted inmates. Even so, it is a sad reality of the prison environment that the volunteer dealing with an unknown or barely known inmate for the first time cannot safely assume that he or she has the best of intentions.

Good and kind staff, especially devout officers, truly desire that the Gospel will make a difference in the individual lives of their prisoners. When an inmate either innocently or calculatingly creates a situation of distress that results in a one-on-one with the volunteer, good and compassionate officers may try to give as much space as possible to the inmate and the volunteer, even offering to step out and close the door and let them have privacy. As a general rule, the volunteer should not accept such an offer of privacy unless they are a priest about to hear a confession. The default option volunteer response should be: "Thank you, officer. That is very kind. But our discussion does not need that level of privacy. So you are welcome to stay with us." If the officer does not understand, the volunteer could point to a chair and make the softly-spoken suggestion: "Would you like to sit here, officer?" If either the officer or the inmate protests, insisting on privacy, the volunteer may very gently respond: "I am sorry but I am not sure if our Church insurance allows for volunteers to be alone with an inmate."

The presence of an officer who shows that level of compassion will not endanger the effectiveness of the spiritual counseling. The officer's presence can be unobtrusively in the room or through a glass wall standing just outside the room. The officer does not need to stand between the volunteer and the inmate, but the inmate should not be positioned between the volunteer and the officer.

Another aspect of physical boundaries is the volunteer's physical person. As a bright-line policy, I always recommend that men minister to men and women minister to women. This is not a hard and fast rule, but it is a point of departure so that any proposal for mixing volunteers and inmates of the opposite sex will be thoroughly evaluated as to the purpose and the risk. Suffice it to say, a woman in a male prison is always at some level of risk; the goal is to keep that risk as low as possible. Ignoring hard facts of life does not reduce risk.

Later in this book, *Chapter 8: Characteristics of Criminal Thinking* looks in detail at the uncomfortable reality that many people in prison—not all, not most, but many—suffer from patterns and habits of thought and action that are different from law-abiding citizens. A hallmark of such patterns is the erroneous formula: *if you show me something I want, it is your fault if I take it from you.* That something can be flashing money, showing off an expensive car, or flaunting one's sexual attractiveness.

I ask female volunteers preparing for ministry at men's prisons to ask themselves the following questions:

+ Am I dressed the way I would be to visit my ailing grandmother at her home or the way I would be to go to an all-night dance club? (The first is a better idea!)
+ Will my clothes and my hairdo and perfume make it easier or harder for the men to focus on the Gospel instead of on me?
+ Am I aware how my style of dress might be perceived by men who could be highly sexualized and could suffer from severe impulse-control problems?

Anyone, whether male or female, going into prison as a volunteer to fill their own personal needs for self-esteem or self-worth should reconsider immediately. Any woman who is going into a men's prison needing to feel attractive and affirmed as a woman is putting herself at great risk. The same would be true of men in a women's prison.

Finally, volunteers must deal with the issue of hugging. A male religious volunteer giving a hug to a male inmate after an emotional sharing on a *Kairos* weekend is not much different than two NFL players hugging on the field after a hard fought touchdown. A female volunteer hugging a male inmate at the kiss of peace at Mass in the prison chapel, however, can be completely different. Good and well-motivated inmates have shared with me the anguish of weeks and months of fighting sexual urges enflamed by just such an innocent hug.

Catholic prison ministry volunteers must always be honest and frank with themselves about the power of the sexual urges in the human psyche and the unintended consequences that can flow from tapping into those urges in prison through touches and embraces that would pass almost unnoticed on the outside. For a man who is dying of thirst, a drop of water is like an ocean. For a man who lives a forced life of celibacy, devoid of female sexual contact, a whiff of exotic perfume or a moment of physical embrace can inflame decades of suppressed passion.

Emotional boundaries. The concept of emotional boundaries is quite simple. The practice of maintaining them, on the other hand, is a discipline that is anything but simple.

People's emotional boundaries allow them to knowingly distinguish between what they feel and what others feel. This can be tricky when one's volunteer ministry activity is compassion, which by definition means to "suffer with" those who are suffering. Catholic ministry volunteers must always be aware of their own feelings about the system, about the prison, about the administration, about the other inmates, about the other volunteers, and about all the other aspects that make up the prison reality. By the same token, volunteers must be aware of the feelings of the inmates they serve and how those feelings are similar and different from their own feelings.

The Eucharistic and communal practices described in detail in *Chapter 6: The Spiritual, Communal and Individual Practices for Cath-*

olic Prison Ministers to Avoid Burnout are geared toward bolstering and sustaining volunteers in consistently giving those they serve back to Our Savior. Volunteers cannot internalize the suffering of their charges. Only the Savior can bear that weight. In a similar fashion, volunteers must also consistently surrender their own emotions about the suffering of their charges to the Savior. The suffering of those we comfort in prison is more than our humanity can bear. Only the Savior can bear that weight, as well.

Healthy emotional boundaries will allow volunteers to know when they are feeling their own anger or are carrying the anger of those they have served, when they are feeling their own disillusionment and despair, or are carrying the disillusionment and despair of those they have served. Sorting out such feelings takes time, quiet, somber reflection, and strong, competent spiritual counseling.

Spiritual boundaries. Our spiritual boundaries are the defining parameters of our personal relationship with God and our faith. Every person's spiritual relationship is different. It is not unusual for prison ministry volunteers to realize that their own image of God—loving, involved, both immanent and transcendent—is being hammered by the counter-images of God held by those they are seeking to serve. Just as firm psychological boundaries allow us to know who we are (often despite wrongful aspersions from others), strong spiritual boundaries allow us to maintain a firm grip on the God of Revelation taught by the Church despite wrongful aspersions against God from others.

Strong spiritual boundaries can only be based and maintained in a strong personal relationship with Jesus Christ, in and through the Holy Spirit. Once again, the Eucharistic and communal practices described in detail in Chapter 6 and the investment of time for quiet, somber reflection, and strong, competent spiritual counseling are key.

I am frequently asked, "So, Dale, what do you say to those people in prison?" The question is rooted in a misunderstanding that prison ministry is mostly about lecturing the wayward. The questioner is usually quite amazed when the answer is, "Actually, I say very little. Over 90% of what I do is listen." Listen to their stories about their lives. Listen to their hardships and their suffering.

Listen to the needs of the ones they love: moms with Alzheimer's, daughters with cancer, children with disabilities, families with problems. Listen to their hopes, their regrets, their struggles with God and with their fellow man.

For Catholic prison ministry volunteers, first and foremost, the task is listening. Really listening. What is called *active listening*. It is absorbing yourself in the other person and soaking in the context of his or her life, his or her stance, his or her body language, and the specific words he or she is saying to you, while synthesizing it all into an understanding of where this person is in his or her relationship with God today. And then it is seeking the guidance of the Holy Spirit as to how you can help that person move deeper, closer, and more profoundly into that relationship with God today.

The formula is simple: Listen. Love. Pray.[14]

Long before their first encounters with inmates, volunteers will have prayed for themselves and for those they will minister to that day, for guidance, and for protection. Volunteers will start the day by praying that all their listening in prison will be through the ears of the Holy Spirit and that all their loving in prison will be through the loving Sacred Heart of Jesus. That is assumed before the formula—listen, love, pray—kicks in.

Once volunteers are facing inmates, their first task is listening: prayerful, active listening. If it is a prayer appointment, or otherwise appropriate, a joint prayer with the inmate can be very powerful as a beginning. Then the volunteer will express the love of God for the inmate. Scripture, the teachings of the Church, the words of our popes, the writings of the saints all provide a deep repertoire of descriptions for the unquenchable love that burns in the heart of God for each of the men and women in prison.

Finally, the volunteer will close in prayer with the inmate: prayers of petition, of intercession, of thanksgiving, of repentance, and of adoration. Depending on what is most comfortable to the inmate, the volunteer may use either well-worn Catholic prayers or spontaneous prayers. The important factor is that the volunteer is serving as a prayer-partner to the inmate. Even if the volunteer offers prayers themselves for the inmate and the inmate's petitions, even if the volunteer leads the inmate in prayer, the prayers made are meant to be the prayers on the heart of the inmate. The volunteer is supporting the inmate in offering prayer, much as Aaron and Hur supported Moses by holding up his arms while the Israelites were in battle.

> As long as Moses kept his hands raised up, Israel had the better of the fight, but when he let his hands rest, Amalek had the better of the fight. Moses' hands, however, grew tired; so they took a rock and put it under him and he sat on it. Meanwhile Aaron and Hur supported his hands, one on one side and one on the other, so that his hands remained steady until sunset. And Joshua defeated Amalek and his people with the sword.[15]

Then, at the end of the day, when the volunteers return to the quiet of their own home, they will hold in prayer each of the inmates that God allowed them to serve that day. The Catholic prison ministry volunteer knows that the work of God is the work of love, an "inside job" motivated and brought to fruition by the power of the Holy Spirit.

The Ultimate Terror

The cool mornings have evaporated. Sticky, humid air squats heavily throughout the un-air-conditioned wings of death row, signaling the advance of another trademark North Florida summer.

By 10:00am the halls are sizzling. My glasses refuse to stay mounted atop the sweaty bridge of my nose. The calendar says it is spring. But in this sun-soaked steel and concrete box, there is no spring. Winter is cold. Then summer is hot. It is as simple as that.

As the footfalls of my rubber soles announce my arrival with squishing noises against the damp cement, a middle-aged man moves to the front of his cell. He is waiting for me. "Man, of all the people that come back here, you are the only one that scares the hell out of me."

"Is that a good thing or a bad thing, brother?" I joke, still not certain whether this is a set up for a punch line or an intro to a deep discussion.

"I don't know," he shakes his head solemnly, indicating that there is no punch line coming. "I just know that you come back here and scare me but nobody else does."

"Is it the way I look or the way I dress?"

He bends over laughing but pursues the original line of his thoughts.

"It is like this, man. Everybody else that comes back here hates somebody. Some folks hate Catholics; some hate Pentecostals. Some hate cops; some hate inmates. They all hate somebody. And they all believe that God hates the people they hate. See, I am fine with that. I understand that. But you—you come back here talking about loving everybody." His eyes grow wide as he makes a sweeping gesture with both arms. "Love the inmates and love the cops, too. Love all the Christians and even the ones that ain't Christian. God loves everybody."

"It is not my idea, you know. I am just sharing with you what Jesus said. We do believe that Jesus is God. So what He said must be true."

"Man, that's too much."

"Why? Why is it too much?"

"It is scary. Listening to you talk scares me."

"Why?"

The lines forming across his face reveal the intensity of the inner struggle. His words come slowly, deliberately. "Look, man. I understand hate. I lived hate. Before I came here, my whole world was hate. It don't matter who is being hated. Hate is hate. And when I hear people talking hate—even if they use other words—I am comfortable with that. It is familiar. But when you start talking about all this love stuff—God loves everybody and all that— man…you terrify me."

"Why?"

"It is like my core is hate. I have been raised to hate. I was born to hate. If I let in what you are talking about, it is like my very core would cease to exist. I don't know who I would be or how to be. It is that scary."

"According to Scripture, the opposite of love is not hate. The opposite of love is fear. Are you afraid of being loved?"

"Let's just say I am not used to thinking of myself or anything else from that perspective."

"You are right. It is a radical departure from what the world has to offer. Maybe that is why it is called the Good News."

"I'm not saying whether it is good or not. I'm just saying that when people come back here talking about a God that hates the people they hate, I know the score. That's a God I understand.

"But when you come back here talking about a God that loves everybody…. Man, you scare the hell out of me. It is terrifying."

The inmate in that story is not the only one who is terrified by the message of a God of love. It is not unusual for the Catholic prison ministry volunteer to find that inside the prisons and jails there is a great deal of misunderstanding, misconstruing, and—in some exceptional case—even potent hostility toward the Catholic faith. But that is the subject of the next chapter.

"I want a laity, not arrogant, not rash in speech, not disputatious, but [men and women] who know their religion, who enter into it, who know just where they stand, who know what they hold and what they do not, who know their creed so well that they can give an account of it, who know so much of history that they can defend it."

Blessed John Henry Cardinal Newman[1]

CHAPTER 4

Effective Pastoral Prison Ministry in a Pluralistic Setting

Anti-Catholicism has been called America's last acceptable prejudice:

> Catholics and Catholicism are at the receiving end of a great deal of startling vituperation in contemporary America, although generally those responsible never think of themselves as bigots. Examples are far too easy to find.... What is striking about these comments is not any individual phrase or accusation, but the completely casual way in which these views are stated, as if any normal person should be expected to share these beliefs.... The attitudes are so ingrained as to be invisible.[2]

It should come as no surprise that the anti-Catholic attitudes so freely shared in the media and the culture at-large are also evident inside the fences of prisons and jails. In areas of the country where Catholics are in a distinct minority, such as many states where Catholics average less than 10% of the population[3], the *accepted truths* most people have learned about Catholicism would horrify most Sunday pew-sitting Catholics. Make no mistake. There are many marvelous pastors, chaplains, officers, wardens, and staff who are fully supportive of the work of their Catholic brothers and sisters. Furthermore, anti-Catholic attitudes have been diluted a bit by the prevalence of Catholics in major population centers, even in the South and West. When people actually meet and experience Catholics, many of the most severe stereotypes and false beliefs start to breakdown.

Prisons, however, are rarely built in major population centers. The siting of most prisons is a political decision based on the desire by politicians to obtain rural jobs and rural votes by building a constituency for them in rural communities, usually those without a strong economic base. Even in the North and East, it is not unusual for the Catholic inmates inside prisons in rural locations to face a shocking level of bigotry—and in rare cases outright hatred—against practicing Catholics. This can be insidious or explicit. It can come from other inmates, from staff, even in exceptional cases from chaplains and religious volunteers. Sometimes, it is systemic.

For example, I am well acquainted with a Catholic nun who served for thirty years as a key spokesperson for the rights of Catholic inmates in her state's prisons. For over three decades, she tried to obtain fish entrees for Catholic inmates on Fridays in Lent. To date, that request has been refused. Instead, the Catholics in that state's prisons are offered USDA surplus peanut butter and stale crackers on Fridays in Lent. Meanwhile, that same state seems to trip over itself making sure that adherents of other religious groups have available to them foods which, though not religiously required, are imbued with religious significance. It appears that the "Mackerel Snappers," as Catholics are frequently and pejoratively called in areas hostile to Catholicism, are not to be treated like other religiously observant inmates.

Mackerel Snappers

Today my prison rounds start at the Work Camp. The men here are hoping to go home soon. Unlike the inmates locked in solitary confinement, these men demonstrate no mental illness or gross behavior problems. They are articulate, focused, and hoping to turn their lives in new directions when they leave prison in a matter of months. Compared to solitary confinement or death row, one could actually call the minimum-security camp a reservoir of hope.

By 9:15 am, we are inside the chapel library of the Work Camp. The Protestant service, housed in the chapel sanctuary, is filled with over 100 men. Our little Catholic service consists of seven inmates—mostly from places very foreign to rural Florida: New England, Miami, Tampa, Puerto Rico. Centers of large Catholic populations. The Catholic men are seated around a brown folding table. We begin with an hour of religious instruction before the Communion service.

"Man," exclaims one fellow in exasperation, "What is the deal about being Catholic in this part of Florida? I cannot believe what I hear about our faith here! I have never seen anything like it before."

As he speaks, the other men are nodding and shaking their heads in agreement with his dismay.

"Welcome to the deep south of rural Florida," I laugh.

"Is it because we are surrounded by small towns?"

"No. I wish it were that simple. When I moved to Tallahassee, the medium-sized city that is the capital of the State of Florida, America's fourth largest state, Catholics told me that the main Christian bookstore had just moved Catholic materials from the occult section to a neutral shelf."

"It is unbelievable," a fellow with a thick Boston accent interjects. "You ought to hear what we have got to listen to about Lent and Ashes. You would think we were worshipping Satan."

"It is not just here," I caution him. "In Tallahassee, I practiced law and represented the county on several major projects. One year, I went straight from receiving ashes at the Co-Cathedral to a meeting at the county offices. As we took our seats around the meeting table, a senior county staff member lashed out at me, 'Our lawyer has dirt on his face. The least we could do is have a lawyer who can wash his face!'"

"What did you do?"

"I explained the meaning of the ashes as a form of penance and acknowledgment of our sinfulness before God. Also, I cited the strong Biblical tradition of wearing ashes as an outward sign that we are creatures made of dust
and that we know we will return to dust when we die. Ashes remind us to be
aware of our dependence upon God for even our very breath."

"What did he do?"

"He cursed me for being a g-d mackerel snapper and expressed his
opinion that the county should have been able to do better in hiring outside counsel. He was of course using an old derogatory term for Catholics
because we eat fish on Fridays in Lent."

"What did you do?"

"I simply said that his stereotype was unfair because I prefer red snapper,
so that makes me a snapper snapper." Everyone at the table laughed!

"How do we stop this?" asks the fellow who started the discussion. "How
do we get these people to understand that the history of the Catholic Church
is part of their history and the history of Christianity?"

"I do not have an ultimate answer to eradicating prejudice and bigotry
against American Catholics," I said, "but in the short run, my suggestion is to
wear the signs of our faith proudly and without apology. Wear those ashes.
Say your Rosary sitting on your bunk. Make the sign of the cross clearly and
unambiguously. We are the emissaries of Christ in the mission field of the
prison. Above all, be proud of being a mackerel snapper."

One of the first conclusions that must be drawn from the reality of
anti-Catholicism in our prisons is the tendency of some "free-world"
(that is, outside of prison) Catholics to doubt the veracity of the faith
of their brothers and sisters in prison is clearly erroneous. Far too
often, I have heard disdain from free-world Catholics in the pew who
refuse to believe that the faith of Catholics inside prison is genuine. In
many, even most, cases, I have discovered that not only is the faith of
prisoners genuine, but it comes at a steep price. There are rarely any
benefits to be obtained by openly practicing your Catholic faith in

prisons and jails. Instead, you might incur penalties for your Catholic faith by being counted out of special "Christian" events—especially at the formal prison chapels—because of the strongly-held belief on the part of some evangelical Protestants that Catholics are not Christians. This prejudice can even result in Catholic inmates being insidiously excluded from consideration for the best jobs and best housing in a prison or jail. Such adverse treatment of Catholics is not universal or guaranteed, but it is common enough to be a concern to Catholic prison ministry volunteers. When it occurs, moreover, although "everybody knows the score," it is virtually impossible to prove in a court of law.

Such insidious discrimination against Catholics are further cloaked in the myth that Catholicism is a small, misguided sect, almost like an occult denomination. The well-accepted true facts about the number of Catholic Christians in the world and in this country and the universality of the Catholic Church's work worldwide do not seem to penetrate inside rural prison fences. The chapels of many rural prisons and jails seem hermetically sealed from the facts of Christian history and the demographics of modern Christianity.

Many years ago, I had the unfortunate experience of a chaplain who sought to protect his "Christian" inmates from the temptations of "non-Christian" faiths, including Catholicism, by eliminating all the "non-Christian" material from the chapel general circulation library. He knew that the U.S. Constitution required him to make all that material available to the inmates. So, he ingeniously designated a closet as the "minority religion library" and emptied all the "non-Christian" materials, like Catholic Bibles and Catholic Catechisms, into that closet. The inmates, who have an incredible knack for descriptively naming people and things, promptly dubbed that space the "cult closet."

The cult-closet materials were only accessible by special request to that same anti-Catholic chaplain. Each inmate making a request for materials from there was immediately inundated with a deluge of materials mailed in from a local Baptist Church.

Out of the Closet

After Mass, the Catholic inmates and those studying the faith gather in the chapel library for the Catholic hour. This is a time of fellowship and instruction. Frequently it also turns out to be a time for correcting the "politically correct" misinformation about Catholicism that thrives in Florida's rural prisons.

Today is no exception. A pleasant middle-aged man who is preparing for Easter initiation into the Church raises his hand. "Since I started studying the Catholic faith, I have been bombarded: Catholics are all going to hell; Catholics are not saved; Catholics are not even Christians. What is all this about?"

"In a word: ignorance," I say as I shake my head. "You were all here a few weeks ago when a non-Catholic fellow inmate explained that in a Protestant service he was being taught that the pope is the anti-Christ and that the ashes worn by Catholics on the forehead at Lent are the mark of the beast from the Book of Revelations. We asked him to show us the Scriptural support for this. Of course, there was not any at all. He had been fed someone's ignorant misinterpretation of the Scriptures. He assumed they knew what they were talking about. They did not."

"Even so," the catechumen stands to raise another issue, "the attacks on Catholics never stop. I have also been challenged with this: if the Catholic Church is the true church, then why are Catholics a minority religion? Why are our materials kept in the 'cult closet' and not put out with the other Christian materials in the prison chapel library?"

We all know that the "cult closet" is the prison slang term for the small storage room where all non-Christian circulation library materials in that prison are kept. It is officially called the "minority religion" library. Evangelical or Fundamentalist Christian library materials for circulation are kept in the main chapel library. Recently, Catholic materials for circulation in that prison were deemed non-Christian and not even allowed to be kept with the Christian lending library.

"Look, don't ask me to explain other people's erroneous conclusions," I say. All I can do is give you the facts. And here are the facts."

"Number one, the State of Florida Department of Corrections has to guarantee freedom of religious practice. That means they must be concerned about minority religions at each prison. That designation has nothing to do with the number of people that practice a faith in the country or in the world. It only looks at the percentage of people of a given faith in a particular prison. Most of the people in this prison are Protestant. So, the State of Florida calls Catholics at this prison a minority religion."

"Does that mean the State of Florida has decided that Catholics are not Christian?"

"No, absolutely not," I waive my hand. "Minority religion status protects denominations too."

"So, why are Catholics in the cult closet and other Christians aren't?"

"I do not have a clue. Let me give you some more facts. Way more than half of all the Christians in the whole world are Catholic. There are 1,200,000,000 Catholic Christians in the world.[4] That is more than twice the total number of Protestant Christians in the world.[5] As for our country, according to the U.S. government as of 2009 there were over 68,500,000 Catholics in the U.S. The next largest Christian denomination in America was Southern Baptist with about 16,100,000 members. All the other Protestant denominations are much, much smaller. So Catholic Christians in America outnumber the next largest Christian group by 4-to-1 and most of the largest other ones by 10-to-1 or more."[6]

"So why are our materials in the cult closet? Why are we treated like a non-Christian religion?"

"I do not know, brother. I can only answer from what is real. And that conclusion cannot be supported by reality."

Another conclusion that must be drawn from such experiences of Catholics in prisons and jails is that the other Christian denominations see Catholics as more of a threat than the non-Christian faiths. My experience of the difference in treatment by some Evangelical and Pentecostal Christians toward Catholics, as opposed to members of non-Catholic faiths, is very similar to the difference in treatment we as a country make between enemy soldiers and enemy spies. Soldiers are known to be on the enemy side and are treated under specific rules and protections that will also protect our own soldiers. We may even think of their service honorably. Spies, on the other hand, are held in especially derisive and vitriolic disregard because they dress and act like they are on our side, but they are really the enemy. When we catch one, we sock it to them.

This appears to be the very way that some non-Catholic Christians view Catholics. They seem to think that Catholics are "pretending" to be Christian, like spies for God's enemy, in order to snatch souls out of heaven to send them to hell. This is frequently implied or even explicitly stated in their television revivals, their literature, their movies, and their sermons. That mistaken suspicion of Catholic motives can justify a tremendous amount of self-righteous bigotry and persecution.

It is unfortunate that suspicions of Catholic motivation stretch far beyond the spiritual realm. It is well known that many Protestant leaders advocated against the election of John F. Kennedy as President of the country because of their stated concern that he would be a spy and a patsy for a foreign potentate—their description of the Catholic pope. They were wrongly fearful that a Catholic President would make the United States subject to a foreign ruler. These grossly outrageous and totally unsupportable suspicions and fears continue to this day. When they are unleashed inside our prisons and jails, they can motivate hatred and violence.

Kill A Catholic For God And Country?

An esteemed jurist from New York once reflected on our human condition saying, "Negligence is in the air."

Perhaps, if he had lived in a rural Florida prison, he might have commented, "Anti-Catholicism is in the air."

We all know where anti-Catholicism comes from: the Protestant Reformation of 500 years ago. Founders of the new Christian denominations justified their departure from the unity of western Christianity by alleging that the successor to St. Peter, that is, the pope, was the anti-Christ and that the Catholic Church was the biblical beast of *Revelation*. I am told that such claims were in the original confessions of faith of the Lutherans, the Presbyterians the Anglicans, and others.

The Scotch-Irish who settled America's Deep South imported these wildly erroneous notions, which are sixteenth-century European political slogans masquerading as theology, and the presses of Catholic hate are still spinning.

The trophy for most notorious Catholic hate publisher has long been held by Chick Publications. Their comic book series demonizing the popes and their tracts filled with blatant, absolute falsehoods about the Roman Catholic faith are supposed to be banned from Florida prisons. That means the material cannot come in through the chaplains. Yet, the material continues to pour in through the prison mailrooms, especially in Spanish. Anyone who naively believes that such acidic hate speech is not serious, needs to spend a few minutes with Christian convicts who have been fueled into a simmering rage at Catholics because of the virulent lies fed to them through Chick Publications.

Some of the more mundane assaults on the Catholic faith may be protected by the fringes of the First Amendment. Americans tend to give religious groups the right to lie rather than turn our courts into arbiters of theological truth. So, for example, a particular newspaper that bills itself as an "independent Christian publication" and is prominently displayed in some prison chapels, falsely, maliciously, and regularly mocks Roman Catholic teaching and tradition as "denominational fantasy" and attacks the Eucharist. Such tripe contributes to the anti-Catholic atmosphere in many prisons, but there's not much we can do to prevent it. We can, however, answer and refute it.

For example, in extreme cases, we must stop the new level of anti-Catholic written hate speech inside rural Florida prisons, promoted by books such as *The Secret Terrorists*. This diabolical book is identified as a publication of "Truth Triumphant Ministries," with post office boxes in Tangerine and Eustis, Florida.

Any reader with an ounce of academic sophistication will immediately recognize this book as sewage with a binding. Not a smidgen of truth appears anywhere in its pages. Yet this despicable "manifesto," which all but explicitly rouses the passions of patriotism to take up arms against the *"true"* enemy of the United States is being read by men in Florida prisons, some with violent histories and legendary lack of impulse control.

Who is this enemy that this anti-Catholic author claims has put "the United States in more danger today than she has ever been"?

According to his moronic drivel, the real enemy is a "secret terrorist organization" called the Roman Catholic Church, especially the pope and the Jesuits. With lies and perversions that exceed all conceivable bounds of fantasy with outright malice, he purports to document his outrageous claims that the Roman Catholic Church was behind the World Trade Center attack and is *the* terrorist organization that threatens the survival of America.

Civil rights lawyers might argue over whether such a hateful, incendiary book should be allowed in a free and decent society. But can anyone conceive of any reason why such vile, abominable material, copyrighted in 2002 and clearly intended to mobilize post-9/11 violence against Catholics in America's South, should be allowed inside our Florida prisons?

Upon verification of the false contents of that book, it was banned and declared contraband in Florida's prisons. My main point here is that Catholic prison ministry volunteers throughout the country bear an affirmative duty to review the materials being disseminated in the chapels of the prisons and jails. Materials that are blatantly vituperative in characterization of Catholic beliefs or are geared to stir up hatred and violence against Catholics must be reported to the local administrations, and in state systems to the central administrative authorities. That is part of the job of protecting our faith inside the fences. But there is much more to do as well.

Catholic prison ministry volunteers must never take for granted the efforts of those who assist in combatting and eradicating anti-Catholic prejudices. Standing up against decades-old and centuries-old prejudices and bigotries is always courageous and needs to be recognized and appreciated as such. Prison wardens, administrators, chaplains, and guards who stand up to the subtle and not-so-subtle anti-Catholic attitudes of the prison subcultures need to be affirmed and thanked. Our goal is joyful cooperation with believers of goodwill for the sake of the Gospel.

WHEN WE VISIT JESUS IN PRISON

We Catholic prison ministry volunteers are blessed with an abundance of direction on how to handle our participation in the pastoral ministry of our bishops and priests when working shoulder to shoulder with non-Catholic Christians and with non-Christians. Not only are we to avoid returning the anti-Catholic attacks with attacks in kind, but we are also instructed to affirmatively build bridges of cooperation and goodwill. Catholic prison ministry volunteers do not engage in tit-for-tat. The core teaching for this approach is found in the documents of the Second Vatican Council:

> Respect and love ought to be extended also to those who think or act differently than we do in social, political, and even religious matters. In fact, the more deeply we come to understand their ways of thinking through such courtesy and love, the more easily will we be able to enter into dialogue with them.
>
> This love and good will, to be sure, must in no way render us indifferent to truth and goodness. Indeed love itself impels [Catholic] disciples of Christ to speak the saving truth to all men. But it is necessary to distinguish between *error*, which always merits repudiation, and *the person in error*, who never loses the dignity of being a person even when [he or she] is flawed by false or inadequate religious notions. God alone is the judge and searcher of hearts, for that reason he forbids us to make judgments about the internal guilt of anyone.
>
> The teaching of Christ even requires that we forgive injuries, and extends the law of love to include every enemy, according to the command of the New Law. "You have heard that it was said: Thou shalt love thy neighbor and hate thy enemy. But I say to you: love your enemies, do good to those who hate you, and pray for those who persecute and calumniate you" (Matthew 5:43-44)[7] (Citations omitted and italics added.)

In that same Second Vatican Council, the Church elaborates specifically on the principles that are to be followed in sharing the work space of ministry with brothers and sisters who are Christian but not

Catholic: the Catholic principles of Ecumenism.[8] Needless to say, these principles are to be fully employed by Catholic volunteers in prisons and jails.

There is a great deal of misunderstanding about Catholic ecumenism. I have encountered ministers of non-Catholic Christian denominations who think that ecumenism means Catholics should participate in the services and rituals of non-Catholic Christian denominations as though they were equivalent to the Catholic services and sacraments. In my opinion, that is not Catholic ecumenism, because such participation portends to recognize a unity that does not in fact exist.

The focus should instead be upon doing together the work which the words of Christ call us to in common, such as relieving human suffering. That is a unity of purpose that exists in fact. As Pope Francis recently stated in his address to the delegation of Salvation Army Leaders:[9]

I earnestly hope that Catholics and Salvationists will continue to offer a common witness to Christ and to the Gospel in a world so much in need of experiencing God's boundless mercy.

Catholics and Salvationists, together with other Christians, recognize that those in need have a special place in God's heart, so much so that the Lord Jesus Christ himself became poor for our sake. As a result, Catholics and Salvationists often meet in the same peripheries of society. It is my hope that our shared faith in Jesus Christ the Savior, the one mediator between God and [humans], will become evermore the firm foundation of friendship and cooperation between us. (Citations omitted)

True Catholic ecumenism recognizes the unity that does exist, although imperfectly: (¶3)

+ All men and women who believe in Christ and have been truly baptized are in imperfect communion with the Catholic Church.
+ All who have been justified by faith in Baptism are members of Christ's body, are rightly called Christian, and correctly accepted as brothers and sisters of Catholic Christians.
+ The separated Churches and Communities, though deficient in some respects, have not been deprived of significance in the mystery of salvation.
+ However, our separated brethren lack Christ's intended perfect unity with the Catholic Church, which is "the all-embracing means of salvation."

The true Catholic ecumenical movement includes: (¶4)

+ Every effort to avoid expressions, judgments, and actions that misrepresent the true state of unity.
+ Dialogue between competent experts from different Churches and Communities.
+ Actions prudently and patiently taken by the Catholic faithful under the attentive guidance of their bishops to promote justice and truth, concord and collaboration, and the spirit of brotherly love and unity.
+ Prayer for our separated brethren.
+ Unceasing work by all the Catholic faithful toward Christian perfection.
+ Preservation within the Catholic Church of unity in essentials.
+ Generous recognition of the truly Christian endowments of our separated brethren, especially of their virtuous works and virtuous lives.

The practice of true Catholic ecumenism includes Church renewal as evidenced by: [¶6]

+ Biblical and liturgical movements.
+ Preaching of the Word of God.
+ Catechetics.
+ The Apostolate of the Laity.
+ The new forms of Religious Life.
+ The spirituality of Married Life.
+ The Church's social teaching and activity.

As part and parcel of this new ecumenism, the Church describes spiritual ecumenism as the effort by all the faithful to live holier lives, including with prayer for the unity of all Christians. [¶7-8] Moreover, there is an affirmative duty on the faithful to understand and study the outlook, history, and spiritual and liturgical life of our separated brethren in order to engage in meaningful dialogue. [¶9] But doing so should never obscure the fact that, "according to Catholic belief, the authentic teaching authority of the Church has a special place in the interpretation and preaching of the written word of God." [¶21] In other words, as we Catholic prison ministry volunteers engage in cooperative and ecumenical activities, we do so as Catholics, bearing the teaching of the Church before us.

One of the most persistent demands on a Catholic prison ministry volunteer is to answer questions concerning the Catholic faith. This will frequently be in response to questions based on misinformation, sometimes even erroneous teaching in other churches about what Catholics do and why they do it. The questions could come from officers, from other staff, from inmates, or even from other volunteers. We Catholic prison ministry volunteers must endeavor to know our faith as well as possible, so as to answer accurately and with sufficient depth.

Responding to such questions should also be done lovingly, with gentleness. One can only imagine how hard it might be for the inquiring person to finally ask the question that has been on his or her mind for years. For example, imagine the plight of a male corrections officer in Florida's highest security prison with over 1,200 solitary cells when, on a Wednesday that seems just like any other late winter Wednesday, he shows up for work only to find out that he is assigned to go with a Catholic volunteer who will be distributing ashes for Ash Wednesday. As one of the escort officers, he will have the flap key to open the food flap in the door of some of the almost 200 solitary cells that have a Catholic inside. He has nothing against the particular volunteer or Catholics, *per se*. He does not know for sure if they are Christian or not; but for his whole life he has heard from the pulpit at his rural non-denominational Christian church that the Catholic ashes distributed on Ash Wednesday are from human remains and are smeared on the forehead of Catholics purportedly as a sign of allegiance to Satan, the Mark of the Beast in Revelation 13:16-18 of the Bible.

Far-fetched? Not at all. Just another day in Catholic prison ministry in the rural U.S. I know. I was there.

Dust to Dust

It is not even spring, but the mercury is pushing eighty at high noon. "Already sweating and it is only Ash Wednesday," I sigh, making my way into the prison guard stations and entry gates.

"What is in the plastic bottle?"

"Ashes, sir." I respond nonchalantly, as though I am back in the Italian Catholic neighborhood of my youth. "Ashes for Ash Wednesday."

"Say what?"

"Ashes," I repeat, pointing to the telltale outward sign on my own forehead. "It is a Catholic thing, sir. The ashes are on the gate pass."

Soon, I am back at the chapel. The chaplain hands me the list of Catholics in the prison. "There are almost two hundred of them. Good luck."

Twenty years ago many of the men in this prison were in general population. That meant Catholics could come to the chapel and receive ashes just like in a church. Those days are gone.

This prison is now all solitary confinement. The 1,200 cells are all lock-down. There will be no ashes for these Catholics unless the ashes come to them.

Solitary confinement has its own rules. The ashes must be administered through the "food flap," the narrow opening in each man's door through which food, toilet paper, clothes, laundry, mops, toilet brushes, and everything else pass between the world inside that cell and the world outside. Only an officer on the wing can unlock the food flap. And he must stand right there until it's relocked. With twelve prison wings I will need help from at least a dozen different guards. Those poor officers are not going to be overjoyed to see me.

The hall sergeant turns the outside lock in the thick metal door of the first wing, banging his key against its huge brass handle. The clanging reverberates up and down the wing stairwells inside, announcing to the officers inside that someone is "on the door." That door will not open until an officer inside keys the companion lock.

The door opens. I enter, identify myself, and announce my purpose. The blank expressions around me are not unfriendly or uncooperative. They are just blank. In few words, I summarize the purpose of the ashes and the method of application. The officers nod. One is assigned to escort me through that wing.

As we climb to the third floor atrium, he pauses, obviously a bit shaken and uncomfortable. He is staring at the Styrofoam cup in my hands that holds the blessed slurry. His pallor has turned pasty white. I am concerned he is having a heart attack.

"No offense, sir," he speaks softly, but with great emotion. "But, I have to know. Just what are those the ashes of?"

He is trying to be very respectful. I can only imagine what he has been told in this part of the country about Catholics. He seems visibly relieved—and confused—at hearing that the ashes are burned palm branches from Palm Sunday mixed with blessed oil and water.

Cell by cell, floor by floor, wing after wing, officer after officer, the food flap is opened. I kneel on the concrete floor before each cell and reach through the opening, taking the hand on the other side. "In the name of the Father, the Son and the Holy Spirit…."

WHEN WE VISIT JESUS IN PRISON

Prison brother after prison brother bows his head and receives that blessed mark which is so uniquely Catholic: "Remember, man, you are dust and to dust you will return."

The interruptions of the daily routines are inevitable. The nurse must distribute meds. Food carts arrive with dinner. Laundry must be collected. The officers patiently juggle priorities while trying to accommodate my mission. Over and over I am asked, and over and over I gently answer, where the ashes are from, what the ashes mean, and why we Catholics wear them at the beginning of Lent.

Finally I am in the last wing. Almost five hours have passed. Eleven escort officers have already learned something new about Catholics. There are thirteen more men to go. My final escort officer listens quietly as I kneel in front of the next open food-flap and pray with the prisoner inside: "Lord, do not face us suddenly with death, but give us time to repent."

"Sounds like a good prayer for all of us," the guard sighs, locking the flap.

"All of us who are dust," I smile. "Have you met anyone that isn't?"

In carrying out the directions of our Church for dealing with separated Christian brothers and sisters, we Catholic prison ministry volunteers must not become impatient at their questions nor become defensive or assume that our faith is being attacked. That moment when the question is asked one-on-one, deep inside a prison fence, may be the first time the inquiring person has been able to ask their questions of a real, live Catholic. Such teachable moments are more than just ecumenical; they are like gold. By the same token, it is important to acknowledge the progress that is being made in many prisons because of the introduction of local and regional professional chaplains of various denominations and faiths with a better understanding of the Catholic faith and because of wardens and administrative staff who see the efforts of Catholic prison volunteers as a contribution to the betterment of the inmates and the staff. In my personal experience over the last two decades, in the very same prisons described in the three articles immediately above, I have observed a 180° change in the institutional attitude toward Catholic prison ministry volunteers.

The attitudes of some rural subcultures that host many prisons may not change so quickly. I had the experience of an officer who was so excited to find out the truth about many Catholic practices that he wanted to get his hands on a *Catholic Catechism*. He dare not accept it in the prison, however, because others from his church who work there might see it. He also dare not have it sent to his house, because his wife or his mother-in-law might see it. Instead, I delivered a catechism to him discretely, wrapped in a brown paper bag, in the disposable diaper aisle of a nearby discount store. Even then it could not be transferred hand-to-hand. Rather, I had to drop it in passing, without discussion or even salutation, in his green plastic hand-basket that the store provided for convenience of customers.

Not all ecumenical events in prison ministry are nearly so dramatic! In most situations, the exchanges of information are routine and low key. But it does help for the volunteer to keep a good sense of humor. That can be especially true when dealing with the questions of inmates who want to save the Catholic prison ministry volunteer from certainty of damnation by rescuing them from the supposedly satanic clutches of the Catholic Church.

Angels Don't Lie

It is a day of regular rounds in solitary confinement. The head chaplain has provided me with a prison *triptik*, a list of the men who have asked to see a Catholic ministry volunteer. On a wing of one hundred men, there may be only one who has requested to see me. But once I am on the wing, almost everybody is "standing on the door" requesting a visit. Standing on the door means face squashed against the little cell door window, yelling or pounding, trying to out-decibel all the other men standing on their doors. The noise can be staggering.

Most are yelling, "Hey, Chap!" or "Over here, Chap!" Some voices are shrieks. Some men just keep throwing their whole body weight against the door, like a battering ram. The metallic booms and screams echo throughout

WHEN WE VISIT JESUS IN PRISON

the atrium of the wing. This wing is one of disciplinary confinement. Human agony in surround sound.

As I circle the second floor catwalk of the wing, a voice yells from my left. "Hey, I have a religious question for you."

I have learned the local vernacular. The voice is from a child of God about to take his best shot at revealing the fatal gross errors of Catholicism. I do not take it personally anymore. It is pretty boring in those cells. I am the catch of the day.

"You get one question of 25 words or less," I laugh as I turn to the partial face in the miniscule window. "Or two questions of less than 10 words each."

The stranger in the cell knows I am on to him. He bites back a smirk and musters a straight face. "Are you one of them Mary worshippers?"

"Nope," I shrug. "That was seven words, so you get one more question."

"Is that all you're going to say?" he blurts out in disgust.

"Yup," I wave good-bye and turn to leave.

"Wait a minute! Gimme a necklace!"

"You know I don't have necklaces," I wave him off over my shoulder.

"C'mon, man. The colored beads."

"Do you mean the prayer beads that we call rosaries?" I pause and turn back toward his cell.

"Yeah. Gimme one of them."

The hook is baited. It is time to let out the line. I stroll back toward his door without haste.

"You know I cannot give you those unless you promise to use them as prayer beads."

"Sure. No problem."

"You know that they are contraband if you wear them." I summarize the rule that prohibits any colored paraphernalia that could be used for gang insignia, including colored rosaries. We must use only jet black beads with breakaway string. "You can only use them to pray."

"Sure. Just to pray."

I am at his door. "What are you going to pray on them?"

He shrugs.

"We Catholics pray Bible verses," I suggest as I shove the rosary through the crack by the wall and into his fingers. "You could pray verses of things that angels have said in the Bible."

"Yeah," he nods in mock relief, "Angels don't lie."

"Then do this," I continue as he holds up the beads to the window. "Say the *Lord's Prayer* on the little beads with space around them and say a Bible verse on each of the beads that are close together."

"What? Man, how many is that?"

"Fifty. But most of us have picked one verse. We just keep praying it over and over. You could do that. It is easier."

"Yeah. Sounds good. What do you use?"

"We use the Gospel of Luke, chapter 1, verse 28," I answer, opening my Bible and reading it to him. "Hail Mary, full of grace, the Lord is with you."

His mouth drops open in astonishment. The hook is set.

"Angels don't lie," I wink. "And it is in the Bible."

It is incumbent upon us Catholic prison ministry volunteers to educate ourselves sufficiently in Church teaching in order to be capable of answering the inevitable questions about the faith. Sometimes the questions will sound like barbs or attacks, but they should always be treated as real questions. And the people making the inquiry should be assumed to be seeking truth in good faith. Their question may sound decidedly more like condemnation or judgment rather than a legitimate inquiry. In that case we should give them the benefit of the doubt: *first*, assuming that no one ever taught them how to properly ask a question, perhaps rephrasing it for them, and *then* answering the question we think they *meant* to ask.

The question about the Catholic devotion of saying the Rosary is a frequent one. In fact, many of the questions we will be asked are the same questions that have been asked by other inmates before, and there is a wealth of resources available to help us bone-up for the most inevitable questions.

I have compiled a goldmine of valuable material for self-preparation to respond to questions and attacks on the faith from non-Catholic Christians wielding poorly understood Scripture citations. You can find them in the following resources:

WHEN WE VISIT JESUS IN PRISON

+ Father Peter M. J. Stravinskas, *The Catholic Response* (Huntington, Indiana: Our Sunday Visitor, 1985). Fr. Stravinskas, at the time of writing this book, was the Director of Public Relations for the Catholic League for Religious and Civil Rights. He offers an ecumenically acceptable reasoned and calm response to Fundamentalist criticisms of the Catholic Church.

+ Father Ronald D. Witherup, SS, *Biblical Fundamentalism: What Every Catholic Should Know* (Collegeville, Minnesota: Liturgical Press, 2001). Fr. Witherup, at the time of writing this book, was Provincial of the U.S. Province of the Sulpicians. His writing responds to fundamentalist attacks that the Catholic Church is anti-Biblical and to fundamentalist attitudes that have crept into some Catholic circles regarding the Bible.

+ James J. Drummey, *Catholic Replies: Answers to Over 800 of the Most Often Asked Questions about Religious and Moral Issues* (Norwood, Massachusetts: C.R. Publications, 1995). In his foreword, the late Charlie E. Rice, Professor Emeritus Notre Dame Law School, calls this book a work of catechesis. Drummey, a renowned Catholic educator and editor of the *Catholic Replies* newspaper column, answers questions about Catholic teaching on the Trinity, Scripture, the Pope, Salvation, Catholic prayers and practices, Mary, the Angels, the Saints, the Sacraments, the Eucharist, the Liturgy, Marriage, Human Life, Morality and numerous other issues.

+ Karl Keating, *Catholicism and Fundamentalism: The Attack on "Romanism" by "Bible Christians"* (San Francisco, California: Ignatius Press, 1988). Keating poses the fundamentalist attacks on Catholicism exactly as they are worded by the attackers and then answers them in clear, detailed and charitable fashion.

+ Karl Keating, *The Usual Suspects: Answering Anti-Catholic Fundamentalists* (San Francisco, California: Ignatius Press,

2000). This supplemental work by Keating adds to the repertoire of attacks and answers.

+ David B. Currie, *Born Fundamentalist: Born Again Catholic* (San Francisco, California: Ignatius Press, 1996) (with a strong endorsement from the Editor of *Catholic Answers*).

Another issue we need to be ready to deal with is the various ideas around the "end of time." While the contemporarily famous Left Behind Series does not explicitly condemn all Catholics to be part of the unfortunate remnant who will be "left behind" in the so-called Rapture, virtually every inmate who has raised the subject of those books (and movies) with me has understood that to be the case.

We Catholic prison ministry volunteers need to be ready to deal with the issues created by popular misconceptions about the Rapture—the bowls, seals and trumpets—and with the pre-Tribulation and Post-Tribulation partisans of the different Evangelical and Pentecostal persuasions. If we can show a facility with the specialized words and phrases used by non-Catholic Christians in discussing such issues, we will have a better chance of being heard on the Catholic position. The following resources can be helpful in learning to address the *Rapture*:

+ Paul Thigpen, *The Rapture: A Catholic Response to "End Times" Ferver* (West Chester, Pennsylvania: Ascension Press, 2001). Thigpen, a former evangelical pastor turned Catholic, draws from Scripture, Tradition, the Catholic catechism, and Church history to reveal the inconsistent teachings and contradictions inherent in popular notions of the Rapture doctrine.
+ Ralph Martin, *Is Jesus Coming Soon? A Catholic Perspective on the Second Coming* (San Francisco, California: Ignatius Press, 1997).

In addition to non-Catholic Christians, we Catholic prison ministry volunteers also rub elbows with many members of non-Christian

WHEN WE VISIT JESUS IN PRISON

religions. The groups most often encountered are Jewish and Muslim. While those groups do not share with Catholics the belief that the Christian Scriptures are Divine Revelation, they do share with us the Hebrew Scriptures and the paternity of the Patriarch Abraham as the Father of Faith, as well as our commitment to justice and to love. In our dealings with Jewish groups, Muslim groups, and all the other non-Christian religious groups, our Church has provided significant guidance. This teaching is found in the documents of the Second Vatican Council:[10]

> The Catholic Church rejects nothing that is true and holy in these religions. She regards with sincere reverence ways of conduct and of life, those precepts and teaching which...reflect a ray of that Truth which enlightens all [men and women]. [And the Church] exhorts her [sons and daughters] that through dialogue and collaboration with the followers of other religions, carried out with prudence and love and in witness to the Christian faith and life, they recognize, preserve and promote the good things, spiritual and moral, as well as the socio-cultural values found among these [men and women]. [¶2]

A powerful example of this approach in action is the activity of the Pro-Life Alliance, a "coalition of nontraditional organizations that have banded together for the protection of the unborn." The group met in conjunction with the 2015 March for Life Rally in Washington, DC. As announced by Aimee Murphy, founder of the group, the alliance's mission is to "work together to abolish abortion" uniting "atheists, pagans, Buddhists, Muslims and Jews" on the issue of the sanctity of human life and dignity."[11]

Such concerted action with respect to crime and punishment based upon shared moral principles and religious beliefs is a natural application of the Church's teaching to the pluralistic environment of ministry in prison.

In regards to specific world religions, with respect to the Muslim faith the Church tells us that the adherents of that faith:

+ Are regarded by the Church with esteem.
+ Revere Jesus as a prophet.
+ Honor Mary, His Virgin Mother.
+ Await the Day of Judgment.
+ Value the moral life and worship of God.
+ Believe in prayer, fasting and almsgiving.

Moreover, despite the violence of the past between Christians and Muslims, the Church "urges all to forget the past and to work sincerely for mutual understanding ... social justice and moral welfare, as well as peace and freedom." [¶3]

With respect to those of the Jewish faith, the Council Fathers remind us that:

+ God holds the Jews most dear, for the sake of their ancestors in faith.
+ Our spiritual patrimony is so great that we should foster mutual understanding and respect.
+ Those of the Jewish faith should never be presented as rejected or accursed by God.
+ The Church, not because of politics but rather due to Gospel love, decries hatred, persecutions, and displays of anti-Semitism directed against Jews at any time, by anyone. [¶4]

With respect to all members of non-Christian religions, the Church reminds us that:

+ We must treat all in a brotherly or sisterly way.
+ We must never discriminate or harass anyone because of race, color, condition of life, or religion.
+ We are to maintain good fellowship and, so far as is possible, live in peace with all people. [¶5]

In similar fashion to the self-preparation expected of us Catholic prison ministry volunteers for handling questions from non-Catholic

Christians, we should be prepared to field questions from non-Christians, as well. My experience is that non-Christian inmates usually present questions about Christianity in general, as opposed to specific questions about Catholicism. The preparation for fielding the more general questions on Christianity at large is referred to as "Christian apologetics." The following works of two well-known Boston College professors in Christian apologetics can be very helpful in this preparation:

+ Peter Kreeft and Ronald K. Tacelli, SJ., *Pocket Handbook of Christian Apologetics* (Downers Grove, Illinois: InterVaristy Press, 1994).
+ Peter Kreeft and Ronald K. Tacelli, SJ., *Handbook of Christian Apologetics: Hundreds of Answers to Crucial Questions* (Downers Grove, Illinois: InterVaristy Press Academic, 1994).
+ Peter Kreeft, *Christianity for Modern Pagans: Pascal's Pensées Edited, Outlined & Explaine*d (San Francisco, California: Ignatius Press, 1993).

For Catholic prison ministry volunteers who want a brief understanding of how to respond to the approaches made to Catholics by members of different non-Christian religions, the following work is quite handy:

+ Albert J. Nevins, M.M., *Strangers at Your Door* (Huntington, Indiana: Our Sunday Visitor Press, 1998).

A seminal work for understanding the faith relationship between Catholics and Jews is:

+ Roy H. Schoeman, *Salvation is from the Jews: The Role of Judaism in Salvation History from Abraham to the Second Coming* (San Francisco, California: Ignatius Press: 2003).

Finally, with Islam openly acknowledged as the fastest growing religion in America's prisons and jails, every volunteer should have a working knowledge of that faith. A valuable resource for that purpose is:

+ Fr. Samir Khalil Samir, SJ., *111 Questions on Islam in the West*, edited and revised by Fr. Wafik Nasry, SJ. (San Francisco, California: Ignatius Press, 2008).

Despite the complexities, the nuances, and the learning we volunteers undertake in preparation for the queries of inmates and staff inside the prison walls, we must always keep in the forefront of our consciousness the fact that knowledge of Catholic and Christian teaching falls on deaf ears without the witness of the lived life. By the same token, when a person revered and renowned on the world stage as someone of holiness and honor sets his or her life as a testimony to the truth of Divine Revelation and of Catholic teaching, incredible things can happen. Such a person was Pope John Paul II.

Pope John Paul II Makes His Final Visit

During the final days of Pope John Paul II's life and those immediately following his death, the electronic media was filled with pictures and testimonies recounting his unparalleled legacy to the Church and the world. As the images reached to every corner of the world, they also penetrated the concrete and steel of Florida's death row. The echoes of his final visit to Florida's most infamous prison unit come to me in the voices of the men who live here.

"Chap, chap, chap," a young man who has never spoken to me before, never even acknowledged me before, waives me down. "I have got a question for you."

"Sure," I respond nonchalantly, trying not to sound surprised. "What's up?"

"Well I have been watching all this stuff on the box about this pope. All the stuff he did. And…well…you know, I ain't no Catholic or nothing like that…but man…he was really something." The prisoner's arms are pumping in broad sweeps as he struggles for the unfamiliar words to express deep emotions. "I know we are all flesh and all that…but that man…wow…he just was really something else."

His glance falls to the floor as he rubs tears from the corner of his downcast eyes. I pause before gently asking, "And what is your question?"

"Him," he motions toward the little plastic black and white TV that has introduced him to the man that over a billion Catholics had called Papa for almost three decades. "Him…how can a man be such a life?"

I realize that this young man has finally experienced what it means for someone to be a father. For a man to selflessly nurture and sustain his children. His tears are the tears of losing a father, cried by one who has never known a father.

"It is really true," I speak very softly. "Today, we are all orphans."

Cell after cell after cell, I am met with similar reactions to the passing of "that Polish Pope." I am barraged with heartfelt questions about the Vatican, about the Catholic Church, about our faith.

Corridors that usually take forty-five minutes to cover will take me two hours today. Everyone wants to speak to me about John Paul. "There is no doubt about it," an elderly Pentecostal man in a wheelchair smiles at me through the bars while gesturing toward the small TV hanging on his wall. "That man is a saint. He is of God."

Three hours later I am standing at the cell of an articulate man of Muslim faith. He, too, feels the need to express his admiration. "The world has never seen such a man in anyone else in my lifetime," he assures me. "Everybody knows it. Look at all the leaders who have flocked to Rome to pay their respects. No one else has ever had such an outpouring of tribute from every corner of the world. He reached out to everyone, even to us."

His finger points to himself, signifying all those of his faith. "And he forgave that guy who tried to kill him, even visited the guy in prison. Incredible. Just an incredible man."

I am finding myself a bit overwhelmed by the constant outpouring of warm sentiment from over a hundred men in a single day. My own deep feelings are looking for expression as I come to the cell of a Catholic brother who is a fervent and regular communicant. He gives voice to my unspoken thoughts. "You know," he beams as our eyes meet in the moment before I remove the host from the pyx and begin to pray. "It makes you proud to be Catholic. After all the garbage we have had to take from the media about the Church for the last several years, it really makes you proud to be a Catholic."

That leads to the very next critical question: What does it mean to become a Catholic?

The answer to that question is the focus of the next chapter.

> "Jesus invites us into God's family. Jesus is the 'only Son of God' (John3:18). We receive our status by adoption."
>
> Cardinal Donald Wuerl[1]

CHAPTER 5

Catholic Prison Ministry as Evangelization

What does it mean to become a Catholic Christian? In a word: *Family*. When we join the ranks of the baptized, we join a family, the Family of God. Cardinal Wuerl shares this experience after celebrating a Sunday Mass:

> "Why do you call us brothers and sisters?" a youngster asked me after Mass. "You're not my brother."
>
> "Ah, but I am spiritually, because we are all members of God's family," I responded.
>
> After he received a nod of affirmation from his mother and father who stood behind him, he said, "Wow, I didn't know that." Then he added, "That's cool."[2]

In the modern world, despite its affluence and abundance, despite electronic gadgets and impressive technological capabilities, individuals are suffering in the depths of aloneness. Isolation is pervasive.

Many folks do not even know who their neighbors are. Spiritual isolation is rampant, as well. Even as that is true in the "free world" (the world outside of prison), the level of isolation and loneliness inside prison is that much greater.

When Catholic prison ministry volunteers step inside the prison fence, they step into a world of broken and severed relationships. Everyone in prison is someone's son or daughter, is someone's grandchild, perhaps even someone's niece or nephew. Many inmates have brothers and sisters and are someone's aunt or uncle. But with the stress and barriers of incarceration, and the social stigmas that attach to the families of wrongdoers, those connections may not be functional or even healthy. In some cases, the connections may be damaged so severely that they no longer exist. Volunteers in prison ministry can visualize themselves as stepping into the center of these broken connections and standing with the inmate amidst a debris field of shattered relationships.

We Catholic prison ministry volunteers bring a message of hope into this desolation. We offer an entire spiritual family, the Family of God, to be in relationship with the inmates, allowing them to become a spiritual son or daughter, spiritual grandchild, spiritual niece or nephew, spiritual sibling. Little by little, the bonds of connectedness can be rebuilt. We are envoys of a large spiritual family sent out to engage inmates, to welcome them into the Catholic family, and to offer God's healing, restorative love. The Catholic term for the process of making this invitation is *evangelization*.

The Family of Faith, with Jesus as its head, also includes the angels and the saints who have gone ahead into eternal life as part of the Communion of Saints. This Family of Faith is the Eternal Family of both the inmate and the volunteer.

WHEN WE VISIT JESUS IN PRISON

The Legacy of August Ninth

At 12:25 pm retired Bishop John Snyder and Fr. Joe Maniangat, the priest for Florida's death row from 1983 until 1999, don the vestments for a special Mass. My wife, Susan, tunes her guitar and sets out the music. Baptismal candle, water, pitcher and small towel are all neatly placed next to the chairs before the altar. Chrism for confirmation is at the corner of the altar. All is in readiness. As soon as count clears, the officers will escort our brother to this prison chapel for his initiation into the Family of Faith.

Unlike the rugged individualism of some understandings of Christianity, our Catholic faith cherishes the reality of community, the Family of Faith. We are surrounded by brothers and sisters in faith throughout the world and throughout time. A cloud of witnesses testifies to the truth of the baptismal moment. Even when to the world we seem alone, the Family of Faith that is the Communion of Saints is standing for us and with us. We are never abandoned.

Today is August Ninth. What a day to be baptized and confirmed! Especially for a man who has spent fifteen years on Florida's death row and just last spring had his sentence reduced to life in prison. The blossoming of faith from the shadow of death—that is the legacy of August Ninth. The prisoner is still fighting to clear his name, to have the facts of his case as he knows them revealed. He has waited many years for the truth to come out. That is also part of the legacy of August Ninth.

As I reflect on this mystery of God's ways, hidden truth revealed by God's hand in God's time, another prisoner comes to mind. He, too, seemed isolated and alone in a solitary cell, standing against insurmountable odds. The time was 1943. The place was Austria. The man was Franz Jägerstätter, a peasant farmer who prayed the Rosary constantly and received Communion daily. His wife and three children could not be with him during those long, dark nights of the soul in prison. He was truly alone with none but his God and his Family of Faith.

Those who loved him wanted to see him spared from further suffering. Friends and family exhorted him to give in, to compromise. Virtually everyone beseeched him to do whatever was necessary in order to get out of prison. But what was necessary was for him to agree to fight for Hitler, which in good conscience he could not do. God nourished Franz in his struggle against the pressure to conform. He prayed and fasted and refused to bear weapons for Hitler. He was beheaded at Brandenburg Prison in Berlin at 4 pm on August 9, 1943. He died, apparently alone and unsung.

To all involved in Franz Jägerstätter's execution, he must have seemed a fool, forgotten before his body even turned cold. But then, against all odds, in the laboring of the next generation of the Catholic Family of Faith, his sacrifice is rediscovered. His story told. The solitary witness of his quiet refusal to compromise moral principles is discussed by the bishops and cardinals of the worldwide Catholic Church at the Second Vatican Council.[3]

Now, decades after that lonely execution, the side entrance door to the prison chapel at Union Correctional Institution in Florida swings open. Our brother is escorted inside. It is time to begin. My wife and I, standing as his godparents, renew our vows of faith as he commits to his. His lifelong name is surrendered, yielding to the name "Christopher'—one who bears Christ. The water pours. The candle is lit. The chrism is touched to the inmate's forehead. For the first time, the consecrated bread, forever changed, touches his lips.

It is August Ninth. The Family of Faith is in jubilation. Aloneness has been vanquished again by Communion.

The victory over aloneness, through membership in the Family of God, is a fruit of evangelization. The means of evangelization is very simple and very specific:

> The first moment of any evangelization originates not from a program, but in an encounter with a person, Jesus Christ, the Son of God. The Church maintains that "it is the same Lord Jesus who, present in his Church, goes before the work of evangelizers, accompanies it, follows it, and makes their labors bear fruit. What took place at the origins of Christian history continues through its entire course." We rely first and always on Jesus.[4]

It is understandable that we prison ministry volunteers might feel a bit confused as to the proper role of ecumenism and the primary role of evangelization as we labor as Catholics inside the prison fences. The Church is very clear in her guidance, however, instructing that these two realities—ecumenism and evangelization—must be held together in a dynamic missionary tension, without succumbing to the temptation to forego either one or the other:

> This teaching does not contradict the universal salvific will of God, who "desires that all [people] be saved and come to a knowledge of the truth" (1 Timothy 2:4); therefore, "it is necessary to keep these two truths together, namely, the real possibility of salvation in Christ for all [humankind] and the necessity of the Church for salvation."[5]
>
> Both these truths help us to understand the *one mystery of salvation*, so that we can come to know God's mercy and our own responsibility. Salvation, which always remains a gift of the Holy Spirit, requires [our] cooperation, both to save [ourselves] and to save others. This is God's will, and this is why [God] established the Church and made her a part of his plan of salvation.[6] [Italics in original.]

So, how is that done? How does a Catholic prison ministry volunteer maintain the core values of ecumenism identified in Chapter 4, while also energetically serving as a witness for evangelization? Cardinal Theodore E. McCarrick, then Archbishop of Washington, DC, addressed this question in the broader perspective of all Catholic ministry in his keynote address to the North American Institute for Catholic Evangelization:[7]

> But how do we preach the Gospel? How do we truly be missionaries in today's world? Here there are three points I want to make.
>
> First of all, we have to know what the Gospel says. We have to take it and read it and understand it, the Gospel in one hand and *The Catechism of the Catholic Church* in the other. We have to appreciate that we cannot just go out and say that "Jesus

Christ is Lord." In today's world we have to know what comes before that and what comes after that....

Secondly, we have to tell it like it is. I think of St. Paul's criticism of those who do not preach the Gospel correctly, who twist it for their own desires or their own projects. Forgive me for being very direct when I say that there really is no place in evangelization for those who tell us: "I will accept this and not that," the so-called "cafeteria Catholics" of today. The Gospel is one piece....

Thirdly, the evangelist must speak from the heart. The evangelist must know what he or she is all about, know what he or she needs to proclaim, the truth of the Gospel, the power of the doctrine, and to build on that a solid foundation of faith. To know what it says and to know what it means ultimately is to let it be alive in us, because if it is not alive in us, it is not alive in what we say, in what we proclaim. To know it well, to accept it all, to live it: these are the marks of the true evangelist.

Do You Believe It?

Most Catholics my age have experienced sponsoring someone for Confirmation or being a godparent for Baptism. In the early sixties, confirmations were done at a younger age than today. I was confirmed in fifth grade and served as a sponsor in 8th grade. The young man involved had helped with my paper route for three years. There is more there than meets the eye. Harsh Michigan winters. Hot humid summers. Wayward dogs and neighborhood toughs. You really get to know someone when you work together in such circumstances. I could vouch for his character and his loyalty. Even for his faith that God would protect us from rabies, frostbite, and heat stroke.

The first taste of god-parenting came at that time as well. My youngest brother was born just a week before my 14th birthday. I was honored to become his godfather, but the relationship has since grown even deeper. We share our faith more readily as adults than we did as youngsters in the Motor City.

WHEN WE VISIT JESUS IN PRISON

These sacramental roles are important. Someone in the community of faith must step forward and speak for the larger Family of God. The godparent must repeat the words of commitment that the new Christian, whether child or adult, will be mentored in the faith. And the sponsor must vouch for the faith of the one to be confirmed. Committing. Vouching. Those are the roles of the godparent and sponsor.

Where faith is alive, there will always be baptisms and confirmations. Hence, there will always be a need for godparents and sponsors. Even in prison. The faith is alive there, but there is more complexity than usual. Prison is not an easy place to choose Catholicism.

Catholics are a minority in most prisons. Anti-Catholic tracts by people like Jack Chick and others promise absolute certainty of hellfire to anyone who is baptized into the Catholic faith. On occasion, well-meaning but misguided ministers from other Christian denominations have argued passionately to men on death row that becoming Catholic will seal their eternal fate in hell at the moment of their execution.

Several men on death row in the prisons where I work are currently enrolled in RCIA. Others are studying Catholic materials to make a decision. Today there will be a baptism and confirmation of one inmate I have been preparing for the two sacraments, but I think to myself, "Who will step up and promise to mentor this man spiritually? Who will vouch for his faith and his courage?" The answer is clear: "Let it be me, Lord."

I have spent months tutoring this young man through the sweltering heat of August and the frigid days of December. I have shared his prayers in the most difficult of circumstances. It is my honor to voice the words of godparent and sponsor in his behalf.

He kneels in his prison whites on the floor inside his cell.

A priest and I stand in the corridor at the cell door.

The priest stretches his hand through the bars, anointing as he speaks the words of the baptismal rite. My new godson responds solemnly and fervently to the questions.

The oils are administered. The blessed water pours from a Styrofoam cup, over his head and onto the concrete floor. A candle and a white cloth are touched by the confirmand and their symbolic significance is explained to him.

"At this moment," Father finishes, "your immortal soul is as white as snow.

You believe that, don't you?"

Our newest member of the Catholic Family of Faith rises slowly while the words of the priest continue to settle in. Finally, wiping streams of water from his face with a worn prison towel, he responds.

"I know you believe it, Father. I know Brother Dale believes it. So, I am able to believe it."

For many Catholics, the word *evangelization* triggers mental images of preachers on television harping for money or screaming on street corners. It seems that most lay Catholics would rather shrug that job off to the ordained and the vowed religious, absolving themselves of any responsibility. After all, they tell themselves, "We are just lay people. That work is above our pay grade." Nothing could be further from the truth.

The duty to evangelize comes with the grace of Baptism as part of the work of the Christian vocation. The role of the laity in this work, according to the Second Vatican Council's *Decree on the Apostolate of the Laity*, is to "enable all people to share in his saving redemption and enter into relationship with Christ." [¶2] This is called the apostolate of the laity and the Church has been very insistent about it,[8] instructing us that:

+ This apostolate was not limited to the times of the early Church; in fact, modern conditions demand that the apostolate be broadened and intensified. [¶1]
+ The laity exercise the apostolate by activity directed to the evangelization and sanctification of men and women. [¶2]
+ They should not cease to develop earnestly the qualities and talents bestowed on them in accord with the conditions of their life in the lay state. [¶4]
+ They should also hold in high esteem professional skill, family and civic spirit, and the virtues relating to social customs. [¶4]

+ The apostolate of the laity and pastoral ministry can be mutually complementary. [¶6]
+ An apostolate of this kind does not consist only in the witness of one's way of life; a true apostle looks for opportunities to announce Christ by words. [¶6]

The Council Fathers strongly call the laity's attention to the fact that proper ecclesial authority, solidarity with their brothers and sisters in the Church, and a life focused upon and enlivened by the sacraments, especially the Eucharist, are indispensable to the lay apostolate:

+ Because the hierarchy entrusts to the laity certain functions which are more closely connected with pastoral duties, such as the teaching of Christian doctrine, certain liturgical actions, and the care of souls, the laity are fully subject to higher ecclesiastical control in the performance of this work. [¶24]
+ The sacraments, especially the most holy Eucharist, communicate and nourish that charity which is the soul of the entire apostolate. [¶3]
+ One's gifts should be used in the apostolate in communion with their brothers and sisters in Christ, especially with their pastors who must make a judgment about the true nature and proper use of these gifts. [¶3]
+ Strengthened by active participation in the liturgical life of their faith community, the laity are eager to do their share of the apostolic works of that community. [¶10]
+ They should all remember that they can reach all people and contribute to the salvation of the whole world by public worship and prayer, as well as by penance and voluntary acceptance of the labors and hardships of life whereby they become like the suffering Christ. [¶16]
+ Promoting Christian friendship among themselves, they help one another in every need whatsoever. [¶4]

Furthermore, training, education and formation are essential to carrying out the lay apostolate, especially when it involves participation in the pastoral ministry of the priests and bishops, as prison ministry does:

+ In addition to spiritual formation, a solid doctrinal instruction in theology, ethics, and philosophy is required. [¶29]
+ In regard to the apostolate for evangelizing and sanctifying men and women, the laity must be specially formed to engage in conversation with others, believers or non-believers, in order to manifest Christ's message to all. [¶31]
+ There are many aids for lay persons devoted to the apostolate, namely:
  • study sessions,
  • congresses,
  • periods of recollection,
  • spiritual exercises,
  • frequent meetings,
  • conferences,
  • books and periodicals directed toward the acquisition of a deeper knowledge of sacred Scripture and Catholic doctrine, the nourishment of spiritual life, the discernment of world conditions, and the discovery and development of suitable methods. [¶32]
+ To cultivate good human relations, truly human values must be fostered, especially the art of living in harmony and cooperating with others and of striking up friendly conversation with them. [¶29]

The Council Fathers remind us that the effectiveness of the apostolate depends in large measure upon the authenticity of the lived life:

+ The success of the lay apostolate depends upon the laity's living union with Christ, which is nourished in the Church by spiritual aids common to all the faithful, especially active participation in the sacred liturgy. [¶4]

+ The very testimony of their Christian life and good works done in a supernatural spirit has the power to draw men to belief and to God. [¶6]
+ The laity must make progress in holiness in a happy and ready spirit, trying prudently and patiently to overcome difficulties. [¶4]
+ Only by the light of faith and by meditation on the word of God can one always and everywhere exercise the faith, hope, and charity that makes it possible to see Christ in everyone, whether a relative or a stranger, and make correct judgments about the true meaning and value of temporal things. [¶4]
+ They are neither depressed by the lack of temporal goods nor inflated by their abundance. [¶4]
+ They have no obsession for empty honors, but seek to please God rather than other humans. [¶4]
+ They are ever ready to leave all things for Christ's sake and to suffer persecution for justice sake. [¶4]

With regard to the role of the Holy Spirit in the lay apostolate, the Council teaches that:

+ One engages in the apostolate through the faith, hope, and charity which the Holy Spirit diffuses in the hearts of all members of the Church. [¶3]
+ The proper attitude of the lay apostolate is poured into one's heart by the Holy Spirit, allowing the laity to express the spirit of the beatitudes in their lives. [¶4]
+ The basis and condition for every successful lay apostolate is learning how to perform the mission of Christ and the Church by basing one's life on belief in the divine mystery of creation and redemption and by being sensitive to the movement of the Holy Spirit. [¶29]

Finally, the lay apostolate inevitably involves living out and acting upon the social justice teachings of the Catholic Church:

+ Wherever men and women lack the facilities necessary for living a truly human life or are afflicted with serious distress or illness or suffer exile or imprisonment, there Christian charity should seek them out and find them, console them with great solicitude, and help them with appropriate relief. [¶8]

+ Since the works of charity and mercy express the most striking testimony of the Christian life, apostolic formation should lead also to the performance of these works, so that the faithful may learn from childhood on to have compassion for their brethren and to be generous in helping those in need. [¶31]

For those who are in remote areas, or locations that are decidedly under-populated with Catholics, as is the case for so many Catholic prison ministry volunteers, the apostolate still obtains and can be exceedingly effective:

+ The apostolate does not need to be practiced in groups, as the individual apostolate, flowing generously from its source in a truly Christian life, is the origin and condition of the whole lay apostolate. [¶16]

+ The individual apostolate has a special field in areas where Catholics are few in number and widely dispersed. [¶17]

+ The laity who engage in the apostolate as individuals, usefully gather into smaller groups for serious conversation, so that an indication of the community of the Church is always apparent to others as a true witness of love. [¶17]

+ By giving spiritual help to one another through friendship and the communicating of the benefit of their experience, the laity are trained to overcome the disadvantages of excessively isolated life and activity and to make their apostolate more productive. [¶17]

As noted above, prison ministry volunteers could feel a bit confused as to the proper role of ecumenism and the primary role of evangelization in their labors inside the prison fences. In his book, *Evangelical Catholicism*,[9] the esteemed Catholic author George Weigel helps in navigating this terrain. He names and describes the process. He explains that since the middle 1600s, since the Council of Trent, our Catholic faith has been focused upon correcting the errors of the Reformation. This mindset, which he calls *Counter Reformation Catholicism*, has prepared Catholics to defend the faith from Reformation-era attacks through training in Catholic catechetics and apologetics. Weigel describes the new era of evangelical Catholicism as being hallmarked by certain characteristics, the first one of which is "friendship with Our Lord and Savior Jesus Christ."

The reality of how this friendship with Jesus plays out inside the prison fences is that we Catholic prison ministry volunteers must still carry with us, and have at the ready, the knowledge to refute Reformation-type attacks on the Catholic Church. Those attacks continue inside today's prisons and must be answered. But defense alone is not enough. We must move into affirmatively sharing the realities of the new evangelization, the realities of personal relationship with our Lord and Savior Jesus Christ and, through that relationship, participation in the Family of Faith. I have found Fr. Larry Carew's retreat for prisoners, described below, to be a beautiful example of how that bridge can be built.

Good News from Christ the Prisoner

Union Correctional Institution, known in shorthand as UCI and nicknamed Raiford after the nearest town in Union County, Florida, has a faith-and-character-based program with more than 100 participating general population inmates. The program, run in J-Dorm, has been going strong for a decade. The problem is there has been no Wednesday night program.

When the administrative chaplain approached me to "volunteer" for a weekly Wednesday program from 4 to 6 pm, I quickly surmised that my Catholic faith is what made me desirable. According to the most recent data, there is not a single registered Catholic in all of Union County, Florida. They must not be counting prisoners, of course. The weekly Catholic Sunday service at UCI pulls in more than fifty inmates. P-Dorm, the death row building at UCI, has at least fifty Catholics. And Father Robert McDermott of our diocese ministers to at least 100 Catholics in the prison complex at Lake Butler in Union County. So, to be tongue-in-cheek, perhaps there are no non-prisoner Catholics in Union County, Florida!

But virtually everyone in Union County is a *saved* Christian, that is, an evangelical or even fundamentalist Protestant, and is attending their church on Wednesday nights, which is their custom. Catholics, however, do not make a point of having church services on Wednesday night. Not even when they are "behind bars" with nothing better to do! And because I am a volunteer Catholic correctional chaplain who lives in Macclenny, just 15 miles up the road in Baker County, I am the best bet to run a Wednesday night program in J-Dorm at UCI.

"So, how long a commitment are we talking about, Chaplain?"

"Well, now." The minister leans back in his chair behind the mountains of paper that are inevitable since the state budget cuts reduced the number of staff chaplains at this huge prison from four to one. "Actually, at least one year. But two years would be better."

"What is the faith complexion of the group? Are any of them Catholic?"

"Actually, no. But they are almost all Christian."

I know what that means in the Bible Belt: Most of them will have been taught since the cradle that the pope is the anti-Christ, the Catholic Church is the whore of Babylon, and Catholics are destined for hell but do not know it.

"What exactly should I teach them, Chaplain?"

"That is entirely up to you. You have free rein within the normal state constraints."

I accept the challenge with trepidation, but by the time my first evening program rolls around, I have discerned exactly what to teach. And, by God's providence, the best possible tool has been put in my hands. The program is called *Healing the Imprisoned: A Retreat*, narrated by Father Larry Carew. Father Larry, a Catholic priest of the Community of the Cross in Danbury,

Connecticut, who is also pastor of Christ the King Catholic Church in Trumbull, Connecticut, has spent 25 years in prison ministry. He knows something that almost no one ever talks about.

Father Larry knows that Jesus Christ did not allow himself to be a lawyer or a scribe or a Pharisee or an earthly physician. He did not allow himself to be an earthly ruler or soldier. He did not allow himself to be a rock star-type celebrity.

Jesus Christ allowed himself to be a prisoner. He was arrested, tried, imprisoned and executed. That means every man and woman in prison has a special connection to our Savior through their common experience with him of condemnation and incarceration. Father Larry's six-session program is in-depth and ecumenical.

The first night, I have some men sitting with their hands over their ears and looking away from me the whole time, presumably so that nothing diabolical can enter their minds. By the end of the first month, however, their hands are in their laps. And, when I am not watching too closely, they are looking at the television screen that projects the DVD of Father Larry's talk. Once we finish the retreat talks, we will move on to the Catholic understanding of the Bible.

For Catholic prison ministers in the Bible Belt, I recommend Father Larry as a powerful tool to break through denominational prejudices. The six-disc set *Healing the Imprisoned: A Retreat* can be ordered from www.communityofthecross.com, specifically at http://www.communityofthecross.com/healing-imprisoned-a-retreat.

....

For the last few years, many of us Catholics, including prison ministry volunteers, have been hearing from the pulpit of our parishes about the *New Evangelization*. This is a new impetus to a longstanding effort of infusing the laity with the urgency of the lay apostolate discussed above, "the power of God for the salvation of everyone who believes and which, in the final essence, is identified with Jesus Christ himself."[10] The actual subject of Catholic doctrine on evangelization is extensively treated in the Church's teaching through Popes Paul VI and John Paul II.[11]

A significant hallmark in the Church's teaching on evangelization is the document *Evangelization in the Modern World (Evangelii Nuntiandi)*,[12] issued by Pope Paul VI to mark the "tenth anniversary of the closing of the Second Vatican Council, the objectives of which are definitively summed up in this single one: to make the Church of the twentieth century ever better fitted for proclaiming the Gospel to the people of the twentieth century" (2). The *New Evangelization* is that same proclamation by twenty-first century Catholics to a twenty-first century world, but Pope Paul's teaching is foundational nonetheless. Pope Paul VI reminds us that the effectiveness of evangelization depends in large measure upon the authenticity of the lived life and the evangelizer's constant efforts to move toward greater holiness themselves:

+ The first means of evangelization is the witness of an authentically Christian life, given over to God in a communion that nothing should destroy, and at the same time given to one's neighbor with limitless zeal (41).
+ Modern people listen more willingly to witnesses than to teachers, and if they do listen to teachers it is because they are witnesses (41).
+ St. Peter expressed this well when he held up the example of a reverent and chaste life that wins over even without a word those who refuse to obey the Word[13] (41).
+ This need for authenticity is corporal as well as individual. It is therefore primarily by her conduct and by her life that the Church will evangelize the world, in other words, by her living witness of fidelity to the Lord Jesus—the witness of poverty and detachment, of freedom in the face of the powers of this world, in short, the witness of sanctity (41).
+ It is often said nowadays that the present century thirsts for authenticity (76).
+ The witness of life has become more than ever an essential condition for real effectiveness in preaching (76).
+ Our evangelizing zeal must spring from true holiness of life (76).

WHEN WE VISIT JESUS IN PRISON

+ Preaching must, in its turn, make the preacher grow in holiness, which is nourished by prayer and above all by love for the Eucharist (76).
+ The world is calling for evangelizers to speak to it of a God whom the evangelists themselves should know and be familiar with as if they could see the invisible (76).

Pope Paul also goes to great lengths to underline the important role of the Holy Spirit in modern evangelization (75):

+ Evangelization will never be possible without the action of the Holy Spirit.
+ In fact, it is only after the coming of the Holy Spirit on the day of Pentecost that the apostles depart to all the ends of the earth in order to begin the great work of the Church's evangelization.
+ It is in the "consolation of the Holy Spirit" that the Church increases.
+ The Holy Spirit is the soul of the Church.
+ It is the Holy Spirit who, today just as at the beginning of the Church, acts in every evangelizer who allows himself to be possessed and led by God.
+ The Holy Spirit places on our lips the words which we could not find by ourselves; at the same time the Holy Spirit predisposes the soul of the hearer to be open and receptive to the Good News and to the Kingdom being proclaimed.
+ Techniques of evangelization are good, but even the most advanced ones could not replace the gentle action of the Spirit.
+ The most perfect preparation of the evangelizer has no effect without the Holy Spirit.
+ The Holy Spirit is the principal agent of evangelization.
+ It is the Holy Spirit who impels each individual to proclaim the Gospel.

✦ It is the Holy Spirit who in the depths of consciences causes the Word of salvation to be accepted and understood.

✦ Now if the Spirit of God has a preeminent place in the whole life of the Church, it is in her evangelizing mission that the Spirit is most active.

In its essence, evangelization always has and always will be the proclamation and teaching of the Good News and of life of the Family of Faith in the Church:

✦ Preaching, the verbal proclamation of a message, is indeed always indispensable (42).

✦ The Word remains ever relevant, especially when it is the bearer of the power of God (42).

✦ This is why St. Paul's axiom, "Faith comes from what is heard" (Romans 10:17), also retains its relevance: it is the Word that is heard which leads to belief (42).

✦ The role of evangelization is precisely to educate people in the faith in such a way as to lead each individual Christian to live the sacraments as true sacraments of faith—and not to receive them passively or reluctantly (47).

✦ A means of evangelization that must not be neglected is that of catechetical instruction (44).

✦ The first Christians readily expressed their deep faith in the Church by describing her as being spread throughout the universe; they were fully conscious of belonging to a large community which neither space nor time can limit (61).

The pope then reminds us that true and effective evangelization always takes into account the human factor, both the world to which we present Christ and the person to whom we present Christ:

✦ Evangelization loses much of its force and effectiveness if it does not take into consideration the actual people to whom it is addressed (63).

WHEN WE VISIT JESUS IN PRISON

+ Nevertheless the use of the means of social communication for evangelization presents a challenge: through them the evangelical message should reach vast numbers of people, but with the capacity of piercing the conscience of each individual, of implanting itself in his heart as though he were the only person being addressed (45).
+ For this reason, side by side with the collective proclamation of the Gospel, the other form of transmission, the person-to-person one, remains valid and important (46).
+ Evangelization does not consist only of the preaching and teaching of a doctrine; evangelization must touch life: the natural life to which it gives a new meaning (47).
+ The work of evangelization presupposes in the evangelizer an ever increasing love for those whom he or she is evangelizing (79).

Pope Paul restates the truth that evangelization is a participation in the missionary work of the Church and is therefore always part of the Church and under the authority of the Church:

+ The whole Church is missionary, and the work of evangelization is a basic duty of the People of God (59).
+ Evangelization is for no one an individual and isolated act; it is one that is deeply ecclesial (60).
+ The evangelizer's action is certainly attached to the evangelizing activity of the whole Church by institutional relationships and by profound invisible links in the order of grace (60).
+ No evangelizer is the absolute master of the evangelizing action, with a discretionary power to carry it out in accordance with individualistic criteria and perspectives; he or she acts in communion with the Church and her pastors (60).

This will, of course, result in true evangelization leading to participation in the sacramental life as true sacraments of faith which are not to be received passively or reluctantly (47)

Pope Paul stresses the role of the laity in this work of evangelization (70-71):

+ Lay people, whose particular vocation places them in the midst of the world, must exercise a very special form of evangelization.
+ Their primary and immediate task is to put to use every Christian and evangelical possibility latent but already present and active in the affairs of the world.
+ Their field of evangelizing activity includes other realities which are open to evangelization, such as human love, the family, the education of children and adolescents, professional work, and the mystery of suffering.
+ The more Gospel-inspired lay people there are engaged in these realities, the more these realities will be at the service of the Kingdom of God and therefore of salvation in Jesus Christ.
+ One cannot fail to stress the evangelizing action of the family in the evangelizing apostolate of the laity.
+ At different moments in the Church's history and also in the Second Vatican Council, the family has well deserved the beautiful name of "domestic Church." This means that there should be found in every Christian family the various aspects of the entire Church.
+ Family ought to be a place where the Gospel is transmitted and from which the Gospel radiates.
+ In a family which is conscious of this mission, all the members evangelize and are evangelized.
+ Such a family becomes the evangelizer of many other families, and of the neighborhood of which it forms part.

Finally, Pope Paul VI identifies two different spheres of human beings and human conditions in the modern world which are susceptible to evangelization: "two spheres which are very different from one another but...are very close by reason of the challenge which they make to evangelization" (55). People who fit the descriptions of both these spheres susceptible to evangelization are certainly present inside prisons and jails.

+ First, the increase in unbelief: a secular humanism which describes the world as self-explanatory without any need for or recourse to God (55):
  • Denies God.
  • Engenders pragmatic, systematic, and militant atheism.
  • Fosters consumerism which seeks pleasure above all else.
  • Thirsts for power and domination over others.
  • Denies the power of God in order to support the power of human beings.

+ Second, nominal Christians who identify themselves as believers but do not practice their religion (56-57):
  • Do not renounce their baptism, but live as though it did not happen.
  • Justify themselves based on "interior religion."
  • Refuse Church authority in the name of "personal independence" or "authenticity."
  • Stand side-by-side with atheistic secularists in mocking religious practice and leading others astray.
  • Resist religion with a kind of inertia and slightly hostile attitude.

In the *New Evangelization*, the Church's teachings in the *Apostolate of the Laity (Apostolicam Actuositatem)* and in *Evangelization in the Modern World (Evangelii Nuntiandi)* are finely tuned and focused upon the world of the twenty-first century:[14]

[John Paul II] made this urgent task a central point of his far-reaching Magisterial teaching, referring to it as the "new evangelization"...affirmed in *Christifideles Laici*: "Whole countries and nations where religion and the Christian life were formerly flourishing...are now put to a hard test and, in some cases, are even undergoing a radical transformation as a result of a constant spreading of indifference to religion, secularism, and atheism. This particularly concerns countries and nations of the so-called First World, in which economic well-being and consumerism, even if coexistent with a tragic situation of poverty and misery, inspires and sustains a life lived 'as if God did not exist.' This indifference to religion and the practice of religion devoid of true meaning in the face of life's very serious problems are not less worrying and upsetting when compared with declared atheism...."

Of most particular importance for the Catholic prison ministry volunteer in the First World is the application of this New Evangelization to the environment inside prison fences, where some have lost or have never found faith in God, but many more have accepted a faith in Jesus that deplores the Catholic Church that Jesus Christ founded:[15]

In its precise sense, *evangelization* is the *missio ad gentes* directed to those who do not know Christ. In a wider sense, it is used to describe ordinary pastoral work, while the phrase "new evangelization" designates pastoral outreach to those who no longer practice the Christian faith....

Everywhere and always, each Catholic has the right and the duty to give the witness and the full proclamation of his faith. With non-Catholic Christians, Catholics must enter into a respectful dialogue of charity and truth, a dialogue which is not only an exchange of ideas, but also of gifts, in order that the fullness of the means of salvation can be offered to one's partners in dialogue. In this way, they are led to an ever deeper conversion to Christ.

If a non-Catholic Christian, for reasons of conscience and having been convinced of Catholic truth, asks to enter into the full communion of the Catholic Church, this is to be respected

WHEN WE VISIT JESUS IN PRISON

as the work of the Holy Spirit and as an expression of freedom of conscience and of religion.... It would not be a question of proselytism in the negative sense that has been attributed to this term.... The work of ecumenism does not remove the right or take away the responsibility of proclaiming in fullness the Catholic faith to other Christians, who freely wish to receive it.

As noted above, the prison ministry volunteer must go beyond defense and move into affirmatively sharing the realities of the new evangelization, the realities of personal relationship with our Lord and Savior Jesus Christ and, through that relationship, participation in the Family of God that is the Church. In short, we Catholic prison ministry volunteers do not engage in the so-called practice of "sheep stealing," which would be the targeting of members of non-Catholic Christian groups. But we are expected to know what we believe and why we believe it and to stand ready to answer questions about it. When such dialogue leads to interest in the Catholic faith by a non-Catholic Christian, we must be ready to either provide instruction in the faith or provide to the inquiring inmate a qualified person that can provide such instruction.

Pope Francis includes this relationship-sourced activity with the least of our brothers and sisters, which according to Jesus Christ includes those in prison, in the concept of the New Evangelization. In his book, *What Would Pope Francis Do? Bringing the Good News to People in Need*, Fr. Sean Salai, SJ, explains:[16]

In particular, *Evangelii Gaudium* [uses the] phrase "new evangelization" to describe Francis's blueprint for missionary closeness in a field-hospital church. Far from *replacing* the new evangelization, Francis preaches his vision of closeness to marginalized people as a *development* of it.

In the mind of Francis, ever conscious of his role as successor of St. Peter, his own closeness to God's people requires that he be close to the teachings of his immediate papal predecessors and to the vision of the Second Vatican Council. By calling on all baptized Christians to be missionary disciples who are close to the needy, he invites us to revisit the new evangelization and Vatican II's universal call to holiness in light of our own experiences of Jesus. Francis writes in *The Joy of the Gospel*:

> The new evangelization calls for personal involvement on the part of each of the baptized. Every Christian is challenged, here and now, to be actively engaged in evangelization. [¶120]

Once again, the exchanges being described here go beyond the *Counter-Reformation Evangelism* that is purely defensive and was described in Chapter 4. The interactions contemplated here are instructional encounters, shared in the context of brotherly relationship, wherein the faith of the Catholic Church is presented in ways that the inquirer can understand and relate to their existing knowledge of Christianity. There are some excellent resources available to help the volunteer prepare for such encounters:

+ Sean Salai, SJ, *What Would Pope Francis Do? Bringing the Good News to People in Need* (Huntington, Indiana: Our Sunday Visitor, 2016). A compelling narrative that intertwines Pope Francis' fresh impetus for grassroots evangelization with Fr. Sean's fascinating personal experiences of Gospel truth, gleaned from ministry on the margins in places as diverse as Times Square in New York City, Third World mission fields, and America's death rows.
+ Most Rev. Victor Galeone (ret. Bishop of St. Augustine), *Joyful Good News for Young & Old* (Houston, Texas: Magnificat Institute Press, 2014). A remarkable tool for offering the basics of the Catholic faith to the uninformed, uninitiated and those in need of a tune-up.
+ Scott Hahn, *Reasons to Believe: How to Understand, Explain, and Defend the Catholic Faith* (New York, New

York: Doubleday, 2007). Scott Hahn was once a Protestant minister who specialized in getting Catholics to leave the Church. Then, when he delved into the basis for Protestant allegiance to the doctrine of sola scriptura (only Scripture), he discovered that the premise stood as an assumption outside of Scripture. Thus began his well-documented and articulate journey to the Catholic faith.

+ Scott Hahn and Leon J. Suprenant, Jr., foreword by Archbishop Charles J. Chaput, OFM Cap, *Catholic for a Reason: Scripture and the Mystery of the Family of God* (Steubenville, Ohio: Emmaus Road, 1998). Working from a dynamic understanding of the Holy Scriptures, the authors produce a combined testimony of their faith journey and explanation of the Biblically-sound Catholic faith.

+ Patrick Madrid, *Any Friend of God's Is a Friend of Mine: A Biblical and Historical Explanation of the Catholic Doctrine of the Communion of Saints* (San Diego, California: Basilica Press, 1996). An excellent handbook to equip the volunteer with the vocabulary for explaining Catholic belief in the Family of God, veneration of relics and of saints, veneration of the Blessed Virgin Mary, and prayers for the Holy Souls in Purgatory.

+ Patrick Madrid, *Why Is That in Tradition?* (Huntington, Indiana: Our Sunday Visitor, 2002). An excellent handbook to equip the volunteer with the explanations and vocabulary for explaining Catholic belief in Church authority, doctrine, the sacraments, sacramentals, and morality.

+ Chantal Epie, *The Scriptural Roots of Catholic Teaching* (Manchester, New Hampshire: Sophia Institute Press, 2002). Epie cuts through the popularly "accepted criticisms" of Catholic belief by accurately and firmly documenting them in the Scriptures.

+ Thomas Howard, *Evangelical Is Not Enough: Worship of God in Liturgy and Sacrament* (San Francisco, California: Ignatius Press, 1984). The author shares his journey from a lifetime evangelical faith to liturgical Christianity, ultimately to the Catholic faith.

+ Mary Elizabeth Sperry, *Scripture in the Parish: A Guide for Catholic Ministry* (Collegeville, Minnesota: Liturgical Press, 2013).

There are also some top-notch resources that can be utilized when actual systematic instruction is in order. A marvelous Catholic self-study program that can be used in prisons and jails is written by Fr. Oscar Lukefahr. His materials are available through the Catholic Home Study Service.[17] The Catholic Home Study Service (CHSS), sponsored by the Vincentian community and the Missouri Knights of Columbus, has been offering free courses on the Catholic Faith for more than seventy years. It is based at Saint Mary's of the Barrens, in Perryville, Missouri. Father Oscar Lukefahr, C.M. is the Director of Catholic Home Study Service.

I have used Fr. Lukefahr's courses to prepare numerous inmates for reception into the Catholic Church. While the inmates find the courses enlightening and interesting, they especially like the fact that there are workbooks and a graded test at the end of each section, and they receive a certificate upon completion of each book.

The current series includes the following nine courses.

+ *We Believe… A Survey of the Catholic Faith*
+ *We Worship: A Guide to the Catholic Mass*
+ *We Live: To Know, Love, and Serve God*
+ *We Pray: Living in God's Presence*
+ *The Search for Happiness*
+ *A Catholic Guide to the Bible*
+ *The Privilege of Being Catholic*
+ *The Catechism Handbook*
+ *Christ's Mother and Ours*

Another source for excellent self-study materials specifically designed for prisons and jails is *Dismas Ministry*.[18] Their materials are available in English and, in some cases, Spanish.

+ *God with Us* (*Dios Con Nosotros*, Spanish) 3-part correspondence course for inmates on the Catholic Bible:
  • Part 1 – Introduction, Pentateuch and Historical Books
  • Part 2 – Wisdom Books and Prophetic Books
  • Part 3 – Gospels, Acts, Letters and Revelation

+ *A Reason for Hope* (*Una Razon para La Esperanza*, Spanish) 3-part correspondence course for inmates on the Catholic faith:
  • Part 1 – The Sacraments
  • Part 2 – The Creed
  • Part 3 – Christian Morality

+ *Pray Always* (English Only) 3-part correspondence course for inmates on Catholic prayer:
  • Part 1 – Prayer in the Old Testament
  • Part 2 – Prayer in the New Testament
  • Part 3 – Prayer in the Catholic Tradition

No amount of printed or mail-order resources, however, can substitute for the evangelizing impact of a flesh and blood person who sets aside their worldly pursuits in order to make the time to come inside the barbwire fences to visit Jesus come in the face of the prisoner.

Love Alone Is Credible

In the statement *Responsibility, Rehabilitation, and Restoration: A Catholic Perspective on Crime and Criminal Justice,* the U.S. Conference of Catholic Bishops (USCCB) acknowledge that the Catholic approach to criminal justice can seem paradoxical. On the one hand, we insist upon accountability and upon the right and duty of the community "to establish and enforce laws to protect people and to advance the common good." On the other hand, we reject naked vengeance and insist upon a restorative justice that protects society while "rehabilitating those who violate the law." No offender is to be considered hopeless and discarded.

The image of this dual concern for both the victim and the offender is reflected in the revelational mirror of the Gospels: the Good Samaritan (Luke 10:25-37), who "did all he could to help a victim of crime," and the Prodigal Son (Luke 15:11-32), which modeled the invitation to conversion and, when conversion is accepted, the embrace with welcome and celebration. Those images paint a paradox of divinely revealed love, which holds us accountable, yet never ceases in seeking our repentance and our return to grace.

For Catholics, this paradox benefits from the sacraments of Penance and Eucharist. These "central Catholic signs of true justice and mercy" teach us that a compassionate community and a loving God seek accountability and correction but not suffering for its own sake. Punishment must have a constructive and redemptive purpose.[19]

The enfleshment of this love in the specific circumstances of the prisons in which I minister takes on many forms. Each is a testimony to the transforming power of the standing invitation to repentance, to accept God's love.

Gerry McMahon, a Catholic layman, recently retired from volunteer Catholic prison ministry at age 90. For over 20 years, every Tuesday he drove more than sixty miles each way from Gainesville to push the Christian literature cart through the confinement buildings. Gerry recruited and trained a new volunteer, Charlie Scheer, to replace him at cell-front.

In addition to bringing the Good News directly to the doors of the hundreds of men locked in solitary confinement, they both return on Saturdays with their guitars. That is when a half dozen Catholic volunteers from Holy Faith and Queen of Peace parishes in Gainesville spend the afternoon with fifteen or twenty general population inmates in a Prayer and Share Group, sharing faith and love. As one inmate describes it, "I had not had a visit from anyone in over twenty years. This group has become my family."

Deacon Ken Cochran is the RCIA director for his parish in Macclenny, Florida. He takes his teaching inside the walls by running a group RCIA for general population inmates in the chapel on Thursdays. The dozens of men who have decided to seek entry into the Catholic Church keep him busy. The inmates' interest in the Catholic faith is not surprising. And I have witnessed the power of the cell-to-cell ministry of the Church in these two prisons.

Bishop John Snyder, who retired as Bishop of the Diocese of St. Augustine in 2001, still drives twice a month from Switzerland, Florida, to make cell-front Communion rounds on death row with Dr. Don and Bill. Retired Bishop Victor Galeone, who served as Bishop of the Diocese of St. Augustine from 2001 to 2011, was succeeded by Bishop Felipe Estévez. Both have maintained a visible presence inside the prisons and Bishop Vic serves as spiritual advisor to a man on South Carolina's death row.

Dr. Don Barnhorst and William Koenig, both volunteers from the Order of Malta, are responsible for weekly Communion rounds at UCI at cell front in death row, disciplinary confinement, psychiatric solitary confinement (crisis stabilization and transitional care) and in administrative segregation. Other regular volunteers at cell front in these two maximum security prisons include Art Gase, Deacon Larry Geinosky, and Robert Mylod (all from the Order of Malta), Deacon Egardo Farias of Miami, and Arnold Leporati, a Notre Dame alum from Jacksonville. Three laymen from Tallahassee—Michael Savage, Peter Cowdrey and Stephen Hammond—make the three hundred miles round trip every month for a day of cell-front ministry. Deacon Ray Aguado comes every few months all the way from Pensacola, a seven-hours' drive each way, to make cell front rounds. And Bishop Gregory Parkes of Pensacola has made that long trip, with his assistant Fr. Paul Lambert, in order to provide sacraments of initiation and communion for men on death row.

All these volunteers are in addition to Fr. Slawomir Bielasiewicz and Deacon Jason Roy, who are the official priest and deacon for these two highest security prisons in Florida.[20] And then there are the countless hundreds of Catholic priests, nuns, and lay people from all over the country and the world, who make the time to correspond with men on death row and in solitary confinement. What is the upshot of all this *New Evangelization*?

One inmate explained his desire to become Catholic this way: "I want to belong to the Church that wants to belong to me."

If he had read St. Augustine and Hans Urs von Balthasar, frequently called St. Pope John Paul's favorite theologian, he might have realized that he was verbalizing a universal spiritual truth writ small: "Buried in the heart of every one of us is the God-given desire to belong to that God Who wants to belong to us."

After reading all this detail about Catholic prison ministry, you might reasonably ask: *How does the Catholic prison ministry volunteer remain engaged over the long-term on the frontlines of such work?* That is the subject of the next chapter.

> "St. Francis...was a Lover. He was a lover of God
> and he was truly a lover of [men and women]. St.
> Francis did not love humanity but [individual human
> beings]. He did not love Christianity but Christ....
> To this great mystic his religion was not a thing like a
> theory but a thing like a love-affair."
>
> G.K. Chesterton[1]

CHAPTER 6

The Spiritual, Communal, and Individual Practices for Catholic Prison Ministers to Avoid Burnout

There is a perennial problem in our culture: people who are in love with the idea of being in love. Such men and women are featured in contemporary literature, movies, and television dramas. Their quest for the ideal of love, without the disappointing entanglements that come with real live flesh and blood people loving one another in real time and imperfectly, result in an endless series of constantly new and hopelessly doomed relationships. The essence of this mode of operation has been crystalized in the phrase: *I love humanity; it is people that I cannot stand.*[2]

We Catholic prison ministry volunteers have ideals and hopes, as we should. We may hope and pray that our prisons and our criminal justice system will one day be operated in a manner consistent with Catholic social teaching. We may strive for the day when capital punishment will be abandoned in respect for the inherent dignity of every human life. We may dream of a time when society at large makes drastic improvements in reflecting God's plan for the common good. These are all good things and great aspirations.

Even so, over the long haul of day-in and day-out participation in the pastoral ministry of the bishops and priests inside prisons and jails, such ideals simply cannot provide us with the energy to continue serving with love. The prison concrete-and-steel world of grime and waste, the incessant assault of banging and screaming, the constant discomfort of noxious smells from raunchy food, un-flushed toilets, and dirty, shabby prison clothes caustically erode our dreams for making the world, even the prison world, a better place.

The long haul, sometimes even the short haul, of prison ministry, however, demands a spiritual power much greater and more potent than our human empathy and compassion, something both beyond us yet already among us, in order to stave off the temptation to cynicism and despair and allow us to continue to love and serve those inside prison fences. That something is not an idea or a mere concept. It is both transcendent and immanent—the person of Our Lord and Savior Jesus Christ, manifested in the Sacrament of Sacrificial Love that we Catholics call the Eucharist.

With Jesus in My Pocket

Grinding. Reverberating. Numbing. Metal against metal punctuates my twenty minute sojourn into the bowels of the prison. Ten massive, steel-barred doors now separate me from the prison entrance. One more security door stands between me and death row. The officer with the key swings it open. He nods. I step through.

The heavy steel bolts clang shut, locking me in on the beige corridor of death row cells. Like a stray cosmic noise from another world, the spongy soles of my *Rockports* announce my arrival with muffled squeaks against the hot, damp concrete.

Fifteen solitary cells stretch to my right.

The men know the fall of my step and the noise of my shoes. Except for four hours per week of yard exercise, this short narrow hall with its six foot by nine foot cages is their whole world. There is nothing to see. All the cells face a wall of steel bar backed by concrete and brick. They cannot even see each other. It is a world of sounds. Nothing—not even the smallest squeak of middle class walking shoes—goes unnoticed.

Men wanting to talk will step to their cell door as I approach. Those who aren't sure, will stand mid-cell, avoiding commitment until we exchange greetings. Those needing their privacy will simply look the other way. A turned head means "not today, thank you." Common courtesy honors the code and moves on to the next cell. I greet each man who looks my way.

"Hey…how are you doing today?"

At least three men on this corridor will ask me to stop. They always do. We are brothers in faith. They know that I am bringing something special for them, that I have Jesus in my pocket.

There are over fifty Catholics on Florida's death row. Most of them, like the three on this corridor, are regular communicants. They are always waiting—not so much for me as for the One whom I bring.

"Good afternoon, brother, would you like to receive Communion today?"

The small waist-level opening in the bars of the cell door serves as a port for physical food and supplies. We convert it to a spiritual portal by taking each other's hands through the opening and stepping beyond time and space into the most sacred moment of our faith outside the Mass itself.

"Let us begin with the prayer Jesus taught us."

One prayer issues from both of our lips. "Our Father…."

As our prayers unfold, I remove the pyx from my shirt pocket. My brother through Baptism stands close to the bars, hands folded against his chest. I hold the consecrated host between us.

"I bring you the real presence of Jesus Christ in the world, both his presence and a sacrament that also symbolizes our unity with you—a unity that is greater than these bars and these walls…."

We complete the rite. I raise the host and say, "The Body of Christ."

In response to his "Amen," I lean forward to place the Host on his tongue.

Suddenly, there is a loud roar.

The lights flicker out as the shriek accelerates into a shrill pitched scream. I freeze like a deer in the dark, caught unawares by the headlights of a car bearing down.

He raises his eyes and steps compassionately into my frozen stare. "The generators for the electric chair," he shrugs. "They test them every week."

The scream stops abruptly. The lights return.

Struggling to regain my composure, I stammer, "We are ... uh, you are ... I mean this ... this is the Body of Christ."

He nods assent, "Amen."

We Catholic prison ministry volunteers, whether or not we are physically bearing the Eucharist to the prison, participate in Christ's most excellent presence in the Eucharist at the parish Mass (or the Mass said in the prison or jail) and then minister to Jesus come into our immediate presence in the face of the prisoner, as described in the document *On the Eucharist in Its Relationship to the Church (Ecclesia de Eucharistia)*[3] by Pope John Paul II:

> To contemplate Christ involves being able to recognize him wherever he manifests himself, in his many forms of presence, but above all in the living sacrament of his body and his blood. [¶6]

This reality allows us volunteers to experience and understand our own labors as journeying from Jesus to Jesus. It is Jesus in his most excellent presence in the Eucharist who feeds and sustains us. It is Jesus present in the Word who teaches us. It is Jesus present in the assembly who provides a community of faith and worship to us. It is Jesus in the face of the prisoner to whom we are sent in service.

As Catholics, we are a Eucharistic people in the deepest and most penetrating sense. Eucharist permeates our reality, our experiences, and our responses. Eucharist is not the glasses we wear, a mere filter through which to view the world. Eucharist is our identity, individually and corporately. We Catholics believe we become that which we consume and are thereby transformed into a Eucharistic people who see the presence of Jesus where we could not see it before:

The Church draws her life from Christ in the Eucharist; by him she is fed and by him she is enlightened. The Eucharist is both a mystery of faith and a "mystery of light". Whenever the Church celebrates the Eucharist, the faithful can in some way relive the experience of the two disciples on the road to Emmaus: "their eyes were opened and they recognized him" (Luke 24:31). (Italics in original.) [¶6]

That presence visible to our Eucharistic eyes includes the sovereignty of Jesus Christ over time. As Eucharistic people, we are consciously connected with our brothers and sisters in faith across the ages:

The Church has received the Eucharist from Christ her Lord not as one gift—however precious—among so many others, but as *the gift par excellence*, for it is the gift of himself, of his person in his sacred humanity, as well as the gift of his saving work. Nor does it remain confined to the past, since "all that Christ is—all that he did and suffered for all [men and women]—participates in the divine eternity, and so transcends all times." (Italics in original.) [¶11]

The most basic and essential rung of every Catholic prison ministry volunteer's effort to avoid the mental and emotional weariness, fatigue, and exhaustion that characterize *burnout* is grasping the lifeline of the Eucharist. In order to sustain our service for the long term, we must build every aspect of it, including the pursuit of holiness upon, within, and through the Eucharist.

Every commitment to holiness, every activity aimed at carrying out the Church's mission, every work of pastoral planning, must draw the strength it needs from the Eucharistic mystery and in turn be directed to that mystery as its culmination. In the Eucharist we have Jesus, we have his redemptive sacrifice, we have his resurrection, we have the gift of the Holy Spirit, we have adoration, obedience and love of the Father. Were we to disregard the Eucharist, how could we overcome our own deficiency? [¶60]

Pope John Paul then notes that "priests are engaged in a wide variety of pastoral activities" and gives special focus to the role of the Eucharist in providing the bond which gives unity to the priest's life and work.

We can understand, then, how important it is for the spiritual life of the priest, as well as for the good of the Church and the world, that priests...celebrate the Eucharist daily.... In this way priests will be able to counteract the daily tensions that lead to a lack of focus, and they will find in the Eucharistic Sacrifice—the true center of their lives and ministry—the spiritual strength needed to deal with their different pastoral responsibilities. Their daily activity will thus become truly Eucharistic. [¶31]

As discussed in Chapter 2, our Catholic prison ministry volunteer service inside prisons and jails is actually a participation in the pastoral ministry of our priest and bishop. Experience tells us that the "daily tensions which contribute to a lack of focus" are definitely a factor in burnout for us prison ministry volunteers, as well. Consequently, Pope John Paul's recommendation to priests of daily participation in the Eucharist as a protection against spiritual burnout should be well-headed by us volunteers. For the priest, it is celebration of the Eucharist as presider. For the volunteer, it is participation in the Mass. Unity is the antidote for the disunity of burnout. Communion is the antidote for the isolation of burnout. Eucharist is the primary element of Pope John Paul's anti-burnout strategy for Catholics:

"It is not a matter of inventing a 'new program.' The program already exists: It is the plan found in the Gospel and in the living Tradition; it is the same as ever. Ultimately, it has its center in

WHEN WE VISIT JESUS IN PRISON

Christ himself, who is to be known, loved, and imitated, so that in him we may live the life of the Trinity and with him transform history until its fulfillment in the heavenly Jerusalem." The implementation of this program of a renewed impetus in Christian living passes through the Eucharist. [¶60 ci*ting, Pope John Paul II, Apostolic Letter* Novo Millennio Ineunte, ¶29.]

The term Pope John Paul gives to our conscious awareness of this Eucharistic reality is *amazement*, and he connects it to the New Evangelization:

I would like to rekindle this Eucharistic "amazement".... To contemplate the face of Christ, and to contemplate it with Mary, is the "program" which I have set before the Church at the dawn of the third millennium, summoning her to put out into the deep on the sea of history with the enthusiasm of the new evangelization. [¶6]

Our conscious awareness of this Eucharistic amazement is the key to protecting ourselves from burnout.

That They May Be One

St. Mary's Catholic Church, Macclenny, Florida: The Saturday vigil Mass usually hosts about fifty people. Most are older members of this small rural church three miles south of the Georgia border.

My wife, Susan, leads the Communion song on her guitar as the graying members of the congregation each take their turn standing before Jesus and responding, "Amen."

Baker County Jail, Macclenny, Florida: It is early Sunday morning. After obtaining the Pyx from the tabernacle at the church, Susan and I arrive at the county jail. The Catholic female federal prisoners sit elbow to elbow around the small oval table in the visitor room. They rise early to make the weekly

Communion service which is wedged between the staff shift change and the 9:00 am Protestant service.

Susan and I stand, taking their hands in a circle of faith and reciting the *Our Father*. They are all in their late twenties to mid-thirties. One just received word her husband is dead. A sudden heart attack. She's not sure who is caring for her young son. Another is hoping to enter rehab and then return to her children. She may have to do hard time instead. Punishment has trumped treatment. Still another is wobbling on crutches.

One by one each woman steps forward, before the most excellent presence of Jesus in the world, bows her head and says, "Amen."

Florida State Prison, Starke, Florida: The massive door to Q-Wing opens for me at 12:30 pm. This is the maximum-security wing where Frank Valdez was killed two years ago. The cell where I regularly gave him Communion is still sealed with crime scene tape.

For the past two hours, Catholic inmates at this prison have been greeting me at the door of their solitary cells. On each wing, an officer opens the food flap, the hole in the middle of the door through which the man is fed. I bring a different food.

One by one, each man kneels on the cement floor in his cell and bows his head before the real presence of Jesus in the world saying, "Amen."

Union Correctional Institution, Raiford, Florida: This huge prison neighbors Florida State Prison. The Catholic Mass here starts at 1:30 pm. Thirty to forty men clad in prison blue pour into the small chapel as the church guitar choir revs up with a spirited rendition of *Shine, Jesus, Shine!*

Fifty minutes later a reverent stream of blue wends its way to the altar rail. For the briefest moment each man ceases to be a criminal or an outcast. Standing before the host, poised in the grasp of the priest, each one is merely and completely a child of Abba.

I listen as the river of blue pauses before the Lord of Hosts and, one voice at a time, speaks the word of faith, "Amen."

Christ the King Catholic Church, Jacksonville, Florida: At 5:15 pm the Teen Mass choir explodes in song, welcoming teens and parents from all over our diocese. With three of our five children already up-and-out, we are happy to make the weekly drive from Macclenny every Sunday so that our two teenagers can participate in the Mass with other teens their age.

When the Communion hymn begins, the dozens of teens who have been standing around the altar through the Consecration file quietly down to the aisles. As the voices of the choir blend into the words of *One Bread, One Body*, I can hear the younger members of our church acceding to the central reality of our faith.

One by one, those who are the future of our church stand before Jesus under the appearance of bread and wine and put it on the line, "Amen."

St. Mary's Catholic Church, Macclenny, Florida: As I return the Pyx to the tabernacle, the waning summer sun casts a myriad of colored shadows through the large stained glass window of *Mary, Mother of Mercy*. It is time to pause and reflect on the day's pilgrimage of faces that is my Church, my Family of Faith, the Body of Christ.

Is it possible? Are we all truly one bread, one body? Genuflecting before the tabernacle in the evening kaleidoscope of shadows, I hear my own voice. "Amen."

Whether bringing Jesus to inmates in a group or one-on-one, it is an awesome experience for a Catholic prison ministry volunteer to serve as an Extraordinary Minister of the Eucharist inside prisons and jails. The privilege of this role involves the volunteer in a direct and immediate connection to the "profound amazement and gratitude" in which the Church and her members hold the mystery of the Eucharist.

Needless to say, no volunteer should ever bring the Eucharist into a prison or jail without first having been duly authorized and commissioned to do so in accordance with requirements of the local Bishop and the supervising pastor. Assuming that those requirements have been met, it is crucial for the volunteer to exert the constant effort to stay out of the way of the relationship between the inmate and God. That means, at the very least, making sure that the primary relationship being nurtured is the relationship with Jesus.

There may be a periodic Mass celebrated in the prison by a Catholic priest with the volunteer serving as lector or as an Extraordinary Eucharistic Minister. With either a Mass or a Communion service done in a gathering, there may be music played by the volunteer or the inmates. The point is that the peripheral stuff is not the central focus. Whether the music is marginal or there is no music at all, that is not the core thing. Whether the cellblock or chapel is elaborate or cinderblock is not the core thing. Whether there are varnished wooden pews or scratched up and dinged folding chairs is not the core thing. The focus is the Eucharist. It is the Eucharist that confronts and answers the most urgent need of the human heart, inside prison as well as outside the walls.

Assume a man has heard good things about a woman and would like to get to know her. So he asks his friend who knows the woman to introduce them. At the moment of this encounter, the friend is expected to make the introduction, vouch for the suitor, and encourage the woman to pursue a relationship with the suitor. If instead, the friend focuses the discussion on himself, the man who asked to be introduced would be quite justified in feeling used by his so-called friend. He might even say, "Some friend you turned out to be!"

The position of the Catholic prison ministry volunteer is very similar. Jesus wants the inmate to get to know him. He is asking the volunteer only to make the introduction and vouch for him. In the context of an inmate who has progressed in the faith enough to receive Communion, Jesus is asking the volunteer to introduce the inmate to a deeper, more fully committed relationship with Jesus—a Eucharistic relationship. If the volunteer uses that precious time to buildup himself and to focus the inmate on the volunteer instead of Jesus, we can see Jesus shaking his head sadly and saying, "Some friend you turned out to be."

The mission of the ministry volunteer is to make the introduction—or reintroduction—to encourage the relationship with Christ, and to get out of the way. As Archbishop Charles Chaput puts it:

Fear and isolation threaten the modern heart because, deep down, people are hungry for a more authentic experience of life. We yearn for truth about our purpose in the world. We long for the deeper life that Jesus in the Eucharist makes possible....

WHEN WE VISIT JESUS IN PRISON

Spectators don't contribute. They merely consume. Too often, in recent decades, we've carried the consumer attitude into the Liturgy. Instead of losing ourselves in worship of the Trinity and love for one another, we're preoccupied by what we are or aren't getting out of the Mass.... We've too often lost our sense of awe, our reverence for Jesus in the Eucharist, and our Christ-centered service to one another....

The Eucharist is about God. It should focus our worship and our hearts where they belong—on him, not on us.... Thus, our musicians...lectors, and extraordinary ministers of Holy Communion—all the wonderful people who serve in these rolls—need to become transparent, humble, and deeply faithful to the Liturgy that the Church defines, so that nothing distracts us from our encounter with God.[4]

In a subtle but potent way, keeping the focus upon Christ, keeping the mission Eucharistic, is very important in protecting the volunteer from burnout. No volunteer can carry the load of human suffering that is intrinsic to the life of the incarcerated. That load must be given to and carried by the One who came for that purpose—Jesus Christ. No volunteer can bear up to the needs and demands of the incarcerated. Those needs and demands must be given over to the One who came to bear those needs and answer those demands—Jesus Christ. Nurturing this awareness in ourselves is the best way for us volunteers to develop and maintain the emotional and spiritual boundaries described in Chapter 3.

A volunteer facing the suffering of an inmate who has developed a relationship only with the volunteer says, "What am I going to do?" A volunteer facing the suffering of an inmate who has developed a relationship primarily with Jesus says, "Let us pray together to understand what God is doing."

It is the difference between worship and social work. Both are good, but they are not the same. When I volunteered one-morning per week with Mother Teresa's sisters at San Gregorio's in Rome, Italy, the story was told of non-believing critics who attacked Mother Teresa because the nuns in her order spend four hours per day in prayer. The critics, so the story goes, calculated how many more dying people per day her sisters could care for if those four hours were spent in the streets rescuing the dying instead of in prayer in the chapel. Mother Teresa explained to the critics that they completely missed the point. She and her sisters were not engaged in social work, but in worship of God, even when in the streets. If they were to stop their four hours of prayer per day, soon they would burnout and not be able to do any work in the streets at all.

In short, those dying in the streets were being introduced to God because Mother Teresa and her sisters were ministering to them for God's sake. They loved their neighbor out of love for God. They were ministering to Jesus present in the stranger, the sick, and the abandoned. Their four hours of prayer per day made it possible for them to do the other hours of prayer through service in the streets. In other words, whether in the chapel or in the streets, the focus is God. The Mother Superior at San Gregorio also shared with me that Mother Teresa would not allow her nuns to be located any place where daily Mass was not available to them.

It has become cliché to say that nothing is impossible for us with God. In practice, however, too many of us are saying, by our choices and the way we allocate our time, that nothing is impossible for God with me. That is getting it backwards and it does not work. This is not to say that the Eucharistic reality does not have social implications. As Pope Benedict XVI instructs us in his Post-Synodal Apostolic Exhortation, *On the Eucharist as the Source and Summit of the Church's Life and Mission (Sacramentum Caritatis)*, quite the opposite is true:[5]

> The Eucharistic mystery thus gives rise to a service of charity towards neighbor, which "consists in the very fact that, in God and with God, I love even the person whom I do not like or even know. This can only take place on the basis of an intimate encounter with God, an encounter which has become a communion of will, affecting even my feelings. Then I learn to look on this other person not simply with my eyes and my feelings,

WHEN WE VISIT JESUS IN PRISON

but from the perspective of Jesus Christ." In all those I meet, I recognize brothers or sisters for whom the Lord gave his life, loving them "to the end" (John 13:1). [¶88]

...The union with Christ brought about by the Eucharist also brings a newness to our social relations: "this sacramental 'mysticism' is social in character.... In the memorial of his sacrifice, the Lord strengthens our fraternal communion and, in a particular way, urges those in conflict to hasten their reconciliation by opening themselves to dialogue and a commitment to justice. Certainly, the restoration of justice, reconciliation, and forgiveness are the conditions for building true peace. The recognition of this fact leads to a determination to transform unjust structures and to restore respect for the dignity of all men and women, created in God's image and likeness. Through the concrete fulfillment of this responsibility, the Eucharist becomes in life what it signifies in its celebration." [¶89]

...In a particular way, the Christian laity, formed at the school of the Eucharist, are called to assume their specific political and social responsibilities. To do so, they need to be adequately prepared through practical education in charity and justice. To this end, the Synod considered it necessary for Dioceses and Christian communities to teach and promote the Church's social doctrine. [¶91]

Once we prison volunteers begin to comprehend the intricate connectedness between the Eucharist and the Church's social doctrine, it becomes easier for us to understand the miscommunications that inevitably result from attempts to explain Catholic social teaching without the foundation of the Eucharist. It is the Church's understanding of the Eucharist that makes it necessary for Christian faith communities to teach and promote the Church's social doctrine.

It is that same understanding of the Eucharist that requires us volunteers in prison ministry to be so transparent, so humble, and so deeply faithful that nothing in our service distracts us or those we serve from encounter with God. In other words, we are to engage whole mind, whole strength, whole heart, and whole soul in the task of holiness. As the bishops of the Second Vatican Council teach us in the *Dogmatic Constitution on the Church (Lumen Gentium)*, this call to holiness is universal:

> Therefore in the Church, everyone whether belonging to the hierarchy, or being cared for by it, is called to holiness, according to the saying of the Apostle: "For this is the will of God, your sanctification." However, this holiness of the Church is unceasingly manifested, and must be manifested, in the fruits of grace which the Spirit produces in the faithful; it is expressed in many ways in individuals, who in their walk of life, tend toward the perfection of charity, thus causing the edification of others....
>
> The Lord Jesus, the divine Teacher and Model of all perfection, preached holiness of life to each and every one of his disciples of every condition.... He sent the Holy Spirit upon [all] that he might move them inwardly to love God with their whole heart and their whole soul, with all their mind and all their strength and that they might love [one another] as Christ loves them. The followers of Christ are called by God, not because of their works, but according to his own purpose and grace. They are justified in the Lord Jesus, because in the baptism of faith they truly become [children] of God and sharers in the divine nature. In this way they are really made holy. Then too, by God's gift, they must hold on to and complete in their lives this holiness they have received. They are warned by the Apostle to live "as becomes saints," and to put on "as God's chosen ones, holy and beloved a heart of mercy, kindness, humility, meekness, patience," and to possess the fruit of the Spirit in holiness.[6]

Miserere Nobis

When I hear Latin spoken today, it's usually by a mature Catholic. Mass prayers in the Church's mother tongue are the province of people my age and older. In the millennial year, the big 5-0 stands as a continental-size divide between those who served Mass in English and those of us who perfected our pre-Vatican II prayers in the traditional language.

It was a different world then. No one had walked on the moon. The first Catholic was elected President. Catholic families had at least five children. (I am the eldest of eight.) Mothers worked at home. And from the moment I became old enough to be an altar boy, I can tell you one of the things my mother was doing. She was drilling me without mercy in the Latin phrases used in Mass.

"Ad Deum qui laetificat juventutem meam." Again. Then it was *"Confiteor Deo omnipotenti...."*

Mom was usually a stickler on bedtimes. But we burned the midnight oil for weeks practicing prayers in what she used to call "the tongue of angels." Her Italian pride could not bear the shame of a rebuke from our stern Irish pastor. I had better come home from this exam with a perfect score or better not to come home! In those days, no one talked about "nurturing" children. We were forged in fire. Just a couple of years later, however, everything changed. My younger brothers learned their Mass prayers in English. I told them it did not count.

Now, forty years later, vivid memories of altar boy boot camp are a common treasure for me and many of my Catholic brothers on death row. That should not surprise me. The average age on Florida's death row is over 40 years old. Almost one-fourth of the men incarcerated there are old enough to be on my side of that great divide. Among the Catholics, the percentage is even higher. Descendants of Poles, Irish, Germans, Italians—they all remember the Latin gauntlet. Sometimes, they will even test me.

"Ite, Missa est!" a voice barks from the bunk of a cell as I pass in the hall.

"Deo gratias!" I fire back, catching an impish altar boy grin flash across a grown man's face.

Today, I bring Communion to a man my age who hails from the heart of New York. I stand before his cell as we carve out the sacred time and space that will hold this sacramental moment. It is more difficult than usual.

The summer heat and humidity is distracting. The noise on the corridor seems louder than normal. The new steel cage-mesh, which has been welded over all the death row cells, makes it harder to connect, harder to see or touch each other. We are both struggling.

"What can we do to make ourselves aware of God's presence in a special way?" I ask, taking his hands in mine through the food-flap opening in the mesh.

He pauses for a moment, then smiles, "Could you say the Agnus Dei?"

"Yes, I can. In the special monthly healing Mass at our church, we sing it."

He shifts his head to make eye contact through the jet-black mesh. "Could you sing it now—here?"

I hesitate. But only for a moment. His suggestion is perfect.

"Agnus Dei…" I begin. *"Qui tollis peccata mundi: miserere nobis."*

The effect is immediate. Within seconds, the entire corridor falls hushed. As the Latin syllables disperse through the hall, cassock-clad memories of High Masses and Benedictions fill both our minds. The Presence of something—Someone—much larger than ourselves transcends the moment. By the third verse, the very air in the place seems to have changed.

"Dona nobis pacem."

Our eyes meet. The prisoner and I have traveled together to another time, another space. We're ready. Now we can begin.

....

Developing and maintaining a Eucharistic consciousness is a process that will develop and maintain our spiritual boundaries as ministry volunteers, as discussed in Chapter 3. The pursuit of holiness is a spiritual quest that goes hand-in-hand with a Eucharistic consciousness and is crucial to protecting ourselves from burnout. The Eucharist is the way, the means, and the destination of true holiness. Our efforts to avoid burnout through this quest start long before our ministry activities commence. The process of training and practicing to live in a Eucharistic way, in pursuit of holiness, while providing service for the Church, is called "spiritual formation."

There are many tools and disciplines available in the Church as roadmaps for the steps taken to move ever deeper into holiness. Prison ministry volunteers who are already tertiaries to a religious order (e.g., the Secular Franciscans, the Dominicans, the Benedictines, etc.) have well-developed guidelines that are closely connected to the primary order's observance of the Liturgical Hours and in the spirit of the order's charisms. Volunteers who are already invested in Catholic organizations (e.g., the Knights of Malta, the Knights of Columbus, Legatus, etc.) may also have available to them a recommended process for daily spiritual growth. For volunteers who are not covered by those situations, there are other avenues.

For example, a brief booklet I still carry around with me offers a guide to spiritual growth for Extraordinary Ministers of the Eucharist. The same suggestions serve quite nicely for us volunteers in prison ministry, even if we are not Extraordinary Ministers of the Eucharist. The book is *The Liturgical Ministry Series: Guide for Extraordinary Ministers of Holy Communion* (Chicago: Liturgy Training Publications, 2007). In the chapter "Spirituality & Formation" the authors, Kenneth A. Riley and Paul Turner, survey the benefits and practices of Sunday and Daily Mass, Habits of Prayer including Praying with Scripture, in Small Groups, the Liturgy of the Hours, Eucharistic Devotions, and participation in Workshops and Retreats on Prayer, the Sacrament of Reconciliation, Spiritual Reading, and Service to the least of our brothers and sisters. One of the fruits of all this prayer is compassion.

When I attended the University of Notre Dame Law School in the 1970s, our class was drilled in a short but important maxim: *Compassion without competence is a cruel hoax.* For the Catholic volunteer in prison ministry, compassion is absolutely essential. But it is not enough. There must also be competence—competence in a wide variety of aspects of the Catholic faith and about Catholic pastoral ministry. Later chapters of this book discuss the parts of that competence, which involve knowing what you don't know, for example, the nuances of medicine or psychology.

The current discussion in this chapter primarily addresses competence from the standpoint of what a Catholic ministry volunteer should know. In the wider perspective of all lay people involved in ecclesial ministry, the U.S. Conference of Catholic Bishops address this subject of formation and maintenance (which they call "continuing formation") in *Co-Workers in the Vineyard*.[7] The broad requirement for preparation for participation in ecclesial ministry, the bishops insist, is that "lay persons who devote themselves permanently or temporarily to some special service of the Church are obliged to acquire the appropriate formation which is required to fulfill their function properly."[8]

The text does not distinguish between those who participate in ministry for compensation and those who are volunteers. In short, if we undertake to perform a service of the Church, we have the affirmative duty to acquire the necessary preparation. This preparation is not just the learning of facts and figures, not just head knowledge. It is a preparation of the whole person. And the duty includes constantly continuing one's state of spiritual readiness.

Every nation knows that establishing a military force capable of defending its boundaries but then failing to maintain the capabilities and readiness of that force is courting disaster. It is no different with the spiritual preparation of the volunteer in prison ministry. Initial formation is only the beginning. Constant readiness and tune-ups come with the territory.

Co-Workers in the Vineyard is an excellent resource. The following is a very brief summary of the formation material presented in it, slightly adapted to the lay volunteer in prison ministry.

The U.S. Bishops identify four areas in need of formation [p. 34]:

+ **Human qualities:** this addresses our ability to form healthy relationships that will be able to communicate God's love.
+ **Spirituality:** this category focuses upon our practice of a prayer life that grounds our service in the Trinitarian life that I refer to as a Eucharistic consciousness.
+ **Knowledge:** this is the learning in theology and pastoral principles we need to acquire to competently serve.
+ **Pastoral abilities:** this piece looks to the raw material that

we bring to the table and asks: Are we suited, by temperament, gifting, and life experience, to participate in ministry in the environment of prison?

In practice, this fourth category must be handled very delicately and with a great degree of respect for each volunteer. The plain fact of our human condition is that not everyone is well-suited to everything. The volunteer supervisor who is responsible to the priest and bishop for screening potential volunteers must prayerfully and thoroughly determine the true gifts and natural abilities of each potential volunteer and match them to the tasks for which they are best suited.

For example, some volunteers have strong administrative gifts but are very weak on interpersonal communication. They will do a great service handling scheduling and reports. They might not be as effective dealing face to face with inmates, who may often also have weaknesses in the area of interpersonal communications. Such evaluations and volunteer assignments must be made and then communicated to the volunteer in a non-judgmental and affirming way.

The bishops also provide specific guidance as to formation in each of the four categories.

+ **Formation in Human qualities:** [pp. 36-37]
  - Goal of human formation: development of human qualities and character that foster a healthy well-balanced personality.
  - Elements of human formation: self-awareness, psychological health, physical health, mature sexuality, insight concerning our own gifts and weaknesses, understanding of family dynamics and the role of the Christian family in the mission of the Church, a teachable spirit, a valuing of diversity, genuine respect and concern for others, and the virtues of Christian discipleship, including the cardinal virtues.
  - Methods of human formation: small-faith communities, affirmation and critique, feedback (from peers and

supervisors), counseling, methods of self-reflection and self-awareness.

+ **Spiritual formation:** [pp. 38-42]
  - Goal of spiritual formation: animate and foster a hunger for holiness, Trinitarian union, and love of God and neighbor, and develop the practices of prayer and spirituality that foster same.
  - Elements of spiritual formation: living union with Christ, devotion to the written Word of God, formation based on the Liturgy and the sacraments, an incarnational spirituality of presence, and a paschal spirituality of loving service. Extremely important for volunteers in prison ministry, the elements of spiritual formation also include: awareness of sin, spirituality for suffering, a Marian spirituality, love for the Church, devotion to the Eucharist, and an ecumenical spirit.
  - Methods of spiritual formation: daily prayer and spiritual practices, spiritual direction, faith sharing and theological reflection, the practice of justice and charity, and study of the lives of the saints.

+ **Intellectual formation:** [pp. 42-46]
  - Goal of intellectual formation: develop an understanding and appreciation of the Catholic faith, including theology and perhaps philosophy, literature and the arts, psychology, sociology, counseling, medical ethics, culture and language, administration, leadership, organizational development, law, etc., as necessary and relevant for effective ministry.
    > Must go beyond catechesis and into theology: must go beyond thorough adult faith formation and into theology, studying the Church's faith in a scholarly way, interpreting that faith according to the witness of Scripture and Tradition, and making it understand-

able to the present time.
> Ecumenical and interfaith dimensions of intellectual formation are particularly important. Ecumenical and interfaith dialogue is an inherent dimension of evangelization.
- Elements of intellectual formation: study should be as broad and deep as possible (guidance is provided by the USCCB Commission on Certification and Accreditation), including the core elements of Scripture and its interpretation, dogmatic theology, Church history, liturgical and sacramental theology, moral theology, Catholic social teaching, pastoral theology, spirituality and canon law.
- Methods of intellectual formation: may include small groups, lectures, discussions, independent research, guided learning projects, theological reflections on field experience, and new technological means of education.

+ **Pastoral formation:** [pp. 47-49]
- Goal of pastoral formation: cultivate the knowledge, attitudes and skills that are directly related to actual ministry and to the pastoral administration that supports actual ministry.
- Elements of pastoral formation: learning the methods for providing formation for others, leading community prayer and preaching, including the Church's norms and the rites for *Holy Communion and Worship of the Eucharist Outside Mass*[9] and *Sunday Celebrations in the Absence of a Priest*,[10] pastoral ministry skills, family mission and family perspectives, effective relationship and communication skills, collaboration with the ordained, discernment of the signs of the times, gift discernment and volunteer ministry management, change management, conflict management, basic pastoral counseling skills, culture and language studies, administration, leadership, organizational development, applicable civil law, and ministerial code of ethics.

- Methods of pastoral formation: classroom teaching supplemented by practical experience in real world situations and mentored reflection of those experiences.

Such learning and training is preparatory to beginning. Once the Catholic prison ministry volunteer has actually begun service inside prisons and jails, then the period of maintenance begins. The U.S. Bishops refer to this as "ongoing formation." [pp. 50-52]

+ **Ongoing formation:**
  - Continues the process of learning and growing throughout the time one serves in ministry.
  - Is not a luxury for when time and resources allow but rather a permanent necessity for every ecclesial minister, whether lay or ordained.
  - Strengthens ministerial identity and enhances ministerial skills.

+ **Ongoing formation can occur:**
  - Through diocesan, regional or national conferences and ministerial associations.
  - Immersion experiences.
  - Further academic coursework and ministry-specific skill training.
  - Continuing theological reflection on the practice of ministry.
  - Diocesan or parish workshops, renewal days, short courses, study weeks, or retreats.
  - Support groups, study groups or book clubs.
  - A relationship with a mentor and/or spiritual director.
  - Teaching and mentoring others.
  - Sabbaticals (for study and research) for lay ecclesial ministers who have given long and significant service to a particular diocesan church.

WHEN WE VISIT JESUS IN PRISON

+ **Special ongoing formation issues for long careers as a volunteer in prison ministry:**
  - May need spiritual renewal if become tinged with weariness, tedium, or even cynicism.
  - May need re-formation before entering into new areas of ministry.
  - Retirement may provide opportunities for rejuvenation through helping and mentoring newcomers.

For those of us Catholic volunteers in prison ministry who are located in parts of the country that are severely under-populated by Catholics, the struggle for continuing formation can be a special challenge. In addition to the difficulty of participating in conferences and ministerial associations, there may not even be the possibility to attend Mass as frequently as desired. We must do the best we can. One Catholic concept that may be helpful is *spiritual communion*:

> It is good to *cultivate in our hearts a constant desire for the sacrament of the Eucharist.* This was the origin of the practice of "spiritual communion," which has happily been established in the Church for centuries and recommended by saints who were masters of the spiritual life. Saint Teresa of Jesus wrote: "When you do not receive communion and you do not attend Mass, you can make a spiritual communion, which is a most beneficial practice; by it the love of God will be greatly impressed on you." (Italics in original.)[11]

Moreover, volunteers should remember the suggestions of the Second Vatican Council regarding the lay apostolate for those isolated in such areas:

+ Gather into smaller groups for serious conversation, so that an indication of the community of the Church is always apparent to others as a true witness of love.
+ By giving spiritual help to one another through friendship

and the communicating of the benefit of their experience, the laity are trained to overcome the disadvantages of excessively isolated life and activity and to make their apostolate more productive.

As Catholics, we also remember to call upon both the example and the intercession of our Blessed Mother, who in her life and person, stands as a model of Eucharistic faithfulness. She, too, was frequently living out the truth of her faith in isolated areas, with minimal support: e.g., giving birth in a stable, fleeing into Egypt, standing almost alone at the foot of the Cross. Our Blessed Mother Mary knows the solitude of faithful Eucharistic witness in action:

In Mary most holy, we also see perfectly fulfilled the "sacramental" way that God comes down to meet his creatures and involves them in his saving work. From the Annunciation to Pentecost.... Obedient faith in response to God's work shapes her life at every moment.... Mary is the great Believer who places herself confidently in God's hands, abandoning herself to his will.... From the Annunciation to the Cross, Mary is the one who received the Word, made flesh within her and then silenced in death. It is she, lastly, who took into her arms the lifeless body of the one who truly loved his own "to the end" (John 13:1). Consequently, every time we approach the Body and Blood of Christ in the Eucharistic liturgy, we also turn to her who, by her complete fidelity, received Christ's sacrifice for the whole Church.[12]

Finally, a key to maintaining Eucharistic consciousness is connectedness through the Church, the Family of God. This connectedness can be across the miles in current time or even across time itself. The symbols and the practices of our faith can serve as a bond to secure the present to the Eucharistic reality.

WHEN WE VISIT JESUS IN PRISON

A Space-Time Continuum

It's 8:15 am on a Monday morning. Today my first stop is a special one-on-one appointment at the Crisis Stabilization Unit, that is, psychiatric solitary. The appointment had to be set up with the sergeant and the medical staff a week in advance.

Upon arriving at the outer-most door, I hold my identification badge up to the security camera. An officer at an unseen desk checks my name against the schedule for the day. Then, one at a time, I work my way through the maze of bolted, solid steel doors. One. Two. Three. Four. Each time a loud buzzing noise announces that the lock is opened. Then there is a thunderous clap as the electronic bolts slam shut behind me.

Finally, I arrive at the short narrow corridor in front of the control room. No chairs. No props. Just gray tile and gray walls. Double security doors seal each end. The sergeant hand-signals me through the window of his control station. Morning count has not yet cleared. He gestures again sympathetically, with a shrug, letting me know that there is nothing he can do. Until the count clears, I will have to make myself at home right where I am standing. Fortunately, I have what I need in my pocket.

As my hidden fingers slide from black bead to black bead, my feet start moving, pacing off the short distance of the hallway again and again. The succession of meditations that flow with each *Our Father* and *Glory Be* dissolve the tight confines of the prison corridor into a special space of connected experiences. "On earth as it is in heaven."

Now it is 1983. The narrow waiting room for cardiovascular surgery is ill suited for comfort. Mother is in open-heart surgery. Dad is sitting quietly in a chair. Most of us children are standing, pacing the room slowly as we pray in one voice from bead to bead. Mom has a special devotion to Our Lady of the Snows. In the middle of a muggy August in Detroit, snow would be too much to ask for. Our plea is much simpler. "Pray for us sinners, now and at the hour of our death."

Now it is 1990. The superheated pre-dusk air is slipping from the grip of a hot August sun as *Hail Marys* start to flow. The Rosary in the Street, Georgia Street, has become a nightly ritual in the crack-prostitution section of downtown Tallahassee. Volunteer prayer warriors pace the curb, bravely calling out their responses to the prayer leader. Passing street people pause to absorb the mysteries, the meditations, and the prayers, including the Fatima prayer: "O My Jesus, forgive us our sins and save us from the fires of hell."

Now it is 1997. The craggy edifice of ancient *San Gregorio*, hulking a stone's throw from the Circus Maximus, has been reclaimed by the little nuns in white. Mother Teresa's sisters work their way from room to room, ministering to the sickest of the refugees that pour into the eternal city of Rome. Sores and diseases rarely seen by American eyes are commonplace within these walls. I am dispatched with two four-foot high dynamos in white to walk across the city for badly needed supplies. The August afternoon heat is peaking. My question about the distances to be covered is nine-tenths plea for mercy. The sisters simply laugh and pull out their beads. It turns out to be about eighteen decades each way. "Thy kingdom come. Thy will be done."

Now it is today. The sharp bang of electronic locks calls me back to the trivial incidents of the prison corridor. An officer steps through the door and welcomes me toward my appointment.

"Sorry about the wait, chap. Been stuck in here long?"

"For decades, sir," I smile, pulling the rosary beads out of my pocket for him to see. "I've been waiting here for decades."

Despite our best intentions and hardest efforts, we prison ministry volunteers may in fact find ourselves slipping into tinges of weariness, tedium, or cynicism. The drive to the prison may seem longer than it was in the beginning. The hectic and sometimes dehumanizing process of clearing security for the umpteenth time, or having the single hour for Catholic time cut to shreds by prison recounts, may start to feel like a mountain that we have no more energy to climb. It may all start to feel like too much. One volunteer described it to me this way: "There is no music anymore. I used to drive to the prison singing. Now, I just clench the steering wheel and my teeth." What does it mean when the music is gone?

For sure, it means the honeymoon is over. But every great marriage has had to navigate the passage from honeymoon to the rest of life. What does the volunteer do when this starts happening? The

WHEN WE VISIT JESUS IN PRISON

following are some possibilities:

+ **Spiritual direction:** None of us can see everything clearly, especially when it comes to ourselves. Not infrequently, those closest to us are also not able to see things as clearly as someone who has the objectivity of a little distance. A spiritual advisor is absolutely essential to the Catholic volunteer in prison ministry. The advisor may be a parish priest, a religious order priest, brother or sister, or a trained lay person. The advisor will prayerfully discern with the volunteer whether the signs of fatigue and burnout are because of a mismatch between the volunteer's gifts and the particular ministry work being done or due to some other factor.

+ **Lack of balance:** We Catholic prison ministry volunteers are usually lay people living in the secular state. One of the characteristics that distinguish the lay state from others, especially for us volunteers with families, is that our participation in pastoral ministry is not our first priority. Our spouse, our children, our elderly parents, our job, even our personal needs might have a higher claim on our time and resources.

That does not necessarily mean there is not any time for ministry work. It does mean, however, that when the demands of family, financial upheaval, or other difficulties, are draining our emotional and spiritual resources, the balance must be restored by first addressing a reduction in volunteer ministry, at least temporarily.

+ **Over-commitment:** Everything takes longer than we think it will take. Every job looks easy until we have to do it ourselves. A volunteer who is dragging himself or herself to a jail or prison must ask whether he or she has overcommitted, taking on more than one person can do. Remember, our volunteer duties must still leave time for our prayer life and liturgical participation that are indispensable to maintaining our spiritual center, our Eucharistic consciousness. To adapt a well-known cliché, if the volunteer is too busy to maintain a spiritual center he or she is just too busy. Period.

Volunteer ministry assignments can accumulate like boxes in the basement or the garage. Cleaning house on a regular basis is an absolute requirement for the long haul. Periodic assessment of ministry commitments, in terms of hours, energy, and trade-offs at home should be as regular as physical checkups.

For the married volunteer in Catholic prison ministry, those checkups should include the rest of the members of the household. In effect, the children and spouse are making a gift of their parent/spouse to God for the service of the Church. And that gift must be willingly made. Their input and desire to make the gift is crucial. In fact, family meetings to discuss and compromise about a parent's volunteer ministry can serve as part of children's formation as kingdom builders in their own lives.[13]

It is possible that all of the above items will check out as green lights: We're good to go! Yet, we may still feel almost too fatigued to go back to that jail, at least not joyfully. In such a case, we prison ministry volunteers must consider the possibility of *compassion fatigue*, which is an extreme form of burnout.

It is well known that the Latin roots of the word *compassion* literally mean: *to suffer with*. We Catholic prison ministry volunteers make a freewill choice in faith to place ourselves at the side of brothers and sisters in prison in order to bring them the Eucharistic presence—the here-and-now presence of the God who *suffers with* them. Even though we serve only as an instrument to bring that presence, the realities of our human condition are such that we suffer with the inmates as well. The toll this takes on a volunteer emotionally, and in some cases psychologically and physically, is called *compassion fatigue*.

The ability to name this phenomenon and to provide counseling for it is relatively new, just in the last twenty-five years. During that time it has also been called *secondary trauma* or *vicarious traumatization*. The renowned expert in this area, Dr. Charles R. Figley, notes that this concept is "associated with the cost of caring for others in emotional pain."[14]

Many people who are not specialists in the psychological and mental-health fields might be under the impression that compassion fatigue would only apply to first-responders, disaster workers, and those providing care in war zones. In actuality it applies to all of us who work with suffering people because, in doing such work, we ourselves suffer. Studies indicate that both humor and "compassion satisfaction," a sense of joy or accomplishment in such work, can be a significant help to those who suffer with the suffering.

Father Forgive Us

3:00 am, December 8. Almost six hours since everyone left. Four hours since my wife and children went to sleep. In the solitude of my living room, the blinking Christmas tree lights pulse with a solitary question: "What have we done?"

The grammar of the eternal defies our puny efforts to diagram cause and effect. The short question cleverly disguises a divine complexity. With each cycle of the tree lights a different mental picture takes center stage. Like the sharply colored fragments of stone adorning the walls of St. Peter's in Rome, fleeting shadows of the last three weeks merge into a vivid mosaic of sorrow and faith.

Phone calls to his family on the day after Thanksgiving. "Your son...your brother...your father...is scheduled to be killed." Echoes of anguished voices, their tears, their grief, linger like the smoke after a bonfire, subtle yet pervasive whispers of wrenching human agony.

Hours of prayer and sharing with my Catholic brother and with his faith-filled family. Their childhood memories. Years of love and companionship. Their sudden confrontation with horror when he was convicted. Their struggle through the darkest of valleys with only the Light of faith. Fragments drawn together into a final walk up the front steps of a massive edifice called Florida State Prison. The Death House. A Golgotha beyond any family's worst nightmares.

And yet, in their hour in the Garden, they choose not to sleep. During their last moments with him, they form a circle. Arm in arm they pray the *Lord's Prayer* and call to mind all those present and far away, friends, loved ones, and strangers who have sent hundreds of cards and prayers, people united in candlelight vigils on bended knee on the grounds outside the prison and across nine time-zones from England to California.

Then, before leaving, they again form a circle and pray for the healing of all those affected by the crimes, especially the families of the victims. Who can imagine such faith?

The noon hour visit by the priest to administer the sacraments and my last four hours with my brother at his cell in the death house blur into that instant when the curtain opens. I am sitting front row left in the witness room. He is stretched out on the gurney with his feet to the right. His arms and legs are strapped down. All he can move is his head. When he looks toward the window, I am staring right into his eyes.

On behalf of his family, who are not allowed to be present, I sign the words "I love you." He smiles, winks in acknowledgment, and speaks his last words on earth.

"I ask that the good Lord forgive me my sins. I would like to apologize to the families of my victims."

Then, before thanking his family and friends who have shown him love and support, he pauses and says to all of us: "I ask the Lord to forgive them, for they know not what they do." In thirteen minutes he is dead. Killed right before our eyes.

Next thing I know, I am exiting in a van, listening to some of the official witnesses chat casually about their Christmas party schedules. Twenty minutes and fifteen miles later, I am walking into the candlelit church where his mother and family have been kneeling in prayer with the priest and my wife for over two hours.

Only a tear in the fabric of time and space can describe the chasm.

First, to the family present in the church and, then, by phone to family not present, I hear my own voice: "It is finished. Your father...your son...your brother...is dead."

I unplug the Christmas tree lights, but it does not help. There will be no sleep tonight.

WHEN WE VISIT JESUS IN PRISON

Thus far, this book has focused upon the Catholic prison ministry volunteer, their relationship with the Church, and the nature of the work they seek to perform inside the prison fences. In the ensuing chapters that focus shifts to the inmates, their needs, the needs of their families, and of the officers and staff who are charged with their care.

The most obvious and burning question at the pivot-point of such a change in focus is very basic: *Why do people commit crime?* That is the subject of the next chapter.

PART II

THE GENERAL
PASTORAL NEEDS

"Look into my heart, O God.... Let my heart now tell you what prompted me to do wrong for no purpose, and why it was only my own love of mischief that made me do it. The evil in me was foul but I loved it. I loved my own perdition and my own faults, not the things for which I committed wrong, but the wrong itself."

St. Augustine[1]

CHAPTER 7

Current Theories on Why People Commit Crime

Why do people break the law? In Book Two of his *Confessions*, St. Augustine struggles to understand why he and his adolescent friends stole fruit from a neighbor's pear tree.[2]

> I was willing to steal, and steal I did, although I was not compelled by any lack, unless it were the lack of a sense of justice or a distaste for what was right and a greedy love of doing wrong. For of what I stole I already had plenty, and much better at that, and I had no wish to enjoy the things I coveted by stealing, but only to enjoy the theft itself and the sin.

Regarding the pears stolen by Augustine and his teenage friends, he notes:

> We took away an enormous quantity of pears, not to eat them ourselves, but simply to throw them to the pigs.... Our real pleasure consisted in doing something that was forbidden.

There appears to have been no payoff for this crime committed by the fourth century teenage hooligans, except the sheer thrill of breaking the law, both God's law and human law. It was merely the thrill of doing what is forbidden.

We need not be Scripture scholars to scratch our head and say, "Wait a minute. That sounds a lot like Adam and Eve in the Garden of Eden eating the forbidden fruit from the Tree of the Knowledge of Good and Evil." Yes, it does sound very similar indeed.[3] *The Catechism of the Catholic Church* puts it this way:

> The "tree of the knowledge of good and evil" symbolically evokes the insurmountable limits that a [man or a woman], being a creature, must freely recognize and respect with trust. [Humans are] dependent on [their] Creator and subject to the laws of creation and to the moral norms that govern the use of freedom.... Tempted by the devil, [Adam and Eve] let [their] trust in the Creator die in [their] heart and, abusing [their] freedom, disobeyed God's command.... All subsequent sin would be disobedience toward God and lack of trust in [God's] goodness. [¶¶396-397]

The iconic symbol of humankind's inclination to evil is the bite taken by Adam and Eve from the forbidden fruit. Even serious scholars dealing with the most serious of subjects, like Augustine, struggle with our tendency revealed in the classic biblical story from Genesis: to partake in evil just because we can. *The Catholic Catechism* names this condition "concupiscence":[4]

> By yielding to the tempter, Adam and Eve committed a *personal sin*, but this sin affected the *human nature* that they would then transmit *in a fallen state*.... [Original sin] is a deprivation of original holiness and justice, but human nature has not been totally corrupted: it is wounded...subject to ignorance, suffering, and the dominion of death; and inclined to sin—an inclination to evil that is called "concupiscence."

Every Catholic volunteer in prison ministry must come to terms with the reality of evil. Even when the specific crimes of the inmates are not known, the volunteer knows that everybody in the prison chapel or the prison dorm most likely did something to hurt another human being (unless they are completely innocent, which is not the norm). In special situations, such as a dorm or prison camp for lifers, the volunteer will know that probably all those inmates did something really bad to other people. In solitary confinement prisons or death rows, the volunteer knows that most likely the inmates have committed horrible crimes, even murder, against other people's loved ones.

Why? Why do people do such terrible things?

Our Catholic faith addresses this issue from the standpoint of morality: God's law is written on every human heart, yet the effects of original sin weaken our will and strengthen our desire toward that which violates God's law. The moral analysis inevitably leads to the issues of culpability, accountability, and repentance. Making this process of moral judgment available to those inside our prisons and jails is a major task of the Catholic prison ministry volunteer.

The Church's approach based on morality parallels the tremendous efforts from a secular standpoint to study and understand why people commit crime. The modern theories are not at all in agreement. In fact, in some ways, they can contradict each other. But they do break down into some well-defined categories:

+ **Nature:** crime is caused by the way criminals are made; evil is in their blood or their DNA.
+ **Nurture:** crime is caused by the way criminals have been treated as children and/or throughout their life.
+ **Physical Environment:** crime is caused by chemical pollution, for example, lead poisoning, or other environmental factors.
* **Society:** "Crime" is only a social construct; objectively, there is no such thing as a crime.

As discussed below, in the context of any particular person each of these theories only partly explains why he or she commits an act that society judges must be punished, i.e., a "crime." The arguments in the professional journals and symposiums continue to rage between adherents of the various theories.

There is a relatively recent development that is proving quite useful in a practical way in the secular effort to deal with people who have committed crimes. It is called the "cognitive thinking approach." Basically, this analysis is more universal than the other secular theories on criminal behavior. It disregards the arguments about whether crime is the result of nature, nurture, chemical dependency , or whatever and simply assumes that *something has occurred* which has resulted in the criminal becoming a law breaker instead of a law-abiding citizen.

The cognitive thinking approach starts from that point. It addresses the ways in which criminals think differently than law abiding citizens and attempts to change that thinking. The cognitive thinking approach, which is the basis for most of the modern secular efforts at treatment and rehabilitation of offenders, is the subject of *Chapter 8: Characteristics of Criminal Thinking.*

The professional vocabulary that attempts to describe how and why people commit crimes is nothing short of a minefield for prison ministry volunteers. The first major distinction of which every volunteer in prison ministry must be aware is the difference between major mental illness and Antisocial Personality Disorder. Both conditions can exist at the same time with respect to a particular person, in other words, a person suffering from a major mental illness can also be diagnosed with Antisocial Personality Disorder. *Chapter 14: The Special Pastoral Needs of Inmates with Mental Illness* deals with major mental illness, e.g., schizophrenia and bipolar disorder. This current chapter is focused upon criminal behavior which is essentially antisocial behavior that violates the law.

Yet even in making that distinction, we stumble upon another issue that is greatly confusing to people who are not professionals in mental health. In the milieu of the public at large, including the legions of television crime shows and murder mystery movies, the terms *antisocial behavior* and *antisocial personality* are used loosely as synonyms for *criminal behavior* and *criminals*. That usage is not faithful to the technical meanings of those terms when employed by mental health professionals. In order to avoid confusion, I will use here the terms *criminal behavior* and *criminal* unless the technical meanings are intended.

The reality is that only a small percentage of the people in prisons and jails, in other words only a small percentage of *criminals* are in fact *sociopaths* or *psychopaths*. Most of the inmates we volunteers will encounter behind bars are normal people who made really bad choices and made stupid mistakes. Regardless of whether an inmate is in the small subset that are *sociopaths* or *psychopaths*, the fact that they are in prison almost guarantees that they were engaged in some level of criminal thinking. That is why the cognitive thinking approach is so universal in its application. That is also why the universal precautions we volunteers should take to protect ourselves from criminal thinking presented in Chapter 8 are so important to heed.

The bible of the mental health professional world in the U.S. for classifying human pathologies in thinking, feeling, and behavior is called "the DSM" which is the abbreviated name for the *Diagnostic and Statistical Manual of Mental Disorders* published by the American Psychiatric Association. In 2013, a major rewriting of this manual was released as the Fifth Edition.[5]

The following definitions are critical to a discussion of criminal behavior, but the definitions are not all from the DSM. As described below, there are many variations in the use of even these technical terms by prominent authors. That is part of what makes the discussion a minefield for us non-professionals.

+ **Antisocial behavior:** harmful behavior in disregard of the dignity or needs of others.
+ **Criminal Behavior:** antisocial behavior that breaks the law.
+ **Narcissistic Personality Disorder:** a disorder defined in the DSM as a pervasive pattern of grandiosity, need for admiration, and lack of empathy, according to certain criteria of thinking and relating.

+ **Antisocial Personality Disorder:** a disorder defined in the DSM as a pervasive pattern of disregard for, and violation of, the rights of others occurring since age 15, according to certain criteria of thinking and behavior.
+ **Psychopathy:** a technical term for the condition of one who is a sociopath or a psychopath.

This definition of *psychopathy* begs the question: What does it mean to be a *sociopath* and a *psychopath*? Based upon my experience in decades of prison ministry at all levels of security and classification, the mental health profession's distinctions between sociopath and psychopath are not always helpful. In fact, many mental health and corrections professionals use the terms interchangeably to refer to someone who does not evidence feelings of remorse or evidence pangs of conscience. Here is an operational definition that has served me well; it distinguishes between the two forms of psychopathy as follows:

+ **A sociopath** will do whatever it takes to get what he wants from you. That could be money, or stuff, or sex. And he does it without evidencing any observable feelings of remorse or pangs of conscience. The payoff, however, is the "what" that he gets.
+ **A psychopath** will also do whatever it takes to get something from you. That could be money, or stuff, or sex, but that is not the primary gain. That is only secondary. The primary gain is your suffering. The suffering can be inflicted through torture, the agony of realizing that one has been "marked" in an elaborate deceit, or even through the ultimate infliction of death. The psychopath also commits his crime without evidencing any observable feelings of remorse or pangs of conscience. The payoff, however, is clear. The "what" that a psychopath gets out of his or her criminality is the suffering of the victim(s).

Adding the term *sadism* (the enjoyment of inflicting pain on another) to describe the pursuit of human suffering allows the following definitional distinctions:

+ **Sociopath:** one who engages in antisocial behavior without evidencing any observable feelings of remorse or pangs of conscience.
+ **Psychopath:** one who engages in sadistic antisocial behavior without evidencing any observable feelings of remorse or pangs of conscience.

Without the benefit of any statistical analysis or professional mental health diagnoses, my operational experience has been that out of every 100 or so inmates in men's prison about four or five may be sociopaths and one or two may be psychopaths. But it is important for prison volunteers to also recognize that close to 100% of those 100 inmates have engaged in criminal thinking.

For us Catholic volunteers in prison ministry, any definitions or analysis of criminal theories must begin with the question of conscience. How does Catholic teaching about conscience square with putting and keeping people in prison? Even more poignantly, with respect to the small subset of criminals who are sociopaths or psychopaths, what difference does it make that they do not evidence any observable feelings of remorse or pangs of conscience? How can that be reconciled with the teaching of our Church concerning conscience?

The key question is "What is conscience?" In *The Sociopath Next Door*, Dr. Martha Stout asserts that "One in twenty-five ordinary Americans secretly has no conscience and can do anything at all without feeling guilty."[6] Dr. Stout's analysis of "feeling guilty" leads her into a probing discussion of the nature of conscience and of the history of humanity's attempts to understand it; she quotes Augustine, Aquinas. and Freud, and her operating definition for purposes of her book is a psychological one:

Conscience is something that we *feel*…. Conscience exists primarily in the realm of "affect," better known as *emotion*…. Psychologically speaking, conscience is a sense of obligation ultimately based in an emotional attachment to another living creature…or to a group of human beings, or even in some cases to humanity as a whole. Conscience does not exist without an emotional bond…and in this way is closely allied with the spectrum of emotions we call "love."[7] (Emphasis in original.)

Every Catholic volunteer in prison ministry will immediately note that this definition is at great variance from the Church's understanding of conscience. *The Catholic Catechism* teaches that:

Conscience is a judgment of *reason* whereby the human person recognizes the moral quality of a concrete act that he is going to perform, is in the process of performing, or has already completed…. It is by the judgment of conscience that men and women perceive and recognize the prescriptions of the divine law.[8] (Emphasis added.)

Moreover, where the psychological definition of conscience as a *feeling* of duty arising out of an *emotional bond* seems to understand that conscience as formed through attachments to others, Catholic teaching understands conscience as *the voice of the natural law implanted in every human heart by the Creator*. In *Gaudium et Spes*, the bishops of the Second Vatican Council teach us:[9]

In the depths of [our] conscience, [human beings] detect a law that [we] do not impose upon [ourselves] but holds [us] to obedience. Always summoning [us] to love good and avoid evil, the voice of conscience when necessary speaks to [our] heart: do this, shun that. For [we humans have] in [our] heart a law written by God; to obey it is the very dignity of [men and women]; according to it [we] will be judged (Romans 2:15-16). Conscience is the most secret core and sanctuary of a [human]. There we are alone with God, whose voice echoes in [our] depths. In a wonderful manner conscience reveals that law which is fulfilled by love of God and neighbor (Matthew 22:37-40; Galatians 5:14).

In his landmark encyclical, *On the Relationship between Faith and Reason (Fides et Ratio)*, Pope John Paul II reminds us that this understanding goes back to the earliest Christians:[10]

The first Christians could not refer only to "Moses and the prophets" when they spoke. They had to point as well to natural knowledge of God and to the voice of conscience in every human being (cf. Romans 1:19-21; 2:14-15).

The pope warns that the voice of conscience can be perverted and muted by erroneous teaching or immoral practices or by a society that renounces objective truth:

Conscience is no longer considered in its prime reality as an act of a person's intelligence, the function of which is to apply the universal knowledge of the good in a specific situation and thus to express a judgment about the right conduct to be chosen here and now. Instead, there is a tendency to grant to the individual conscience the prerogative of independently determining the criteria of good and evil and then acting accordingly. Such an outlook is quite congenial to an individualist ethic, wherein each individual is faced with his own truth different from the truth of others.[11]

Consequently, Church teaching recognizes an affirmative duty to form one's conscience in accordance with God's law and the Scriptures. *The Catholic Catechism* confirms this duty:

Conscience must be formed and moral judgment enlightened.... The education of conscience is indispensable for human beings who are subjected to negative influences and tempted by sin to prefer their own judgment and to reject authoritative teaching. The education of conscience is a lifelong task. From the earliest years, it awakens the child to the knowledge and practice of the interior law recognized by conscience…. In the formation of conscience the Word of God is the light for our path; we must assimilate it in faith and prayer and put it into practice.[12]

There is no "get out of jail free card" morally just because we did not form our conscience properly. Cardinal George Pell addresses this truth head on:

Christians have no entitlement to define sins out of existence, to deny or ignore fundamental teachings of faith, by claiming that their consciences [which can sometimes be mistaken through their own fault] are free…. Individual conscience cannot confer the right to reject or distort New Testament morality as affirmed or developed by the Church.[13] (Bracketed language in original.)

Accordingly, there is a dual reality to the Catholic understanding of conscience. Pope Benedict XVI enunciates these two prongs in his encyclical *On Integral Human Development in Charity and Truth (Caritas in Veritate)*. Conscience starts out as something received from the Creator, the voice of the natural law written on every human heart:

Likewise the truth of ourselves, of our personal conscience, is first of all given to us. In every cognitive process, truth is not something that we produce, it is always found, or better, received. Truth, like love, "is neither planned nor willed, but somehow imposes itself upon human beings."[14]

The second aspect is the duty upon each human person to properly develop the gift of conscience:

WHEN WE VISIT JESUS IN PRISON

The human person by nature is actively involved in his own development. The development in question is not simply the result of natural mechanisms, since as everybody knows, we are all capable of making free and responsible choices. Nor is it merely at the mercy of our caprice, since we all know that we are a gift, not something self-generated. Our freedom is profoundly shaped by our being, and by its limits. No one shapes [his or her] own conscience arbitrarily, but we all build our own "I" on the basis of a "self" that is given to us. Not only are other persons outside our control, but each one of us is outside his or her own control. *[People's] development is compromised if [they] claim to be solely responsible for producing what [they] become.*[15] (Italics in original.)

Likewise, people's moral development evidences an improperly formed conscience if they claim no personal responsibility for what they become:

Conscience enables [us] to assume responsibility for the acts performed. If [we] commit evil, the just judgment of conscience can remain within [us] as the witness to the universal truth of the good at the same time as the evil of [our] particular choice.... In attesting to the fault committed, it calls to mind the forgiveness that must be asked, the good that must still be practiced, and the virtue that must be constantly cultivated with the grace of God.[16]

An important role of us Catholic prison ministry volunteers in dealing with inmates is to first engage them in the process of educating and correcting any errors in the formation of their conscience. All or part of this education may be in the context of preparation for the Sacraments of Initiation (Baptism, Confirmation, Eucharist). In some cases an inmate may already have been initiated into the faith sacramentally but has not yet incorporated the Church's teachings regarding formation of conscience. Either way, as an inmate's conscience is corrected and conformed to truth, the volunteer assists him or her in the continuing process of conversion that allows those incarcerated the power of the Holy Spirit to convict them of sin and yet draw them into repentance.[17] The Sacrament of Reconciliation is of course the primary vehicle for this process. On the continuing journey of sanctification, the volunteer becomes a traveling companion to the inmate in the lifelong work of cultivating the practice of virtue and of awareness of the presence of God.

Forty Days and Forty Nights

Rain has been falling for over a week. The St. Mary's River, which usually wends quietly and unnoticed behind our church, is cresting at more than six feet over flood stage. Flash flood warnings for Macclenny and Baker County are not apocalyptic, but they sure have riveted everyone's attention. We all hope the rain will stop soon.

The parking lot of the prison is at least four inches under water. I find myself straddling the curbs and tiptoeing along the crest of the speed bumps in order to avoid the ankle deep wavelets.

"You gonna make it, chap?" calls out a slicker-clad officer from the steps of the building. "It might be easier to swim than to walk."

"I'll say. Up in Baker County we are ready to start bringing the animals into the ark two-by-two."

"Yeah, same thing down in Lake Butler. Be careful, chap," he continues, reminding me that water will be inside the building, too. "You know how slippery the floor gets in spots when it rains."

"Thanks," I answer distractedly, while checking the security of the plastic lid on my Styrofoam cup filled with the slurry of blessed ashes and holy water.

Once on a wing, I wait for the officer to open the first man's food flap.

"Do you have to be Catholic to get those?" a voice calls out from behind the door of the cell next to a Catholic who has just received his ashes. "I want some!"

"You do not have to be Catholic," my voice exhales forcefully as I pull

WHEN WE VISIT JESUS IN PRISON

myself up from kneeling on the wet concrete. "But you have to be willing to repent. These ashes mark the beginning of Lent, forty days of fasting and prayer."

"Forty days! Why forty days?"

"We are allowing God to cleanse and prepare us for the mysteries of Good Friday and Easter. When God cleansed and prepared the world for Noah and his family, it rained for forty days and forty nights. Forty is the Biblical time period for cleansing and preparation."

"So what I got to do?"

"For starters," I tap my finger on his window, pointing to the pictures of nearly naked women adorning the walls of his cell, "Those have to come down."

"No way. I'm not ready for that yet."

"Fine. Put it off. But don't wait too long. It has already been raining for two weeks. Don't let God's cleansing flood of judgment catch you holding on to your favorite sins!"

How does the Church's mission of conversion, repentance, and sanctification, square with the theories of why people commit crime?

The secular theory that there is no such thing as objective crime—that crime is only a social construct that benefits the ruling elites—does not fit well at all with Catholic teaching. That is not to say that society has no responsibility to the individual. Quite to the contrary. As discussed in Chapter 1 of this book, the Church has a strong social justice teaching that incorporates solidarity and social responsibility. But the Church also teaches that there is objective truth that God has revealed and individual responsibility to follow it.

Every individual is held accountable to that truth, regardless of whether society honored its moral duties or not. Every person of faith understands with outrage the maxim: *Who steals more, the one who comes with a gun or the one who comes with a briefcase?* Every Catholic who understands the Church's social teaching is perplexed and outraged that the same voices that condemn humane treatment for the imprisoned poor shrug helplessly at the theft of hundreds of billions of dollars by the already rich—to the destruction of families and lives across the entire nation. That is not right. It is not just. And, just as surely, the crimes of the rich do not remove personal responsibility from the poor for crimes they themselves commit. So we Catholics must work toward a more just society and toward laws that punish crime without regard to class or wealth. And inside prisons and jails, we must call all offenders, even if they are mostly or even exclusively poor, to accountability and repentance.

With respect to the theories that look for causes of criminality in social environmental factors (e.g., family and social influences), and in physical environmental factors (e.g., lead poisoning in center cities, water pollution by arsenic and other heavy metals, etc.), a Catholic can consider such factors as mitigating of culpability to the extent that the ability of the criminals to understand right and wrong, to control their decisions, or to control their behavior was impaired through no fault of their own. But the objective evil of the acts done must still be faced and repented. And the defects in conscience that may have resulted from such factors need to be corrected.

Finally, the firm purpose of amendment that is part of the Sacrament of Reconciliation must incorporate the corrected conscience into a personal commitment to avoid such sin in the future. Much of this is material rightly dealt with between the inmate and the priest in the sanctity of confession. The Catholic volunteer in prison ministry should always be extremely prudent in avoiding discussion of confessional material. The best guideline may be to stick to the principles of Catholic teaching in the inmate's preparation and allow the priest and the inmate to work-out the specific application of those principles to the inmate's life and choices.

The theories that look for causes of criminality in nature are the most difficult to address. In real life application, most modern theorists would posit some combination of nature and nurture in the mix of causation of criminality. It is unfortunate, however, that most popular discussions of the nature argument have to do with crimes committed by people who are said to have no conscience:

Psychopaths are social predators who charm, manipulate, and ruthlessly plow their way through life leaving a broad trail of broken hearts, shattered expectations, and empty wallets. Completely lacking in conscience and in feelings for others, they selfishly take what they want and do as they please, without the slightest sense of guilt or regret.[18]

Does God create people without a conscience? How could that possibly square with Catholic teaching? First, it is important to recall the difference between the psychological understanding of conscience (as something that one *feels*) and the Catholic understanding of conscience, the voice of the natural law impressed upon every human heart by the Creator. Frequently, when Catholics ask what is to be done with sociopaths and psychopaths, we are working with the psychological definition of conscience. From a Catholic standpoint, however, there is no such thing as a person without a conscience.

I speak around the country and the world on issues concerning crime and punishment. People in the audiences will ask: *What are we supposed to do with criminals if they do not feel remorse?* They are making a thinly veiled reference to psychopaths. My answer can be very uncomfortable to them: For the Catholic, a criminal's ability to *feel* remorse or to *feel* anything else has nothing to do with verifying whether or not the person has a conscience. If the person is a human being, they have a conscience as understood by Catholic teaching. Period. End of discussion.

Furthermore, dramatic displays of remorse by criminals are highly over-rated and the absence of them can be hugely misused in the criminal justice system. A true psychopath can provide on demand an academy award-worthy display of remorse. It means nothing to him or her.

Based on the fact that the condemned did not show remorse, many governors in death penalty states will justify not considering commuting to life in prison a death sentence where the inmate is claiming innocence. It is a difficult question that a lot of "free" people (those outside of prison) never consider: How does a condemned person show remorse for a crime that he or she did not commit?

Given the dramatic difference between the Catholic understanding of conscience and the psychological understanding of conscience, what is the task of us Catholic prison ministry volunteers in ministering to a true sociopath or psychopath in prison? What can be accomplished with a person who is incapable of *feeling* repentance? The answer, in my experience is: Actually a great deal.

When coupled with the absolution received through the Sacrament of Reconciliation, an inmate can obtain forgiveness of sins even though his contrition is born of the fear of eternal damnation and not from an emotional revulsion for his sin. Feelings are not necessary. The contrition of fear, called "imperfect contrition" or "attrition," together with sacramental absolution in the sacrament, will suffice for the Church to forgive sin.[19]

As part of the sacrament, however, the inmate must also have a firm purpose of amendment to sin no more and take steps to make that commitment a reality. Pope Benedict XVI points dramatically to this reality in the encyclical *On Christian Hope (Spe Salvi)*:

> We must free ourselves from the hidden lies with which we deceive ourselves. God sees through them, and when we come before God, we too are forced to recognize them. "But who can discern his errors? Clear me from hidden faults" prays the Psalmist (Psalm 19:12 [18:13]). Failure to recognize my guilt, the illusion of my innocence, does not justify me and does not save me, because I am culpable for the numbness of my conscience and my incapacity to recognize the evil in me for what it is. If God does not exist, perhaps I have to seek refuge in these lies, because there is no one who can forgive me, no one who is the true criterion. Yet my encounter with God awakens my conscience in such a way that it no longer aims at self-justification and is no longer a mere reflection of me and those of my contemporaries who shape my thinking, but it becomes a capacity for listening to the Good itself.[20]

Benedict also recognizes, in that encyclical, the powerful role that fear of eternal damnation can play in bringing about such an awakening of conscience, through the power of the Last Judgment:

From the earliest times, the prospect of the Judgment has influenced Christians in their daily living as a criterion by which to order their present life, as a summons to their conscience, and at the same time as hope in God's justice. Faith in Christ has never looked merely backwards or merely upwards but always also forward to the hour of justice that the Lord repeatedly proclaimed. This looking ahead has given Christianity its importance for the present moment. In the arrangement of Christian sacred buildings, which were intended to make visible the historic and cosmic breadth of faith in Christ, it became customary to depict the Lord returning as a king—the symbol of hope—at the east end, while the west wall normally portrayed the Last Judgment as a symbol of our responsibility for our lives—a scene which followed and accompanied the faithful as they went out to resume their daily routine. As the iconography of the Last Judgment developed, however, more and more prominence was given to its ominous and frightening aspects, which obviously held more fascination for artists than the splendor of hope, often all too well concealed beneath the horrors.[21]

How can this decision, this revival of conscience, be made by someone without an emotional (psychological) conscience? Perhaps inadvertently, Drs. Robert Hare and Paul Babiak provide a very modern metaphor to understand how the volunteer can facilitate this outcome:[22]

Think of Spock in *Star Trek*. He responds to events that others find arousing, repulsive, or scary with the words *interesting* and *fascinating*. His response is a cognitive or intellectual appraisal of the situation, without the visceral reactions and emotional coloring that others normally experience. Fortunately for those around him, Spock has "built-in" ethical and moral standards, a conscience that functions without the strong emotional components that form a necessary part of our conscience. (Italics in original.)

Through catechesis, the Catholic prison ministry volunteer educates the inmate on the reality of life after death, of eternal punishment, of forgiveness of sins, and of the requirements of God's law. A person who has no ability to feel empathy or sympathy can still make an informed decision to choose salvation in order to avoid the pains of hell. Salvation is available to everyone, even sociopaths and psychopaths. That is our Catholic faith.

And, as Pope Benedict reminds us, the heavy lifting is the power of prayer. In prison ministry, that can be prayer by the volunteer, by the inmate, and by the Church:

> For prayer to develop this power of purification, it must on the one hand be something very personal, an encounter between my intimate self and God, the living God. On the other hand it must be constantly guided and enlightened by the great prayers of the Church and of the saints, by liturgical prayer, in which the Lord teaches us again and again how to pray properly.[23]

But what about...?

Last week marked my first ever trip to Cody, Wyoming, a town just minutes from the East Gate (U.S. 14) to Yellowstone National Park. When we receive guests in Florida, deference to certain local proclivities is expected: trips to the Mouse (Disney World), to rub the coquina walls of Fort Marion (St. Augustine), and to ride the glass bottom boats through the alligator-pitted river (Wakulla Springs, where the Tarzan movies of my youth were filmed).

WHEN WE VISIT JESUS IN PRISON

So I consented to the touristy regimens of my local experts, including the Buffalo Bill Cody Museum and the Plains Indians Museum. I begged off on the Wild Sheep Museum.

Aside from those few tourist mandatories, all pursued in snow flurries and chill breezes of less than 25 degrees, the trip was deadly serious: the annual statewide meeting of the Wyoming Catholics United for Life. Usually, this once-per-year gathering hosts speakers and topics more typical of religious Right to Life Conferences. This year the subject was all about capital punishment and the concept of God's mercy.

In the course of an intense day, the statewide audience heard the riveting testimony of a mother whose son at college had been brutally abducted, tortured, and murdered in a gang thrill-kill. As she wrapped up the description of her journey to forgiveness, it seemed impossible for there to be any oxygen left in the hotel, let alone the room.

Then, Fr. Augustine Judd, a Dominican priest and theologian, delivered two one-hour presentations on the Catholic Church's history with, and theology of, capital punishment, culminating with the Church's modern day application of that tradition: moral exercise of the state's power to execute only obtains when bloodless means are not sufficient to protect innocent life in society.

I was there to share the story of our family's journey from my first career, as a Wall Street finance lawyer, to our death row ministry. Then, in a second talk, I brought the audience up close to death row and the death house. Finally, in the evening keynote at dinner, I was asked to share my personal journey with respect life and my change of heart on the death penalty—a change that took place in the late 1980s, at least a decade before my wife and I came into death row ministry.

The participants were incredible. Fully engaged. Brimming over with questions and encouragement. I marveled at their stamina in the face of such a deluge of difficult talks. As the dinner ended and a closing benediction was given, many lined up to share their appreciation and ask more questions of the speakers. That is when a very serious and concerned lady approached me.

"Thank you for your stories. It was all quite incredible, this whole day. But I have a concern. Don't we need the death penalty for the ones who are sociopaths, who have no remorse, the ones who are…."

"I think the term you are looking for is 'intrinsically evil.'"

"Yes," she takes my hand in a gesture that is clearly more forceful than she meant it to be. "Yes, the ones who are intrinsically evil, who have no remorse. Who are cocky and brazen about the horror they have done. Don't we need the death penalty for those ones?"

"Are you Catholic?" I ask gently.

"Yes, but why should that matter?"

"Because as Catholics we do not believe that anyone is intrinsically evil, no matter how sociopathic they are. We believe that everyone is susceptible to the power of the Cross and Resurrection and can be redeemed."

"What?"

"The notion of predestination to hell, which is what it means to be intrinsically evil, is from John Calvin. It is part of a theory of double predestination: that some people are predestined by God for heaven, and others are predestined by God for hell. As Catholics we do not believe that."

""What do we believe?"

"We believe that God creates and predestines everyone for heaven, but we get to choose whether or not we accept the gift."

"So, these people get off scot-free without eternal punishment?"

"Only if they repent."

"But what if they just repent to avoid hell?"

"We Catholics call that imperfect contrition—repentance out of fear of the loss of Heaven and of the pains and punishments of hell. And, yes, we believe that can be a sufficient route to salvation. It is not as good or as pure as perfect contrition, repentance out of the horror of the harm we have done to others and the offense of our crimes to a pure and perfectly loving God. But we believe that imperfect contrition and sacramental confession can result in salvation and that everyone, no matter how perverse his or her sins are, is capable of repentance."

"Well, let me tell you, brother, if that is true, God and the Church are a lot more merciful than I am!"

"Amen."

A final distinction that every Catholic prison ministry volunteer must bear in mind is the difference between narcissistic personality traits and Narcissistic Personality Disorder, also referred to as NPD. While individuals diagnosed with NPD will exhibit narcissistic personality traits, it does not follow that everyone who has narcissistic traits is at the level of NPD. For the volunteer facing an inmate and experiencing their way of relating to others, it can be too easy to treat the actions and attitudes attributed to narcissism as the equivalent of the sociopathy of NPD. It is not always the case and should not be assumed.

In *The Object of My Affection Is in My Reflection: Coping with Narcissists*, Rokelle Lerner, considered by many to be the most eloquent at describing narcissism and how narcissists affect the people who live and work with them, offers some keen insights into the narcissistic personality:[24]

> They are charming, that is, until you get to know them; that's when you're at risk of becoming one of their victims…. They're spoiled and wounded children, desperately in need of someone to be in awe of them…. Narcissists are actors playing a part… expert liars and, even worse, they believe their own lies…. They rarely, if ever, admit fault and they never say they're sorry.

We volunteers who came of age at the time of the movie *Love Story* should cringe at the memory of that flick's famous line: "Love means never having to say you're sorry." That is an axiom for the narcissist who feeds off of others—emotionally, physically, and psychologically—and then reinterprets this parasitic behavior as love by claiming that *taking care of myself is the best way to take care of others.* Our consumer culture, hedonistic media, and pervasive dysfunctional parenting have contributed to the formation of a torrent of people with narcissistic personality traits. Ms. Lerner, however, distinguishes narcissistic personality traits from the diagnosis of NPD, pointing out that only 1% of Americans have NPD but that the number with narcissistic personality traits is much, much higher.

For those who are not NPD, narcissistic traits can be dealt with by facing the fears and emptiness behind the behavior and bringing the healing power of the Holy Spirit and the sacraments to bear. For the one person out of one hundred who is diagnosed with NPD, the recovery of emotional and relational health is much more difficult. But even sociopathy is amenable to the saving grace of Calvary.

The God I Know

Part of my responsibility as a Catholic Correctional Chaplain on Florida's death row is making myself available to the inmates for one-on-one pastoral counseling. Such counseling is never initiated by me. Usually it is at the request of the inmate. In rare instances, it can also be at the request of officers and staff who are looking out for the welfare of a particular inmate.

For example, on one occasion, officers were very concerned that a particular inmate, who had suffered the loss through death of important friends and family members, might be despondent enough to attempt suicide. They ask me to see him pastorally. I agree, so long as the inmate is willing to come voluntarily. He does.

The officers escort him in chains and black-box handcuffs from his cell down to the main floor counseling room and lock us in together. The inmate and I are sitting quietly across the table from one another as he sizes me up.

"I'm not one of your flock, you know," he finally speaks in a rather dismissive tone.

"Yes, I know." I smile and nod.

"So what the heck do you want with me?"

"I want to convince you that your life is a gift from God, and that even in here your life is a gift of great value."

"What!" he glares at me with a rapid succession of rolling-eye rim shots. "Exc-u-u-use me! I assumed you were a Christian, but I must have been mistaken!"

"No. No mistake. I am a Catholic Christian."

"You Christians are the ones who want to kill me!" The black-box cuffs make a dull thudding noise as his hands beat the table, punctuating his words. "You Christians are the ones who insist on having the death penalty! And you have the nerve to come in here and tell me my life is a gift? What kind of a Christian hypocrite are you?"

"My turn?" I ask gently after allowing the energy from his tirade to dissipate.

"Have at it!" He snorts in disdain. "This should be good!"

"Not all Christians support the death penalty. In fact, the overwhelming majority do not. But we are in a country, and in a particular part of the country, where many Christians mistakenly believe that this practice is mandated by God's will."

"That would be the same God that you want to tell me about?" he speaks while pretending to crane his sight to the hallway, as though he wants the officers to end this pointless meeting. "This God that you want to tell me about thinks my life is a gift?"

"I cannot speak for others." I shrug with all the innocence that can be mustered under the circumstances. "I can only tell you about the God I know. And the God I know is mercy within mercy within mercy. God treasures your life and does not desire the death of a sinner."

"So now I'm a sinner am I!" He again feigns the search for release and rescue by the hall officers; but this time he is smirking, obviously intending to pull my chain a bit.

"No worries," I laugh. "I am a sinner, too."

"So, Chaplain Sinner, cut the crap and give it to me straight. What do you want from me?"

"I want to convince you that your life is a gift from God, and that even in here your life is a gift of great value."

"That's your story and you're sticking to it, huh?" He shakes his head as though we are wasting our time.

"Actually, that is God's story, and God doesn't change it."

"This God that *you* know." His emphasis is effectively sarcastic.

"Yes, the God I know."

"Well don't get your hopes up. I'm not going to pray, and I'm not going to read from your stupid book that all you Christians quote from to kill me."

"You mean that 'some Christians' quote from to kill you, right?"

"Sure, if you say so."

So, does that mean you would like to meet with me regularly?"

"I wouldn't say 'like.' But it will be okay."

In the course of the next three years, that man became a godson to me and my wife. But not all my pastoral endeavors on death row have started out so well.

An infamous criminal on the row requested to begin seeing me pastorally. I was almost paralyzed at the thought. Surely, this required someone with much more training, much more experience, much more something.

Surely, God would not ask me to see a man pastorally when just the thought of his crimes, the thought of holding his hands in prayer, the hands that did those unspeakable things to other peoples' loved ones, moved me to a nauseating horror and revulsion. All the crimes represented by death row are horrible. All the crimes are revolting. But these particular crimes were the stuff of my worst nightmares. Surely, I was not the guy to do this.

"I don't think you get to pick, Dale." The kindly priest, almost as grey in the hair as I have become seemingly overnight since starting death row ministry, is my pastoral advisor. "I don't think you get to decide who God can ask you to serve."

"But there has to be a limit, a boundary, a something that even God can't ask me to go beyond."

"Well, there isn't in this regard, not when it comes to bringing the Good News to the people who need it most. Can you think of anybody who needs the message of Jesus more than this fellow?"

"No. Of course not. But why me?"

"We don't get to ask that question. Jesus eradicated that question for all time when He went to the Cross willingly and said, 'Not my will, but thy will.' If anyone had the right to scream, 'Why me?' it was him. But He didn't. And so, we don't get to ask that either. The reason he is sending you is because this man asked for you. If you refuse, you are not saying 'no' to the inmate, you are saying 'no' to Christ."

"Well, it's a little late for that, don't you think?" I feel sheepish at how sarcastic my tone is, but in fact it does feel like God is taking me a lot deeper than I ever intended to go.

"In fact it is *far too late* for that." The priest places his hand so gently on my shoulder that he feels like a father speaking to his teenage son. "I think

WHEN WE VISIT JESUS IN PRISON

you said 'yes' to this a long time ago, but you didn't know it yet. You said 'yes' when you were baptized and confirmed. You say 'yes' every time you receive the Eucharist. Now, you are finding out what that 'yes' means."

By the conclusion of my first pastoral with the infamous inmate, word has spread through the entire building. Not just the inmates, but also the staff are somewhat shocked that I would entertain the possibility that such a man is capable of forgiveness and redemption. As I clear the security checkpoint to exit the death row building, I notice that two officers are standing between me and the entrance to the quarter-mile long fence tunnel that leads to the front of the prison. I greet the two officers because I know them well and they have always treated me well. They do not return my greeting. As I step within arm's reach of them, they do not budge an inch. I realize they are not there to make sure I am able to leave. In fact, they are there to block my path.

"You are way off track on this one, chap." The younger officer who towers over me speaks with arms rigidly folded while expertly aiming his tobacco stained spit just a centimeter from my shoe. I know instinctively that his marksmanship with the spent tobacco juice is not a threat, but it is meant for emphasis.

"We usually support your work in this building." The older, shorter officer takes up his portion of the presentation. "You know we are supportive of your efforts. But this one is a mistake. God wants him in hell."

In the moment's pause before responding, I pray to the Holy Spirit for the words. I know that both these men are strong biblical Christians. That is what we have in common…that and our horror at the crimes done to other peoples' loved ones.

"I hear you." My hands are raised in a gesture of surrender. "But I do not have a choice."

"Sure you do," snaps the younger officer. "Nobody is making you see him."

"Jesus doesn't give me a choice. Jesus says he leaves the ninety-nine righteous in the desert and goes out seeking to save the one who went astray."

"I never read that in the Bible!" The younger officer stiffens with resolve, but I look squarely at the older officer who I know is a deacon in his church.

"Yeah…" he shakes his head disgustedly and drops his arms to his side. "Yeah…it's in there. I've read it."

"I do not have a choice, sir." I am speaking softer now to two officers who themselves are feeling dejected and burdened by the weight of the Gospel's demands. "If I come here as a minister of the Gospel, I have to be willing to go after the sheep Jesus would go after. And Jesus would go after him."

No more words are exchanged. The two officers, crestfallen with heads shaking, simply step away, leaving me unobstructed from the gate to the outside.

For over a year that inmate and I meet for pastoral counseling. It never gets easy or casual. But God, in His infinite mercy to my brokenness, allows me to know with absolute clarity that this man can be forgiven and can someday see heaven.

God's greatest desire is that no one choose hell.

Jesus' *Parable of the Lost Sheep*:

> The tax collectors and sinners were all drawing near to listen to him, but the Pharisees and scribes began to complain, saying, "This man welcomes sinners and eats with them." So to them he addressed this parable. "What man among you having a hundred sheep and losing one of them would not leave the ninety-nine in the desert and go after the lost one until he finds it? And when he does find it, he sets it on his shoulders with great joy and, upon his arrival home, he calls together his friends and neighbors and says to them, 'Rejoice with me because I have found my lost sheep.' I tell you, in just the same way there will be more joy in heaven over one sinner who repents than over ninety-nine righteous people who have no need of repentance." (Luke 15:1-7)[25]

Advances in medical science and in our ability to view the functioning of specific portions of the brain have raised new issues about criminal responsibility, issues that no ethicists would have conceived of just a few years ago. The problem, succinctly put, is this: *Do we assess criminal responsibility against someone who knew that what he or she was doing was wrong, knew that it broke the law of society and of*

God, but he or she lacked the impulse control to refrain from doing it?

A case in point could be a condition called *frontotemporal dementia* or *frontotemporal lobar degeneration*. This condition, which can be caused by disease, by drugs or by brain injury incurred in physical impact, can impede or disable the brain's inhibitions against acting on emotions and impulse. The symptoms generally become more profound over years of deterioration and can begin much younger than dementia or Alzheimer's disease. Some of the symptoms can be dramatically similar to psychopathy, including inappropriate behavior, loss of empathy, loss of judgment and inhibition, and repetitive compulsive behavior.

What is our punishment response to a person who could not overcome the impulse to do wrong? These are the 21st century challenges facing criminal law and Christian ethics as science and technology makes it possible to view the actual mechanics of how free will is activated in the various lobes of the human brain. As a society, we have not yet learned how to deal with people with medical conditions that result in serious impulse control issues. We are still learning how to both keep society safe and treat such a criminal with dignity.

Almost everyone in prison has been, and many still are, engaged in criminal thinking. The relatively recent method of treatment and rehabilitation using cognitive thinking disregards the arguments about whether crime is the result of nature, nurture or whatever. It assumes that something has occurred which has resulted in the criminal becoming a law breaker instead of a law-abiding citizen. It addresses the ways in which criminals think differently than law-abiding citizens and attempts to change that thinking. That is the basis for most of the modern efforts at treatment and rehabilitation of offenders and is the subject of the next chapter.

"If I go to visit him, I cannot call him 'the Monster' but will have to treat him as if he were Christ, even if he is guilty. 'Every time you visit a prisoner, you come to visit me!'"

Bishop Robert Baker and Fr. Benedict Groeschel, C.F.R., incorporating the words of Pope John Paul I from a Christmas homily when he was Cardinal Albino Luciani of Venice[1]

CHAPTER 8
Characteristics of Criminal Thinking

Almost everyone in prison has been, and many still are, engaged in criminal thinking. The relatively recent method of treatment and rehabilitation using the cognitive thinking approach assumes something has occurred that has resulted in a criminal person becoming a law breaker instead of a law-abiding citizen. It addresses the ways in which criminals think differently than law-abiding citizens and attempts to change that thinking. That is the basis for most of the modern efforts at treatment and rehabilitation of offenders. Before turning to the details of such efforts, this chapter first looks at the mindset of the Catholic prison ministry volunteer entering a prison or jail.

As developed in detail in earlier chapters, all of us Catholic prison ministry volunteers need to be conscious of the fact that in visiting the prisoner we are visiting Jesus Christ, who has come to us in the face of the prisoner. A common misconception can be that this reality only applies if the prisoner is in prison as punishment for a crime that was not too bad or if he or she had an understandable reason for doing it: joy riding, for example, or stealing food for his or her family, or prostitution to buy medicine or pay for a parent's or spouse's chemotherapy treatments. The prisoner is still culpable, but not too hard to forgive.

There are definitely people in prison for such more easily forgivable offenses. But many of the inmates we volunteers encounter in prison are there for inflicting much more serious harm on other people. How do we really know whom we are dealing with? And should it matter?

First of all, none of us should ever ask an inmate what his or her crime was. That is treacherous territory. Sometimes an inmate must intentionally keep their crimes a secret in order to protect themselves from physical harm in prison. So, how do we know whether we are sitting across the table from someone who embezzled from a bank to protect his or her family from foreclosure or a serial murderer who tortured his or her victims? And even if an inmate confides the nature of his or her crimes to us—or a guard, another inmate, even another prison minister does so—we still might not be getting the complete truth. Many inmates have copped a plea to a much lesser offense in exchange for rolling over on a codefendant for the actual crime. Others may have been framed, received poor legal counsel, even given a false confession for some reason. The short answer is that we volunteers must let go of any need to know for sure the real harm done by any particular inmate.

From the pastoral and spiritual standpoint, that is not a problem, it is a good thing. This is exactly the point being made by Pope John Paul I, when he was Cardinal Albino Luciani of Venice, about visiting the so-called *Monster of Marsala* in an Italian prison:

In a Christmas homily, [the future pope] made the point that God in Jesus made himself small "not only in order to become our brother but so that we ourselves would feel more brotherly towards [one another]." Going further, the future pope claimed, "The culmination of love of our neighbor is that Jesus

WHEN WE VISIT JESUS IN PRISON

even agrees to be found in the guise of the prisoner." He then got very specific, mentioning a notorious criminal who was nicknamed the "Marsala Monster" for his heinous crime of killing three little girls.

The then cardinal said, "If I go to visit him, I cannot call him 'the Monster' but will have to treat him as if he were Christ, even if he is guilty. 'Every time you visit a prisoner, you come to visit me!' Love of my neighbor, however much he hurts me, even though he may be my enemy, does even this.... This is what it truly means to be Christian and to practice fraternity."[2]

So, as heroic as Pope Paul I might seem, treating prisoners as if they were Christ is cut and dry. But what do we volunteers do in terms of knowing the precautions to take if we do not know the various levels of dangerousness of the inmates we are dealing with? When you think about it, medical and dental professionals deal with a very similar situation all the time. Every single person that enters their office or medical facility for services may be carrying contagious diseases that are transmittable by blood or other bodily fluids. In fact, only a small percentage of patients present such infectious risks, but there is no way to know which patients carry the danger and which ones do not. So, medical and dental professionals follow what are called *universal precautions*.

The precautions are called "universal" because they are taken with every patient. The dentist wears gloves and a mask for drilling on the teeth of every patient. No one takes it personally. There is no intent to besmirch the patient who is not infected. In fact, universal precautions protect not just the medical and dental professionals but also all their patients. Because the precautions are universal, they apply to everyone, and everyone accepts them without inferring any negative connotation from them.

We volunteers in prison ministry have no way of knowing if a particular inmate is one that would try to manipulate us into criminal activity or prey on us physically or psychologically. Such inmates are probably in the small minority. But the prudent prison ministry volunteer will take no chances and will employ safeguards in all situations, in order to not become a victim of crime or an unwilling accomplice in a criminal enterprise.

So, just like a doctor or dentist, every volunteer in prison ministry should follow what I call the *universal precautions for jail and prison ministry*. These precautions do not involve wearing a physical mask or donning physical gloves. But in a similar way, the volunteer and others involved in prison ministry or working or living at the particular institution are all protected.

The first universal precaution in prison ministry is that no volunteer should ever provide any personal information to an inmate. Personal information would of course include addresses, phone numbers, and work locations. Most everyone would agree on the sense of this precaution with respect to intentionally sharing personal information. But often people give out personal information without intending it.

For example, a prison ministry volunteer sits down for a one-on-one Bible study at the prison chapel with an inmate. The volunteer could be providing a wealth of personal information to the inmate or other inmates in the area without even knowing it. The inmates will notice immediately if the volunteer is wearing an unusually expensive ring, or keys for a luxury class vehicle, or clothing logos that suggest wealth or powerful connections. The radar of every inmate, both male or female, whether or not sociopathic, is highly attuned to a woman volunteer's perfume or clothing that is stylish and expensive.

Even more dangerous can be a list of the names of the volunteer's children or grandchildren inside the Bible cover. Or a bookmark or piece of clothing that names places the volunteer recreates or vacations.

Some volunteers naively assume that because the inmate they are ministering to has received a long or a life sentence, personal information can be shared without risk. They forget that intelligence on "free" people (those outside prison), including addresses, children's names, children's schools, and locations of places for family recreation, are bought and sold inside a prison as commodities. That information can also easily end up in the hands of former partners in crime who are still on the outside and still doing harm. Volunteers should never provide any personal information about themselves or anyone in their family or church to any inmate.

The second universal precaution is that no volunteer should ever do a favor for an inmate. Often an inmate might request a volunteer to do what seems like a minor thing, e.g., calling the inmate's mom to see if she is still sick. This might seem like a harmless request. But it is not something the volunteer can or should ever do.

First of all, the phone call to mom may in fact be a signal for a preplanned event, such as an escape or the commission of a crime on the outside. The recipient of the call may not even really be "mom."

Secondly, the act by the volunteer would violate the rules of the institution. In fact, the point of the request may have nothing to do with the actual state of mom's health, but instead be aimed at compromising the integrity of the volunteer. So the universal precaution in prison ministry is that no volunteer should ever agree to do anything that breaks the rules for an inmate, even if the request seems like a minor matter, even if the request seems to "makes sense" to the volunteer as something helpful.

No prison ministry volunteer should ever be calling an inmate's relative to find out if they are still sick, or contacting any relative, friend, or pastor of an inmate because the inmate would like a visit from them. No prison ministry volunteer should be contacting an inmate's lawyers, investigators, reporters, or expert witnesses about anything, ever. And no prison ministry volunteer should be contacting law enforcement authorities on behalf of an inmate, including local, state and federal police. The requests can be as extreme as "call my dying grandmother and tell her I love her" or "notify the feds that I am being blackmailed by the warden." The volunteer's answer is 'no.'

It is very important, however, for the volunteer to distinguish between contacting outside authorities on behalf of an inmate, which should not be done, and contacting outside authorities because of what the volunteer has personally witnessed. For example, if a volunteer witnesses the beating of an inmate by officers, or the use of chemicals and electric prods as punishment on an inmate who is already under control, [3] or the deprivation of food and water from an inmate as punishment, the volunteer has an affirmative duty to report this factual information to the proper authorities. This should be done, of course, and especially in the case of new volunteers, in close consultation with the volunteer's pastoral authority, Church supervisors and ministry colleagues, both to protect the volunteer in the process and to avoid serious mistakes.

In such a case, it is important that the volunteer employ the Catholic social teaching on *subsidiarity*, which directs them to present the information to the most local level, where it will be effectively handled, e.g., the prison's inspector general, or warden, or the sheriff of the jail. If there is a reasonable belief based on facts (and not on a general suspicion of authority at large) that the information will not be effectively handled at the local level, then reporting of abuse to outside authority is necessary. This must also be done prudently, addressing it first to higher-ups within the system before reporting to ombudsman-type positions at large.

The goal is to stop the aberrant behavior and keep it from happening again. Most often, that is best achieved within the system without creating a media event. Just like other human organizations, the staff and administration of prisons and jails will be strongly tempted to circle the wagons when confronted by a media onslaught. If the abuse can be dealt with effectively through the mechanisms designed for such purpose within the system, that is the preferable route for relief.

If the system has no such mechanisms, the creation of such mechanisms should be a high priority for the representatives of the Church in dealing with the elected and appointed officials of the applicable governmental agencies. Transparency of institutions in their activities with vulnerable populations, especially people under their total control, is another core value of Catholic social teaching. The greater the transparency of the institution to review from the outside, the less likely it is that abuse will occur on the inside. Without such transparency, unimaginable acts of abuse and torture can occur. The Arthur G. Dozier School for Boys in Florida's panhandle is a horrific example

WHEN WE VISIT JESUS IN PRISON

of the evil that can happen when institutions holding vulnerable populations lack transparency. [4] All of us Catholic prison ministry volunteers should work with our ministry teams and our host institutions to develop greater transparency and stronger accountability by staff and volunteers in the care of inmates.

A third universal precaution in prison ministry is that no volunteer should ever discuss with an inmate prison procedures, geographic details, or details about other prisoners, staff, volunteers, or officers. This is especially true about security procedures and prison gossip. The requests for details that a calculating inmate can slip into a casual conversation are nothing short of amazing. We volunteers who are on our toes will be quick to recognize danger in such a request, whether the inmate intends harm or not.

There should never be any discussions with an inmate as to which officers are on duty at the front gate or in other portions of the prison, or as to security procedures such as pat-downs and searches. Personal information about other inmates, about officers, and about other staff or volunteers is also strictly off-limits. It does not matter if the inmate used to attend the same church as the volunteer or the person in question. The inmate is not attending that church now; he or she is in prison. And nothing good can come from handing personal information about anybody at any time to an inmate. If the inmate is truly concerned about someone's well-being, tell them they can pray for others in general.

No prison ministry volunteer should ever provide information to an inmate about geography, roads, distances, commercial facilities, retail outlets for food, gas, or clothing, or about commercial deliveries to the prison. The inquiring inmate may in fact be innocently seeking information about when the bread truck makes deliveries because he loves fresh bread. It is more likely, however, that the bread truck could be part of an escape attempt. Killing the bread truck driver and donning his clothes could be part of the plan. There is no way we volunteers can know the true motives of the inmate requesting the information. That is why this precaution is "universal." If we always follow it, we do not have to guess at the inmate's motives. We just know that we never, ever, under any circumstances provide such information to anyone inside a prison or jail.

A fourth universal precaution in prison ministry is that no volunteer should ever accept anything from an inmate as a gift. Nor should we ever accept anything from a family or friends of an inmate as a gift. While we might want to believe that such a gift is simply an expression of gratitude for the volunteer's services, it is much more likely that the gift is a way of attempting to manipulate us into feeling duty-bound to break the rules for the inmate. People who live free on the outside could not imagine the *prison value* carried by very small gifts inside prison and jail. For inmates who have access to virtually nothing, even the smallest of gifts can justify exorbitant expectations of return favors.

New prison ministry volunteers would be shocked to their socks at the forbidden acts an inmate might feel a volunteer is obliged to perform if they have accepted even a small gift. The inmate could expect sexual favors for himself or for friends of his on the outside. The inmate could expect that the volunteer owes it to him or her to create a distraction of staff while the prisoners move contraband past a checkpoint, or to lie to staff about the prisoner's whereabouts at a particular time on a particular day.

The smallest of gifts from an inmate's family could justify in his mind the expectation that the volunteer will smuggle drugs or weapons into the prison, even hidden in body cavities, or assist in an escape attempt. An inmate might even demand that the volunteer threaten, shoot, or kill someone on the outside. All these things have happened!

If the inmate believes that the volunteer owes him or her something because of a gift, the refusal by the volunteer to carry out such favors could result in a sense of betrayal. In the inmate's mind, the betrayal could justify violence against the volunteer or the volunteer's family. In fact, in order to protect the honor of the inmate, he or she may feel obliged to initiate violence against the repudiating volunteer who "took advantage" of him. Again, no prison ministry volunteer should ever accept anything from an inmate or their family as a gift. Inside prisons and jails there is no such thing as a gift.

WHEN WE VISIT JESUS IN PRISON

Sometimes it can be helpful to have a quick checklist for purposes of memory. This is a bullet-point summary of specific universal precautions for jail and prison ministry. You should print these out and go over them every time you enter a prison, no matter how long you have been doing so. I still do.

+ Never provide any personal information to an inmate, about yourself or anyone else.
+ Never agree to do anything that breaks the rules of the prison or institution.
+ Never agree to contact any relative, friend, pastor, or advocate of an inmate.
+ Never discuss prison procedures with an inmate.
+ Never discuss geographic details with an inmate.
+ Never discuss details about staff and officers with an inmate.
+ Never accept anything from an inmate as a gift.
+ Never accept anything from an inmate's family or friends as a gift.

You may feel awkward about having to refuse so many possible gifts and requests. The best way to affirmatively protect yourself is to learn the proper procedures at the institution for obtaining the information being requested by the inmate. How do inmates contact relatives to inquire as to their health? Or contact their hometown pastor to request a spiritual visit? Usually it is done through the chaplain or a classification officer. Be ready with the information. But don't do it for them.

How do inmates contact their lawyers and advocates? Usually that is done through the classification officer or the warden's office. Be ready with the information. But don't do it for them.

How does an inmate's family and friends obtain the geographic information to drive to the prison or jail for a visit? In this day and age, most institutions have driving directions on their website, which are accessible by family and friends but not by the inmates in the prison. Know this answer before the question is asked. But don't provide the information.

How do inmates learn about prison procedures? That is handled by the staff, and only on a need-to-know basis. Be ready to answer kindly and authoritatively that such discussions are not allowed and could result in sanctions against both the inmate and the volunteer. If the inmate insists that "no one is listening," smile and answer light-heartedly, "Is this your first day in prison? Someone is *always* listening!"

After developing an instinctive grasp of the universal precautions for prison and jail ministry, one of the first hurdles to be surmounted by the prison ministry volunteer is terminology. Part of this challenge is the professional terminology of classifying and diagnosing criminal behavior itself. Another part of it is the language of prisons and jails.

Every prison and jail will have its own local *dialect* of slang terms that refer to things that are particular to that institution. These terms will usually be less than charitable references to the most prevalent menu items (also, likely to be the cheapest and least appealing), to particular staff positions that are responsible for unwelcome services (e.g., passing out reprimands or rationing toilet paper), and the like.

Many volunteers who have served in the military find that the informal prison process of naming the familiar and the repetitive is very similar to what they experienced in the armed forces. Home-turf nomenclature is just what people do in such situations. The volunteer should keep an open ear to the terminology, but only use it when the words are consistent with professionalism and setting a good example. For example, in one facility the inmates called the officer assigned to check for dust on the property lockers and bunk posts "locker-top Suzy" even though the officer was male. Volunteers should not repeat such nicknames, even in conversation among themselves.

Other prison terminology is more global in its use, like a language common to prisons and jails at large. A volunteer may encounter some of the following prison slang terms at many different types of facilities.

+ **On the phone:** when inmates in separate cells communicate through the HVAC system by yelling into the air vents.
+ **Comodophone:** when inmates in separate cells communicate through the plumbing system by yelling into their toilets.
+ **Kiting:** writing notes that are passed between inmates in violation of prison rules.
+ **Frequent flyers:** inmates who have returned to prison multiple times for new crimes or violating parole.
+ **Getting some streets:** when an inmate fakes illness or files a frivolous lawsuit in order to get a trip outside the prison so he or she can enjoy seeing the sky, trees, and people.
+ **Prison smarts:** the constant ingenuity shown by inmates in designing and making contraband and weapons from what appear to be innocuous, worthless objects.
+ **Getting over:** when an inmate successfully manipulates staff, officers, or volunteers.
+ **Trick-bags:** set-ups that inmates plan to trap another inmate, staff, officer, or volunteer into believing that they must do the inmate's bidding or face loss of their safety, position, or job.
+ **Hard volunteers:** volunteers who are despised by the inmates because they are without sympathy or empathy.
+ **Soft volunteers:** volunteers who are easily manipulated because they have sympathy with the inmates and emotionally bond with them.
+ **Mellow volunteers:** volunteers who are respected by the inmates because they connect with them through empathy but make all their decisions rationally, without emotion.

There is also a somewhat universal terminology that is not prison slang, but refers to important realities inside the fences. For example:

+ **Verbal deception:** when a person lies outright in speech or in written word.

+ **Situational deception:** when a person creates a diversion that is not real but is staged to distract authority while an ulterior motive is accomplished.
+ **Apathy:** when a person is devoid of either sympathy or empathy and is cold and uncaring.
+ **Empathy:** when a person understands and identifies with another's thoughts and feelings, not as shared emotions but as an intellectual and objective understanding of the other's experience.
+ **Sympathy:** when a person pities or feels sorry for another, and actually enters into the other's emotional state.
+ **Fraternization:** when a person ceases to maintain a professional boundary in relation to another and instead becomes a friend or companion.
+ **Institutionalization:** the mental and emotional condition that can occur when someone has been confined in an institution away from society for so long that they no longer are able to function socially or initiate normal human activities.
+ **Prisonization:** the condition of institutionalization resulting from prolonged incarceration, especially in solitary confinement.

Rest assured, from the very first moment we volunteers step inside a prison fence we are under scrutiny. The inmates and the staff are scrutinizing us, looking for any indication that we are either "hard" or "soft" or "easy to get over." The staff knows that a volunteer who appears prone to sympathy—as opposed to empathy—is easily suckered into the pit of fraternization. Fraternization is almost always a fire-able offense for officers and staff, and it usually results in expulsion for volunteers. The world inside the fences is a minefield. But it is a minefield that can be learned and navigated.

Too Good To Be True

Apalachee Correctional Institution, called ACI, is a massive prison just fifty miles west of Tallahassee, near the town of Sneads, Florida. It sits on the west side of the Apalachicola River, well into the rolling hills of the panhandle, barely into the central time zone. In a concession to the lion's share of prison staff and administration that commute from the Eastern Time zone, the prison keeps its clocks on Tallahassee time. This is the place where I will be introduced to prison ministry as a volunteer chaplain. My route there takes me out of Tallahassee, west on Interstate 10, then once across the river, exiting on State Road 286 north to Highway 90. About two miles later the prison jumps into view from the highway. In good weather, it is about an hour's drive each way.

The prison is divided into two camps, a west and an east unit. I am serving in the west unit which has its own beautiful chapel building, constructed years ago with donated funds and materials. It is even topped by a white steeple. Not every camp has a chapel building. The inmates and staff at this camp are fortunate to enjoy such a beautiful place of worship. As I enter the chapel for the first time, the thought occurs to me that some inmates do not know how to properly express that appreciation. Hand painted signs adorn both sides of the chapel entry door warning: "Don't be cussin er smokin!"

Programs for larger groups of inmates are conducted in the chapel sanctuary which holds about 250 people. I will be holding Bible studies in there with groups of 20 or more once a week. But that space is far too large for the prayer-counseling appointments that I will be conducting in one-on-one sessions. The card room in the chapel serves as my base of operations for prayer ministry. It is about four feet wide and ten feet deep. It is ringed with shelves six layers high and serves as the storage closet for Christmas cards, Mother's Day cards, Father's Day Cards, greeting cards, birthday cards, thank-you cards, get-well cards, and bereavement cards. Every possible kind of card that the inmates might need, all sorted, counted, labeled, and filed in neat piles on the shelves.

Chaplain Counselman, the man who invited me to come to his prison as a volunteer, is my mentor and supervisor. He assures me that the card room will not be allowed to cause problems for my service as a prayer minister.

"We will make it clear that none of your prayer partners are allowed to ask you for cards." His seriousness clues me that this is not a small matter. "The inmates are not allowed to have money. But cards are a commodity that can be traded like money. If the inmates think by coming in to see you, they can get cards from you, well…" His voice trails off. "We just cannot allow that to happen."

"And is that for security, too?" I attempt to change the subject by pointing to the small shatterproof glass window that has been inserted into the otherwise solid fire door of the card room.

"We have to assume that some inmates' motivations are not the best," he speaks matter-of-factly, as if to remind me that prison is a place where there are criminals. "So, there are no spaces in this building that are closed to public view. Not even in counseling."

Over the next two years, my twenty-to-thirty-minute prayer meetings settle into a rhythm. The card room itself becomes a sanctuary of sorts. One after another, a new face appears in the chair facing me. We open with prayer for guidance from the Holy Spirit and with Scripture. Then I ask each new face the same question: *What would you like Jesus to do for you today?*

And during the brief interlude after one leaves and before the next comes in, I pray: *Lord Jesus, give me your words for this man today. Give me your eyes to see him as you do, your heart to love him as you do, and your Spirit to lead him ever closer to you.*

The weekly Bible studies in the chapel sanctuary swell in attendance to as many as forty or fifty men. For security reasons, we must break the group into two smaller cohorts. I teach one during the week. My two new volunteers recruited from parishes in Tallahassee teach the other group on Saturdays while I am in prayer counseling.

Even so, the weekly need for prayer appointments at ACI soon outstrips what can be offered on Saturday. I am picking up the spillover with morning sessions on Thursdays and Fridays. I start to think of myself as a seasoned veteran of sorts. I start to feel comfortable, relaxed, at home. Never a good thing to do inside the prison fence.

It is always a joy to see my regulars in the prayer appointments, but nothing quite matches the exhilaration of the new face, the new soul coming to Christ from the darkness of the prison compound. Because I am still relatively new myself, with only a couple of years in prison experience, I always assume that every new prayer partner must be on the verge of an explosion of spiritual grace. My thinking is: *Why else would someone go through all the trouble to obtain a work absence permit to come in for prayer?*

The fellow who disabuses me of that misconception really does not stand out from the others in any way. He shows up at chapel for the weekday Bible study and expresses a need for prayer as soon as possible. He says he has been in prison for fifteen years and is dealing with a deep and personal loss. He says that because of his work he needs an early appointment, really early—earlier than I usually schedule them. I know I will need to get special permission and that he and I will be the only ones in the chapel that early in the morning.

He shows no affect and does not make eye contact. I am so delighted to have him finally turning to Christ that I ignore the red flags that should tip me off to ask more questions. I could ask about his job. Turns out he is a houseman, an inmate who sweeps and cleans in his dorm. If I found that out, I would know that there is no reason for him to need a 7:30 am appointment in the chapel. I do not ask.

The administration approves the early prayer appointment and I show up on time, obtain the chapel keys, start the coffee pot, and joyfully wait for my new prayer partner to show. And wait. And wait. And wait.

By 9:00 am I know something is wrong. Count is still delayed and even the chapel clerks who regularly show up at 8:30 am have not arrived. The curt response to my calls to the control room and the dorm every 30 minutes yield no information.

Finally, at almost 10:00 am, an escort of officers led by a white-shirted lieutenant enters the chapel. The burly lieutenant, who easily towers over me by at least eight inches, summons me to the front of the building and explains that I must stand with him while the officers "shake down the entire building" searching for contraband. Later I will learn that they are searching for weapons.

Not a word of explanation is offered until they complete their work, down to emptying coffee cans of grounds, checking that the cardboard inside unopened toilet tissue rolls is really empty, and removing the plastic facades off every fluorescent light in the place.

"You must have a guardian angel, chaplain," finally the lieutenant addresses me. "Today is your lucky day."

"I'm not sure I understand, sir."

"How well do you know the inmate who you were scheduled to see this morning?"

"Not well at all, sir. It was a first appointment."

"And could well have been your last, chaplain."

"I'm not sure I understand, sir."

"The man you had an appointment to see has a very bad gambling problem. He has run up a huge amount of debt to other inmates right here in this prison and they figured out that he has no way of paying them back—ever."

"And that has to do with me…how…?"

"He needed a transfer fast, like today, or he was sure to be dead meat. You were supposed to be his transfer ticket."

"How? I cannot get him a transfer."

"No, chaplain, not for you to *get* him a transfer," the lieutenant is shaking his head in dismay at how incredibly little I understand. "You were supposed to *be* his transfer, to be his hostage if you were still alive, or to be the reason he gets shipped out to maximum security this morning if he killed you."

"How…how do you know this?"

"This morning, other inmates in his dorm who couldn't figure out why he would want a prayer appointment, saw him remove something from inside his mattress and slide it inside his sock and pant leg. They rushed to warn the dorm sergeant, who called control, and we intercepted him halfway across the yard coming to see you."

I mean to respond but no words will come out.

"It was a real good shiv," the lieutenant smiles at my frozen expression that revels a sudden indoctrination into deeper prison reality. "About eight inches long and sharp as a razor. I figure he would have tried to stick it in about right here." His pointed finger stops just short of touching my chest right outside my heart. "And even on a guy your size, it would have done the job with one stab."

I know he is not being mean. He is teaching me a lesson that I will never forget, and he is willing to take all the time I need to let it sink in. Finally, I dare to respond.

"How do I thank the inmates who...."

"Saved your life?" he finishes my sentence. "You don't and you never will. If anybody finds out who tipped the officers, either your gambler or the inmates he owes money to will go after them. Inside prison we have to live without knowing a lot of things for sure. All I can tell you now is that the warden is on the phone with Tallahassee and he expects you in his office in five. You better be moving. This chapel is closed today."

"Yes, sir," I turn to gather my few personal items.

"And chaplain," the lieutenant's tone suddenly sounds almost fatherly, "You were lucky today. Don't expect to be lucky twice."

As regards the professional terminology of classifying and diagnosing criminal behavior, volunteers who delve into the material may be shocked to find a huge dispersion of professional views and opinions. A landmark text in this area, recently updated to incorporate the last two decades of research, is Dr. Stanton E. Samenow's *Inside the Criminal Mind*.[5] Dr. Samenow focuses upon methods to rehabilitate a person who is incarcerated because of having indulged in criminal behavior. He repudiates any approach that enables the criminal in casting himself/herself as a victim in their own mind because he believes that this reinforces the tendency to avoid taking personal responsibility for the harm done.

Dr. Samenow's assertions reflect the need for an analysis that allows for a solution, action steps that can be taken to help the individual who is already in the criminal justice system. This viewpoint is important when holding his work side-by-side with Catholic teaching. Catholic moral teaching about our vulnerability to sin and the experience shared by St. Augustine from his youth line up well with the notion that criminal behavior is connected to the wrongful desire to do whatever is forbidden. That goes back to the *Garden of Eden*.

It has been said that our Catholic efforts to improve the common good are synonymous with improving culture and society in order to make it easier for people to choose to do the right thing. That is not in conflict with holding the individual responsible for choosing the wrong thing. Some would argue that we must choose to focus only on the role of culture and society; others would argue that we must focus only on the error of the individual, the criminal. Our U.S. Catholic bishops call us to focus upon both, challenging us to break out of political paradigms that offer only false, extreme solutions, and instead to see that crime demands not only punishment and accountability but also rehabilitation and restoration.

In fact, the Catholic moral answer to sin, when a person chooses wrongly against God's law, is conversion and repentance. We work from the Greek word *metanoia* which means, literally, to change one's heart. As Pope Paul VI states in his *Apostolic Constitution On Fast and Abstinence (Paenitemini)*:

> The kingdom of God announced by Christ can be entered only by a "change of heart" ("metanoia") that is to say through that intimate and total change and renewal of the entire [person]— of all [his or her] opinions, judgments and decisions—which takes place in the light of the sanctity and charity of God, the sanctity and charity that were manifested to us in the Son and communicated fully.[6]

In this reference, Pope Paul is using the biblical concept of "heart" which is the center of man's being, the source of his actions. So even as Catholics work diligently to give effect to the Church's social teaching in our world, we are also responsible to challenge those who have engaged in criminal activity, calling them to accept responsibility and to change their "opinions, judgments, and decisions." As Catholics we are coming from a Christian spiritual and sacramental basis. In doing so, we are challenging individuals who have engaged in harmful behavior to change their criminal thinking, that is, their ways of forming opinions, making judgments, and arriving at decisions. The Catholic approach of repentance and conversion by the individual does not conflict with Dr. Samenow's focus, as a psychologist, on criminal thinking.

Likewise, his dismissal of cultural and social factors, because they offer scant benefit in arriving at a therapeutic approach to change those who have already fallen into crime, does not affect our commitment to Catholic social teaching. Mr. Boyd Sharp, whose work is addressed extensively below, provides an excellent summary of how we must hold together in dynamic tension both the need to improve social conditions and the individual's responsibility for change:[7]

> We are not denying that many conditions contribute to a person choosing to commit crimes. Conditions such as childhood abuse, poverty, unemployment, homelessness, parental drug use, sexism, racism, and living in a ghetto must be addressed and eliminated, however, not when treating the criminal....
>
> We believe that as a society and as human beings, these things should be addressed. We should do everything in our power to help people obtain a good life. However, in treating criminals, we cannot get sidetracked by these issues, because then we will not be able to help them change their thinking and behavior.

In parallel to Dr. Samenow's work, and in large part as a result of it, the professionals like Mr. Sharp, whose responsibility is to redirect criminals into productive lives, have developed a method of treatment and rehabilitation using cognitive therapy to change the thinking of criminals. The secular nature of this cognitive therapy does not deter our support. As Catholic prison ministry volunteers we augment that process by bringing to bear the firepower of the Holy Spirit, who convicts us of sin, the Good News of the Gospel, which offers us hope of change, and the transforming reality of the Eucharist, which provides us the means and the map to true freedom from criminal thinking. We do not negate the secular therapeutic approach to change criminal thinking; on the contrary, we bring the power to achieve transformation at levels far deeper than the therapy by itself could ever hope to touch. That is what *metanoia* is all about.

As Pope John Paul II teaches in his *Post-Synodal Apostolic Exhortation, On the Encounter with the Living Jesus Christ: the Way to Con-*

version, Communion and Solidarity (Ecclesia in America):[8]

> In speaking of conversion, the New Testament uses the word *metanoia*, which means a change of mentality. It is not simply a matter of thinking differently in an intellectual sense, but of revising the reasons behind one's actions in the light of the Gospel. In this regard, Saint Paul speaks of "faith working through love" (Galatians 5:6). This means that true conversion needs to be prepared and nurtured through the prayerful reading of Sacred Scripture and the practice of the Sacraments of Reconciliation and the Eucharist. [¶26]

> Since "no one can serve two masters" (Matthew 6:24), the change of [heart and] mentality (*metanoia*) means striving to assimilate the values of the Gospel, which contradict the dominant tendencies of the world. Hence there is a need to renew constantly "the encounter with the living Jesus Christ," since this…is the way "which leads us to continuing conversion." [¶28]

The general concepts of *cognitive treatment* to correct criminal thinking are fairly accessible to even those of us who are not mental health professionals. An excellent resource in this regard for volunteers in Catholic prison ministry is Boyd D. Sharp's *Changing Criminal Thinking: A Treatment Program*. This book is available for purchase online and through the American Correctional Association.

It is extremely important to note that such a resource is only for a prison volunteer's understanding. A volunteer that is not licensed by the host jurisdiction to provide mental health treatment should never attempt to provide mental health services of any kind, including those described in the book, not even in a guarded or indirect way. Such an endeavor could be dangerous for the volunteer, the inmate, and, if the inmate has a violent delayed reaction to clumsy therapeutic attempts, possibly for staff and other inmates. Even if no one is physically injured, the volunteer could face sanctions under state law for

WHEN WE VISIT JESUS IN PRISON

such unauthorized mental health activities.

In understanding the concepts of criminal thinking and the cognitive treatment for it, the following definitions are important (these definitions are extensively based upon the work of Boyd D. Sharp):[9]

+ **Criminal thinking:** is the system of erroneous thoughts, logic, and emotions that result in criminal activity.
* **Criminal masks:** is the system of false faces that criminals use to present themselves to the outside world.
+ **Criminal tactics:** is the system of behavior and responses that criminals use to avoid accountability for their behavior.
+ **Criminal belief system:** is the unified overall system consisting of criminal thinking, criminal tactics, and criminal masks.
* **Cognitive treatment:** is a current approach to help inmates change their criminal thinking, without regard to causation.
+ **Prosocial model:** is a method of psychological analysis of human thinking and behavior that places normal people on a spectrum of healthy, constructive thinking.
+ **Antisocial model:** is a method of psychological analysis of human thinking and behavior that places antisocial people on a spectrum of unhealthy, destructive thinking.

A critical distinction made by Mr. Sharp is between the *prosocial model* and the *antisocial model*. In a random sampling of people in society, there is a spectrum distribution of ways of thinking. He estimates that about 65% of the population consists of what he calls "prosocial thinkers"—healthy constructive thinkers. Some of these are "internal prosocial thinkers" who make up 25% of the population (owning completely the responsibility for their thoughts, feelings and actions). For these people there is no significant erroneous thinking.

The next category is still not problematic: "external prosocial thinkers" who make up about 40% of the population. They dabble in the game of blaming things on others and occasionally use lies to get what they want. They know what is really true, however, and do know their responsibility. Erroneous thinking may be present as much as 20% of the time in this group, but internal and external controls prevent any run-ins with the law.

The next 10% of people are "antisocial thinkers" who engage in erroneous thinking about 40% of the time. The boundary between taking personal responsibility and blaming everyone and everything except oneself begins to blur. This category includes people who may have had run-ins with the law. Danger signs are everywhere.

The next category of "antisocial thinkers" makes up about 10% of people and they take a small but significant step toward the destructive end of the spectrum. In this group, the majority of their thinking excuses their destructive behavior; actually about 60% of their thinking is erroneous. Because everything is everybody else's fault, personal responsibility drops off dramatically. They experience run-ins with the law, repeated confrontations with authority, and arrests. Their ability to distinguish lies from truth is almost gone. Destructive consequences become palatable if the harmful actions obtain the satisfaction they seek.

The next demarcation in the spectrum of "antisocial thinkers" is actual criminal thinking. The people in this group make up about 10% of the population and criminal thinking consumes between 80 to 100% of their thoughts. There is no remorse except when it is feigned for self-serving purposes. Lying is reality for them.

The final category based on this model, the remaining 5% of "antisocial thinkers" are true psychopaths and sociopaths. There is no intention in this model to distinguish between psychopaths and sociopaths. Mr. Sharp's spectrum has nothing to do with the DSM categories addressed earlier in this book. From the viewpoint of cognitive therapy for criminal thinking, the only difference between a psychopath and a sociopath is whether the researchers themselves have degrees in sociology or psychology. Mr. Sharp does note that at this far end of the spectrum besides "having lost all ability to feel remorse or guilt, they actually become sadistic…they get delight in watching other people squirm." That last element meets my operational distinction between sociopaths and psychopaths.

What are the differences between the way "prosocial" (healthy, constructive) people think versus the way "antisocial" (unhealthy, destructive) people think? The differences can actually be very acute. The following is a list of some differences between the two models of thinking, taken from an article in *Corrections Today*,[10] which references the work of Boyd D. Sharp and of Samuel Yochelson and Stanton Samenow:[11]

Criminal Thinking vs. Healthy Thinking:

- closed off to input and feedback of others vs. self-critical; receptive to feedback from others
- blames others for own conduct vs. accepts accountability and responsibility for behavior; does not blame others
- false, inflated self-image maintained at others' expense vs. realistic self-assessment
- reacts to normal workaday life with scorn and lack of effort vs. seeks balance of enjoyment and responsibility in everyday routines
- will not put in effort without immediate payback vs. ability to postpone immediate gratification for long-term benefit
- fails to deal realistically with time vs. good planning and time management
- fails to learn from the past vs. ability to learn from past experiences
- denies fear in self and attacks fear in others vs. identifies realistic danger without undue anxiety
- uses power and external force to control others vs. has collaborative and respectful relationship with others
- views self as center of the universe vs. able to take others' needs and desires into account
- views self as above the rules vs. able to function within the expectations of the system
- perceives all people and objects as possessions vs. respectful of the rights of others

+ gives words private meanings to avoid responsibility vs. communicates without manipulations
+ lacks empathy vs. exhibits empathy with others
+ denies and minimizes situations vs. accepts present and past realities

Mr. Boyd also lists examples of typical criminal thinking for denial—*Don't Blame Me!*—taken from a 1998 study: [p. 97]

+ **It is all right to fight/lie/steal/take drugs:**
  • **Moral justification:** to protect friends or take revenge for our family.
  • **Euphemistic language:** when you are just joking/giving someone a lesson/just borrowing/just doing it once in a while.
  • **Advantageous comparison:** when others are doing worse/when other acts are worse.

+ **You can't blame me if:**
  • **Displacement of Responsibility:** I live under bad conditions.
  • **Diffusion of Responsibility:** The whole gang was involved/friends asked me to do it.
  • **Distorting Consequences:** No one was really hurt.
  • **Attrition of Blame:** If I misbehave, it is the fault of my teacher/parent.
  • **Dehumanization:** Because it is all right to hurt those who deserve it.

Other characteristics of criminal thinking include the use of anger to avoid uncomfortable emotions or interactions, the habit of assuming that one knows what other people are thinking, manufactured obfuscation through contrived confusion, feigned helplessness, sidetracking to avoid uncomfortable realities, and splitting and antagonizing others to create a conflict as a diversion from facing the facts.

The cognitive approach deals with such denial and others aspects of criminal thinking head on. Sharp uses the treatment of addiction as an analogy to explain the process. [p. 100]

[Therapists often] focus on clients' freedom of choice and their need to accept the responsibility for their behavior.... Most professional counselors working with alcoholics and addicts were looking for the symptoms—the reasons why the person drank or used. Not until we quit looking for the symptoms or cause and began focusing on the fact that alcoholics drank because they were alcoholic did we begin to be able to assist alcoholics into recovery. We believe the same is now true of the criminal.... They commit crimes because they are criminals!

And that is what has to be changed. [p. 150]

We come now to the [therapists] most difficult and exacting area of working with the criminal: being effective agents of change.... It requires us to hold the criminal responsible and accountable and yet remain detached from the outcome of our efforts. The challenge [for therapists] is how one can be cursed, manipulated, and abused—yet remain firm, friendly, and fair.

The treatment involves challenging the inmate to discard the false faces (called *masks*) that he or she uses to control and manipulate others. They are called to accountability for the tactics they use to avoid facing the truth about themselves and about the harm they have done. And they are gradually led out of the criminal belief system that is their complex web of self-deceit, knit together by criminal thinking, tactics, and masks. This is the task of the cognitive therapist. It is a major overhaul of the inmate's ways of thinking and being in the world.

The task of us Catholic volunteers in prison ministry is to bring faith and spirituality to the inmate navigating this passage from anti-social to prosocial thinking. When the power of spiritual conversion is added to the prosocial way of thinking, inmates can truly feel that they have experienced the *metanoia* promised by the Church.

Given the reality of criminal thinking, it is very important for us volunteers to protect ourselves from manipulation. An excellent resource in this regard for volunteers in Catholic prison ministry is a recent book by Gary Cornelius, a corrections professional who has spent a career studying and teaching inmate behavior, *The Art of the Con: Avoiding Offender Manipulation*. This book is available for purchase online and through the American Correctional Association. The author details every aspect of staff and volunteer vulnerability to inmate manipulation. In doing so, he touches upon a very sensitive subject that almost no one discusses: the use of "attempted suicide" as criminal manipulation. Why would an inmate fake suicide as a manipulation? Based upon Mr. Cornelius' experience, he lists some specific reasons that would never occur to most volunteers:[12]

+ To elicit sympathy from staff.
+ To avoid a court appearance.
+ To obtain a housing relocation.
+ To bolster an insanity defense.
+ To get a trip or transfer to a hospital (where confederates may be waiting to assist in an escape).
+ To go on a transport to a mental health facility or psychiatrist and attempt to escape.
+ To obtain preferential staff treatment.
+ To seek sympathy and compassion from a previously unsympathetic spouse or family member.

Mr. Cornelius reminds us that all suicide attempts or suicidal behavior must be taken seriously and followed up with staff involvement and mental health care. He does note, however, that "Truly suicidal people usually feel sadness and regret following an unsuccessful suicide attempt. Their failure may result in more depression. Manipulative offenders do not feel relief or regret from a self-destructive act, but feel energized and angry." [p. 107]

WHEN WE VISIT JESUS IN PRISON

Part of what makes his book such a valuable resource for volunteers in prison and jail ministry is his acronym approach to avoid inmate manipulation: CHUMPS. He tells us that the dictionary definition of *chump* is a foolish person, exactly what the volunteer does not want to be. So, the acronym provides a way to remember the crucial principles for avoiding being a chump to inmate manipulation, which are: [p. 110]

C = Controlling yourself and not being complacent.
H = Helping offenders to help themselves.
U = Understanding the offender subculture and understanding yourself.
M = Maintaining a safe distance.
P = Practicing professionalism in adhering to policies and procedures.
S = Stopping yourself from being stressed out so you are not vulnerable.

The actual details and stories shared in the development of the CHUMPS model are well worth the read.

The last subject in Mr. Cornelius' list is stress—a crucial factor for all those working in the prison environment, whether as employees or as volunteers. Over the last thirty years, the researchers and professionals have recognized and tried to assess the severe stress involved for those who work in corrections. Volunteers can experience the same sources and effects of stress as those who work as officers and staff. The landmark report *Addressing Correctional Officer Stress: Programs and Strategies* was produced by the National Institute of Justice in 2000.[13]

Stress that is unmanaged or poorly managed is a ticking time-bomb inside prisons and jails. Stressed-out volunteers are prone to mistakes, inattention, vulnerability and emotional compromise. The following are a sampling of the stressors and possible solutions that may be applicable to volunteers.

+ **Too many and too heavy responsibilities; too many inmates needing ministry**
  - Tell your pastoral or volunteer supervisor that you need help.
  - Do less and do it better.

+ **Offender demands and arguments**
  - Know who the especially short-fused and manipulative inmates are and where they are located.
  - If they always snare you in the chapel after the service, arrange for the chaplain or staff to shield you until they leave.
  - Either avoid them altogether or structure your time to minimize contact.

+ **Offender threats**
  - If an inmate has been clear that he has it in for you, do not give him or her the opportunity to act on his threat.
  - Arrange for someone else to serve that inmate's area and make yourself scarce.
  - Do continue to pray for the inmate, but only do it from a distance.

+ **Cramped working conditions and substandard buildings and equipment**
  - Be realistic about the stress from working in heat and humidity, cold and dampness.
  - If you are working in segregation units, be realistic about:
    > the stress of standing and kneeling on damp concrete,
    > the physical effects to you of the strong chemicals that must be used by staff for cleaning and sanitation in such confined and densely populated conditions,
    > the constant infestation of insects, and
    > the mold and grunge on the cell doors and food flaps.

- Limit your time in such conditions in order to manage your physical and psychological stress.

+ **Excessive noise and unpleasant odors**
  - Be realistic about the stress from constant screaming, screeching, and grinding.
  - Be realistic about the stress from unpleasant odors, especially in segregation units, from un-flushed toilets, feces and urine on the catwalks, and unwashed inmates.
  - Be realistic about the stress of ministering to those suffering in hospital cells and to the odors that attend end-stage diseases.
  - Limit your time in such conditions in order to manage your physical and psychological stress.

+ **Inmates who are manipulative, mentally ill, aggressive, or under influence of substances**
  - Know the true risks of ministering to such inmates and know how to best minimize those risks.
  - Know your options of self-protection if an incident occurs.
  - Limit your time in such conditions in order to manage your physical and psychological stress.

+ **Emergencies: fire, escape, hostage situation, etc.**
  - Be aware that such situations can occur.
  - Do not obsess about such possibilities.
  - Make sure you know what to do if such an emergency arises.

+ **Organizational stress**, including problems with the institutional chaplain or your pastoral supervisor or lack of clear guidelines for your assignments in terms of where, when, how and the objectives to be achieved or communication problems with the administration, the staff, the pastoral supervisor or fellow volunteers or grievance filed against you by an inmate.

- Utilize sound problem solving with healthy interpersonal dialogue.
- If an impasse is reached, be realistic about the stress on you from that situation and evaluate your ability to continue effectively as a volunteer at that institution.

It is well known in the world outside the prison fences that severe stress is a killer because of the residual toll it takes on the human body. Inside the prison fences, stress can kill much faster because in addition to the damage to one's body stress takes the volunteer's attention off the dangers always at hand. All of us volunteers are responsible to be honest and open with our pastoral and volunteer supervisors about the impact of the prison-induced stress on our ability to safely perform our duties. And every volunteer supervisor is responsible to plan and arrange the volunteers' duties and activities with an eye to managing and minimizing their stress.

The facts in this and the preceding chapter are not warm and fuzzy, not endearing, not even comfortable. The volunteer needs to know the truth about the strange world inside jails and prisons and about the people who inhabit them. This is not to dissuade or discourage volunteers but rather to empower and protect them.

Whenever we Catholic volunteers in prison ministry step inside the barbwire fence, we are making ourselves a "stranger in a strange land" for the sake of the Gospel and the Church. It is a noble endeavor that is only possible through God's grace. It offers the transformation of continual conversion not just for the inmates but also for us. Father Pierre Raphael, Catholic priest and chaplain for Rikers Island prison in New York City, shares this in a concise and powerful way.

The adventure is a daily one. Unceasingly I am led to the essential questions about evil, illusion, suffering, pardon, the mystery of the cross and of salvation. The fact of being a stranger, of coming from far away, of having had to adapt myself, of being somehow in exile as the prisoners are, has brought me closer to them. Like them, I am continually obliged to rub up against a strange environment, a culture, a way of life. No doubt with time there comes an acclimation, an adaptation, an acceptance, a greater facility of acceptance. But it is still the case that the prison often makes me think of Jacob's wrestling match.[14]

The story of Jacob wrestling with the angel is recounted in Genesis. It is generally believed that Jacob was in the process of attempting reconciliation with his brother Esau from whom he had been estranged for two decades. Jacob stole Esau's birthright through deceit of their dying father, Isaac. Jacob does not know whether Esau, who is bearing down with an army of 400 men, seeks to destroy him in vengeance or welcome him in reconciliation:[15]

> Jacob was very much frightened. In his anxiety, he divided the people who were with him, as well as his flocks, herds and camels, into two camps. "If Esau should come and attack one camp," he reasoned, "the remaining camp may still escape." (Genesis 32: 8-9)

Every inmate facing re-entry into society after prolonged incarceration for crimes committed against family, friends and strangers will hear their own fears in Jacob's prayer:

> Then Jacob prayed: "God of my father Abraham and God of my father Isaac! You, LORD, who said to me, 'Go back to your land and your relatives and I will be good to you.' I am unworthy of all the acts of kindness and faithfulness that you have performed for your servant: although I crossed the Jordan here with nothing but my staff, I have now grown into two camps.
>
> "Save me from the hand of my brother, from the hand of Esau! Otherwise, I fear that he will come and strike me down and the mothers with the children. You yourself said, 'I will be very good to you, and I will make your descendants like the

sands of the sea, which are too numerous to count.'" (Genesis 32:10-13)

Jacob must wrestle his way past an angel in order to continue on the path toward his brother Esau. The angel strikes Jacob on the hip, inflicting a wound that leaves him limping for the rest of his life. Jacob's story is one of struggle, perseverance, the search for reconciliation and the lingering effects of that struggle. Every man and woman who has endured prison will recognize that limp. Inmates too have been left with an invisible limp from the struggle to leave behind their identity as an offender and make it back to the place of their home. Every one of them who has overcome criminal thinking and plumbed the deep waters of grace through personal encounter with Jesus Christ and living enfleshment of the Eucharist will be able to say, like Jacob: "I have seen God face to face, yet my life has been spared" (Genesis 32:31).

Like Father Pierre, every Catholic prison ministry volunteer steps into the midst of that Jacobean struggle by the inmates.

What are the pastoral needs that are presented to the volunteer as part of that struggle? That is the next subject of this book, beginning with the needs of the inmates themselves.

> *"Having failed once, I was literally terrified that I might fail completely this time and lose the last thing I still clung to, my faith in God."*
>
> Fr. Walter J. Ciszek, SJ, prisoner in a Soviet gulag[1]

CHAPTER 9

Pastoral Needs of Inmates

What does it feel like spiritually to be in prison? Fr. Walter Ciszek was an American Jesuit priest who was sentenced to a Soviet gulag, a forced labor concentration camp, in Siberia in World War II. He remained in prison there for 23 years and credits his faith and his prayer life for having survived. But that is not where his prison spirituality started:

> I was so desolate that even prayer seemed impossible. I felt endangered and threatened anew, but I could find no light or consolation in prayer. I found myself instead reproaching God for not sparing me this new ordeal. I found myself wondering why God permitted it to go on, day after day, without finding some way to end it, or helping me to find a way to step back from the downward path I seemed to be moving along.[2]

While incarceration in an American prison is surely not as horrible as the tortures of the Soviet gulags, it is amazing that Fr. Ciszek's description of his spiritual crisis at the beginning of imprisonment sounds so similar to the crisis many inmates describe in adjusting to prison. The questions are brutal to the soul, especially for those facing long or life sentences.

+ Is this really God's will for me?
+ How could God let this happen to me?
+ How could God let this continue?
+ How could God let me do the things
    that got me into this fix?
+ Where was God?
+ Where is God?
+ Is there really a God after all?

Fr. Ciszek found the answers to his questions, but he did not come by them easily. It was a grueling spiritual and mental process that led him to the truth:[3]

The simple soul who each day makes a morning offering of "all the prayers, works, joys and sufferings of this day"—and who then acts upon it by accepting unquestioningly and responding lovingly to all the situations of the day...has perceived with an almost childlike faith the profound truth about the will of God....

The temptation is to look beyond these things, precisely because they are so constant, so petty, so humdrum and routine, and to seek to discover instead some other and nobler "will of God" in the abstract that better fits *our* notion of what God's will should be.... It is the temptation faced by everyone who suddenly discovers that life is not what he expected it to be. The answer lies in understanding that it is these things— and by these things alone, here and now, at this moment—that truly constitute the will of God. The challenge lies in learning to accept this truth and act upon it, every moment of every day.

WHEN WE VISIT JESUS IN PRISON

A very plain description of the task facing us Catholic volunteers in prison ministry is to assist inmates in making the spiritual journey from their feelings of desolation, described by Fr. Ciszek at the beginning of his imprisonment, to the simple truth he arrived at, lived day-in and day-out. This is no small task. Even more daunting, our task is to be accomplished despite the role of social and economic forces in crime and despite the part played by criminal thinking for each individual inmate. We must allow those realities to move us to deeper levels of compassion in the awareness that *but for the grace of God, there go I.* Yet this awareness is to be held side-by-side with the reality that we are progressively nudging inmates always deeper into the drastic changes of thought and judgment called conversion.

Such a task could indeed be labeled a "mission impossible," but Jesus assures us in Scripture that "What is impossible for human beings is possible for God."[4] And we stand on a long tradition of pastoral service to the imprisoned, as described in *The Oxford History of the Prison:*[5]

> The largest single group of Roman prisoners whose sources provide extensive detail for life in Roman prisons are the Christians…. Among Christians, the duty of visiting prisoners was recognized as soon as the persecutions began in earnest in the second century [the 100s AD]. It was inspired by Jesus' prediction that at the Last Judgment, those who had visited prisons would be counted among the righteous (Matthew 25:36), and by other scriptural texts (Hebrews13:3)….
>
> The acts of the martyrs were read by later Christians, along with the books of Job, Psalms, Lamentations, Isaiah, and Zechariah, and these shaped later Christian attitudes toward both the use of prisons and the needs of prisoners.

In Hebrews 13:3, we are instructed:

> Be mindful of prisoners as if sharing their imprisonment, and of the ill-treated as of yourselves, for you also are in the body.[6]

It is important not to miss the tie-in of this duty with the Eucharistic reality of our unity in the body of Christ. In his Apostolic Exhortation, *On the Eucharist as the Source and Summit of the Church's Life and Mission (Sacramentum Caritatis)*, Pope Benedict XVI makes the same connection:

> The Church's spiritual tradition, basing itself on Christ's own words (cf. Matthew 25:36), has designated the visiting of prisoners as one of the corporal works of mercy. Prisoners have a particular need to be visited personally by the Lord in the sacrament of the Eucharist. Experiencing the closeness of the ecclesial community, sharing in the Eucharist, and receiving Holy Communion at this difficult and painful time can surely contribute to the quality of a prisoner's faith journey and to full social rehabilitation..... I ask dioceses to do whatever is possible to ensure that sufficient pastoral resources are invested in the spiritual care of prisoners.[7]

For sure, resources include people and time. But what about money? Doesn't the word *resources* usually include money? Is the pastoral care of inmates so important that we should be willing to even spend money on it? If so, doesn't that imply that we should be willing to spend money on taking care of inmates physically, mentally, and medically, as well?

Does expending resources on convicted offenders who are incarcerated mean that we do not care about the victims of crime? Evidently the popes and bishops do not think so.

Am I My Brother's Keeper?

When I see one of my casual friends every weekend at church, we usually waive politely from a distance. Not today. He is headed for me with purpose and mission.

"Read your columns," he winces. "Sounds like you're for the inmates."

"No question about it," I nod. "I'm definitely for the inmates."

He shakes his head disgustedly, "I knew it. You're against the officers."

"Oh no," I respond. "I'm for the officers, too."

"What? That's preposterous. You can't be for both!"

"I have to be for both," I place a hand on his shoulder in emphasis. "Jesus is for both."

He steps back apace throwing up his hands, "Then who is the bad guy?"

I pause. He will not like my answer.

"See there," he jumps into my hesitation, thumping a pointed finger against my chest. "Even you know you cannot be for both sides. Who is the bad guy?"

"I am for both," I explain slowly. "I must be because Jesus is for both. The bad guys are you and me. We are the voters and the taxpayers who treat both the officers and the inmates unjustly."

"What kind of drivel is that?" his tone wanes to incredulity.

"We are responsible for the inmates' care and the officers' working conditions. When it comes to corrections officers and inmates in Florida, we have subjected them both to tremendous injustice."

"That is nonsense."

"No it isn't. When I walk into a prison with Jesus in my pocket, I spend the entire time surrounded by brothers and sisters in Christ. Some are wearing brown because they are officers. Some are inmates wearing blue and some are inmates wearing orange because they are on death row. But all of them are in unjust conditions because you and I would rather spend money entertaining ourselves than pay the money necessary to treat them justly."

"What is unjust…what injustice?"

"How much time do you have?" I ask, realizing that all the cars in the church parking lot are gone except his, mine, and the priest's.

"This can't take long. Shoot!"

"Okay. Take the case of those with intellectual disability and the mentally ill. Our state is in contempt of court for its refusal to provide for the intellectually disabled. And our severely mentally ill are mostly wandering the streets of our inner-cities without community care."

"What's that got to do with anything?" his eyes roll in an exaggerated rim shot.

"It is all connected. You and I refuse to pay the money necessary to care for the severely mentally ill in their communities. Sooner or later, many of them get in trouble. Then we throw them in jails and prisons without the mental health services to properly treat them. Essentially, we punish them for being sick, for needing treatment."

"Fine. Assume you're right. What has that got to do with the officers?"

"Then we tell the officers, 'Here, take them. Keep them out of our sight. We are not going to provide the money to adequately treat them. We are not going to give you the tools or the expertise to properly care for them. They are your problem.' That is injustice to both the inmates and officers. They both deserve much better."

"What is your point?"

"I don't think Jesus would be pointing at either the officers or the inmates today. I think Jesus would be pointing at you and me, challenging us to be fairer to both of them by stepping up to our duty to care for all our brothers and sisters justly. Jesus told us we must take care of each other."

"But that would mean paying out more money."

"Did Jesus make an exception if it costs us money?"

Too often, we Christians struggling with the realities of incarceration stumble into political arguments about whether the care of our brothers and sisters should be done through programs that are supported by taxes or through other mechanisms. That misses the point. The critical issue is not whether our Christian duty to care for each other is done through taxes or through other means of support. For centuries, the Church itself and the religious orders served humanity in meeting such needs, especially when government could not do it or government did not even exist. The critical point is that the Gospel

　　　　WHEN WE VISIT JESUS IN PRISON

makes it incumbent upon all of us who profess Christ to take care of our brothers and sisters. Getting stuck in endless arguments about *how* to do it does not satisfy our duty to *get it done.*

In later chapters, this book will deal with the issues of inmate medical illness, mental illness, and rehabilitation for re-entry into society. For purposes of this chapter, it is important to note that our Catholic understanding of the Eucharist consistently brings us back to the social aspects of our faith. As detailed in Chapter 6 of this book, Pope Benedict specifically elaborates on the social ramifications of our Eucharistic faith in *On the Eucharist (Sacramentum Caritatis).* That social aspect provides texture to our pastoral efforts inside the prison fences. We Catholic volunteers in prison ministry allow those social realities to move us to depths of compassion in our pastoral service while avoiding the pitfall of removing culpability from inmates for their wrongful moral choices. What is important to remember is that we also serve as a voice outside the prison fences, to testify to the truth of Church teaching about crime and punishment on behalf of the incarcerated, who cannot speak for themselves.

Our U.S. Catholic bishops are very clear in their guidance in this regard. Based upon their words in *Responsibility, Rehabilitation, and Restoration,*[8] volunteers in Catholic prison ministry are guided as follows:

+ *A Catholic approach to crime and punishment begins with the recognition that the dignity of the human person applies to both the victim and the offender (p. 2).* Pastoral ministry inside prisons and jails will always affirm and maintain the dignity of the human person for both victims and offenders. With inmates who suffer from criminal thinking and have committed violent crimes against the physical person of their victim, this can be a difficult truth to accept. But it is a key step in repentance and conversion.

+ *The common good is undermined by policies that give up on those who have broken the law (p. 1).* Catholic pastoral ministry inside prisons and jails never gives up on anyone; not because the crimes were not really that bad but because the power of redemption through the grace of Jesus Christ is that great.

+ *The ways to overcome violence are not simple (p. 4).* We volunteers in Catholic prison and jail ministry know and understand this reality and eschew political platitudes and catch phrases that oversimplify our complex social situations.

+ *The Catholic approach accepts the notion that we can reach out to victims without supporting vengeance (p. 2).* Pastoral ministry inside prisons and jails will reject populist slogans that claim vengeance is necessary to support victims of crime. We must be creative and invested in bringing about healing for the victims of crime without giving them the false hope of vengeance.

+ *There are many Catholics in prisons and jails in the U.S .(p. 3).* We volunteers in Catholic ministry know that it is tough to be a practicing Catholic in many of the country's prisons and jails; so we are supportive and present to assist those inside in the practice of their Catholic faith. But we also stand for the truth outside the prison fences.

About fifteen years ago, I offered a prayer at the *Prayer of the Faithful* in our parish for "our Catholic brothers and sisters on death row." At the end of Mass, a group of angry parishioners gathered outside the church and rebuked me for lying in church because "we all know there are no Catholics on death row." Catholic prison ministry volunteers must serve as credible witnesses of the truth to their fellow Catholics, who have never been, and may never be, inside the prison fences.

+ *Even if the death penalty were proven to be a deterrent to crime (which it has not been proven to be), the Catholic bishops would still oppose its use because there are alternative means to protect society available to us today (p. 7).* Without even realizing it, many of our brothers and sisters on the outside of prisons have substituted utilitarian pragmatism for morality in dealing with criminal justice. That means our brothers and sisters living inside the prison fences have a pastoral need to be visible and heard through our voices proclaiming the value and dignity of their human lives.

WHEN WE VISIT JESUS IN PRISON

+ *Also affected by crime are the children left behind by incarcerated parents (p. 7).* Many parents in prison have a pastoral need to know that the needs of their children are being met. This will be dealt with extensively in the later chapters of this book.

+ *African American children are at least nine times more likely to have a parent incarcerated than white children (p. 7).* The response of the Catholic volunteer in prison and jail ministry to such a horrible statistic is the compassion of *but for the grace of God, there go my children.*

+ *Too often, the criminal justice system neglects the hurt and needs of victims or seeks to exploit their anger and pain to support punitive policies (p. 8).* We volunteers in Catholic prison and jail ministry must resist the social pressure to endorse (even informally) the polarized policy clichés of conservative or liberal pundits and seek, instead, to find avenues for true healing for victims of crime and their communities and also the rehabilitation of criminals and their families.

+ *Prison inmates have high rates of substance abuse, illiteracy, and mental illness. Such realities require multi-dimensional responses to meet the needs of those in our prisons and jails (p. 10).* Inside the prison fence, we volunteers in Catholic prison ministry must be clear about the pastoral nature of our mission and mindfully work around such limitations.

Outside the prison fence, we are to be a voice of reason to the vengeance-crazed mentality that conflates alcohol and substance abuse treatment of offenders with lack of concern for the victims of crime.

+ *The U.S. imprisonment rate is highest in the world, even when compared to the rate in other western countries (p. 8). One area of criminal activity that seems to respond to treatment is substance abuse. The savings to taxpayers from quality substance abuse treatment versus imprisonment are significant, as much as three to one in a recent RAND Corporation study (pp. 12-13).* As credible resources to those on the outside who are seeking volunteers' judgment and knowledge about solutions to crime, volunteers need to make themselves available to others, especially at their parishes and in social situations, with the facts about programs that work.

+ *Inmate access to worship services and religious formation is a significant element in rebuilding the lives of inmates and changing their behavior, and it is guaranteed by the U.S. Constitution (p. 13).* Inmates have a deep pastoral need for spirituality, and we volunteers in Catholic prison and jail ministry know that our work is important to the kingdom and to society here and now. We invest the preparation and the energy that is merited by a task of such great weight.

Many Catholic bishops have spoken regionally to the pastoral needs of inmates, as well. As noted previously, the Catholic bishops of the southern U.S. have issued a series of pastoral letters on the subject of crime and punishment in the southern part of our country. In the fifth letter in that series, called *Prison Conditions*,[9] they instruct us as follows:

+ We must stop the practice of putting so many people in prison. Our policies must emphasize alternatives to incarceration for nonviolent offenders.
+ All of us must work to improve the jails and prisons in our communities. All prisoners should be safe from violence while incarcerated. There should be regular ongoing Catholic ministry in every prison and jail.
+ Even when an offender is especially callous and commits a horrendously violent crime, he or she retains their humanity and possesses a dignity, worth, and value that must be recognized, safeguarded, defended, and promoted.... Even though inmates have broken the law, the work they are required to do in prison must be worthwhile or compatible with human dignity.
+ While society must protect the community from those whose mental illness causes them to become aggressive or

WHEN WE VISIT JESUS IN PRISON

violent, society has an obligation to insure that offenders receive proper treatment of their mental illnesses. There must be a dramatic increase in treatment for mental illness.

+ All prisoners should have the opportunity to participate in substance abuse programs.
+ Racism and discrimination must be eliminated from the criminal justice system.
+ The Gospel calls us to minister to families of the imprisoned, especially to children who lose a parent to incarceration.

In the words of our southern bishops, we hear echoes of the statement by the U.S. Conference of Catholic Bishops. Reality is standing on the side of the bishops: the massive U.S. incarceration system is simply not sustainable. Without even addressing moral teaching, sheer economics is already playing a role in reducing the number of incarcerated Americans.

The American phenomenon, referred to worldwide as *mass incarceration*,[10] is being recognized by both the political left and right as too costly for federal and state budgets to sustain. From 1980 to 2008, the number of incarcerated Americans tripled, with the number of federal inmates having risen about 8 times in that period.[11] Mandatory minimum sentences for nonviolent drug offenses have resulted in an explosion of inmates on both federal and state levels. The result is a catastrophic economic cost for state and federal incarceration of $80,000,000,000 per year.

Widespread incarceration at the federal, state, and local levels is both ineffective and unsustainable. It imposes a significant economic burden—totaling $80 billion in 2010 alone—and it comes with human and moral costs that are impossible to calculate.

As a nation, we are coldly efficient in our incarceration efforts. While the entire U.S. population has increased by about a third since 1980, the federal prison population has grown at an astonishing rate—by almost 800 percent. It's still growing, despite the fact that federal prisons are operating at nearly 40 percent above capacity. Even though this country comprises just 5 percent of the world's population, we incarcerate almost a quarter of the world's prisoners. More than 219,000 federal inmates are currently behind bars. Almost half of them are serving time for drug-related crimes, and many have substance abuse disorders. Nine to 10 million more people cycle through America's local jails each year. And roughly 40 percent of former federal prisoners—and more than 60 percent of former state prisoners—are rearrested or have their supervision revoked within three years after their release, at great cost to American taxpayers and often for technical or minor violations of the terms of their release.[12]

The effects of mass incarceration have been especially devastating for African-Americans.

+ There are more African-American men now incarcerated in America than were held in slavery in 1861.[13]
+ A black man in America is 3.6 times more likely to be incarcerated than a black man in South Africa just before apartheid ended.[14]

All of the foregoing facts affect pastoral ministry inside the prison fence. The inmates know that society spends more money to keep them in prison than it would have cost to put them through college. They know that the system treats the poor and minorities differently from those who are well-healed and politically connected. They know more than any volunteer could possibly learn about how society gives them and others a raw deal. That is why we volunteers must be aware of the social and economic inequities in order to be effective pastorally.

If we volunteers in a prison or jail dismiss such inequities as mere fabrication or illusion, we have just made ourselves useless for pastoral ministry in that facility. Instead, we should knowingly acknowledge the reality of such inequities That stance allows us to lovingly challenge the inmate to focus on the immediacy of the moment: "Here we are—two people with different life experiences and different challenges and opportunities in our past. What shall you and I do now? Where shall we start from today?"

That is the point of departure from which the deeper pastoral needs of the inmate can be addressed. First and foremost in any realistic assessment of such deep pastoral needs of men and women in prison is grief—the grieving of the innumerable losses that are inherent to incarceration. I can hardly name all the losses, but certainly the following come to mind:

+ **The loss of freedom of movement.** Once inside the fences, inmates no longer have the ability to go where they want whenever they choose. I have been with men who have just been released from prison. Frequently they say, "Let's go somewhere, anywhere. It doesn't matter where. Let's just go."

  Those of us who have never experienced such a drastic loss of freedom cannot even comprehend what it means. No trips to the store, to church, to the gas station. No hopping in the car for a quick spin to clear one's head or to listen to the radio away from the stress at home.

  There is no walking anyplace either. No taking the dog out for a nightly constitutional around the block. No sauntering through town for window shopping or strolling to the ice cream shop after dinner. No stepping out or stepping in.

+ **The loss of choice.** Prison does not allow choice. All the clothes are fungible, down to the shoes and underwear. Even commodities like toothbrushes, toilet paper, and toothpaste are all one brand, one flavor, one texture. Food is barely edible and is all the same.

  Inmates do not get a choice of color, fabric, or style. Even haircuts are frequently set by staff order to be certain lengths for specific times of the year. There is no choice as to bunkmates, cellmates, roommates, or co-workers. There is no choice on work assignments, on rising and sleeping times, or on which building one is assigned to as a dorm. There is no choice as to which prison one is sent to. And there is absolutely no choice as to the staff that supervises the dorm, the work stations, or the rec yard.

Those who have just been released from prison after even modest periods of incarceration can be effectively paralyzed by the need to make normal decisions. Making choices is a function of freedom. Choices take energy and judgment. Inmates are usually punished for trying to make any choice other than the choice to obey immediately, without thought or question.

+ **The loss of relationships.** Most people living free in society would be hard pressed to make a list of all the people they are in relationship with. Closest relationships would include a spouse or significant other, parents and grandparents, children, grandchildren, and closest friends. For most inmates in prison, that list has been all but scratched off.

But day-to-day life in a free society includes innumerable other relationships with co-workers, church members, neighbors, professional and medical service providers, customer service people at gas stations, post offices, doctor and dentist offices, barber shops, hair salons, nail salons, clothing stores, shoe stores, personal cosmetics stores, newspaper and cable service people, plumbers and electricians, lawn-care and nursery specialists, etc. When a person steps inside a prison or jail, everyone who provides such services is either staff—and prohibited from being friendly—or another inmate, who is not to be trusted without risking life and limb. Casual social relationships are gone.

+ **The loss of a sense of well-being.** Most people in free society possess, at some level and to some degree, a basic sense of well-being. This can be either a feeling that all is well or, more often, that even if all is not well, we all know how to take care of ourselves. For example, we may feel physically strong, but we know that if we get sick we can go to a doctor or hospital. In fact, we can be so accustomed to a sense of well-being that it becomes an assumption that is only noticed if it ceases to exist and is replaced by anxiety.

Any sense of well-being in a prison or jail is usually an illusion. One's physical and sexual integrity is always on the line and can be seized in a moment by the new, stronger inmate just admitted to the prison. There is no guarantee that an inmate can see a doctor or that the inmate will obtain the needed medicine even if they are seen by one.

Another inmate can manipulate staff to obstruct medical callouts for even serious illness in order to compel sexual favors. An inmate who has caught the eye of a powerful prisoner can be forced to choose between giving in to the illicit sexual demands or being blocked from antibiotics or chemotherapy. Inside the prison fence, there is no such thing as a sense of well-being.

✦ **The loss of positive stimulation.** The healthy stimulation of positive discussions, sharing positive thoughts, even planning and acting on positive impulses, is a fabric of our days in free society. We can minimize our time spent interacting with people who generate negativity and maximize our exposure to people who are uplifting and positive. How do inmates do that inside a fence that forces them to interact with a population where many of the people are routinely engaged in criminal thinking and criminal attitudes?

I have repeatedly experienced inmates expressing the anguish of living in an environment where they are drowning in negativity, where many of the other inmates are hateful and nothing meaningful can ever be discussed without the risk of accidentally infuriating someone who can become homicidal. There is plenty of stimulation to be had in prison, but almost none of it is positive or healthy.

✦ **The loss of a sense of self.** Most of us human beings have a sense of who we are as a person. That sense of self can be framed by our emotions, character traits, strengths, weaknesses, likes and dislikes, etc. Too often, I have listened to men in prison struggling to reestablish some sense of who they really are in light of the crime they have committed. "I could not have done that! I mean, the person I was before it happened could not have done that. But I did it. Who am I really?" The emptiness of losing any sense of one's true identity can leave a gaping hole inside.

The losses in incarceration just enumerated, and so many others, are true losses in every sense of the word. True losses need to be grieved. The process for grieving and overcoming deep losses is well known, but not easy to avail oneself of inside a prison or jail, where any sign of weakness or emotion can render one a target of predators. Suffice it to say, one of the deepest pastoral needs of inmates is the need to grieve their losses occasioned by incarceration.

All people, even free people in open society, experience the loss of loved ones that come with normal human life. The deaths of parents, spouses, siblings, close relatives, or children are all instances of losses that are experienced by human beings at large. Such losses are referred to as "natural losses." All losses, even natural losses, "can profoundly challenge what gives our life meaning and pleasure."[15]

Inmates experience such losses from within prisons and jails. The grief of the bad news itself is frequently compounded by the longtime lack of contact between the inmate and the deceased before the death. The pain is deepened by the inability of the inmate to be present for surviving family members. When experienced in loneliness from inside a prison fence, even natural losses can be very hard to move beyond.

The unique losses of incarceration including, in many cases, the loss of a significant relationship, can be so wrenching as to constitute a trauma. Severe traumatic losses can sap all of someone's energies and coping skills for a long time, as John Schneider points out in his book *Finding My Way: Healing and Transformation through Loss and Grief:*

We focus on what no longer exists, what is missing now, or what will never be. It can be painful to find out how alone we are, the price we are paying for our achievements, our secret passions, our betrayals or our procrastinations.[16]

The death of a relative, or other person who is significant in an inmate's life, usually results in a phone call from the family to the prison. The call is forwarded to the prison chaplain, or if there is no chaplain, the appropriate officer. The person fielding the call usually has the duty to inform the inmate of the death in an encounter called *death notification*. In a massive prison with thousands of inmates, death notifications can be a major portion of the chaplain's job duties. They are never to be taken lightly. Death notifications can drastically increase the risk of inmate suicide or can result in an act of violence towards others.

Usually a place separated from the routine hustle and bustle of the prison at large, such as the chaplain's office, is designated for death notifications. That is partly for control of the situation and partly to show respect for the privacy of the offender who will be receiving the bad news. Even the most callous of men and women can be expected to shed tears at the death of a loved one, especially a spouse, parent, or child. In prison, those tears need to be shed in the safety of a private situation, so as not to make the emotionally distraught inmate a target for predators.

Under even the best of circumstances, tremendous caution must be exercised in anticipation of the emotions that can be released in someone who is informed that he or she will never see their mom or dad or child or wife again. Depending on the behavior record of the inmate involved, prison procedures may require the presence of one or more officers, even if the meeting will take place in the chaplain's office. For an inmate who has only a short time left until release, the death of a loved one can seem especially cruel, as though God and the system have it in for him. The rage can be intense.

Even more devastating is the case of an inmate who would already have been released except that an officer wrote him up for a petty disciplinary infraction (e.g., having too many postage stamps, having an extra spiritual book on his shelf). If the infraction caused the inmate to lose 30 days of "gain time" (time earned for good behavior) and his mother died 15 days before his release, that officer's actions could be interpreted as the reason that the inmate was not able to hug his mother goodbye in the hospital before she died. It would not be unheard of, in the grip of powerful grief and rage, for that inmate to leave the chaplain's office and head straight to that officer to hurt or kill her. So, competent administration and staffing of death notifications is both humane and crucial to safety and security in prisons and jails.

Most volunteers will never be asked to handle death notifications, but every one of us volunteers in prison ministry should be extremely careful never to inadvertently jump the gun by passing such information to an inmate. For example, if a chaplain has been out sick for three days, the formal death notification may not have occurred. We might see a note in the chapel or hear from an officer in the hall that so-and-so's mother passed away. Trying to be empathic and supportive, we could express condolences to the inmate at the bible study in the dorm dayroom. We will have unintentionally made a death notification, without the protective systems in place to handle and control the situation. We will be held responsible for whatever happens because of that mistake.

Unless someone in charge informs us that an inmate has had a death notification by staff, we should never bring up the passing away of an inmate's relative or friend. If the inmate brings up the subject in an exploratory way—as if fishing for information that we might have—our answer is always, "If anything had happened, I am sure that the Chaplain would let you know as soon as possible."

We volunteers in Catholic prison ministry are rarely trained or equipped to serve as grief counselors, at least in prison. That role is best left to the prison chaplain and the mental health staff. But we do need to be familiar with the process of grieving a loss. Even an inmate who is burdened with aspects of criminal thinking or is sociopathic is still susceptible to human grief and emotions about his or her own losses, especially traumatic ones. Our role is to provide a spiritual answer that can address such losses and help inmates find meaning to their suffering. For the Catholic volunteer that means introducing them to the Paschal Mystery.

Paschal Mystery is a shorthand term for specific aspects of the Eucharistic reality that is core to Catholic faith. As such, it refers to Jesus' passion, death, and resurrection—the reality in human history of God-become-man suffering, dying, and overcoming death. This reality is embodied in the Holy Sacrifice of the Mass. But as Pope John Paul II instructs us in the encyclical letter *Rich in Mercy (Dives in Misericordia)*, the message of the Paschal Mystery, the message of God as the One who suffers with us, who has thrown himself in with the lot of suffering humanity, is not limited to Catholics or even just to Christians:[17]

> The Paschal Mystery is the culmination of this revealing and effecting of mercy, which is able to justify [human beings], to restore justice in the sense of that salvific order which God willed from the beginning in [them] and, through [them], in the world. The suffering Christ speaks in a special way to [people], and not only to the believer. The non-believer also will be able to discover in him the eloquence of solidarity with the human lot, as also the harmonious fullness of a disinterested dedication to the cause of [humanity], to truth, and to love. And yet the divine dimension of the Paschal Mystery goes still deeper. The cross on Calvary...emerges from the very heart of the love that [humans...have] been given as a gift, according to God's eternal plan. God...does not merely remain closely linked with the world as the Creator and the ultimate source of existence. He is also Father: He is linked to [humans], whom he called to existence in the visible world, by a bond still more intimate than that of creation. It is love which not only creates the good but also grants participation in the very life of God: Father, Son and Holy Spirit. [¶7]

Pope John Paul is clear that God's being for us is not limited to matters dealing with the next life; to the contrary, God is present with us in the grief and the hurts that are part of human existence in this earthly life:

The cross is the most profound condescension of God to [humans] and to what [humans]—especially in difficult and painful moments—look on as [their] unhappy destiny. The cross is like a touch of eternal love upon the most painful wounds of [humanity's] earthly existence. [¶8]

The pope goes so far as to point out that the message of the Paschal Mystery specifically includes the poor, the prisoners, and the suffering:

It is the total fulfillment of the messianic program that Christ once formulated in the synagogue at Nazareth and then repeated to the messengers sent by John the Baptist.... This program consisted in the revelation of merciful love for the poor, the suffering, and prisoners, for the blind, the oppressed, and sinners. In the paschal mystery the limits of the many sided evil in which [human beings] become a sharer during [their] earthly existence are surpassed: the cross of Christ, in fact, makes us understand the deepest roots of evil, which are fixed in sin and death. [¶8]

This is truly Good News for those grieving the losses of incarceration and of the death of loved ones. But how, specifically, are they to understand the suffering and pain of their losses? Pope John Paul elaborates on this in his apostolic letter *On the Christian Meaning of Suffering: (Salvifici Doloris)*:[18]

The Cross of Christ throws salvific light, in a most penetrating way, on [human] life and in particular on [human] suffering. For through faith the Cross reaches [men and women] *together with the Resurrection*: the mystery of the Passion is contained in the Paschal Mystery. The witnesses of Christ's Passion are at the same time witnesses of his Resurrection.... [¶21]

Suffering, in fact, is always *a trial*—at times a very hard one—to which humanity is subjected.... Those who share in Christ's sufferings have before their eyes the Paschal Mystery of the Cross and Resurrection, in which Christ descends, in a first phase, to the ultimate limits of human weakness and impotence: indeed, he dies nailed to the Cross. But if at the same time in this *weakness* there is accomplished his *lifting up*, confirmed by the power of the Resurrection, then this means that the weaknesses of all human sufferings are capable of being infused with the same power of God manifested in Christ's Cross. [¶23] (Emphasis in original.)

In and through the Scriptures dealing with suffering, Pope John Paul leads us to the understanding that human sufferings, including the sufferings of those in prison, including their sufferings through grief and loss, can be infused with the power of Calvary. The weakest human moments are imbued with God's greatest power:

In such a concept, *to suffer* means to become particularly *susceptible*, particularly *open to the working of the salvific powers of God*, offered to humanity in Christ. In him God has confirmed his desire to act especially through suffering, which is [human] weakness and emptying of self, and he wishes to make his power known precisely in this weakness and emptying of self. [¶23] (Emphasis in original.)

We volunteers in Catholic prison ministry need to be ready for the almost reflexive *faith vs. works* challenge to the Paschal Mystery by non-Catholic Christians. A Christian who has been schooled in the consciousness of *saved by faith, not by works* may fear that the Paschal Mystery means believers are trying to merit redemption by suffering themselves instead of relying on the redemptive sufferings of Christ. Pope John Paul seems to anticipate this misplaced concern by explaining the cosmic reality of the Paschal Mystery—a dimension of divine love which supersedes space and time:

> Does this mean that the Redemption achieved by Christ is not complete? No. *It only means* that the Redemption, accomplished through satisfactory love, *remains always open to all love* expressed in *human suffering*. In this dimension—the dimension of love—the Redemption which has already been completely accomplished is, in a certain sense, constantly being accomplished. Christ achieved the Redemption completely and to the very limits but at the same time he did not bring it to a close. In this redemptive suffering, through which the Redemption of the world was accomplished, Christ opened himself from the beginning to every human suffering and constantly does so. Yes, it seems to be part of *the very essence of Christ's redemptive suffering* that this suffering requires to be unceasingly completed. Thus, with this openness to every human suffering, Christ has accomplished the world's Redemption through his own suffering. [¶24] (Emphasis in original.)

Yet, the pope explains, this cosmic reality continues to work within the space and time of human history through the body of Christ, the Church:

> For, at the same time, this Redemption, even though it was completely achieved by Christ's suffering, lives on and in its own special way develops in the history of the [human race]. It lives and develops as the body of Christ, the Church, and in this dimension every human suffering, by reason of the loving union with Christ, completes the suffering of Christ. It completes that suffering *just as the Church completes the redemptive work of Christ*. The mystery of the Church—that body which completes in itself also Christ's crucified and risen body—indi-

cates at the same time the space or context in which human sufferings complete the sufferings of Christ. Only within this radius and dimension of the Church as the Body of Christ, which continually develops in space and time, can one think and speak of "what is lacking" in the sufferings of Christ. The Apostle, in fact, makes this clear when he writes of "completing what is lacking in Christ's afflictions for the sake of his body, that is, the Church" (Colossians 1:24). [¶24] (Emphasis in original; citation added.)

Perhaps of special importance to those suffering the losses of incarceration, as well as natural losses in prison, is Pope John Paul's further teaching on the role that suffering can play in developing our interior spirituality:

Down through the centuries and generations it has been seen that *in suffering there is concealed* a particular *power that draws a person interiorly close to Christ*, a special grace. To this grace many saints, such as Saint Francis of Assisi, Saint Ignatius of Loyola, and others, owe their profound conversion. A result of such a conversion is not only that individuals discover the salvific meaning of suffering but above all that [they] become a completely new person. [They] discover a new dimension, as it were, of [their] *entire life and vocation.*

This interior maturity and spiritual greatness in suffering are certainly the *result* of a particular *conversion* and cooperation with the grace of the Crucified Redeemer. It is he himself who acts at the heart of human sufferings through his Spirit of truth, through the consoling Spirit…. Suffering is, in itself, an experience of evil. But Christ has made suffering the firmest basis of the definitive good, namely the good of eternal salvation. By his suffering on the Cross, Christ reached the very roots of evil, of sin and death. He conquered the author of evil, Satan, and his permanent rebellion against the Creator. To the suffering brother or sister Christ *discloses* and gradually reveals *the horizons of the Kingdom of God....* For suffering cannot be *transformed* and changed by a grace from outside, but *from within.* And Christ through his own salvific suffering is very much present in every human suffering, and can act from within that suffering by the powers of his Spirit of truth, his consoling Spirit. [¶26] (Emphasis in original.)

We volunteers in Catholic prison ministry who are serving as a prayer partner and spiritual advisor to an inmate who is struggling with suffering need to understand that this process is not didactic, but is, instead, experiential. We can set forth the concepts, but the inmate will only grow in understanding through the spiritual process of growth in participation in the sufferings of Christ. It is a faith walk, not a head trip. As Pope John Paul points out:

However, this interior process does not always follow the same pattern. It often begins and is set in motion with great difficulty. Even the very point of departure differs: people react to suffering in different ways. But in general it can be said that almost always individuals enter suffering with a *typically human protest* and *with the question "why."* [They] ask the meaning of [their] suffering and seek an answer to this question on the human level....

Gradually, *as individuals take up [their] cross,* spiritually uniting [themselves] to the Cross of Christ, the salvific meaning of suffering is revealed before [them]. [They] do not discover this meaning at [their] own human level but at the level of the suffering of Christ. At the same time, however, from this level of Christ the salvific meaning of suffering *descends to [human] level* and becomes, in a sense, the individual's personal response. It is then that [men and women] find in [their] suffering interior peace and even spiritual joy. [¶26]...

This is the meaning of suffering, which is truly *supernatural* and at the same time human. It is supernatural because it is rooted in the divine mystery of the Redemption of the world, and it is likewise deeply *human*, because in it the [people] discover [themselves, their] own humanity, [their] own dignity, [their] own mission. [¶31] (Emphasis in original.)

In addition to the need to deal with the grief of losses from incarceration and losses of loved ones, we volunteers should expect that inmates will need healing in their relationship with God, with others, with themselves, and in their understanding of who God is.[19] An example of an excellent program that facilitates this process is *Healing the Imprisoned: A Retreat* designed and narrated by Father Larry Carew.[20] The program is suitable for ecumenical as well as Catholic audiences. I have used the program effectively with groups as small as six inmates and with groups of over 100 inmates. Fr. Larry scopes in on the power of the Holy Spirit to heal and restore the following areas of brokenness in individuals:

+ **Session 1 – Coming to know Jesus, the prisoner.** This module elaborates on the Scriptural record of Jesus' experiences as an inmate. For example, his arrest, his arraignment, his betrayal by his friend, his abandonment by his friends, the agony of his mother, the false charges and false witnesses, the politics of a politically valued execution, the role of public opinion from the crowds, the beatings and humiliations, and ultimately his horrific public execution. Most inmates have a general knowledge that Jesus was a prisoner, but have rarely experienced the bond of identity with Jesus through his in depth experiences of their life as an inmate.

+ **Session 2 – Inviting Jesus to heal lingering wounds and scars of childhood abuse.** It is almost cliché to discuss the correlations between criminal behavior as an adult and child abuse in early life. When dealing with inmates who are enmeshed in criminal thinking, the connection must be presented very carefully to avoid it being manipulated into a free pass from culpability. Fr. Larry presents the wounds and scars of abuse as an emotional and spiritual prison from which Jesus wants to free each person. He warns of the dangers of abused children becoming abusive men and women and implores each member of the audience to throw themselves on Christ's mercy for healing from this scourge.

+ **Session 3 – Meeting the man in the middle: Salvation as God's forgiveness.** Identifying with Jesus and naming the effects of abuse (both as the recipient and the agent) inevitably lead to the issue of repentance and conversion. For Catholics, sacramental Confession needs to be made available. For non-Catholics, the need is addressed from the evangelical standpoint.

+ **Session 4 – Encountering the risen Christ: Salvation as healing love and new life.** The full effects of the Paschal Mystery are presented in a personal and profound way. The audience is challenged to step into the changed life of the new man in Christ, energized by healing love and a personal relationship with our Risen Savior.

+ **Session 5 – Rejecting spiritual power and experience which does not come from God; and coming into the empowerment of the Holy Spirit.** It is amazing how many Christian men and women in prison, either before coming to prison or since, have dabbled or practiced in the occult: Séances. Witchcraft. Tarot Cards. Ouija boards. Numerology. Psychics. Sorcery. Spells and charms. This module details the harm and the danger occasioned by availing oneself of spiritual powers and experiences that are not of God and leads the audience through a reaffirmation of the baptismal-like renunciation of the powers of Satan. Fr. Larry also details the Scriptural promises of the gifts of the Holy Spirit and the impact on the lived life of encountering the person, power, and presence of the Holy Spirit.

✦ **Session 6 – How the sins of our "fathers" distort our image of God and healing our image of God; coming to know the love of our Father in heaven and recognizing ourselves as God's beloved children.** A universal truth of prison ministry is that men and women describe God the same way they describe their natural father. In this module, Fr. Larry explains the ways that the failings of our natural fathers can distort our notions of what God is like. He details the attributes of the Father that Jesus revealed and leads the audience in prayer for healing of their image of God.

In addition to the need for healing, conversion and repentance, every inmate has a need for correct teaching about the Catholic faith. We Catholic volunteers, who are a primary source of such information, should know our faith well enough to answer questions about Catholicism and Catholic practices correctly. Formal catechetical instruction (such as RCIA) is highly desirable and frequently welcomed by both the non-Catholic inmates seeking knowledge about the faith and by the Catholic inmates who want to learn more. Such programs must always be conducted in accordance with the rules and disciplines of the local bishop and pastoral authority concerning instruction in the faith. In the prison and jail environment, the need for religious instruction is critical. Fr. David Shilder puts it this way in his excellent book, *Inside the Fence*:

> To face the challenge of a secular, materialistic age that is by and large devoid of moral and sacred teachings, it is absolutely necessary for the chaplain to [emphasize] religious education.... This is not a luxury. This is an absolute necessity if we

are to prepare the minds of the inmates for the fight against secular ideas, philosophies, and habits that brought them to prison in the first place.[21]

The physical environment for such instruction can vary from a greeting card storage area, which I used in a Florida panhandle prison for five years, to a more formal setting that resembles a "free-world" (outside the prison) classroom. The physical setting can be helpful, but far more important is the substance of instruction. For higher level, even college level, instruction in such subjects as Catholic theology, philosophy, and Church history, we volunteers may be able to structure cooperative arrangements between the facility administration and outside resources. For example, Fr. George Williams, S.J., is the Catholic chaplain for California's massive San Quentin prison. A recent article in *America* magazine described how he has pulled together a cooperative program with nearby universities and theological unions to bring post-secondary level Catholic instruction inside the prison walls.[22]

As noted by Fr. George in the *America* article, primary in Catholic prison activity is the role of the sacraments, including Confession and Eucharist. Every Catholic volunteer should work with their pastoral supervisor to ensure that Catholic sacraments are regularly available to the inmates, and they should assist in making the Holy Sacrifice of the Mass, or a Communion Service, at the very least, available weekly. In addition to the constitutional right of every inmate to participate in the worship services of his or her faith, American Correctional Association policies are clear that correctional institutions should provide "appropriate facilities and support services for individual and group religious activities" and should allow "observance of periodic special or ritual activities."[23]

From a Church standpoint, the canonical rules that apply in the free-world to Eucharistic services and the role of Extraordinary Ministers of the Eucharist are fully applicable inside prisons and jails as well. Catholic prison ministry volunteers should be familiar with and abide by those rules and any supplemental disciplines issued by the local bishop or pastoral authority.

In addition to formal instruction, we Catholic volunteers should ensure that sound, authorized Catholic materials are available to the inmates at the prisons and jails in which we serve. To the extent possible, given the resources available, we should assist in making available devotional materials for practice of the Liturgy of the Hours and for daily prayers and meditation. We should engage on a regular basis in prayer, ourselves and with others, including inmates, for God's protection and fostering of the work of the Church in prisons and jails. It can feel challenging to phrase and construct Catholic prayers for such an environment. Fortunately, there are some excellent resources for prison ministry specific prayers, for example Ann Ball and Maximilian, SFO, *Prayers for Prisoners*, and Lois Spear, OP, *God Is with You: Prayers for Men in Prison*. The aim of all of us Catholic volunteers in prison ministry is the work of redemption: redemption of inmates, redemption of staff, and—because of our Catholic concept of spirituality of place—redemption of the facilities themselves.

The Redemption of Hell

Sitting in the Basilica of St. Francis in Assisi in Italy, I am reminded that one of the greatest mysteries underlying our faith is the concept of redemption. The walls and ceilings of this overwhelming edifice are covered with frescoes by Giotto, visual depictions of scenes from the *Old Testament,* the life of Christ, and the life of Francis of Assisi. Notwithstanding the two felled ceiling vaults, destroyed by an earthquake in 1997, this basilica is a monument to the spirituality of St. Francis and the beauty of God's creation.

This magnificent thirteenth-century church is located on a steep rise, just outside the city walls. In one of those not so uncommon paradoxes that are sprinkled throughout God's ways, the very hill that supports this church has itself been redeemed. Before the year 1230 AD, the plot of ground beneath this basilica was known as *Colle d' Inferno,* the Hill of Hell. This was the place of public executions for the city of Assisi. Our Catholic understanding of reality invites us to see the grace of God's saving hand moving through the temporal world—not to destroy it, but rather to redeem it. That grace is remarkably apparent in the history of the Hill of Hell.

Francis of Assisi died in 1226. His body was initially buried in the church of St. George, the parish where he had attended school. God had a different story in mind. Almost immediately, throngs of pilgrims from all over Europe began the journey to the gravesite of St. Francis. The relatively diminutive church of St. George was totally overwhelmed. A much larger church was needed. But where would it be placed? There was no large tract of buildable land available inside the walls of the medieval city. The church would need to be located outside the walls but as close to the city as possible, preferably adjacent to it. The premier site of the Hill of Hell was obvious.

Not unlike the city of Jerusalem in the time of Jesus, Assisi staged their executions in public on the closest hill outside the wall. This allowed all the residents to assemble on the walls and fearfully witness the defining power of those in authority to destroy and extinguish what only God can give—the gift of human life. The Hill of Hell, Assisi's version of *Golgotha*, stood empty and available just outside the corner of the city wall. On March 30, 1228, the Hill of Hell was offered to Pope Gregory IX as the place to build the new church of St. Francis.

When the construction of the lower portion of the church had been completed in 1230, it was time to consecrate the now sacred site. Gregory IX, formerly Cardinal Hugolino, a dear friend and supporter of Francis, knew that an intermediate step was necessary before the formal act of consecration and the interring of Francis' remains. In the papal bull *Is qui ecclesiam suum*, dated April 22, 1230, the Hill of Hell was formally redeemed. Henceforth it would be known as *Colle d' Cielo*, the Hill of Heaven.

Almost 800 years later I find myself sitting in the lower church atop the Hill of Heaven. The spirituality of this place is palpable, a legacy of the hundreds of millions of pilgrims who have journeyed to this ground from every corner of the earth over the last millennium. My thoughts turn to the plots of ground south of Highway 16 between Raiford and Starke in north Florida, ground dedicated to the living hell of death row and solitary confinement—and to the death house and execution chamber, our modern version of *Golgotha* and the Hill of Hell, the place where our legal killings are now performed.

I cannot help but wonder: is redemption still possible? Can the hell hills of Florida be redeemed just like the hell hill of Assisi was redeemed?

There are inmates with special pastoral needs because of their circumstances, their condition or their limited physical and mental abilities. Those inmates will be addressed in later chapters. The two major groups of people, other than inmates, with pastoral needs related to prisons and jails are the prison staff and families of the inmates. Those needs are dealt with in the next chapter.

"The physical, psychological, moral, and spiritual health of children is intimately linked to the health of families. In Christian terms, the family is sacred and holy, a 'community of life and love,' which prepares, nourishes, and sustains the youngest members of the Church in their task of building up the kingdom of God. In social terms, families are the 'first and vital cell of society,' the building block of community."

The U.S. Conference of Catholic Bishops[1]

CHAPTER 10
Pastoral Needs of Families of Inmates and of Staff

The age-old adage is that nobody comes to prison alone, because every inmate takes their family to prison with them. The wisdom of that notion goes far beyond the physical entrance into the prison when family members visit. It also refers to the drastic changes in a family's life when one of their loved ones is incarcerated. The impact can completely alter life as the family knew it. Some people assume this is only true if the incarcerated family member is a parent. In fact, the trauma is also severe when the family member who becomes a prison inmate is the child.

Carol Kent and her husband are world-class speakers in the evangelical traditions. Their life was picture perfect. They could never have imagined that their son would go to prison. But when the phone call came a half-hour after midnight, the normal life that was all they had ever known was forever shattered. Their wonderful son had been arrested for murdering his wife's first husband, in an act he mistakenly considered his protective duty. In the book *A New Kind of Nor-*

mal: Hope-Filled Choices When Life Turns Upside Down, Carol Kent courageously shares her family's journey through the ordeal of her son's arrest and imprisonment. She takes the reader with her in the search for a "new kind of normal life" after her son is convicted and sentenced to life in prison without possibility of parole. She describes her initial days after that call: "I wanted to curl up and die."[2]

The Kents cling tenaciously to their faith as they fight the feeling that the earth has opened up and swallowed them alive. Carol turns to the image of another mother, one who is reported in the Bible as knowing the agony of a son who is vilified as a criminal: Mary the Mother of Jesus.

> My son can never be compared to the son of God, but I can identify with the panicked thoughts that must have been in Mary's heart at that moment [hearing that Jesus was arrested]. She was a mother in pain. *But He's my son. No! No! No! Please let me get through to him. I must be near my boy. He needs his mother. I want him to see my love. It will give him strength.*[3]

This courageous woman makes a vow that she will survive; that, in faith, she will choose to live in God's mercy and grace. The rest of the story is her candid and forthright accounting of the perils and pitfalls, joys and victories in living out that commitment.

A prior, shorter account of her journey was published as *When I Lay My Isaac Down: Unshakable Faith in Unthinkable Circumstances.*[4] Available with that edition is a DVD set, study guide, and discussion questions, dealing from the standpoint of Christian biblical faith with the trauma to an inmate's family.[5] These are a tremendous resource for parish and diocesan support groups for families of inmates. Subjects discussed include:

+ *An Unexpected Journey:*
  The Power of Unthinkable Circumstances
+ *Why Didn't God Do Something?: The Power of Heartache*
+ *But Where is the Lamb?: The Power of Faith*

✦ *Embracing the Upside-Down Nature of the Cross:*
The Power of Joy

One of the issues for families of inmates that Carol Kent address-es: families of the incarcerated rarely tell anyone that they have a loved one in prison. They do not mention it at work, at school, or even at their church. She recommends that they step out in faith and share their story with fellow believers as part of the process of healing from their trauma. The part of this effort that is incumbent on the rest of us is to provide a safe place for that sharing and for spiritual and emo-tional support to take place. That can be easier said than done.

First of all, there is a reality to the fear of sharing such information in the workplace. There could be a loss of employment by the family members if the crime committed is particularly heinous and well-pub-licized. Secondly, the social ramifications could also be severe. There could be deep shame and stigmatization for the family members in school and social groups. But there should not be shame and stig-matization at a Christian church, especially at a Catholic Christian church, the very place where all come together to worship the God that taught us to pray: *forgive us our trespasses as we forgive those who have trespassed against us.*

It is not unusual for parish leadership to be afraid of sponsoring a support group for families of the incarcerated. This can be rooted in the false impression that none of the families in that particular parish have loved ones in prison. So, the erroneous thinking goes, hosting such a group will only serve to attract people from outside the parish, people who already have a strike against them because their family has criminals in it. The phrase I have heard is: *such a program is just a magnet for undesirables.*

The first leg of that faulty logic is disproved by factual reality. One would be hard pressed, even in the most affluent suburban loca-tions, to find a parish in the United States where no one has a loved one in prison. This author knows of a parish in an affluent suburban area where the leadership consented to holding a support group for inmates' loved ones, using the Carol Kent program, on the condition that only members of the parish could attend. Also, it could not be publicized anywhere except in the weekly parish bulletin. The parish leadership expressed certainty that no one would show up because there were no families of inmates in that parish. What a shock when two showed up for the very first meeting, four for the second meeting and—before it was over—more study sheets and a second meeting table were needed. America holds 25% of the world's inmates. Anyone looking for a U.S. parish that has no members with loved ones in prison is on a fool's errand.

The second leg of that erroneous logic is shamefully ignorant. Carol Kent never dreamed she would be visiting her son inside the barbed wire fences. I have met hundreds of families who never dreamed they would be visiting their loved one in prison, dozens who never dreamed they would be sitting in the visiting park at death row. The reality is that, but for the grace of God, every one of us could have someone in our family in prison. Moreover, the spiritual reality for the Catholic volunteer in prison ministry is that every baptized person in prison is our brother or sister in the Body of Christ. We are immersed in spiritual family members in prison. And, likewise, we are surrounded by their natural families outside the prisons.

An excellent resource for ministry to the families of the incarcerated from a Catholic perspective, available from Dismas Ministry, is *Keeping Hope—A Resource for Families and Friends of the Incarcerated* by Karen Heuberger and Ron Zeilinger.[6] The content is based on actual interviews with spouses, family members, friends, prison ministers, and the incarcerated. It also includes specific directions for questions to ask and procedures for visiting and writing inmates.

Not By Bread Alone

The sun and cows are still asleep. But amidst acres of fog and farmland, Florida's weekend rendition of *Field of Dreams* begins. Headlights appear to the east and to the west. They are coming.

They are from everywhere. Florida. America. Some are from Europe or Asia. One by one, the vehicles pull behind each other, dim to their parking lights and wait. The first ones arrive at about 4:30 am. If it is a major holiday like Christmas or Thanksgiving, they start to come at 1:00 am. The wait is not short.

At 6:30 am, the gate is unlocked. The small processing center is opened. First come, first served. But this is not the entrance. This step is just to get a numbered pass. They must return at 8:30 am and present their pass at the prison across the street. Only then will they be admitted to the triangular room with numbered tables where men clad in orange will be escorted to their side. This is the visiting park for Florida's death row.

For twenty, thirty, and more years they have come. Children. Mothers. Fathers. Sisters and brothers. Some have driven all night. Some have come by bus or plane. In a real sense, these visitors are also the victims of crime. The prize for their hours of journey and waiting is simple enough: to sit for half a day with their son, their father, their brother—a loved one who made a terrible mistake.

A wife, who is fighting the world to stay faithful to her marriage vows, kisses her husband's forehead. A fifteen-year-old daughter holds her father's hand. A mother or father places an arm around their son and shares God's Word. Families struggling to deal with their worst nightmare meet here and find ways to support and sustain each other. For over thirty years, this weekend tradition has been the most sacred event in the death row unit. No one has ever threatened to harm anyone here. No one would dare. This is holy ground.

Or at least it was. Florida has proposed terminating such visits. Soon only brief discussions by telephone through a thick plate of glass would be allowed. Today is my second day on death row since the men have started dealing with this news.

"Good morning, brother," I greet one of my regular communicants.

"Would you like to receive Jesus today?"

His discomfort is clear. "I'm not sure," he pauses. "Wouldn't that be eating?"

Most of the men I have talked to on death row yesterday and today are not eating. "Why are you not eating?" I ask.

"Brother Dale, why eat? We live twenty-four hours a day in these small cages. Do you know how hard it is to stay sane and positive living in a cage? Do you know how important it is to have something positive to do or to think about? Since last August, they have taken everything away: our knitting, our painting, our pens, our library books. Now, they are taking away our visits with our families. My mother is seventy years old. She travels a thousand miles to come here to visit. For what? To talk on a wire and look at me through a glass? Like a specimen in a zoo?" He shakes his head, "Why eat?"

"Then let us pray," I begin. We read Psalm 91.

He whispers, "Amen."

"It is not just bread," I assure him. "It is not just eating."

"Just bread wouldn't be enough," he sighs. "And I really need Jesus today."

"Then let us begin, in the name of the Father, the Son and the Holy Spirit…."

Thankfully, largely due to the influence of the churches and synagogues in Florida, the state did not terminate contact visits on death row.

As traumatic as it is for a parent to have a child incarcerated, the ramifications for the family are that much more devastating if one or both parents are sentenced to prison. There could be a drastic change in the family's economic condition if the incarcerated parent helps to support the household, or a major change in the family parenting structure, or a deep and long-lasting trauma to the rest of the family from the pain of separation from the incarcerated member. It is difficult to imagine all the profound ways a child's life is affected when a loved one goes to prison, especially if the incarcerated family member is a parent.

Some of the concrete effects can be as follows:

+ Increased risk of growing up in poverty.

+ Increased risk of substance abuse.
+ Increased risk of mental illness.
+ Increased risk of acting out.
+ Increased risk of poor performance in school.
+ Increased risk of juvenile delinquency.

As bad as it can be for children in a two-parent family when one parent is incarcerated, it can be even more terrifying when both parents are—or the only parent in a single parent family is—sent to prison. As more mothers are incarcerated, more children from single parent homes are left parentless. The statistics tell a horrifying tale.[7]

+ In 2007, 1.7 million minor children had a parent in prison, an 82% increase since 1991.
+ Approximately half of children with incarcerated parents are under ten years old.
+ 22% of children of state inmates, and 16% of children of federal inmates, are under five years old.
+ One in 43 American children has a parent in prison.
+ One in 15 black children and 1 in 42 Latino children has a parent in prison, compared to 1 in 111 white children.
+ In 2007, there were 809,800 parents incarcerated in U.S. state and federal prisons, an increase of 79% since 1991.
+ In 2007, 52% of all incarcerated men and women were parents.
+ In 2004, 59% of parents in a state correctional facility and 45% of parents in a federal correctional facility reported never having had a personal visit from their child(ren).
+ Children of incarcerated parents typically live too far from their parents to see them very often.
  • In 2004, 62% of parents in a state correctional facility and 84% of parents in a federal correctional facility were housed more than 100 miles from their place of residence at arrest.
  • Only 15% of parents in a state facility and about 5% of

parents in a federal facility were housed fewer than fifty
miles from their place of residence at arrest.

+ Two-thirds of the incarcerated parent population
  is non-white.
+ From 1991 to 2007, the number of incarcerated mothers
  increased by 122%, compared to a rise of 76% for incarcerated fathers.
+ The vast majority of children of male prisoners are living
  with their mothers, but only 37% of the children of incarcerated women are living with their fathers. Most of these
  children are living with grandparents or other relatives.
+ One of every nine women in prison (10.9%) has a child
  living in foster care.

The collateral harm to children from our policies of increased
incarceration of parents is well documented:[8]

+ While many children experience adversity before their
  parents are sent to jail or prison, arresting and incarcerat-
  ing parents introduces trauma and hardship of its own into
  children's lives.
+ Sending parents to jail or prison can disrupt bonds between
  children and their parents, lead to children being separated
  from their siblings, trigger residential instability, and cause
  children to be alienated from friends and ostracized by
  peers.
+ The arrest and incarceration of parents also takes an emotional toll on children, leaving some psychologically traumatized, fearful, anxious, withdrawn, socially isolated,
  grieving, or possibly acting out their feelings in disruptive
  ways.
+ Incarceration of parents can result in enduring social and
  economic hardships for the family members who care for
  their children.
+ Even after accounting for other factors, putting parents in

prison can significantly increase the odds of their children living in chronic poverty, which is associated with a wide range of adverse outcomes for youth.

Children of incarcerated parents also may be susceptible to the fear of growing up to be incarcerated; severe depression and acute separation anxiety; severely impaired emotional development; acute traumatic stress reactions; and survivor guilt. Acting out their feelings in disruptive or destructive ways can include violent behavior, drug abuse, and teen pregnancy.

The alert reader will be quick to recognize that the above descriptions of the collateral damage on children and the anguish to parents precipitated by the incarceration of a loved one spell out losses that are at the level of *trauma*. Chapter 9 of this book dealt with the need of inmates to address the losses and trauma of incarceration. How does a family face the losses and trauma of the incarceration of a loved one?

In his book *Helping Traumatized Families*, Dr. Charles Figley addresses the ability of families to recover from severe stress or trauma. He characterizes healthy families as able to help traumatized members recover from such events as follows:[9]

+ Detection of the signs of stress or trauma. Family members know each other well enough and are present enough to each other to detect when one of the members is suffering from stress or trauma.

+ Confrontation (of the cause of the stressor, not of the family member). This is done by assisting the family member to connect-the-dots from the stress or trauma reaction back to the causative event.

+ Urging retellings of the causative event. Other family members initiate and encourage retelling of the event, as the suffering family member struggles to come to terms with five crucial, almost existential, questions:

- What happened?
- Why did it happen?
- Why did we act as we did when it happened?
- Why have we acted as we have since it happened?
- Would we be able to cope better if it happened again?

+ Facilitating Resolution. Family members suggest and help test bigger picture frames of reference for the event.

Figley notes that the healthy family, the functional coping family, is indicated by the following skills:[10]

+ Acceptance that the family is being forced to handle a highly stressful or traumatic event.
+ Quickly refocusing from a particular family member to a situation that the entire family must cope with.
+ Quickly shift out of blame mode and into problem-solving mode.
+ High level of tolerance and patience with one another in facing the crisis.
+ At least some of the family members are highly expressive of commitment and affection, and the family in general makes extensive use of communication on all matters.
+ Family members have a high sense of cohesion and are willing to share the load to get through taking on duties and burdens that normally fall on others.
+ Access and efficiently utilize resources from within and outside of the family.
+ Refrain from use of alcohol, drugs, or prescriptions as a means to cope with stress.
+ Refrain from physical violence against themselves or members of the family.

In reading the two books by Carol Kent mentioned above, we can readily see how, in combination with their strong Christian faith, the healthy family characteristics noted by Dr. Figley were evident as her family struggled to come to terms with the lifetime imprisonment of her son.

But what happens when the family itself does not have healthy coping abilities? What happens when the traumatic event is that one or both parents are incarcerated? Where is the healing family in that case? Can we look to secular society at large to fill this role? Probably not. Secular society seems at times to exhibit the characteristics of a dysfunctional family, unable to cope with trauma of this sort. For example, in connection with the trauma and stress caused to family members by the incarceration of a loved one, even a parent, the public square seems infested with the language of:

+ Denial: The family of the perpetrator is not allowed to be stressed or traumatized; only the victim of the crime is entitled to that.
+ Blame: The family must have done something wrong or the perpetrator would not have committed a crime; somehow the family members deserve to pay the consequences.
+ Intolerance: Family members of criminals are anathema and are to be treated as lepers.
+ Lack of commitment or affection: Any attempt to ameliorate the effects of incarceration on the family of the perpetrator are met with condemnation, as if those trying to help the family of the inmate are taking the side of the bad guy against the victims of the crime.
+ Lack of communication: Any attempt to give voice to the plight of the family members of the incarcerated is characterized as coddling criminals and their "ilk."
+ Rigidity in social roles: Attempts to restore services or support for family members of the incarcerated are characterized as trying to take away the punishment for the crime—as if the punishment of the whole family is part of the sentence.

In short, at our current stage of social and human development, secular society at large does not have the will to stand-in as a functional coping family for healing the traumatized loved ones of the incarcerated. That plants the hope of children with incarcerated parents firmly in the lap of the family of last resort, the Family of God. The Catholic principle that applies is *solidarity*. From the standpoint of its social teaching, the Church holds families among the highest of social priorities. The Church does this not just for healthy families but to encourage healthy families to reach out in love to those who do not have the blessings they do. As *The Compendium of the Social Doctrines of the Church* puts it:

> *The social subjectivity of the family, both as a single unit and associated in a group, is expressed as well in the demonstrations of solidarity and sharing not only among families themselves but also in the various forms of participation in social and political life.* This is what happens when the reality of the family is founded on love: being born in love and growing in love, solidarity belongs to the family as a constitutive and structural element.
>
> This is a solidarity that can take on the features of service and attention to those who live in poverty and need, to orphans, the handicapped, the sick, the elderly, to those who are in mourning, to those with doubts, to those who live in loneliness or who have been abandoned. It is a solidarity that opens itself to acceptance, to guardianship, to adoption; it is able to bring every situation of distress to the attention of institutions so that, according to their specific competence, they can intervene. (Emphasis in original.)[11]

The Church is telling us that intact families have a Gospel duty to intervene in service and attention to the suffering of those who are "impoverished," "orphaned," "in mourning," "in doubt," "in loneliness," and "abandoned." That list certainly is met by most families with someone in jail or prison. The Church specifically calls our attention to the activities of guardianship and adoption. Just in case we read such words but still do not hear the Church's voice shouting *children of the incarcerated*, Pope John Paul II says it plainly in his Apostolic Exhortation, *On the Role of the Christian Family in the Modern Word (Familiaris Consortio):*

> An even more generous, intelligent, and prudent pastoral commitment, modeled on the Good Shepherd, is called for in the case of families which, often independently of their own wishes and through pressures of various other kinds, find themselves faced by situations that are objectively difficult.
>
> In this regard it is necessary to call special attention to certain particular groups that are more in need not only of assistance but also of more incisive action upon public opinion and especially upon cultural, economic, and juridical structures in order that the profound causes of their needs may be eliminated as far as possible.
>
> Such for example are the families...of those in prison.[12]

How do we Catholic Christians support families who "find themselves faced by situations that are objectively difficult" regarding incarceration of one or more of their members? As is usually the case, the best place to start is from similar things that are already being done and being done well. For example, almost all congregations and Catholic parishes have established programs for outreach to various groups of people who are suffering themselves, who are affected by the suffering of loved ones, or who are caring for suffering loved ones. Yet, many church communities have not considered it necessary to create outreach programs to prisoners and others affected by incarceration, especially the spouses and children.

Successful parish and diocesan outreach programs for pastoral ministry in hospitals and nursing homes can provide a basis for structuring ministries of visitation in jails and prisons. Likewise, experience with ministries of comfort and support to families who have a loved one suffering from cancer or other disease can provide a basis for ministries of comfort and support to families with a loved one in prison. Experience with ministries of bereavement and grief support for families who have lost a loved one can provide a basis for ministries of bereavement and grief support for families whose loved one has received a long or life sentence or a death sentence.

In many cases, the parental rights of the incarcerated parent, even of mothers, are quickly severed by the state (this will be discussed in detail in Chapter 13 of this book). But even when the parental rights have not been severed, incarcerated parents have no control over the detrimental effects of incarceration on their children. Incarcerated parents have no say, for example, about where the prison of their incarceration is located or how their children will be cared for on the outside. For us Catholics who are seeking to engage in Pope John Paul's *generous, intelligent and prudent pastoral commitment, modeled on the Good Shepherd* with respect to children of incarcerated parents, some of the following programs can be effective:

+ Work in cooperation with the prison administration to create structured parent-child visiting programs.
+ Organize community-based mental health and bereavement services outside the prison walls to provide counseling for children of inmates.
+ Work with the prison administration and mental health professionals to design and teach classes for inmates on how to parent effectively, even when one is inside prison.
+ Work with the prison administration to create child friendly visiting areas that will enhance children's experience of visiting their parents.
+ Organize mentoring programs to assist children whose parents are in prison in making positive life choices.
+ Organize caring families to serve as sponsors to assist children monetarily whose parents are in prison primarily because of financial difficulties.
+ Organize church homework and tutoring centers to assist children of parents in prison in core math and language skills.

Family visitation with loved ones in prison is crucial to holding families together and preparing inmates for successful re-entry. Until recently, it has been very difficult to assess the national situation with respect to prison visitation policies. Policies can be significantly different from one state to another. Even in states with large systems, the actual implementation of standardized rules can range across a wide spectrum from prison to prison. And within a state, the policies can vary widely from one county jail to another. The new development of contracting with for-profit companies to run some jails and prisons has only exacerbated this problem.

Three young lawyers from Yale Law School have published a comprehensive compilation of national practices in "Prison Visitation Policies: A Fifty-State Survey":[13]

> This memorandum presents a summary of the findings from a survey of prison visitation policies in the fifty states and in the system run by the Federal Bureau of Prisons. We embarked on the project with two primary goals. First, we wanted to provide for relatively easy state-by-state comparisons across a group of common visitation-related categories. Second, we hoped to identify similarities and differences across states in the categories we tracked....
>
> The lives of prisoners and their families are deeply affected by visitation policies and, to date, there has been no comprehensive effort to compare these policies across all of the fifty states. We believe the dataset presented here is the first of its kind to explore the contours of how prison administrators use their discretion in prescribing visitation policies. This comparative analysis has many uses, both in identifying best practices and in uncovering policies that warrant concern as a matter of law or policy.

Such a resource can be very valuable for us Catholic volunteers working through parish outreach programs to improve visitation for inmates and their families. Such efforts can also benefit from the models available from programs that are already up and running. Many have been started in just the last few years. For example, in the effort to create child-friendly visiting areas that will enhance children's experience of visiting their incarcerated parents and help the children's caregivers know how to handle parental incarceration, *Sesame Street* has produced *Little Children, Big Challenges: Incarceration*. A written booklet summarizing this program, *A Guide to Support Parents and Caregivers*, is available online.[14] The actual production of the program can be performed in prison visiting parks, even by actors clad as Sesame Street characters. Just such a production was recently conducted by staff (with nametags instead of costumes) on a visitation weekend at the visiting park of Florida's highest security prison, Florida State Prison in Starke, Florida. It included the participation of the wardens and chaplains.

Bridges of America, a non-profit organization that is a leading provider of substance abuse treatment and work release programs in the State of Florida, whose mission includes helping families survive incarceration, has partnered with others to offer the *Little Children, Big Challenges: Incarceration* program for families of inmates in Central Florida. Their President and CEO, Ms. Lori Constantino-Brown, described the program as follows:[15]

> As we all know, it is difficult to maintain family relationships when an incarceration is in the mix. For the inmates, by the time they are imprisoned, they have often damaged their relationships with family members. And for family members, it may be tough to make the long trips for visits or there may be resentments that now-single mothers or dads are raising children alone. But for the youngest family members, the incarceration of a parent or another trusted and beloved family member can be a time of frustration, loneliness, and sometimes embarrassment....
>
> We are thrilled to be working with Sesame Workshop and deeply honored to be one of the locations at which *Little Children, Big Challenges: Incarceration* is being piloted. Family sup-

port and reunification is critical to the reduction of recidivism and this speaks directly to caring for the needs of the youngest victims of incarceration.

The Florida Department of Corrections announced in an August 24, 2013 press release that it was deploying the *Little Children, Big Challenges: Incarceration* program:[16]

> The resource helps children, inmates, families, and caregivers cope with the reality of incarceration.
>
> In Florida, there are 64,475 children under 18 who have an incarcerated parent. Nationwide the number of children with an incarcerated parent has increased nearly 80% in the past 20 years. Nearly 2.7 million children have a parent in state or federal prison, yet few resources exist to support young children and families with this life-changing circumstance....
>
> The Florida Department of Corrections is the third largest corrections' system in the United States, with over 100,000 inmates and over 120,000 offenders who are serving either probation or parole. Those with family support are less likely to re-offend and re-enter the corrections' system.

The *Little Children, Big Challenges: Incarceration* materials are permeated with the healthy family coping characteristics noted by Dr. Figley above. Human experience indicates that family-to-family mentoring of how to apply such methods in the grind of day-in and day-out family life is crucial to a family's success. That kind of mentoring, from a faith standpoint, can be an excellent way for Catholic families to live out the challenge presented to us by the *Compendium of the Social Doctrine of the Church* and by Pope John Paul II in *On the Role of the Christian Family in the Modern Word (Familiaris Consortio)*.

The new interest of state and federal governments in strengthening family systems for inmates is not solely based on faith principles but also on the burgeoning costs of incarceration. As I noted earlier in this book, the current system of mass incarceration in the United

States is not economically sustainable. Yet, there are still long-standing practices that work at tremendous cross-purposes to the stated goals of successfully reducing our prison populations and expenditures. For example, the *Little Children, Big Challenges: Incarceration* materials describe the importance of "televisits" between children and incarcerated parents in cases where the child is not able to physically visit the parent in prison. It is more than unfortunate that such video-conference meetings between parent and child require a level of technological capabilities that most prisons do not have at this time.

If a child is so young or so far away from the incarcerated parent as to make physical visits impracticable and if televisits are not feasible, the *Sesame Street* materials recommend frequent phone calls between the child and the incarcerated parent. In much of the U.S., however, that is easier said than done because of the unjust telephone charges for phone calls with inmates. For decades, the exorbitant charges for family phone calls with prisoners have been one of the most effective ways to punish inmates' families for guilt by association. The rates are so ludicrous that they amount to punitive pecuniary fines. As a society, we readily acknowledge that it is barbaric to punish the family of an inmate for guilt by association.[17] Yet in practice, that is exactly what we do under different nomenclature, e.g., "inmate telephone rate charges."

It can be cheaper for a person outside prison to call Singapore from their cell phone than it is to speak to someone in prison in the U.S. For a 15-minute call, an inmate's family could be charged more than $17. But this is not punishment just for punishment's sake. According to an article posted by Bloomberg News, this immoral practice is all about private profit for Wall Street tycoons.[18] The article notes that the two companies that dominate over 80% of the market for inmate phone calls are both owned by New York private equity firms.

One of the most visible entities in fighting for affordable inmate family phone calls is Citizens United for the Rehabilitation of Errants (CURE), a non-profit grassroots organization founded in Texas in 1972 by Charlie and Pauline Sullivan, two Catholic lay people.[19] CURE became a national presence in 1985 and grew into an international movement in 2004. Not surprisingly, the movement's mission is simple and, as stated, is consistent with Catholic teaching:

> We believe that prisons should be used only for those who absolutely must be incarcerated and that those who are incarcerated should have all of the resources they need to turn their lives around.

Although CURE is active on many important prison and jail issues, it is a critical participant in the consortium fighting to correct the greed-driven injustice of inmate telephone call charges.[20] In large part due to that campaign, the Federal Communication Commission's proposed rulemaking process[21] moved into the phase of a workshop in Washington, DC, on July 10, 2013, in order to collect information in the areas of Consumers and Public Policy, State Actions to Reform Inmate Calling Services, and the Mechanisms and Systems to Provide Inmate Calling Services.[22]

The battle to arrive at fair and just inmate telephone call charges is a model for the efforts to correct injustices in other aspects of our prison and jail systems. Frequently, the reason that things are structured as they are has to do with money going into somebody's pocket. The efforts made by people of good will to change the system to work more justly are never attacked for the real reason: the loss of profits to a particular interest group. No one ever says in the public square that such-and-such a change to our criminal justice system must not be made because it will crimp the profits of some Wall Street tycoons.

Instead, the proposed improvements to our criminal justice system are usually criticized as changes that are *soft on crime* or *coddle criminals*. As I will discuss in detail in Chapter 15 of this book, vested financial interests are part of the reason why improvements to our criminal justice system are so difficult to make. To accomplish meaningful change, the financial interests underlying the injustices must be painstakingly documented and exposed to the scrutiny of daylight. The tedious political and legal mechanisms necessary to correct the process must be faithfully followed through to completion by a broad coalition of like-minded people.

Same Time Next Year

For over a dozen years, my annual rituals include February, April, and May pilgrimages to the discount stores across rural north central Florida from Jacksonville to Lake City, to Gainesville to Starke. Each year I need about 1,400 Valentines' Day Cards. Mothers' Day Cards—about 900. Fathers' Day Cards—about 700.

Prison regulations are strict. No sparkly stuff. No ribbons or fancy whatnots. No cards with 3-D popups or glued inserts. No plastic. No metal. No foil. No wood. And no envelopes that are not white, light yellow, or light blue.

No cards with alcohol or drinking themes. No cards with pictures of young children. No cards that are overly romantic or suggestive.

It gets harder every year to find cards that meet the prison limitations—even for Mothers' Day. So every year, I greedily hunt down hundreds of 50 cent cards in the special bins across Florida's less-travelled county roads.

Timing is everything. If one shows up just a day or two after the cards have been put out on shelves at a particular store, there can be eight or twelve or even twenty-four of a kind. I still remember vividly an awkward moment with my then high-school senior son. He was keeping me company on such a pilgrimage from store-to-store when I unexpectedly hit the jackpot in the discount card section of a remote shop. As I gleefully filled my hand-basket with dozens of sets of twelve each of prison-qualified Valentines' Day Cards, I must have looked a bit like Blackbeard the pirate scooping up gold coins.

My son lovingly looked at me with concern, and asked: "Dad, are you sure this is spiritually healthy?"

Be that as it may, there is nothing quite like the experience of stepping to the checkout line in a discount store with hundreds of cards for one of those three holidays.

"How many mothers have you got?" is among the politest comments I have received from disgruntled clerks who must hand scan the bar code on the back of every card individually.

The comments about Valentines' Day Cards usually amount to statements of disbelief that a short, round, post-middle-aged man would have so many women to send cards to.

Invariably, I use the opportunity to mention that the cards are for the men on Florida's death row to send to their loved ones. That is guaranteed to kill the conversation for a moment or two. Then, it gets really interesting, and many of the store patrons move closer to listen in.

"So, you are against the victims and in favor of the criminals!"

"No." I always make eye contact and speak gently. "Actually I have become aware that the many victims of these horrible crimes frequently include the innocent family members of the perpetrator. So, the cards are for them—the children, the mothers, the fathers, the brothers and sisters, the wives—most of whom have done nothing wrong."

"So, how come they get to be victims?"

"Nobody goes to prison alone. They always take their family to prison with them. And when a man goes to death row, he takes his family to death row with him."

"But his crime victim is not getting to send any cards to her mom or her young'uns or her husband. What about that!"

"You're right. And I cannot fix that, although I would if I could. So, I do the little bit that I can by trying to relieve the suffering of some of the other innocent victims of the crime."

A few clerks register indifference. Some simply say that they are totally against what I am doing but have to check me out because they need their job. Some clerks have thrown the cards back at me and refused to check me out. One left the premises after telling her manager that either she or I would have to leave the store. There is no doubt in my mind that such strong emotional reactions are rooted in the horror of the personal loss of a loved one to a violent crime. Our society has not even tried to learn how to bring healing to those who have suffered such a loss.

There are some clerks, however, who express surprise that people on death row even have families and loved ones. They seem a bit shaken at that, and then are fine scanning the cards.

Several times each year, as I leave a store and tote my bags to the parking lot, someone will approach me from behind. A man, an older woman, a couple who appear married. They always speak softly and deliberatively, as though pushing out the words with great effort.

"Our son is in prison….""My dad is in prison….""My brother is in prison…." "My grandfather is in prison….""My mother is in prison….""Our daughter is in prison…." These are all followed by a heartfelt sigh: "Thank you."

In discussions of those who are severely affected by our incarceration policies, even more invisible than the families of inmates are the men and women who stand side-by-side with the inmates inside the prison and jail fences: the "corrections officers," also called "peace officers," and sometimes (usually by people who haven't been in a prison) "guards." It is not unusual for career officers inside prisons to speak of their retirement date as *my EOS*, prison slang for *my end of sentence*. I was standing on the quarterdeck in a maximum security wing of Florida State Prison when the following exchange took place:

> The blue-clad inmate, standing shackled and back-cuffed next to the Sargent's desk, is being moved to another wing. That is a routine procedure that occurs dozens of times per day in a prison of 1,400 solitary confinement cells. The brown-clad sergeant stands next to him, wing-keys firmly in hand, waiting for the hall officer to unlock the wing door from the outside. There has been an incident on another wing, so the two will be waiting for a while before the wing door can be opened. The inmate and the officer have known each other for years and are enjoying a little bit of smack-talk to kill the time.
>
> Inmate: "Man, I got another dime to do in this hole 'fore I gets home. Must be nice you gettin' home every night for a hot cooked."
>
> Sergeant: "I've been in here longer than you and have another dime-and-a-half before I EOS out of here. Give me any lip and I'll trade places with you, so I can leave for good a nickel 'fore you do."
>
> Inmate: "No way, man. Bad 'nough livin' here. But working here, too? I ain't 'bout dat."
>
> Sergeant: "Yeah," laughing heartily, "That would be real punishment."

WHEN WE VISIT JESUS IN PRISON

When society talks about the stresses of prison conditions, the heat, the humidity, the noise, the fear, the whole sordid picture of human suffering that exists inside the barb wire fences, the discussions rarely touch upon the uniformed human beings who must endure such conditions. The ones who hold the keys, the officers and staff who spend their days and nights subjected to those stresses.

One of the extreme stresses for corrections officers, especially in the South, is the intense summer heat and humidity inside prisons without air-conditioning. Corrections officers in Texas even announced in a press release their intent to join in a lawsuit by inmates against the state for inhumane conditions of heat and humidity:[23]

> The union that represents Texas' correctional officers on Thursday announced its support for lawsuits filed over the deaths of at least 14 convicts in sweltering state prisons, saying the lockups should be cooled to relieve unbearable and dangerous conditions....
>
> McGiverin [attorney for the inmates] said that many of the older Texas prisons are actually cooler than the dozens of newer ones built during the 1980s and early 1990s that are basically "a series of hot boxes for people to bake in."
>
> Both he and Lowry [representative of the officers] criticized prison officials for their recent decision to spend more than $700,000 on six new pig barns equipped with a "climate-controlled environment" to ensure the hogs don't overheat or get cold in the winter. The barns will be for mothers to birth their piglets, officials said.
>
> "It's despicable that state officials care more for their livestock than their people," McGiverin said. "The management of this system is grossly indifferent.... It's a travesty."

The Austin *American-Statesman* article mentions that Texas is claiming that prisons in Louisiana, Mississippi, Florida, and Alabama are also not cooled. This "everybody else is doing it" defense may or may not carry the day. The article points out that monitoring has revealed Louisiana prison heat indexes as high as 110 degrees in July and early August, and "a temperature log at the Hutchins State Jail outside Dallas showed heat indexes of 150 degrees July 19, 2011, among other readings reaching well over 100 degrees at other times that same day."

Meanwhile, the death row inmates in Louisiana's Angola Prison have also sued in federal court over the heat, claiming that "the heat index—or how hot 'it feels'—on Death Row reached 195 degrees Fahrenheit on more than one occasion in the summer of 2011," and that in the summer of 2012, "the index was above 126 degrees on 85 days between May and August."[24] It defies logic that anyone would try to justify such inhumane working conditions. Yet the very same politicians who pound their fists about law and order will turn around, without missing a beat, and deprecate the officers who must guard the criminals inside the prisons. Does any elected official have the courage to say that although corrections officers are inside a building or a fence and not out in the streets, they are not sitting at plush desks in some air-conditioned state office park like most elected officials are? It is not unusual, especially in election years, for prison staff and volunteers to shake their heads at the reporting of inane political statements made by legislative or gubernatorial wannabes, sighing knowingly to each other: "Obviously they have never worked in a place like this."

What is it like to spend every day in an environment where letting your guard down and trusting a human being to be truly human can cost you your life? What is it like to be on the line every day, without any weapon for self-protection, face-to-face with the people who society does not trust with freedom? What is it like to be the daily verbal punching bag for the inevitable inmate rage, spawned by inadequate toilet paper rations and cheap by-products served as disgusting, barely edible food? What is the stress like when one must be humane but can be fired for being friendly?

In a quarter-century of prison ministry, the overwhelming majority of officers that I have met are people who have entered their profession for the right reasons and with the goal of serving professionally, competently, and safely. Some have described their job as, "I'm

WHEN WE VISIT JESUS IN PRISON

here to make sure the inmates are safe while they pay their debt to society, and to keep society safe by making sure they are in here and not out there."

That approach does not set well enough for some politicians, who mount their campaigns by stoking vengeance in the hearts of voters. As will be discussed in Chapter 16 of this book, there is a strong neo-Calvinistic vein in American society today that believes loss of freedom is not punishment enough, that prisoners must suffer as much as possible during their incarceration as well. Politicians who cater to that vengeance stir up the crowds against reasonable food costs, reasonable activities, and any form of rehabilitation.

The inmates who are angry at being used this way by politicians and society have no one to take it out on except the officers who share their space. Then, when the inmates strike back at society, which always means striking back at the officers, the very same politicians act as though it is the corrections officers and prison staff who are the problem. A constant among corrections officers I know is feeling unappreciated for their contribution to criminal justice and feeling like a convenient whipping boy for both the inmates and the politicos.

It is our elected officials who have engineered mass incarceration and have designed a system of criminal justice that no one can afford to pay for. It is our legislatures and governors who have mandated that prison food be served at costs less than what is paid to feed animals. It is our politicians campaigning for reelection who have promised to do the impossible in terms of ending crime and then, after being elected, beat down the corrections officers and staff because the impossible cannot be done.

The job stress on police on the streets has been well-studied and documented. A significant factor in the occupational stress of police work has been identified as the job interference caused by politics.[25] My experience is that the same can be said of the work done by the officers who walk the beats inside our prisons and jails.

So how does the Catholic volunteer in prison and jail ministry serve the needs of the staff as well as the inmates? I have asked officers and staff that very question. Here are some answers.

✦ **Do not take security personally.** Security is not about the volunteer; it has nothing to do with whether the officer thinks the volunteer is trustworthy or a good Christian. Security is about security which, by definition, means that everyone is to be treated the same: as a potential risk for introducing contraband or weapons inside the secure perimeter of the facility.

Volunteers should never react to security with indignation or disrespect. In fact, they should be as helpful as possible. For example, if one usually carries a pyx with consecrated hosts into the facility, do not begrudgingly wait for the officer to ask for you to open it. Present the pyx and open it for the officer while explaining what the contents are. In non-Catholic parts of the country, it may also be a good idea to ask, "Do you want me to remove the hosts so you can see the metal bottom?" Usually the inspecting officer will say, "no thank, you." But if the pyx is large and the officer is not used to Catholic practices, it is much better for the volunteer to respectfully move the consecrated hosts into the other hand than for the officer to unceremoniously dump them on the table.

I recently stood at the shakedown table (search station) for entry into a maximum security prison while an 88-year-old retired Catholic bishop was being cleared.

"I'm sorry, bishop," the Catholic sergeant apologized softly in the midst of the pat-down search. "I have known you my whole life and you are here every week. But I've got to check you every time."

"Absolutely," replied the bishop, as though simply speaking the obvious. "I would be upset if you didn't do your job. You are keeping all of us safe, including me, by doing your job thoroughly. I do not want to be surprised by a weapon that someone else smuggled inside!"

Officers do not appreciate volunteers acting as if the officers are ogres just because they are doing their job. Show appreciation for their conscientiousness.

✦ **Do not expect special treatment.** Sometimes a volunteer thinks that because they are at a facility frequently or on a regular basis, security should cut them a break. This indicates the volunteer's lack of understanding of basic security analysis. In fact, the security reality is just the opposite. The more often someone enters a facility, the more familiar they are with the security and operational procedures and the longer and more significant their relationships are with the inmates and the staff. That increases their threat level as a security risk. That familiarity and comfort makes it more likely that they may try to pull off something just once, like smuggling in a cell phone so a prisoner can make a "very important" phone call.

It is not security's job to assume that a volunteer has the best of intentions as demonstrated by long-term commitment. Security's job is to assume that a volunteer has been patiently faking the best of intentions to build up a comfort level until the right time that will allow them to assist in an escape attempt.

✦ **Do not expect things to stay the same.** One of the greatest vulnerabilities of security is familiarity. As people enter a prison or jail multiple times they develop a familiarity with the steps and the procedures. That allows for human ingenuity to fashion ways to defeat the system. The counter measure is to routinely and systematically change procedures. So, for example, on Monday only plastic bags could be used to bring in holy cards. On Tuesday only paper bags could be used and plastic bags are now contraband. On Wednesday no holy cards can be carried in at all, but must be mailed to the chapel instead.

Is there a constitutional right for Catholic inmates to have holy cards which are not laminated?[26] Absolutely. Does the U.S. Constitution require that holy cards be allowed to enter the prison by the means that are easiest for the Catholic volunteer? Not at all. The convenience of the volunteer is not even relevant operationally, let alone constitutionally.

✦ **Do not be impatient.** Prisons and jails are top-down hierarchies that respond to power. That means when we Catholic volunteers enter a prison or jail we are entering into powerlessness in a very meaningful and tangible way. Assume that two deputy-sheriffs in uniform from a local county, two high-level administrators from the prison system's regional office, two lawyers making legal visits from a nearby city, and two Catholic volunteers with their pyxes for Communion rounds are all in line to enter a prison. Assume that the volunteers arrived first. Who will enter the prison last? The volunteers.

We volunteers rarely have any power; we are last on the power list. When Jesus said the last will be first, he was not talking about the security gate at a prison. Equally powerless are inmate's visitors who are family and friends. As between visitors and volunteers, it will usually be first-come, first served. But even in this case, the gate sergeant may put the volunteer behind the visitors. The Catholic volunteer smiles and steps aside to make way for the other to go first.

Waiting on Jesus

Many years ago, I found myself standing in the hot August sun at a Florida panhandle prison, staring at a locked gate that separated the yard from the chapel. Forty-some inmates stood on the other side of the gate waiting for an officer to open the lock so they could process into the chapel for the regularly scheduled weekly bible study. At the time, I was at the tail end of a hot-shot legal career in which anyone responsible for making me wait, let alone wait in sweltering heat and humidity with hungry mosquitos, would pay dearly. It was fortunate for me that God intervened.

My silent prayer—basically, "God, you have got to be kidding!"— was reframed by our Father in heaven as a prayer for patience. The answer to prayer came in the thought, "See those inmates in blue? They have to deal with this all the time. They are watching you very closely to see how you handle it. Be sure in your own reactions to model the words and deeds of my Son. And oh—by the way—welcome to working for me."

When a burly sergeant who had been otherwise engaged finally showed up with the key after almost an hour, he grunted, "Been waiting long?"

"Not at all, sir." I responded, pointing to the sweat drenched men in blue. "Time goes fast when you're waiting on Jesus."

✦ **Do not ask the officers "why?"** When an inmate asks me why a particular rule prohibits what seems to be a harmless activity, I answer, "Don't know. Nobody asked my opinion."

I know that must be how an officer feels when we volunteers ask questions about rules and procedures that have been handed down from on high. "Why do we have to leave the chapel during lunch?" "Why does the system do a master count statewide during my RCIA class?" "Why are real turkey legs not allowed for the Thanksgiving meal?" Why? Why? Why?

Surely the officer wants to say, "Why are you asking me?" But that would not help with maintaining the sense of authority that must be maintained to do the job. So, not surprisingly, the answer is usually a bit brusque. What did we expect?

In all honesty, the dumping of such a question on a line officer is really just a thinly veiled gripe, a statement in question form that shows that we disagree with the rule or decision. Nobody cares if we disagree, and the response will usually convey that, at least viscerally.

✦ **Do not make the officer's job harder.** The officer has clocked in and will clock out. This is his or her job. It is not a social event. It is not a charity event. This is where they work. Officers will know in short order which volunteers make their job more difficult and which volunteers are alert to the situations around them in order to be as little trouble as possible.

My advice to new volunteers is to always be a good guest. Be flexible and be attentive to your surroundings. Always try to offer to do what officers will have to ask you to do. So, for example, if you are walking across the compound to the chapel and from around the corner come three officers escorting an unruly inmate, you do not need to wait to be ordered to step away from their path. The astute volunteer will begin to move out of their path while saying, "Sir, would you like me to move over here?"

We volunteers need to evidence an awareness that we are in a prison. In prison, people can be dangerous. We need to make sure we are not a concern to the officers, especially when the staff is handling a crisis situation.

+ **Do not forget that officers are human beings.** Most written materials on the pastoral needs of staff in prisons and jails drive home the point that even though someone is wearing a uniform he or she is still a human being. That reality should be chock full of meaning for the volunteer in Catholic prison ministry.

Human beings have good days and bad days, days of saintly patience and days where every single little thing went wrong before they even arrived at work. There are children with problems, elderly parents with illness, marriages that are struggling, losses being grieved like the death of a loved one, financial and personal pressures, etc.

No volunteer should be interrogating an officer about the state of their personal life. What we should do is always give officers and other staff the benefit of the doubt and treat and greet them as we would want to be treated and greeted on an off day. Rarely will anyone respond badly to a genuine smile and genuine warmth.

We volunteers must maintain a professional relationship with staff. But that still allows, over time, for sincere questions, like: "How are you today, sir?" "How was your day off, ma'am?" Or in cases where one knows about an event, "How was your daughter's wedding, Lieutenant?" "How is your grandson doing in the hospital, Captain?" Or, respectfully and with a smile of course, "I was thinking of you Saturday when Notre Dame whooped your team!" A prison is a professional work environment and warm interaction proper to such an environment will usually be well received.

+ **Do not forget that officers are spiritual beings.** It is important for we Catholic volunteers in prison ministry to govern our actions and words inside the fences in a way that will make it comfortable for officers and staff to approach us about spiritual things. If an officer shares a personal crisis, like a sick child or dying parent, we should be ready to provide comfort, hope, and reassurance based on our faith.

We can offer to pray for the officer or the personal issue they share with us, and when appropriate we can offer to pray with the officer, either on the spot or separately at a different time. Many prison staff will appreciate our offer to put their loved one on a prayer list at church or our suggestion to find direction and encouragement from a particular Bible story or Psalm. In such situations where we are reaching out to either a non-Catholic Christian or a person of different beliefs, a maximum of sensitivity to those differences and to the comfort of the other is in order. This is not the time for us to score theological or doctrinal points. It is a time to gently apply the healing balm of our faith to the wounds of all God's people. Not infrequently, after a person has experienced unconditional love and acceptance in such a crisis, a time will come later, in the calm after the storm, when questions will be presented to us volunteers about what we believe and why we believe it.

There may well be times when a particular officer or staff member is manipulating schedules or security to interfere with delivery of Catholic services inside the prison or jail. There may even be rare instances of abusive language directed at us based on misunderstandings or prejudice about the nature of our Catholic faith. These events must be dealt with, of course, but not right then and there. In fact, any attempt to correct officers or staff on the spot can be interpreted as insubordination and can result in our permanent expulsion from the facility. That does not help those we have come to serve.

The wiser more effective way of dealing with such events is for us to return to our vehicle or home and write down exactly what happened, what was said, and who was involved. Then, that information should be provided to our pastoral authority or supervisor so it can be handled by those Church officials charged with the duty of protecting the Church's prison ministry. The problem may be severe. In situations where security is being manipulated to deny Catholic inmates' access to the Holy Sacrifice of the Mass, lawsuits in federal court may be necessary. But such decisions are made in bishops' conference rooms, not at prison security gates.

Catholic parishes should not overlook the opportunity to minister to the officers and staff of prisons and jails specifically. Many parishes have extensive experience with ministries that support health care professionals, first responders, teachers, and many other workers. Those models can translate well to ministry for corrections officers and corrections medical staff.

Brothers and Sisters at the Doors

Father Aldrich was no pansy. His towering Teutonic frame dominates my memories of Franciscan minor seminary. He was passionate about Truth.

"What is the most important job a friar can have in this monastery?" he asked one morning.

"Guardian," blurted one classmate.

"Disciplinarian," offered the next.

"Cook," guessed another.

"Wrong," Fr. Aldrich shook off each offering like a catcher waiving off signs from a rookie pitcher. Finally, we could guess no more. It seemed we had exhausted the list. "It is Brother Porter," he said. "Brother Porter sets the tone for the whole monastery every day. His smile and gentle manner can make the day a pleasant one for every person here. His is the most important task of them all. A holy Brother Porter can make this a holy building."

We were sure the priest was joking. None of us had even thought to include the gentle brown-clad Friar whose duty was simply to open the doors to chapel, to chow, to study hall, to guests. Truth eludes the undiscerning eye—especially truth hidden in plain sight.

As many doors as there were in the monastery, there were far fewer than the number of doors in a men's prison I visit regularly. And, at every single locked prison door is stationed a corrections officer, a Brother or Sister Porter. One of them is the first one to greet me at the entrance to each building, each yard, each wing.

The sergeant at the prison entrance is responsible for every single person or article that moves in or out of that prison all day long. The stories of ingenious attempts to smuggle weapons and escape paraphernalia into prisons are legion. Yet this officer never fails to greet me warmly, even encouragingly. When I asked him once how he maintains an upbeat attitude in the face of constant stress, he smiles: "I believe in the power of positive thinking. You have a good day."

The officer with the key for the fence tunnel to death row must make a few hundred foot trips per day, from the guard shack to the gate. Rain. Heat. It doesn't matter. Yet, she's always glad to be of help, always has a friendly word. At the other end of the tunnel is the building control officer. She never fails to smile and wish me a good morning.

The wing officers are inundated with routine tasks. Endless paperwork is the least of it. Nurses must be escorted, inmates pulled for showers, psychiatric or medical appointments. Food and cleaning articles must be distributed, laundry collected. In the middle of it all, I show up to distribute Communion.

"Good afternoon, chap," smiles a wing sergeant. "Thank you for coming today."

On entering another wing, I ask if it's a good time. "Any time you come to bring God to these men is a good time," responds the desk officer warmly.

The higher the level of wing security, the greater the imposition of my presence on the workday of the officers. One wing requires an officer to be physically present with me the entire time. If several men need to talk or pray, that can chew up valuable time from the officer's day.

"I'm sorry this took so long," I apologize to the officer who has patiently escorted me through a very high security wing. "It seemed like every single man was trying to connect with God today."

"I'm not surprised," he smiles back. "I'm not just standing here observing, you know. I'm praying for you and each man as you talk. It's incredible to watch my prayers being answered just a few feet away!"

Some days I wonder if gatekeepers like these could turn even a prison into a holy place.

Quite aside from the typical pastoral needs of inmates in general, there are categories of inmates with very specific needs. In the next chapter we begin to look at some of those groupings and their particular pastoral needs.

PART III

SPECIFIC
PASTORAL NEEDS

PART III

SPECIFIC
PASTORAL NEEDS

"*I have a dogmatic certainty: God is in every person's life. God is in everyone's life. Even if the life of a person has been a disaster, even if it is destroyed by vices, drugs, or anything else—God is in this person's life. You can, you must, try to seek God in every human life. Although the life of a person is a land full of thorns and weeds, there is always a space in which the good seed can grow. You have to trust God.*"

Pope Francis[1]

CHAPTER 11

Pastoral Needs of Newly Arrived Inmates, Inmates Facing Long or Life Sentences, and Inmates Facing Serious Illness and/or Death

Part III of this book moves to a quicker tempo, with a survey of some of the specific needs of various categories of inmates that volunteers will encounter inside the prison fences. Some needs are a function of medical and mental conditions. Others are driven by the specifics of inmates' sentence or familial relationships. Regardless of such specific needs of a particular inmate over time, however, all of them will have experienced their reception into the massive penal system. When we volunteers in Catholic prison ministry are serving at local jails or state reception centers, we will constantly encounter newly arrived inmates. What can we expect to be specific needs of male and female inmates who have recently arrived? To prepare for the answers to that question, we might imagine ourselves facing the same situation.

It is important to distinguish the adjustments to prison life over the long haul from the adjustments that are faced by those who are newly arriving into the system. Usually prison life does not start with being escorted to a long-term prison facility. Most often, an inmate, after arrest and booking, is held at the *local pokey*, the jail in or near the courthouse where he or she will be tried and sentenced. If found guilty, the inmate's charges could result in a sentence of six months at that jail, or ten, twenty, thirty years or even life in a state or federal prison. As a volunteer imagines being in that first jail cell, facing that uncertainty, what do they think would be hardest to deal with? Above and beyond the physical environment of the jail itself, what would be the most difficult emotions to face?

The two most prevalent emotions of inmates at the intake end of the justice system seem to be *anger* and *fear*. This is basically true regardless of whether the inmate is predominantly pro-social or is in fact fully invested in criminal thinking. We will first look at the predominantly pro-social inmate sitting in jail, awaiting trial or sentencing. In our example, this inmate is a college student who is charged with a DUI homicide after a sorority party.

+ **Anger at oneself.** The emotion of anger at oneself is pervasive. The self-accusatory question "How did I allow this to happen?" can be wielded by the predominantly pro-social inmate who made a bad or stupid mistake. Telltale signs of this anger at self are revealed in statements such as, "I should have known better" or "What was I thinking?" Guilt that fuels this anger could be expressed, as: "How could I do this to my parents?" or "What will my younger sister think? She has always looked up to me."

+ **Anger at the system.** This anger may be aimed at a much broader target than the justice system. In this example of a college student who committed a DUI homicide after a sorority party, the anger may be directed at the educational system which allows such parties, the *Greek system* which the inmate feels created the pressure on her to participate in such parties, and on the justice system which does not seem to understand that she is a good person and never meant to hurt anyone.

WHEN WE VISIT JESUS IN PRISON

+ **Anger at God.** There is no shortage of anger at God expressed by those in the intake cells of the criminal justice system. The rage at God can be directed at the existence of freewill in the inmate: "Why did God let me do this?" Or at freewill in general: "Why did God let Eve bite that apple?" It can be directed at God's laws of physics that govern material reality: "Why did God let the accident happen?" Or even at God's mistake in the creation of the inmate: "Why did God make me this way? Why couldn't he have made me different?"

+ **Fear of being convicted.** Frequently sharing cell space with anger is the inmate's consuming fear of being convicted of the crime. Even a predominantly pro-social inmate may be terrified by the effects a conviction will have on their life. In this example of a college student who committed a DUI homicide after a sorority party, such effects are real. A conviction, with or without a prison sentence, could render her life's dreams to rubbish. The consequences are real. The fear of those consequences can be severely debilitating.

+ **Fear of receiving a long sentence.** Most inmates sitting in jail pending trial can rationalize that a sentence in jail of a few months, maybe even of a year, would not be too bad. The logic is basically, "I have already done one month in here. I just have to do that again a few times." The prospect of a long prison sentence is a whole different story. The fears are real. "How long will it take for my boyfriend/girlfriend/spouse to drop me and move on?" "How long will it take before my family starts to forget me?" In this example of a college student who committed a DUI homicide after a sorority party, there is the additional terror of being sentenced to prison as a young woman. Those fears are real, as well, and will be discussed in chapter 13 on the special pastoral needs of women in prison.

+ **Fear of being abandoned by God.** This is a complicated fear because it expresses itself in at least two ways. The first manifestation may be expressed as a fear that by receiving a guilty verdict and a prison sentence, the inmate will deserve it *when* God abandons her. A second manifestation can be expressed as the erroneous belief that the inmate will only receive a guilty verdict and a prison sentence *if* God has abandoned her. In the powerful maelstrom of swirling emotions in the jailhouse cell pending trial, these two conflicting fears can stand side-by-side. In this example of a college student who committed a DUI homicide after a sorority party, one can easily understand how the young inmate might have both these fears.

+ **Fear of hoping to be set free and then being sentenced to prison.** In my experience, many inmates report that during the time pending trial, there is a battle raging in their emotions. There can be a deep-seated desire to believe they will be found not guilty and set free. This desire is matched by the dark fear of daring to hope for such an outcome and then facing the disillusionment of being found guilty and sentenced to prison. The bitterness of such a disappointment is so repugnant that any sense of hope is shadowed by that fear of loss. This is especially the case if the inmate will experience a prison sentence as proof of God's abandonment, the same God that is the source of their hope.

+ **Anger and fear at the unknown.** It is well known that studies show the stress levels of the inhabitants of World War II London diminished after the actual bombings of the city commenced. Fear of what the bombings might be like was a greater stress than dealing with the actual bombings.

Human flesh *should* quiver at the specter of sitting in a jail cell pondering the anger and fears that I have just listed. It is understandable that the inmate in such a situation may find themselves fearful of how this horrible event will turn out and angry about having to wait to learn the outcome. The stress can be crushing. In this example of a college student who committed a DUI homicide after a sorority party, the young woman may not possess coping skills sufficient to handle this pressure.

Now let us investigate how these fears and angers play out in the jail cell pending trial for another young woman inmate who is in fact fully invested in criminal thinking. Let us take the example of a thirty-two-year-old middle-class teacher who has been charged with statutory rape after being impregnated by her fourteen-year-old student.

+ **Anger at oneself.** The emotion of anger at oneself is pervasive. The self-accusatory question is not "How did I allow this to happen?" but rather "How did I allow myself to get caught?" Telltale signs of this anger at self for failing to keep the crime undetected are revealed in statements such as, "I should have waited to get pregnant until he was old enough to marry me."

+ **Anger at the system.** This anger may be aimed at a heartless and stupid system that fails to recognize that the inmate is not bound by the petty mores of society. It may be directed at the justice system that does not seem to understand she is a good person and did nothing wrong, that she has not hurt anyone but has made her victim's (she calls him her "lover's") life better.

+ **Anger at God.** The rage at God in this case can be directed at the unfairness of allowing the inmate to meet her soul mate before he is old enough for society to accept the reality of their eternal love. The inmate's anger is not at God's mistake in the creation of the inmate but at God's mistake in allowing society to be so blind and unjust.

+ **Fear of being convicted.** This inmate may also have a consuming fear of being convicted of the crime. A conviction, with or without a prison sentence, could severely impede her duty to spend her life with her soul mate, the victim of her crime, and to raise their child together.

+ **Fear of receiving a long sentence.** This inmate may also be able to rationalize that a sentence in jail of a few months, maybe even of a year or two, would not be too bad. The logic is basically, "We cannot get married until he is sixteen, so I can wait in here as well as wait out there." The prospect of a long prison sentence is a whole different story. The fears are real: "How long will it take for my lover to be brainwashed by his family and his guidance counselors into dropping me and moving on?" and "What will happen to our baby?" There is the additional terror of being sentenced to prison as a female rapist.

+ **Fear of being abandoned by God.** This inmate may already be sure that God has done worse than abandoned her. Since God brought her and her soul mate together, and that is why she is in this situation, then God is in fact a sadist. Worse than abandonment, God is the author of her suffering and is entertained by it.

+ **Fear of hoping to be set free and then being sentenced to prison.** This inmate also has a battle raging in her emotions. She has a deep-seated desire to believe that she will be found not guilty and set free because she in fact has done nothing wrong. This desire is matched by the dark fear of daring to hope for such an outcome and then facing the disillusionment of wrongfully being found guilty and sentenced to prison. In this case, she may express a profound belief in the victory of love—not of God or of virtue but of her right to share love with the victim of her crime.

+ **Anger and fear at the unknown.** This inmate may in fact express anger and fear at the unknown outcome of her situation. It will most likely focus on society's malevolent attempt to tear her and her soul mate apart.

As we volunteers in Catholic prison ministry face either of these two women in the examples above or in the hundreds of other possible situations that fall into one or the other scenario, our assignment is amazingly similar. That can seem counterintuitive with respect to a young female college student charged with a DUI homicide after a sorority party on the one hand and a thirty-two-year-old middle-class woman who has been charged with statutory rape after being impregnated by her fourteen-year-old student, on the other. But God is not limited by our sense of justice or our intuition.

The two major emotions each woman is presenting are anger and fear. With respect to their anger, we volunteers simply receive it. There is nothing we can say or do about it. I benefited greatly from learning the distinction between *receiving anger* versus *absorbing anger*. We can think of anger as a storm of gale-force wind pummeling a sailing ship on the ocean. If the ship leaves its sails up in an attempt to capture the energy of the winds, i.e., to absorb the storm, the winds will tear the ship apart. So, instead, the wise captain orders the sails to be dropped and stowed so that the gale blows over the ship without the ship catching the force of the storm. *Receiving* the anger in this metaphor is the process of letting the anger blow over us without trying to *catch* or *absorb* it, without trying to explain it, ameliorate it, or deny it.

That means we volunteers listen but do not allow ourselves to get energized or affected by the anger. We listen attentively, looking for the footprints of God that are in every person's life. We listen actively in order to be empathetic to the inmate and to focus on his or her specific needs for prayer. The wise ministry maxim *listen, love, pray* needs to be applied with full force.

To carry forward the metaphor of the hurricane at sea, we Catholic volunteers are also prayerfully attentive for the eye of the storm. We look for openings where there may be receptivity on the part of the inmate to truth, to conviction of sin, to repentance, and to conversion. These steps cannot be forced or imposed, but they must be carefully discerned. In appropriate cases, we may introduce the inmate to the Eucharistic consciousness that shapes and energizes our own spiritual life.

The other major emotion both women in the examples above are presenting is fear. It has been said so often as to be in danger of being trite, but the most frequent command in the Bible is "Fear not."[2] We Catholic volunteers stand with each of these two women and say. "Do not be afraid."

At first blush, that response can seem a bit arrogant to some, but in fact it is the stance of the Christian faith. This stance does not predict that the inmate will avoid a conviction or a prison sentence. This stance does not promise that the inmate will avoid the consequences of such developments, if they occur. Such preposterous assurances are the province of fortune tellers and psychics, not of Catholic volunteers.

The faith stance—Do not be afraid!—promises that the God of Scripture will never abandon or forsake anyone, including the inmate, no matter what he or she has done. As Pope Francis directs us in his address to participants in the National Meeting of Italian Prison Chaplains:[3]

> The Lord is close, but tell [the prisoners] with your actions, with your words, and with your hearts that the Lord does not remain outside; he does not remain outside their cells, he does not remain outside the prison; rather, he is inside, he is there. You can say this: the Lord is inside with them; he too is a prisoner; even today, he is imprisoned by our egoism, by our systems, by so many injustices, for it is easy to punish the weakest while the big fish swim freely in the sea. No cell is so isolated that it is shut to the Lord, none. He is there, he weeps with them, he works with them, he hopes with them, his paternal and maternal love reaches everywhere.

This brings us back to the maxim *listen, love, pray*. It is God's love, God's *agapē*, incarnated through the volunteer's Christian love for the inmate, in and through Jesus Christ and under the power of his Holy Spirit, that dispels fear. As John reminds us in his first letter: There is no fear in love, but perfect love drives out fear because fear has to do with punishment, and so one who fears is not yet perfect in love (1 John 4:18).[4]

How and why would we volunteers push this idea of God's unconditional love, especially for the second woman in our example? The answer is very simple. We do it because God does it for us and asks us to do it for them:

> We love because he first loved us. If anyone says, "I love God," but hates his brother, he is a liar; for whoever does not love a brother whom he has seen cannot love God whom he has not seen. This is the commandment we have from him: whoever loves God must also love his brother. (1 John 4:19-21)[5]

For purposes of the exercise we are engaged in here, let us assume that after two years in the local pokey, each of the women discussed above are found guilty at trial and sentenced to twelve years in prison based on mandatory minimum sentences in the laws passed by the state's elected politicians. They will each get credit for time served— their two years in the jail during the pre-trial and trial proceedings. So, each one is looking at a "dime," a ten year prison sentence.

At the trial and sentencing of the college student convicted of DUI homicide after a sorority party, there were scores of witnesses asking for leniency in sentencing: her family, her pastor, her sorority sisters, her professors and classmates, her high school teachers and band mates from the school's marching band, her fellow volunteers from numerous public service agencies that she has volunteered with for years. All offered tearful and compelling testimony of her excellent character and her compassion for fellow human beings. The judge was almost apologetic at the sentencing, noting the overwhelming evidence that the twenty-year-old college student is an upright and compassionate person who had simply made a horrible mistake. The judge explained that when the intoxicated young women left the sorority party, climbed behind the wheel of her one-and-a-half ton vehicle, and then ran a stop sign, t-boning another vehicle whose three innocent passengers were all killed, the will of the people of the state, as imposed by their elected leaders, require her to serve a minimum of four years for each life taken. With the families of the dead victims of the accident holding up pictures of their three dead children, the judge acknowledged their loss and pointed out that the legislature had removed all judicial discretion in crimes such as this. The judge had no choice but to impose the minimum mandatory sentence of twelve years in state prison. The former college co-ed will be thirty-two years old before she tastes freedom again.

At the trial and sentencing of the thirty-two-year-old middle-class woman who has been convicted of statutory rape after being impregnated by her fourteen-year-old student, the primary voice for leniency was her now sixteen-year-old boyfriend who sat through the trial holding their baby in his arms. Though now old enough to have consented to marrying his lover, the statutes governing the crime forbid any such considerations. He will be twenty-six when she is released. The baby will be almost eleven year's old. The former teacher will be forty-three. The young man has been pilloried at school and dropped out. A hearing has been set in family court to determine the fate of the baby. When handing down the woman's sentence, the judge acknowledged that by sending her to prison, as impossible as it seems, a horrible situation has been made much worse. But there was nothing he could do.

Each of those women is then shipped from their local jail to a state prison system reception center. Some of the uncertainties they faced sitting in jail have now been resolved or, more accurately, replaced by new uncertainties. As we volunteers imagine being one of those inmates on the nighttime bus trip under armed guard from the local jail to the state prison system reception center, what might be some of those new worries and uncertainties?

Upon arriving at the state prison system reception center, the inmates will shuffle inside in shackles and handcuffs for classification and, ultimately, assignment to one of the state prison facilities. Each level of classification involves different levels of restrictions on freedom. Each prison is a different distance from home and has its own reputation for violence and harassment. As a volunteer imagines

WHEN WE VISIT JESUS IN PRISON

being one of those inmates being processed and strip-searched, what are the emotions that come to mind? Other than the physical experience of the shackles cutting into her ankles, of the cuffs cutting into her wrists, and of hearing all the degrading jokes and comments from other inmates, what fears are the hardest to deal with? What are the most difficult emotions to face?

In my experience, the reports of inmates as to their interior struggles with the reception process focus again upon anger and fear. Anger at feeling humiliated and disrespected. Fear of being stripped in front of officers of the opposite sex and even of being physically brutalized. And anger and fear at the unknown: to what level of classification and which prison will they be assigned.

Soon those uncertainties are replaced by new ones. Once the reception process has been completed, the inmate is assigned an identification number and a classification status and is assigned to a specific state prison. Now there is another ride, on another prison department transport bus, being shipped from the reception center to the state prison that will be the inmate's new home for the next decade. The new prison home could be either one mile or five hundred miles from the inmate's real home and loved ones.

As we volunteers imagine being one of those inmates that first night in the state prison, we can feel the disorientation caused by sudden immersion into such a hostile and hard environment. There is the assault on the senses by strange smells and unfamiliar noises. There is the enforced darkness at lights out. There is the unfamiliar regimen of the most basic body functions, such as meals and toilet. What would be the hardest to deal with? What would be the most difficult emotion to face?

In my experience, the reports of inmates as to their interior struggles upon entering the first prison assigned as their new home again focus upon anger and fear. Anger is almost secondary to fear, however. Fear of being raped. Fear of dying at this prison. Fear of having their loved ones call it quits on them, of never seeing their children or parents again because it is too far and too difficult to travel back and forth to this prison. And there is always the fear of the unknown, the parade of horrible possibilities that one can imagine might happen during their time in this prison.

As we volunteers in Catholic prison ministry face either of the two women in the examples above, or any inmate who has recently arrived into the prison system we serve in, our assignment is very similar to our task at the local jail. The two major emotions the inmates experience will be anger and fear. With respect to the anger, we *receive it* without *absorbing it*. We listen, love, and pray. With respect to the fear, we stand with the inmate and say, "Do not be afraid." And it bears repeating that we are always prayerfully attentive for openings where there may be receptivity to truth, to conviction of sin, to repentance and conversion, and to introduction to the Eucharistic life. These steps cannot be forced or imposed upon anyone, especially not an inmate newly arrived to state prison. Instead they must be carefully discerned over time.

In their efforts to listen, love, and pray, we volunteers may be helped by knowledge of some typical slang terms that prison inmates use to describe their sentencing, their experiences, and their prison conditions. We may encounter some of the following slang terms at many different types of facilities:

+ **All day:** a life sentence.
+ **Attitude adjustment:** a physical assault.
+ **Badge:** a correctional officer.
+ **Big house:** prison.
+ **Boot camp:** an alternative form of incarceration, usually for juveniles, that is modeled on military training and may substitute for or reduce the inmate's prison sentence; also called "shock incarceration" or "scared straight program."
+ **Bum rap:** an erroneous conviction.
+ **Booty check:** body cavity search for contraband.
+ **Brake fluid:** psychotropic medications, such as Thorazine.
+ **Bug:** an inmate whom the other prisoners consider to be insane.

- **Buggin' out:** an inmate's loss of control of his or her behavior.
- **Bullet:** a one-year prison term.
- **Cadillac:** the narrow garbage cans to be used as receptacles for cigarette butts, usually in the yard or outdoor visitation areas. Bronze colored ones are called "golden Cadillacs" and stainless steel ones are called "silver Cadillacs."
- **Convict code:** the unwritten rules that all inmates must abide by or face retribution from the other inmates at the prison.
- **Deuce:** a two-year prison term.
- **Nickel:** a five-year prison term.
- **Dime:** a ten year prison term.
- **Quarter:** a twenty-five year prison term.
- **Mandatory quarter:** a life sentence (eligible for parole) with a mandatory minimum of twenty-five years.
- **Dis:** to disrespect someone.
- **Doo rag:** a scarf or bandana worn around an inmate's head; also called a "rag."
- **Drop a dime:** to inform on someone.
- **Dr. No:** a doctor at the prison infirmary who denies all requests for medication and treatment.
- **Jacket:** an inmate's prison file with the classification office.
- **Free world:** the world outside the prison fence; also called the "streets" or the "world."
- **Getting short:** an inmate with less than one-year left before release.
- **General population:** the classification status that allows an inmate to live and work in a prison with regular contact with other inmates and with some freedom of movement inside the facility.
- **Good time:** time credited against an inmate's sentence for good behavior, working certain jobs, or participation in certain programs.

- **Hole:** the special control unit where an inmate is placed for breaking the rules; also called the prison "jail."
- **House:** an inmate's cell.
- **Ink:** a tattoo.
- **Lifer:** an inmate who is doing a life sentence or, because of age and length of sentence, is expected to die in prison.
- **Limbo:** the time served in the local jail waiting for trial and sentencing.
- **Lockdown:** a security event when all prisoners in a dorm, prison area, or entire prison are confined to their cells because of a crisis.
- **Ma:** a girlfriend who stands by her man.
- **Nurse Ratched:** a nurse at the prison infirmary who appears to take delight in denying requests for treatment or medication while still charging the inmate's account a co-pay fee for being seen by the nurse.
- **On-the-House:** an on-the-house write up or on-the-house "DR" is a disciplinary report filed by an officer against an inmate, according to the inmate without any basis in fact.
- **Pulling a train:** serving consecutive sentences.
- **Classification:** the level of security assigned to an inmate by the prison system, e.g., minimum, medium, or maximum security, line-of-sight only (must always be under eyeball surveillance of an officer), etc.
- **Reception Center** or **Diagnostic Center:** institution for receiving inmates into a prison system where the inmate is held temporarily while evaluated for classification and special needs.
- **Retired:** a prisoner with a life sentence without possibility of parole.
- **Shank:** a homemade inmate weapon, usually composed of hard material that can be used to cut, slash, or stab; also called a "shiv."
- **Sleeved:** an arm completely covered in tattoos.

- ✦ **Stand-up con:** an inmate that has demonstrated by conduct, over time, that he or she honors the convict code.
- ✦ **Yard:** prison yard for exercise.
- ✦ **Write up:** the disciplinary report filed by an officer charging an inmate with a breach of prison rules; also called a "DR" (short for "disciplinary report").
- ✦ **Yellow brick road:** the yellow painted lines on walkways in the prison within which all inmates must walk, usually single file and on the right.

As we volunteers in Catholic prison ministry strive to assist inmates in facing and overcoming the fears and anger of their new situation in prison, there may be an exceptional case where we feel called to provide help in a special and more committed way to a particular inmate, to extend ourselves for this inmate beyond what is possible for the inmate population at large. For some reason, we feel moved to attempt to make a life-changing spiritual impact on the particular inmate's journey with God.

The mere sense of a desire to do such a thing, however, does not mean it is a good idea. It may or may not be a good idea. The impulse must be vetted with an abundance of caution. Such a reaction to a particular inmate is exceedingly rare and must be based upon significant experience with the particular inmate over time, experience that establishes in all situations the particular inmate as a new man or woman in Christ.

This reality must be apparent to all who deal with the inmate, not just us. Such a special commitment to a particular inmate must pass muster with the many eyes on the situation. I have had only a few situations like this in my entire time in prison ministry, and I recommend that before acting on such desires, a volunteer should present his or her observations and conclusions for verification by the prison chaplain, by the psychology and counseling staff, and by officers and administrative personnel. Any single reservation by any of those staff should be treated as an absolute veto of any attempt on our part to treat a particular prisoner in a "special" way regarding their spiritual development. If we are reluctant to run our desire to work more intensely with a particular prisoner by all those independent observers, that is a pretty good indication that—on some level—we are acting out of sentiment and not out of reality.

Even if the intention to attempt to spiritually assist a particular inmate in a deeper way than usual passes muster with all those objective observers, our actions must remain in full compliance with all the rules and regulations of the prison and must safely protect us and our loved ones from harm in the event that everyone was wrong about the inmate in question. A good sociopath can fool everyone for a long time. Yet, there must always be room for prayerful discernment, confirmed by many others, that in a particular case, God is asking for a deeper commitment by the volunteer to the inmate in question.

A Christmas Inside

It is the Saturday before Christmas.

Our family is well into the four-hour drive from our home in Jacksonville to a large, medium security prison near Pensacola. West of Tallahassee, the land turns hilly. We are passing near the prison where I met him years ago. His courage astounded me. His faith humbled me.

By the time we reach Bonifay, the weak December sun is climbing over the eastern horizon. We line up for the visitor gate, waiting our turn to disgorge identification and the contents of our pockets, remove our shoes, walk through the metal detectors, and raise our arms high for a full body pat down search.

It was a little unnerving for my wife and children the first time they were searched this way. Now we are all used to it. The female officer who searches the children is polite and always remembers us. "You're that unusual family. The ones that aren't really the inmate's family."

"We're family sure enough," I laugh. "We're called a Christian mentoring family. But truth be told, the man we're visiting teaches us more than we could ever teach him."

She smiles a knowing look. The officers know what most of us don't: The

WHEN WE VISIT JESUS IN PRISON

difference between some of those on the inside and many of us on the outside can be a thin line indeed. As thin as one or two drinks or a weapon that was too handy in a fit of anger, but also thin enough for Christians to find family inside the razor wire fences.

About eleven years ago, a prison chaplain asked me to become a spiritual director and prayer partner with inmates at his prison. One of the first men that came in for an appointment eventually became my new brother in Christ. At the end of five years, our weekly prayer-partner hours had brought us as close as brothers.

When he came to prison, convicted at nineteen years old of first-degree murder, my new brother had suffered more trauma than most people would even hear about in three lifetimes. His childhood was unspeakable. The culture of his upbringing in an isolated South Georgia county was violent and rife with prejudice, hatred, drugs, and alcohol.

"I was raised to hate Catholics," he confessed to me matter-of-factly the first time we met. "But when I heard how you talked about my Jesus at the chapel, I knew you couldn't be my enemy."

Making Jesus his Jesus had cost him dearly, more than most of us will ever have to pay. By his own admission, he came to prison like a caged wild animal. But in a six-man cell in the *Rock*, Florida's most infamous prison for violence and death, he was introduced to Jesus. In the mid-eighties he embraced Jesus on a *Kairos* weekend. His family disowned him and denounced him for it. And Satan wasted no time in attacking him on other fronts. He was served with divorce papers and lost any parental rights with respect to his two children. When Jesus walked into his life, everyone else in his life walked out.

After five years of praying one-on-one, and another three years of correspondence with him, my wife and I discerned that this man deserved the Gospel promise of a new family. Here was clearly a case of a new man in Christ who had forsaken all for love of God. For the next several years our family corresponded with him and accepted his phone calls. Finally, we received approval to visit as his family, a Christian mentoring family.

It is Christmas time, the time of special visits with loved ones. He has saved his canteen money for a Christmas picture. We gather around him, arm in arm, in the photo corner of the prison visiting park. "Make it a good shot," he chides the inmate with the Polaroid camera. "This is my family Christmas picture."

Note: *My family continued as a Christian mentoring family for the man in this story all the way through his parole in 2009. At his trial in the 1980s, he had missed the Florida electric chair by one-jury vote, 7 to 5 for life. A tie vote would have allowed the judge to sentence him to death. We picked him up at the prison near Miami when he was paroled after more than 28 years in prison. He has made the difficult adjustment to the free world in such a profound way that one parole commissioner, in a public meeting, thanked him for reflecting well on the parole commission process. He is now happily remarried and working at a Christian ministry.*

We volunteers in Catholic prison ministry will meet inmates who have no hope of ever leaving prison, except when their body is shipped out for cremation or burial after they die. The sentence of life in prison without possibility of parole can be a moral and humane alternative to capital punishment when the convicted person is not capable of living in the "free world" without doing harm to others. Even so, what is the hope that can be offered to an inmate who is facing a life sentence without possibility of parole?

And what about the de facto life sentence as a result of illness? What is an inmate's reaction to being informed that he or she has a terminal illness and will die in prison? Other than the normal human emotions that accompany notification of a terminal illness, what would be hardest to deal with? What would be the most difficult emotions to face? The two most prevalent emotions of inmates facing the specter of spending the rest of their natural life in prison seem to be, no surprise, *anger* and *fear*. The anger can be focused on many different aspects of the situation:

+ There may be anger at the system's inability to be merciful and allow release from prison for a compassionate death. No one is entitled to mercy which is, by definition, an unmerited gift. But if the system *could* provide for mercy, surely an inmate who is no threat to society and is incapacitated through cancer or dementia could be released to die a quiet death with family.

+ There may be anger at the prison system's dysfunctional medical treatment, which failed to diagnose the illness in time to treat it. Cancer left undiagnosed. Kidney disease left untreated. The list goes on and on. In some cases, the inmate has paid co-pay after co-pay from the limited funds in their account, only to have a Nurse Ratched or a Dr. No dismiss their complaints of physical pain out of hand as lacking credibility just because they are an inmate. Then, suddenly, the inmate is informed that the spot which has been hurting for two years is a huge internal tumor that is now inoperable and has metastasized. Would any of us not be furious?

+ There may be anger at God, for allowing the inmate to be born at all and then allowing him or her to live what seems, in their eyes and perhaps in the eyes of many, to have been a worthless and purposeless life.

The fears triggered by the thoughts of dying in prison, whether due to illness or to a life sentence, usually center upon loneliness and abandonment. There is the fear of dying alone in a cell and even of no one on the outside claiming the inmate's body. That goes hand-in-hand with the fear of being buried in an unmarked grave on the prison property, without even a nameplate on the marker—just the inmate's prison number. Although all chaplains and staff will do everything in their power to hold a dignified and religiously proper burial service at the prison graveyard, the expectation of having one's body lay unclaimed and nameless in a prison grave is considered the ultimate indignity, the loudest and most shattering statement that the inmate's life (and death) mattered to no one.

What are we volunteers in Catholic prison ministry to do in the face of such overbearing, ultimate issues of dying in prison? With respect to the anger, we *receive* it without *absorbing* it. We listen, love, and pray. In doing so, we attempt to gently and lovingly lead dying inmates to the crucial question: "What shall we do now? Where shall we start from today?"

When an inmate can let that question in, it becomes possible to turn the energy of anger and fear into productive spiritual endeavors. The prime task for an inmate who is grappling with the reality of spending the rest of their life in prison is the grieving of the loss of their life. The grieving of such losses was discussed in Chapter 9 with respect to a loved one. This loss is even more personal and immediate. This is the loss of one's own life in prison, with no hope of release and real concern about the meaning of one's very life. Can we volunteers imagine what that means?

Imagine all the things a person hopes for—new love, new beginnings, new adventures, new business prospects, new experiences, new places—all suddenly dashed to bits. In the moment of realization when it finally sinks in, the inmate who will die in prison is hit by the bolt of lightning that is their new reality. All of a sudden there is no more "new" anything, ever again. Just prison. Just barbwire fences and guards. Just security cameras and strip searches and lousy food and no privacy for the rest of one's life. That is it, until the day he or she drops dead. (The Neo-Calvinist vein in modern American culture that believes such losses are not really punishment unless society also affirmatively forces physical suffering on the inmates is discussed in *Chapter 16: Religious Constraints that Affect Prison Ministry and Restorative Justice*.)

As noted in Chapter 9, we volunteers in Catholic prison ministry are rarely trained or equipped to serve as grief counselors in prison. That role is best left to the prison Chaplain and the mental health staff. But we do need to be familiar with the grieving of losses and to be ready to provide a spiritual answer that can help inmates find meaning to their suffering. For we Catholic volunteers that means introducing inmates to the Eucharistic consciousness and to the Paschal Mystery. This includes helping inmates see that the meaning of their lives is not just physical but also spiritual, that spiritual reality trumps dust. As Pope John Paul II reminds us in *On the Christian Meaning of Suffering: Salvifici Doloris*:

WHEN WE VISIT JESUS IN PRISON

This discovery is a particular confirmation of the spiritual greatness which in [human beings] surpasses the body in a way that is completely beyond compare. When this body is gravely ill, totally incapacitated, and the person is almost incapable of living and acting, all the more do interior *maturity and spiritual greatness* become evident, constituting a touching lesson to those who are healthy and normal.[6]

For those inmates who are simply dealing with the reality of aging and ultimate death by natural causes inside the prison fences, the words of Pope John Paul II challenge them to see the wisdom of experience as a gift to be shared:

Arriving at an older age is to be considered a privilege: not simply because not everyone has the good fortune to reach this stage in life but also, and above all, because this period provides real possibilities for better evaluating the past, for knowing and living more deeply the Paschal Mystery, for becoming an example in the Church for the whole People of God.... Despite the complex nature of the problems you face: a strength that progressively diminishes, the insufficiencies of social organizations, official legislation that comes late, or the lack of understanding by a self-centered society, you are not to feel yourselves as persons underestimated in the life of the Church or as passive objects in a fast-paced world but as participants at a time of life which is humanly and spiritually fruitful. You still have a mission to fulfill, a contribution to make. According to the divine plan, each individual human being lives a life of continual growth, from the beginning of existence to the moment at which the last breath is taken.[7]

Moreover, our Church gives us specific advice on pastoral care for the elderly, advice that obtains as fully in the prison context as it would in the "free" world. In *The Dignity of Older People and Their Mission in the Church and in the World*, James Francis Cardinal Stafford, writing from the Vatican as President of the Pontifical Council for the Laity, describes the plight of all the marginalized elderly with terms that will be immediately familiar to volunteers in prison ministry to aging inmates:

> Older people suffer not only by being deprived of human contact, but also from abandonment, loneliness, and isolation. And as their interpersonal and social contacts are diminished, so their lives are correspondingly impoverished; they are deprived of the intellectual and cultural stimulus and enrichment they need. Older people experience a sense of impotence at being unable to change their own situation, due to their inability to participate in the decision-making processes that concern them both as persons and as citizens. The net result is that they lose any sense of belonging to the community of which they are members.[8]

The community to which the elderly inmates in prison belong is their faith community inside the walls and the Family of God that transcends the walls. The Church calls on us to combat their isolation and the fatalism that can creep into their thoughts and beliefs:

> The ecclesial community has the responsibility to purify this fatalism by helping to develop the religious faith of older people and by restoring a horizon of hope to it.... It is the duty of the Church to announce to older people the Good News of Jesus...to give older people the chance to encounter Christ... to instill older people with a deep awareness of the task they too have of transmitting the Gospel of Christ to the world and revealing to everyone the mystery of his abiding presence in history. It is also her duty to make them aware of their responsibility as privileged witnesses, who can testify—both before human society and before the Christian community—to God's fidelity: he always keeps the promises he has made to [us].[9]

For those who are facing death in prison by old age, the risks of despair and fatalism are magnified drastically. But inmates still have a mission field and a world that is the object of their witness. Their mission field is the prison. The people to whom they share the witness of the Gospel are the other prisoners, the officers and staff, the volunteers that come into the prison. That world and that mission can provide a redemptive understanding of inmates' role in the Family of God as they serve out their time in prison for the rest of their natural life.

I Give, Therefore I Am

Years ago in the streets of Tallahassee, the itinerant mentally ill taught me a tremendous lesson. As payee for several of them, I handled their government disability funds. Most of the meager monthly amount went for rent, utilities, and food. But it was possible for me to save some for them for Christmas. I had expected them to joyfully splurge on themselves in a Christmas shopping binge.

"What would you like to do with your Christmas money?" I had asked one of my charges, a tall man in his mid-fifties who had been no different from any of us "normal" people until a physical brain injury in an accident. He paused thoughtfully, pushing out his left cheek with his tongue.

"Ya know," he looked down shyly, rubbing his ear as he spoke, "Since I gotten sick, I've never been able to buy any presents for my friends."

In response to my astonishment, he began shuffling his feet and stuttering apologetically.

"R-r-really, Mister Dale, I-I-I just want to g-g-g-ive presents to my friends. That-at-at's all I want for Christmas."

I grabbed him in a bear hug. "We are going Christmas shopping for your friends!"

I should not have been surprised. Our Catholic faith teaches that we are each made in the image of God. That is the basis for the dignity of human life. Of all the traits manifested by that God, perhaps none has been more pronounced than God's propensity to give gifts—even the gift of God's only begotten Son. By grace, it is in our nature to give.

Our Pope John Paul II has challenged us to recognize this dignity, this image of the Giver, in every human being. He has specifically challenged us to see "that the dignity of human life never be taken away, even in the case of someone who has done great evil. Modern society has the means of protecting itself, without definitively denying criminals the chance to reform."

Now I walk the corridors of Florida's death row with the memory of my friend and the teaching of my Church in hand. How do my brothers on death row live out the image of God the Giver?

I have been amazed. As they sit for hours on end in their cells, many allow their time to be redeemed and the image of God to be expressed by preparing gifts for others. One elderly fellow shows me a picture of a six year-old girl who is dying of cancer. The image of the Giver in him wants to surprise her. With an ear-to-ear toothless grin, he proudly displays the sweater he is knitting for her. Another death row inmate hand-paints a replica of a traditional Catholic picture for his daughter. He himself is Protestant. But the image of God in him reaches beyond doctrine to give a gift that will inspire and encourage her while her father is on death row. Still another inmate meticulously crafts Bible verses in calligraphy to send to the mission fields. A mentally retarded young man spends long hours writing letters of spiritual encouragement to tired ministers of God's Word. Yet another is drawing a clown card in color for a third grade CCD student.

Recently, a Florida newspaper reported the effort by some in Florida to prohibit death row inmates from having the instruments they need to give to others, to replace Godliness with idleness. My Catholic response is absolutely clear: The dignity of human life, the image of God the Giver, must never be taken away, even in the case of someone who has done great evil. We must protect society without denying criminals the chance to reform.

While not a grief counselor *per se*, we volunteers in Catholic prison ministry should be familiar with the classic understanding of the five stages of grief. The five discrete steps in the grieving process, first enumerated as such by Dr. Elisabeth Kübler-Ross,[10] are generally acknowledged to be guidelines, with individual variations in inten-

WHEN WE VISIT JESUS IN PRISON

sity, in the order that a person experiences them, even in whether a person experiences all five stages.[11]

+ **Denial:** Usually this phase immediately follows the intellectual knowledge of the loss. It is similar to the body going into shock after a physically traumatic event, but in this case the emotions and the psyche are numbed in shock due to a traumatic loss. We volunteers in Catholic prison ministry need to understand that this numbing is normal and expected and that the time each person needs to absorb the fact of the loss is very individual.

It is counterproductive, and can even be harmful, for us to demand that a person in this stage of grief "get over it" and face reality. That would be like demanding an injured football player get back in the game even though his body is in shock from a concussion. I have been told by men on death row that it took years for them to let in the reality that they were going to be executed.

+ **Anger:** Experiencing anger at the magnitude of a loss can be essential to healing. That does not mean that we should act out on that anger. Rather, the anger needs to be acknowledged and shared with a safe person, like a grief counselor or a volunteer who knows how to receive the anger without absorbing it. We volunteers in Catholic prison ministry need to understand that this anger is a normal and healthy indication of the progression of the healing process. Anger can provide the energy necessary for the suffering person to reconnect with themselves and with the world in their new situation.

Shaming people for their anger in the process of grieving severe losses can be harmful and interfere with the healing process. Rather, we Catholic volunteers should be helping to direct the energy of inmates' anger toward spiritual growth, toward participation in the Paschal Mystery.

+ **Bargaining:** While bargaining can be a normal step in the grieving process for all people, it seems to be an especially poignant step for those in prison. The overwhelming majority of them have come to prison based upon plea bargains. Bargaining is what they do when confronted with powers beyond their control.

"God, get me out of this life sentence and I will do...." What? Anything? Rather than argue with an inmate who is navigating this step in the grieving process, we volunteers in Catholic prison ministry should treat it as a fertile period for exploring discussion on the nature of God as revealed by Jesus Christ in Scripture. Is God a sadist who delights in the suffering of his people? Is God a despot who sits at a zap buzzer seeking to zap any of us as soon as we make a mistake? Is God a relentless super-accountant sitting at a calculator machine, netting pluses and minuses moment by moment of our life? Is God a blackmail artist holding out on us until we put just enough on the table to entice him to do our will? Who is God? What does Jesus say? What does our Church say?

For those inmates who have expressed doubt as to God's existence in the first place, the question can gently be put: "Then who exactly are you bargaining with?"

And if an inmate has expressed belief in God's existence but disbelief in God's omnipotence, then the question can be put: "Why are you bothering to bargain with a God who you claim has no power to help you?"

+ **Depression:** This is the stage where grief hits full force like a Mack truck. This stage is not necessarily depression in the clinical sense. Rather it describes the experience of the person being inundated with the reality of their loss. It is often like being inundated by a huge wave at the beach. Frequently, it will knock inmates off their feet. They may lose their balance and struggle to regain a firm footing. They may fall and find it hard to get up.

I have witnessed well-meaning Christians chastising an

WHEN WE VISIT JESUS IN PRISON

inmate for experiencing this phase of grief with the admonition that anyone with real faith would not be sad. Such a statement is a total denial of our earthly humanity. When the body is punctured, it bleeds. When the psyche is punctured, it grieves. That is how God made us.

It can be very uncomfortable to be present to an inmate who is in this stage of the grieving process. We volunteers may feel helpless because we cannot make the sadness over the loss go away. All we can do is suffer with the inmate in prayer and in faith as this stage of grief is navigated. We must stubbornly resist the temptation to make ourselves feel better by shaming the inmate for not feeling better faster.

+ **Acceptance:** This final stage has nothing to do with liking the new reality of dying in prison but is more along the lines of a "radical acceptance" which disagrees with the state of affairs but says "it is what it is." This is the stage where the inmate says, "Doggone it, this is the way it's gonna be. I'm gonna be in prison for the rest of my life. I'm gonna die in prison. Now what do I do with that?"

With respect to the fears triggered by the thoughts of dying in prison, whether due to illness or to life sentences, we volunteers have to focus upon the core issues of loneliness and abandonment, standing with the inmate in prayer and saying, "Do not be afraid."

For those of us who feel called to put legs on those prayers, there are concrete efforts that could be made. For example, *The Five Wishes,* created and disseminated by the non-profit organization *Aging with Dignity,*[12] is a declaration that "expresses how you want to be treated if you are seriously ill and unable to speak for yourself. It deals with all of a person's needs: medical, personal, emotional and spiritual." The organization offers the ability for groups to design customized versions of the declaration for specific situations.[13] We volunteers in Catholic prison ministry at a specific institution or in a statewide or federal system could work with the prison or system administration to create a document for inmates who will most likely die in prison in that system. We would also need to work with the administration to put procedures in place to ensure that an inmate's wishes will be applied.

The inmate population in U.S. prisons is getting older, and is getting older at a faster rate:

> Some estimates indicate that the population of inmates over the age of 55 increased as much as 282% between 1995 and 2010, representing a growth rate seven times greater than that of the total U.S. prison population during the same period.... More recent estimates indicate the population of older adult prisoners increased 204% between 1999 and 2012. The number of prisoners age 64 and up increased 62.7% in just three years between 2007 and 2010—a dramatic contrast to the mere 0.67% increase of the total prisoner population during the same period. By 2013, prisoners age 55 and up sentenced to one year or greater under state or federal jurisdiction accounted for 17.9% of all prisoners, over twice the percentage reported in 2010 and 2011.[14]

Consequently, a deep need in the prisons and jails is hospice care for the increasing number of aging inmates who are facing terminal illness in custody. Over the last several decades, hospice programs around the country have developed well-tested programs to coordinate the work of doctors, nurses, mental health professionals, spiritual advisors, and hospice volunteers:[15]

> It is currently estimated that approximately 3,300 inmates in the U.S. die each year from natural causes.... It is estimated that in the U.S. there are currently 75 prison hospice programs. The Federal Bureau of Prisons runs six of these programs.[16]

Suddenly, even politicians who have built their political careers with "tough on crime" slogans are lining up to support prison hospice programs. Why? I hate to say this, but for many of them I think it is merely to save money: "A growing body of literature [indicates that] implementation of prison hospices have the potential to reduce agency costs."[17]

Inmate end-of-life care is becoming a more common issue to be addressed by prison ministry volunteers. It is important to emphasize, however, that in a prison hospice program most of the lifting, diaper changing, and bedpan alley work is done by inmate volunteers. Some may be surprised to hear that inmates claim the use of their time as hospice workers in prison is redemptive. For example, a recent article in *The Denver Post* reports:[18]

> In a prison where executioners once administered a poison cocktail to condemned men, nurses now feed morphine into the arms of the dying for their comfort. Men convicted of brutal crimes minister to the physical needs of the ill and elderly and sometimes find redemption in the role of caretaker.
>
> "I've learned that there is more to life than just taking from people," said Wayne Rose, 40, a career bank robber who cared for dying fire-starter Robert Bryan for five months until he died in January. "I want to leave here a better person. I get a good feeling out of it."

The other greatest fear of inmate's dying in prison is that no one outside the prison will claim the inmate's body. That is the fear of being buried in an unmarked grave on the prison property without even a nameplate on the marker—just the inmate's prison number. Although we volunteers in Catholic prison ministry can bring the answer of faith and the promise of eternal life to address the spiritual trauma of such a situation, there is not much we can do to alleviate the physical facts. But a Catholic parish can do amazing things when they set their mind to it.

Church at Its Best

It is Saturday morning in Winter Haven, Florida. The 10:00 am sun pours in from a cloudless sky over the citrus trees behind the church. Orange specks peer brightly from among the bright green leaves. The sloping roof of St. Matthew's Catholic Church answers in its own hues of deep green. All a beautiful backdrop for the unusual event in the portico of the church.

The rear door of the hearse swings open. Six pallbearers receive the casket. A crowd of about seventy parishioners is present to partake in the solemn funeral Mass that acknowledges this deceased as one of us, a Catholic brother in Christ. What is unusual is that none of these people is related by blood to the man who has died, and almost none of them have ever met him face-to-face. Yet, here they are, and here is the former inmate's body.

A white cross-bearing cloth is draped over the coffin. The pastor, Father Ruse, begins a blessing and leads the procession inside. The simple brown-varnished box containing the remains is positioned in front of the altar astride the towering beauty of a white Easter Candle. All the symbols proclaim life. The Holy Sacrifice of the Mass begins.

Ricky, the deceased, was executed by lethal injection at Florida State Prison. Father Ruse was his spiritual advisor. After four years of monthly visits and five weeks of deathwatch weekly visits, Father Ruse was with him at cell front for the five hours prior to Rickey's execution.

My wife and I served as a support for Father Ruse and the members of his pastoral team who participated in the vigil and prayers that surrounded this event. Father never came alone to Florida State Prison. In a very real sense, all these people from his parish who are gathered here today came with him. This is a piece of the mystery of our Church. This is our Family of Faith.

I have heard it said that the Eskimo language has no word for orphan because any child who loses its parents is immediately absorbed into another family. There are no orphans. This Catholic Family of Faith is the same reality in the spiritual realm. There are no abandoned members of our family. No one from this family should ever end up in *Boot Hill*.

Boot Hill is the ultimate statement that a human life did not matter to anyone. It is the ultimate degradation for those who have already been relegated to the bottom of the pile. *Boot Hill* is the state administered pauper's graveyard for those who die in prison at Raiford or Starke, with no one to even claim their body. I have been told that men have been removed from the execution chamber, declared dead by the medical examiner, and sent directly to *Boot Hill*. There is no more effective pronouncement by the world of the worthlessness of a human life.

These good people of St. Matthew's of Winter Haven are taking a stand this morning for the value of human life, not just in general but in the particular case of this man, Rickey, who some considered to be valueless. They are taking this stand at the cost of their personal resources of time, energy, and money. They are throwing down the gauntlet in the face of the culture of death, choosing to see Rickey not as his worst deeds, but rather as God sees him, a human being made in the image and likeness of God.

Through the course of the funeral Mass, prayers are offered for Rickey's victims and their loved ones and for Rickey and his loved ones. Some of the songs sung are the same as those that Ricky and Father Ruse sang with other prison chaplains at his cell front just hours before his execution. Ricky's final words are shared.

In closing the homily, Father Ruse says it all: "This is church at its best."

It cannot be too often repeated that we Catholic volunteers in prison ministry are always prayerfully attentive for openings where there may be receptivity to truth, to conviction of sin, to repentance, and to conversion. Such steps cannot be forced or imposed upon anyone, however, not even an inmate who is ultimately facing death in prison. Instead they must be carefully discerned. This is the case even when the inmate's death is imminent.

About a decade ago, I had the experience of being requested as spiritual advisor by a non-Catholic Christian who was scheduled for execution. The man had no interest in becoming Catholic, but was very interested in why I was bringing the Good News to the men on Florida's death row. In short, he wanted to know what it is that we Catholics believe that would make one of us do such a "crazy" thing. In prayerful discernment and with input from my seasoned spiritual advisor, it became clear that this man needed to hear about the very saint who epitomizes such a deep love for Christ that what the world considers "crazy" can sometimes be the only thing that makes sense.

So, sitting in a cell in the Florida death house, ten feet from the execution chamber, this man and I, with six weeks left for him to live, set out on a journey of discovery about that little man from Assisi who "knew how to die because he knew how to live."[19]

An Instrument of His Peace

7:20 pm. We have been sitting in the witness room seats for one and a half hours—at that time the longest wait in that room in the history of Florida executions. We sit in absolute silence, without motion or distraction. We stare at our own reflections in the glass window: reflecting on the man who will be lying behind the closed curtain, stretched out on a gurney on the other side.

Almost six years ago, I met this then very angry man on death row. During the ensuing weeks, months, and years, he and I became friends, like brothers. He asked me to be his spiritual advisor if his death warrant were signed. Even the expected can be unexpected when it actually happens.

7:21 pm. Still waiting. I can see the reflections of the victim advocates and the survivors of the victim—tense with apprehension that a stay may be in the works. Superimposed over them are the reflections of the defense lawyers in the second row, tense with apprehension that a stay may not be granted. The two sets of images meld into a collage of our community, torn against itself by adversarial interests and homicidal violence, seeking redemption through an adversarial process that promises restoration through more homicidal violence.

Studying the reflections of the witnesses, I realize that every single person seated in that witness room is white. Remaining unseen in this drama is the black man on the other side of the window. He was used to being unseen.

Through a childhood in the black migrant labor camps, he learned that white contractors had the guns and the dogs. The blacks did what they were told or met the business end of both. A black man in those times and place survived by hiding—hiding one's desires, feelings, even rage—and appearing compliant. This man's crimes were crimes of rage. His life experiences did not justify them, but they sure explained where the rage came from.

Over the last several years, however, he became a man of peace, actually a peacemaker who mentored younger men on his death row wing in controlling their anger, letting go of resentments and hate, and living without rancor.

7:22 pm. Still waiting. When I first heard about his death warrant on the Friday before Christmas, I mailed him a package of spiritual materials, including a copy of the Peace Prayer of St. Francis of Assisi. He loved that prayer the first time he read it. All our deathwatch appointments began with that prayer and were peppered with discussions about the life of the little man of Assisi.

"Now that's a white dude what had his stuff together," he had sighed. "Why can't more of you white people be like him?"

During the last few hours before the execution prep procedure began, we paged through a book filled with stories of St. Francis and pictures of Assisi, Greccio, Gubbio, and Rome. He also loved the Canticle of the Creatures and read it aloud to me and the prison chaplain just a few feet from the execution chamber: "Be praised, my Lord, for our sister, Death, whom no living man can escape. Woe to those who die in mortal sin. Blessed are those whom she will find doing your holy will, for to them the second death will do no harm."

My brother knows the second death means the Last Judgment, promised by Jesus as the solace of those afflicted by unjust societies. He admonishes me and the chaplain to be ready for our own death so we will not be condemned in the second death.

"I'll see you again, man," he smiled as we clasped hands for the last time just before the strap-down team came in. "I knew I wouldn't never see justice in this world. But there will be Justice, his Justice, and I will get to speak in his Court on his Day, when it really matters."

7:23 pm. The curtain opens. Whatever the reason for the delay, the execution will now proceed. He is asked if he has any last words.

"Yep," he replies. "Later."

Another group of inmates that have special pastoral needs are those who are agitated or aggressive. For the most part, inmates burdened with such problems are now housed in administrative segregation units, which used to be called solitary confinement cells. The needs of those inmates are the subject of the next chapter.

> "The issue we face is not the dichotomy of being and not being, but that of righteous and unrighteous being.... Indeed, [humans] alone are motivated by the awareness of the insufficiency of sheer being, of sheer living. [Humans] alone are open to the problem of how to be and how not to be on all levels of their existence."
>
> Abraham J. Heschel[1]

CHAPTER 12

Pastoral Needs of Inmates in Confinement

What is it that makes one a human being? Is a person truly human without interaction with other human beings? Is a person truly human without caring for other human beings? Rabbi Abraham Heschel, a Jewish theologian who met with Pope Paul VI concerning Catholic-Jewish relations and the Second Vatican Council, suggests that biblical revelation leads us to a different essential question than the one William Shakespeare posits in *Hamlet*.

Hamlet famously asks whether it is better to be alive or to be dead: "To be or not to be."[2] Heschel suggests that such a focus is in the province of animals; that biblical revelation leads human existence to the question of *how to be* and *how not to be*.

> [Human beings] achieve fullness of being in fellowship, in care for others. They expand their existence by "bearing the burdens of others...."

Animals are concerned for their own needs; the degree of our being human stands in direct proportion to the degree in which we care for others. The central problem in terms of biblical thinking is not: "What is 'to be'?" but rather "How to be and how not to be?"[3]

Mere being versus *human being* is at the core of the battle over the explosion of what are called "segregation unit" cells in our prisons and jails. When people are forced to exist in a six-foot by nine-foot space with a stainless steel shelf for a bunk, a stainless steel toilet-sink in one corner, a single fluorescent bulb for light, a solid steel cell door with an immovable six-inch by eight-inch plastic window, and are fed through a hole in the cell door, are they being cared for like an animal, a *merely being*? Or are they being cared for like a person, a *human being*? To be a human being or not to be a human being: that is the question posed by every solid steel cell door in a segregation unit.

Some segregation units have steel-barred doors with the vertical bars spaced so tightly that they still must have a food flap. In some states, as in Florida, death row is operated as a form of segregation unit. Whether the door to the cells is solid steel or barred, as it is on death row segregation cells, there are some things that do not change. One of them is the heat.

....

How Hot Is Hell?

Although the execution chamber is housed at Florida State Prison, most of the 400 men on Florida's death row are on the other side of the New River, at Union Correctional Institution (UCI).

UCI is a prison complex—a campus of buildings containing every level of security and classification: death row, disciplinary solitary confinement, protective custody, medical hospital, close custody, general population, even psychiatric solitary confinement. The prisoners and staff together total almost the population of my home town. When the planned construction of

WHEN WE VISIT JESUS IN PRISON

additional solitary cells is completed, UCI will be larger than my city.

The escort for my first visit to UCI is Fr. Joe Maniangat. He has been coming to UCI twice a week for almost sixteen years. As we enter the massive beige structure that houses most of Florida's death row, a young female officer hands each of us a personal body alarm or "pba," an electronic device to clip on our belts. If we cease standing vertically, the black plastic box will sound an alarm. Another pod station and four heavy steel doors later, we are "on the row." It is as hot as I have imagined hell to be, but with higher humidity.

Florida's August sun has been beating down for hours on the exterior wall and windows along the left side of the corridor. There is no shade because there are no trees. Trees obstruct the view from the gun towers. Trees are a security risk.

Along the right side are the fifteen solitary cells, each with a ventilator fan in its back wall. The unintended effect is that the superheated air from the outside face of the wall is sucked in through the windows and circulated across the walkway into the cells. In effect, I have stepped into a solar convection oven.

Cell by cell we greet the man inside. All are dressed only in their undershorts, the attire of choice in a solar oven. Until we approach, most are lying on the concrete floor of their cells in a vain effort to find relief from the heat. It is useless.

The scene is the same—corridor after corridor, wing after wing. And these are just the hundreds of men on death row. There are hundreds more in administrative confinement in the next two buildings. I never imagined the impact of Florida's summer heat on thousands of men locked in solitary steel cages in concrete boxes of buildings. No porch to retreat to for relief. No shade to be found…anywhere. Only relentless heat, twenty-four hours a day, seven days a week.

Within minutes, Father Joe and I are drenched in perspiration. We still have hours to go. As the sweat pours and the prayers flow, I find myself examining the men on the other side of the bars. Some look grandfatherly. A few are covered with tattoos.

One who takes Communion has obscenities etched in his shoulder. The next, too young to shave, looks like a neighbor kid who would mow your lawn. My pervading experience is one of unreality.

Fr. Joe has a warm smile and a greeting for every man, Catholic reading material for anyone that wants it, and sacraments for those who are Catholic.

After 150 cells, barely a drop in the bucket, Fr. Joe and I lean against the cool of the metal door that leads off the row, waiting for the control station to release the locks.

"These are God's children, our brothers," he smiles, placing a gentle hand on my soggy shoulder and wiping his brow with the other. "That is the teaching of our Church." Then, moving his head in a sweeping gesture toward the hellish heat around us, he continues in a voice heavy with sadness and dismay, "But that also means society's supposed to treat them with dignity and respect."

In order to competently discuss the issues presented by the explosion in the number of segregation unit cells in our prisons and jails, it is important to be familiar with the vocabulary of the modern forms of solitary confinement.

+ **Bean flap:** feeding hole in a segregation unit cell door which is usually covered by a locked steel flap; also called the "food flap."
+ **Control unit:** high security housing units such as segregations units, administrative segregation units, and protective custody units.
+ **Day room:** a highly restrictive group room where inmates in segregation are allowed for short periods to watch television as a break from the monotony of their segregation cell; usually the inmates are shackled, in handcuffs, and secured to the bench by chains during the time in the day room.
+ **FT:** usually in segregation units, short for "feces thrower;" an inmate with a history of flinging feces, urine, or other body fluids at officers, staff, or volunteers.
+ **Frog-walk:** slang term for the awkward walking motion of inmates being moved into, out of, or from one administra-

WHEN WE VISIT JESUS IN PRISON

tive segregation cell to another, because of the restrictions imposed on their body movement by the pounds of manacles, shackles, waist chains, black-box handcuffs, and other security hardware they are required to wear outside their solitary confinement cell.

+ **IED:** slang term for an improvised device set by an inmate, usually in segregation units, to fling feces, urine, or other body fluids at a passing officer, staff, or volunteer; also called a "roadside bomb."

+ **Segregation unit:** a unit containing special cells that are highly restrictive regarding allowed inmate personal property and interaction with other inmates, with little or no freedom of movement. When the cells are single-man cells, it is also known popularly as "solitary confinement" or an "isolation unit."

+ **Administrative segregation unit:** a segregation unit, especially one where an inmate can be assigned pending a determination as to whether he or she has violated the rules or even without the administration having to prove a violation of the rules; also refers to supermax institutions; also referred to as "ad seg" (for administrative segregation).

+ **Supermax:** a building or prison where inmates are held in single-cell segregation units, twenty-three to twenty-four hours per day: also known popularly as "solitary confinement."

+ **CM or Close Management:** a politically correct term for supermax or segregation unit, usually as part of a structured behavior modification program that allows the inmate to earn back privileges and eventually return to general population.

+ **MM or Maximum Management:** a politically correct term for highly restrictive segregation units that involve sensory deprivation of light and sound, intended for stays of extremely short duration when necessary to bring an out-of-control inmate under control.

- **Protective custody:** a segregation unit to which an inmate is assigned for his or her own protection.
- **Restricted Housing:** generic term for segregation units of various kinds.
- **Sign in:** an inmate's request to be placed in protective custody.
- **Yard:** prison yard for exercise, which in segregation units usually refers to single-man, fenced, dog kennel-type areas that are for outdoor breaks from the inside cell.

It has been said that the solutions to each century's social problems becomes the next century's social problems. In terms of a dynamic, that insight offers a plausible explanation for the mushrooming number of segregation cells in our prisons and jails. Segregation cells offered an answer to a horrendous problem: violence in prisons and jails being instigated and perpetrated by violent inmates and by gangs. In some ways, this strategy has worked.

According to the Bureau of Justice Statistics, homicide rates in state prisons dropped 93% from 1980 to 2002:

> State prison homicide rates dipped sharply from 1980 (54 per 100,000) to 1990 (8 per 100,000). By 2002 prison homicide rates had declined further, down to 4 per 100,000. Homicide rates in local jails...declined slightly from 5 per 100,000 in 1983 to 3 per 100,000 in 2002.[4]

The lower level of rates of homicide inside both prisons and jails in U.S. states has continued through the latest available numbers. The average annual mortality rate due to homicide per 100,000 local jail inmates during the ten years from 2000–2009 was 3.[5] The average annual mortality rate due to homicide per 100,000 state prisoners during the nine years from 2001–2009 was 3.8.[6]

Margaret Noonan, lead statistician of the reports by the Bureau of Justice Statistics that document drastic reductions in violence in America's prisons and jails, credits popular misconceptions for public surprise that our prisons are safer than our city streets:

> "People seem to think that homicides are an epidemic in correctional facilities, and I hate to break their little hearts, but they're really rare," Noonan said. "Most people who go to prisons don't die. They go to the facility, they serve their time, and they get out."[7]

In 1980, the homicide rate inside the barb wire fences was almost five times the rate in the free world. Now, for more than a decade-and-a-half, the murder rate inside the country's prisons and jails is lower than in the free world.[8] Most corrections professionals and politicians assert that a major factor in reducing the homicide rate in prisons has been the use of segregation cells for violent offenders. An article in *USA Today* credits the use of segregation cells to house violent offenders for part of the success in reducing prison violence.

> "Gang violence inside prisons has long been a major source of homicides," said Michelle Lyons with the Texas Department of Criminal Justice. "In the mid-1980s, Texas began pulling confirmed gang members out of the general population and placing them in solitary confinement," Lyons said. "The drop in murders was almost immediate."[9]

The drive for segregation units for violent and vulnerable offenders has fueled a drastic increase in the use of solitary confinement cells. "Between 1995 and 2000, the growth rate in the number of people housed in segregation far outpaced the growth rate of the prison population overall: forty percent compared to twenty-eight percent."[10]

Speaking at *Re-evaluating Administrative Segregation: The Human, Public Safety and Economic Impact*, a plenary session held at the American Correctional Association's (ACA) 2013 Winter Conference in Houston, Kenneth McGinnis, director of Corrections Programs, CNA Institute for Public Research, acknowledged the tremendous growth in use of solitary confinement; but he reminded the assembly why we have administrative segregation units in the first place:

> "As we begin this discussion, it's important to reflect on the reason that administrative segregation exists today," McGinnis said. He explained that administrative segregation evolved as a result of a 10-year period of violence in the late 1970s and early 1980s. "There is no debate in my mind that administrative segregation was the reason we were able to stabilize and regain control of the prisons in the late 1970s and early 1980s...but there's also no doubt that these facilities have grown tremendously."[11]

But there is another side to the story. The first chapter in that other side is the plight of the mentally ill in the grips of solitary confinement. At that same panel of the same conference in Houston, Ron S. Honberg, J.D., director of policy and legal affairs for the National Alliance on Mental Illness (NAMI) spoke after McGinnis:[12]

> Honberg indicated that many people with mental illnesses have difficulty functioning in the community, let alone in a correctional environment. While individuals are placed in administrative segregation for many reasons, Honberg highlighted growing evidence that long-term solitary confinement is harmful, particularly for people with pre-existing mental illnesses....
>
> NAMI adopted a draft policy that opposes the use of administrative segregation for people with mental illnesses, emphasizes treatment and rehabilitation to alleviate aggressive behaviors, and states that if segregation has to happen at all, there should be a defined time limit.[13]

In today's U.S. corrections industry, both private and public, the battle is raging over administrative segregation. As succinctly phrased by the monthly online newsletter of the American Corrections Association, the challenge is:

WHEN WE VISIT JESUS IN PRISON

Previously referred to as "isolation" or "solitary confinement," the use of administrative segregation raises questions of how to ensure safe, humane and constitutionally-sound facilities that are in the best interest of the inmate in segregation, the general inmate population, corrections professionals and the general public.[14]

Speaking at the ACA's follow-up session on administrative segregation, *Segregation: Controversial and Complicated*, the 143rd Congress of Correction in National Harbor, Maryland (Summer 2013), Christopher B. Epps, president of the ACA and Commissioner of the Mississippi Department of Corrections, assessed the magnitude of the issue:

"It is fair to say that we are faced with a new crisis...." Epps cited the increased amount of litigation surrounding the disproportionate number of mentally ill inmates in segregation as a major need for reform. "Corrections professionals know better than anyone else the pressure of administering safe, humane, clean, and constitutionally-sound facilities," he said. "It is time for us to look at segregation and examine its uses, benefits, and effects on the incarcerated. If corrections professionals ignore this important topic, we risk others making the decisions for us."[15]

After Epps and others spoke, Dean Aufderheide, Ph.D., Director of Mental Health for the Florida Department of Corrections, endorsed the call for ACA standards on the use of segregation:[16]

+ Define what types of mental illnesses are not suitable for functioning in segregation, and have mental health staff conduct screenings;
+ Provide access to structured in-cell and out-of-cell mental health treatment for those in segregation;
+ Create an individualized mental health services plan by a

multidisciplinary treatment team—a "one size fits all" strategy will not be effective and must be adaptable based on the changing needs of the inmate; and

+ Identify mental illness early, as early identification prevents deterioration.

The plight of the mentally ill in solitary confinement is dealt with in more detail in Chapter 14: Special Pastoral Needs of Inmates Dealing with Mental Illness and Other Special Needs. But for we volunteers in Catholic prison ministry who are moving cell to cell, door to door, on the tier of an administrative segregation wing, there is no way to know if the next face visible through a small Plexiglas cell door window will be a person who is mentally ill or someone who is being driven to the edge of insanity by the conditions of his or her confinement.

A Face in a Window

Confinement. Corridors of thirty cells, fifteen per side. These cells have solid steel doors instead of bars. The doors are mounted on a track so that they slide open sideways. When the doors are shut, there are only two openings.

One is the feeding hole, a rectangular slot at belt height in the middle of the door. It is large enough to admit a feeding tray or a toilet brush. Because a bottom-hinged steel flap is padlocked shut over this hole (except at mealtimes), the opening is called the "flap."

The other opening is the unintentional vertical slit, about a quarter-inch wide, that results from the imperfect marriage of the door and the wall. Called the "crack," the slit runs from top to bottom. The flap is only opened for those receiving Sacraments. As we move cell to cell, the crack is the medium of communication between us and non-Catholics.

Each door has a small, wire-reinforced Plexiglas window. It's too narrow and too short to fit a man's entire face. We can either see his mouth and nose or his eyes and nose, but we can never see his whole face.

Confinement is where a man goes when he breaks the rules in prison. The inmates call confinement "jail." Some men spend thirty days in confinement. Some spend years.

I know a man who spent three years in one of these cells. After three years, he was moved from confinement to a regular maximum security cell with five other prisoners. One of them brought my new friend to Jesus Christ.

That was many years ago. My friend is still in prison. His efforts to live his faith in the most hostile of environments, refusing to return evil for evil, ministering to the new men, and constantly walking with Jesus in the midst of so much darkness, humbles me and shames my easy faith. As Fr. Joe and I work from flap to flap, crack to crack, my friend and his three years behind that steel door are on my mind. Are there other men like him in these cells—men who are ready to accept the gift of Good News?

One young man asks to go to confession. Father puts his ear by the feeding hole. I step two cells away to give them privacy. Then, I hear a man's voice from behind me. "Brother, if you're a man of God, please talk to me."

It is a tall black man in the cell behind me. His face is scrunched against the crack. I move to the crack and ask him if he is a Christian. He nods "yes." I ask him if he would like me to lead him through a prayer. He chokes back a wobble in his voice and says, "Please."

I tell him to put his hand on the window, and I place my hand on the outside of the window, opposite his. He places his ear by the crack. I place my face by the crack. We pray.

We pray forgiveness. We pray healing. We pray deliverance. We pray protection. We pray hope and perseverance. We pray the Name that is our Victory. We pray the Blood that is our Protection. We pray the Empty Tomb that is our Hope. We pray the Spirit that is our Strength.

After we finish, he whispers through the crack, "Thank you, brother. I needed to pray so bad, but I didn't know how to get back. Thank you."

Industry insiders are not the only ones severely concerned about the dangers of administrative segregation. Evangelical Christians have gone on record against it at the highest levels. On June 19, 2012, Pat Nolan, President of Justice Fellowship,[17] a division of Prison Fellowship founded by Chuck Colson, testified before the Senate Judiciary Subcommittee on the Constitution, Civil Rights, and Human Rights on the subject of Reassessing Solitary Confinement: The Human Rights, Fiscal, and Public Safety Consequences. He surprised many with a piece of historical information that is not well known: Chuck Colson started Justice Fellowship because of his horror at the realities of solitary confinement. The following quotes are taken from Pat Nolan's testimony.[18]

> This is an important topic to our ministry because it was after witnessing the horrid and brutal conditions of Walla Walla Prison [the Washington State Penitentiary] that our founder Chuck Colson added reform of the justice system to the work of Prison Fellowship.
>
> Chuck had gone to Walla Walla to preach the Gospel and lead a Bible study. The prison had been locked down for over nine months in retaliation for the murder of a correctional officer. During those long months, the prisoners were confined to their cells, forced to brush their teeth and drink water from their toilet bowls.
>
> During those nine months they were allowed out of their cells only once every fourteen to twenty days to "shower...." They were to run to the shower room, through the running showers, and back to their cells without stopping.
>
> Chuck was the first outsider to enter the prison after the lockdown ended. At his Bible study one of the inmates challenged Chuck to "tell the world what you have seen here," and Chuck said he would. A large number of the press was waiting outside the prison gates as Chuck exited. He told them about the conditions inside the prison and said, "You can't treat inmates like animals and then expect them to live decent lives after they are released." And he committed to work to reform the system, and from that searing experience he founded Justice Fellowship, the part of the ministry that I lead.

Pat Nolan then recounted his experience as a California legislator passing the bill that financed that state's infamous Pelican Bay super-max facility:

> I was the floor manager for the bill which authorized the construction of Pelican Bay, California's "Supermax," the first state facility in the U.S. designed exclusively for isolating prisoners. I say my support of the bill was "ironic" because the facility was sold to the legislature as being needed to house the "worst of the worst" inmates, not for those prisoners suffering with mental illness.
>
> The justification for the extremely high costs involved in constructing and operating the Supermax was that moving the most violent prisoners to a single facility would make the other prisons safer. Sadly, the reality has been very different.
>
> *Solitary confinement is not limited to extremely violent inmates.* The number of extremely violent prisoners was far less than the prisons officials had estimated. These officials didn't want the legislature to find out that there were a large number of empty beds in such an expensive facility.
>
> So, they did what any good bureaucrat would do: They filled the beds with prisoners who weren't the "worst of the worst." They widened the net to include additional categories of prisoners. They added inmates who were incorrigible (i.e., difficult to manage). Most of these are mentally ill. By definition, someone who is psychotic has difficulty understanding and following orders. These prisoners are not bad, they are sick.
>
> However, many corrections officers find them difficult to manage and write them up for violations of policies. After several "shots," they sent them to isolation. This makes the officers' jobs easier, but it also exacerbates the underlying mental illness of the inmates, driving them deeper and deeper into mental illness....
>
> The decision to send someone to solitary is most often made with no chance for the inmates to plead their case or

appeal the decision. When the decision is made to transfer an inmate to isolation they are not afforded an opportunity to let their family know where they are. This causes great anxiety. They are suddenly unable to contact their loved one, which causes deep concern that they have been stricken by a serious illness or have been badly injured. The inmate arrives at the "hole" without any of their belongings and no money on their account to make a call or buy a stamp to let their family know where they are.

Victims of sexual assault are often placed in solitary. The scandal of rape in prison has begun to be addressed because of the leadership of Congress in passing the Prison Rape Elimination Act. One of the common practices that should be corrected is placing victims in "protective custody." The attacker is often left in the general population, while the victim is in solitary. This is unjust. In solitary the victim loses many privileges, including calls home and visits, and they are prevented from participating in education classes and religious services.

After describing the reaction of outsiders to the horrors of Pelican Bay, Nolan proceeds to discuss the horrendous effects of prolonged solitary confinement on all inmates, even if they did not start with severe mental illness:

Spending years in isolation without being touched by a human being is unhealthy. During what often ends up as years in solitary, inmates are not touched by another human being, save when they are being moved by corrections officers, at which times they are loaded down with literally pounds of manacles and shackles, with guards on either side of them. As they shuffle through the cell block, the inmates avoid eye contact [with visitors] because they are unsure how to react to a "free person".

Other witnesses with training in psychology can explain in proper medical terms the impact that this isolation has on people, even the strongest personalities. But I can tell you my observation is that these men are deteriorating quickly. They look like whipped dogs.

Then in a twist that turns the incongruities of administrative segregation into a *Clockwork Orange*-type horror, Pat Nolan presents the insanity of the result:

Straight from solitary to the street. When their sentence is finished, these men who are deemed so dangerous a moment before are frog-walked to the gate and released—turned loose with no preparation. That is a practice that is horribly dangerous to the public, and also frightening to the inmates.

Having had no control over any aspect of their lives, even such a small matter as when they can exercise, they are then set loose with hundreds of key decisions confronting them.... Hans Toch, a noted criminologist, warns that "Supermax prisons may turn out to be crucibles and breeding grounds of violent recidivism….. [Released prisoners] may become 'the worst of the worst' because they have been dealt with as such."

Mr. Nolan closes his testimony with the specific recommendations of the *Justice Fellowship* with respect to reforming the use of administrative segregation in U.S. prisons and jails:

1. Limit solitary confinement to cases of clear danger of violence that cannot be controlled in other settings.
2. Review each case individually each month to determine whether solitary is still appropriate. The policy should be to transfer inmates out of segregation as soon as possible. (The American Correctional Association requires such reviews in their standards for accreditation).
3. Provide opportunities for inmates in segregation to engage in productive activities, such as education, treatment, and religious programs.

4. Allow inmates in segregation to have regular and meaningful human contact.
5. Carefully review each case for mental illness before confining an inmate in isolation. Evaluate mentally ill inmates at periodic intervals, with the reviews performed by psychiatrists who are not employed by the corrections department.
6. Allow inmates to challenge the decision to send them to segregation units.
7. NEVER release inmates directly from solitary confinement to the streets. Allow gradual decompression, with increasing opportunities for the inmate to make choices.

Nolan's testimony concludes with the assertions that because Christians must speak for those who have no voice, "we are compelled to call out for reform in the overuse of solitary confinement." As we have seen in the social justice teaching of the Church, Catholics are also called to do so. Our U.S. Catholic bishops have spoken loud and clear on this subject:

As of 1997, thirty-six states and the federal government have constructed "supermax" prisons. These facilities isolate prisoners considered most dangerous and confine them to small cells by themselves for twenty-two to twenty-four hours each day....
Regardless of who runs prisons, we oppose the increasing use of isolation units, especially in the absence of due process and the monitoring and professional assessment of the effects of such confinement on the mental health of the inmates.[19]

Are there alternatives to the overuse of administrative segregation cells that will still keep our prisons safe? An editorial in *America* magazine listed the consequences of prolonged solitary confinement and then identified some proven alternatives.

Studies have shown that prolonged isolation actually changes how the brain works and can result in impairments and abnormalities akin to a traumatic injury. Psychological effects can include auditory and visual hallucinations, delirium, self-mutilation, insomnia, paranoia, uncontrollable feelings of rage and fear, post-traumatic stress disorder, and an increased risk of suicide. Most prison suicides occur in solitary confinement....

In order to confront the problem of prison violence the focus must shift from punishment to prevention. Great Britain did just this, beginning in the 1980s, with impressive results. Instead of humiliation and confrontation, which only made things worse, the British reduced the use of solitary confinement and allowed their most dangerous prisoners to have more opportunities for work, education, programming, and mental health treatment. As a result, the need for solitary confinement in British prisons became negligible. The National Institute of Corrections...has already helped Mississippi reduce its restricted housing population by seventy-five percent and prison violence by fifty percent.

Other federal and state prisons should follow suit. Respect for the human dignity of prisoners demands no less.[20]

CNA is a private sector company that specializes in analyses and solutions for public sector operations.[21] Through the company's Safety and Security Division, their Corrections and Detention Programs deal with a broad spectrum of corrections issues, including the management of administrative segregation. Mr. Ken McGinnis, who spoke on administrative segregation at the ACA Conference in Houston, was involved in the restructuring of the use of administrative segregation in the State of Mississippi (mentioned as a model of improvement in the *America* editorial above). In a recent article on the subject, he explains the need for and the possibilities achievable through reform of our administrative segregation practices:

In June 2012, the Bipartisan Commission on Safety and Abuse in American Prisons reported to the Senate Committee on the Judiciary that, in their opinion, increasing the use of high-security segregation is counterproductive, often causing violence inside facilities and contributing to recidivism after release. During the Congressional hearing, Senator Richard Durbin of Illinois added that this type of unit can be extremely costly when compared to traditional correctional housing....

CNA has been an active participant in this debate on the usefulness, appropriateness, and effectiveness of these units... by leading assessments of these units in several jurisdictions. These assessments help to ensure that administrative segregation units operate consistently with national standards, operate in the most efficient and effective manner possible, house only those inmates who absolutely require such placement, and provide access to mental healthcare and other services. For example, CNA staff worked with the JFA Institute[22] to assess the Parchman Segregation Unit within the Mississippi Department of Corrections. The outcome of this review has been cited by many as a national model for reviewing, assessing, and reforming the administrative segregation function......

Ultimately, CNA believes that independent assessments of administrative segregation units are critical to ensuring that the units operate safely, efficiently, effectively, and humanely as a tool for managing high-risk offenders in today's correctional environment.[23]

The success story for the Parchman Segregation Unit within the Mississippi Department of Corrections is getting a great deal of attention in corrections circles, because the outcomes are counterintuitive. The changes made and the results obtained were reported in the *New York Times*:

PARCHMAN, Mississippi.—The heat was suffocating, and the inmates locked alone in cells in Unit 32, the state's super-maximum-security prison, wiped away sweat as they lay on concrete slab beds.

Kept in solitary confinement for up to 23 hours each day,

allowed out only in shackles and escorted by guards, they were restless and angry—made more so by the excrement-smeared walls, the insects, the filthy food trays, and the mentally ill inmates who screamed in the night, conditions that a judge had already ruled unacceptable.

So it was not really surprising when violence erupted in 2007: an inmate stabbed to death with a homemade spear that May; in June, a suicide; in July, another stabbing; in August, a prisoner killed by a member of a rival gang.

What was surprising was what happened next. Instead of tightening restrictions further, prison officials loosened them.

They allowed most inmates out of their cells for hours each day. They built a basketball court and a group dining area. They put rehabilitation programs in place and let prisoners work their way to greater privileges.

In response, the inmates became better behaved. Violence went down. The number of prisoners in isolation dropped to about 300 from more than 1,000. So many inmates were moved into the general population of other prisons that Unit 32 was closed in 2010, saving the state more than $5 million.[24]

Against the backdrop of this national—even international—conversation about solitary confinement, we volunteers in Catholic prison ministry step to the door of a confinement cell. In the moment that the face inside the cell peers through the small window at the "free person" standing outside the cell door, the studies and professional conferences all seem quite distant. The immediate existential issue is the face in the window. Who is this person inside the cage? What does he or she need from us today? How can we dignify the humanity of the person on the other side of the cell door? How can we help deepen that person's relationship with God?

As inhumane as the overarching realities might be, the moment of connection between the person inside the cell and the person outside the door is deeply human. What does a person in solitary confinement need?

Please flush. Many solitary confinement cells have toilets that cannot be flushed from inside the cell. The reasons that support this restriction are as varied as "making sure the occupant cannot flush contraband before the officers can get the door opened" to actual experience of inmates clogging the building's plumbing by flushing towels or pillow cases down their cell toilet.

Regardless, the presenting need that often confronts the volunteer on an administrative confinement tier is a series of notes in every cell door window with the hand-scrawled request "Please Flush." If the time is 8:00am and breakfast was served through the food-flaps at 6:00am, the stench of 50 or 100 un-flushed toilets on the wing can be quite impressive.

As with everything else inside prison, we volunteers do not act on impulse. For example, we do not simply jump up and push all the flush buttons. First, we request permission from the tier officer or wing sergeant. Why?

It is possible that staff has not flushed the toilets because of information that an occupant of one of those cells has made a shiv to stab a night shift officer when the cell door is opened for showers. That would mean the reason no toilets have been flushed on the wing is that a high-security extraction team, called a goon-squad, is headed to the wing for a shakedown to search every cell for a shiv. If we were to jump up and push the flush buttons outside each cell, the security team will never know if a shiv was flushed. The unhappy security team will make sure that the "too eager to help" volunteer never flushes a toilet in that prison again.

Assuming the officer-in-charge nods approval for us to flush the toilets, then we may proceed to do so, but only very carefully. Solitary cell inmates frequently hand wash their underwear in their toilets. If we are merrily traversing the tier pushing all the flush buttons without first confirming, cell-by-cell, that the inmate inside that cell wants a flush, our intended corporal work of mercy could become an unintentional act of extreme provocation because the brand new underwear that took years for the inmate to get was just flushed down the commode!

Human Interaction. It is a safe assumption that most of the inmates in an administrative segregation unit are craving human interaction. Even if they do not want spiritual interaction, there is usually a desperate need to communicate with someone, anyone, who is not wearing a uniform. The moment of interaction can be as simple as asking them how they are, how their family is, and would they like to pray for anything? Usually the inmate will ask if we will be coming back (either later that day or in the future). Never say "yes" unless the answer is certainly "yes."

In wings that have a high prevalence of mental illness, we must be especially careful about ways an inmate inside the cell can hurt a person in front of the cell door. For example, by sticking a pin or pen point through the hearing holes in the cell door window one can puncture a volunteer's eardrum.

We should also be on the lookout for schemes to shower "free people" like us who are walking in front of the cell door with excrement, urine, or other body fluids. A food tray lid or other plastic surface lying on the floor partially outside the cell door and partially inside it can be such a trap. Unnoticed in the business end of the tray lid, sticking out just in front of the cell door, is the payload of urine or excrement. When a person passes in front of the cell, the cell occupant stomps down with their full body weight on the portion of the lid inside their door. Mechanically the bottom of the door acts like an inverse fulcrum, and the payload is projected all over the person in front of the cell. Needless to say, this may be hilarious for the inmate and not much fun for the naïve volunteer.

Prayer. A constant need for inmates in administrative segregation is for prayer. We volunteers do well to respond to such a general request with the question: what would you like to pray for today? Usually the inmate will list the needs of friends and family, especially children and parents. When we are able to listen intently and then include in the prayer we say in front of the inmate all the people he or she mentioned, the inmate will know that someone who really cares (and listens) has visited their cell.

Spiritual material. We volunteers covering solitary confinement cells will constantly be asked for reading material. As with everything else in confinement, we begin by requesting approval from the officer-in-charge. "Is anybody on this wing restricted from receiving religious material to read? Are books allowed or just magazines? Do the staples have to be pulled before we give them magazines?"

Perhaps the most powerful way for us to understand the needs of the inmates inside a cell is to imagine ourselves inside that cell. I have done this many times as a prayerful exercise in preparation for a day of rounds in solitary confinement. But nothing imagined came close to the reality of being locked in a solitary confinement cell at a local jail two hundred miles from home.

From the Inside Out

The phone call came a few weeks before Christmas. A Catholic inmate on Florida's death row had been returned to local court for a new trial. This man, who has always claimed innocence, was undergoing his sixth retrial and was housed in the local jail on their "red dot" wing, the high security administrative segregation wing.

Evidently, the local sheriff had decided that no pastoral services could be provided to the inmates in administrative segregation by local clergy or lay ministers. When the inmate and his family objected to this deprivation, the

WHEN WE VISIT JESUS IN PRISON

reported response of the sheriff was, "Let that guy who does it on death row come and do it here."

The wording sounded more like a challenge than an invite. This was especially so in light of the exchange that had occurred just days earlier between me and the state attorney on the case. I had been asked to provide a letter to the court about my experiences with the inmate as a pastoral advisor. This resulted in a phone call to me from the state attorney.

"May I assume that you are against the death penalty in all cases?" he asked.

"Of course I am," I responded innocently, "I am Catholic."

He informed me in no uncertain terms that plenty of Catholics, including his own wife and her whole family, support the death penalty.

Although I am inclined to look askance at conspiracy theories in general, the connect-the-dots function in my brain kept linking that exchange with the state attorney to the sheriff's insistence that only I could provide the pastoral services for this inmate at his jail. I wanted to stop thinking of that possibility as I contemplated the 200-plus mile drive to his jail. Unfortunately, my brain does not have the software for a "disable conspiracy theories function" option.

At the same time, I also knew that the inmate involved is a faithfully practicing Catholic who receives the Sacraments regularly. He had been stuck in that jail for almost six months awaiting retrial. Someone needed to bring Communion to him. I hoped the priest would do it.

After thorough discussion with our pastor, who served as the Catholic priest for death row, it was clear that his pre-Christmas calendar did not allow for the trip. I made the call to the jail chaplain. He was reluctant about my visit.

"Now, as a general rule, chap," he spoke very deliberately, "we don't encourage non-staff pastoral visits to the red dot wing. But, if you are determined to come, that will be fine."

Upon my arrival, the recently constructed detention facility seemed larger than life, sitting in the middle of a field in the middle of 100 miles of Florida-nowhere. As I climbed the front stairs, my mind's voice sounded like a cheerleader rallying me to the moment: "After all, this is the 21st century. What could really happen?"

The gentle jail chaplain greeted me at the front desk and escorted me to the control desk of the red dot wing. He informed the sergeant who I was and whom I was there to see. Then he patted me on the shoulder and said good-bye.

"You are welcome to stay with me at cell-front," I offered as he turned to leave. He just smiled weakly and waved good-bye.

The control officer escorted me to the front of the very last cell at the very end of the red-dot wing. That was my man. As the guard unlocked his food flap, I noted that the door on the cell immediately across the hall was wide open. I could tell that the cell was vacant, but for some reason, the gaping open cell-door felt unnerving.

About fifteen minutes into the pastoral visit, two jail guards suddenly appeared on either side of me at cell front.

"Sorry for the inconvenience chaplain," they spoke matter-of-factly. "We need to escort a dangerous man off the wing. So you'll need to step into that cell across the hall until we're done. It's for your own protection."

As I stepped into the cell, one of them barked an order and the solid steel door slammed shut behind me. There was a loud bang inside the walls as the electric bolts secured my new cell door shut. For a moment, time and breathing stopped. My heart stopped. I was standing in a six by ten-foot maximum-security solitary cell in a local jail in rural central Florida, hundreds of miles from home. My senses were frozen in the moment as dual tracks of thought fought for dominance.

"Stay calm; don't panic," whispered my wiser self. The antagonist in me, however, had a cascade of questions: "Is this a coincidence or am I in deep, deep trouble? How many people know I'm here? How do I get a message outside for help?"

My internal tug-of-war was interrupted by voices echoing down the hall from adjoining cells. "The chap is in jail!"

"That chap gonna' get gassed."

"Naw, they just gonna' beat 'em."

"Somebody teachin' that boy a lesson."

"That chap is de-e-e-a-d meat!"

The one thought, that should have been my first, finally forced its way into my consciousness. "Pray." Prayer brought a sense of calm and lucidity.

WHEN WE VISIT JESUS IN PRISON

Some operating assumptions fell into place.

Absent irrefutable evidence to the contrary, there was no plot and no conspiracy. The state attorney and the sheriff had nothing to do with this. It was just a coincidence. And anyway, they probably know I'm a lawyer. In corrections, even those who don't fear God usually fear the power of the law. I would be fine.

Also, there was a lot to be learned from this experience. I studied my new environment. A stainless steel toilet filled the rear corner of the cell. The stress of the past few minutes had caused me to need such facilities very soon. Yet, at any moment someone could look through that little window in the door or open the food flap and view me poised gloriously on the throne. How many hundreds of times have I stepped to the front of a solitary cell only to inadvertently catch the man inside on his toilet? An eerie sense of nakedness gripped me.

Even if I used the toilet without being seen, I knew it cannot be flushed from inside. How many thousands of times do inmates in solitary bang on their window, begging me to push the outside flush button from the hall? I never realized how degrading that is. "You will wait," I told myself, while starting to bounce from foot to foot.

My view from inside the cell through the small cell-door window was limited to the inmates in the two cells immediately across the hall. I made hand signs. They extended their little pocket mirrors through their open food flaps. This allowed them to see up the hall. Images in those mirrors are called *spooks*. They signaled back to me that no one was coming to let me out yet.

I have always watched the men in solitary signal back and forth with hand signs. On death row, there are no cells across the hall to signal. During my first several years ministering on death row, the men would hold their mirrors out through the cell bars to see the world outside. They could see my spook coming down the hall. Then a wire mesh was welded over their bars. No spooks to view, and no one to signal. I had no idea how dramatic an isolation that mesh creates. No wonder it causes such depression and despair.

Sitting on the cell's metal bed frame, I attempted to gauge time without looking at my watch. Had five minutes passed? Maybe ten? Seconds seemed like hours. When I finally checked to verify that fifteen minutes has passed, I find it had only been three. This is what time feels like in a solitary cell.

Painting and calligraphy are no big deal to those of us who have countless possible activities competing for our attention. But from inside this cell, the importance of purposeful activity is magnified beyond anything I could have imagined. Forced idleness behind a steel door would drive me insane.

It seemed like a long time of staring at blank walls and dancing from one foot to another before a loud bang signaled the opening of "my" cell door. My crash course in solitary confinement was over.

"Hey, chap," laughed my Catholic inmate through his open food-flap as I stepped out into the hall. "Now you're one of us."

"Almost," I waved to him, before turning to the wing officer. "By the way, sir, where is the visitors' bathroom?"

Prayer is a deep and abiding need in solitary confinement. Knowing that is a far cry from being able to teach an inmate how to pray in the sense of *praying constantly*. For one thing, there is barely enough time for me standing at the crack or the food-flap to be able to teach much of anything. But with the right tools, it can be done.

An excellent resource for instructing Catholics how to pray without ceasing is *Praying Constantly: Bringing Your Faith to Life* by Fr. Benedict Groeschel, C.F.R. Part of what makes this an ideal resource is that the book is basic enough to be left with the inmate in a cell for self-study. It also gently kneads into the dough of prayer a proper theological understanding of prayer's role in the Catholic life in all circumstances.

We volunteers in Catholic prison ministry will usually encounter many more non-Catholic Christians than we do Catholic Christians in cell-to-cell outreach. An excellent ecumenical resource for spiritual development in solitary confinement is the work and materials of the non-profit ministry *Spiritual Formation in Segregation*.[25] Founded by James Rundell, a longtime member of the American Catholic Correctional Chaplains Association, the organization responded to the escalating numbers of inmates in solitary confinement by developing and providing easy to use instructional modules on building the spiritual life. As described in an article from the Diocese of Wichita and carried by the *Catholic News Agency*: [26]

WHEN WE VISIT JESUS IN PRISON

Rundell has designed a program for the men to help themselves. The pilot program, called "Spiritual Formation in Segregation," is an ecumenical program for men in long-term segregation. It incorporates prayer, scriptural reflection, personal discernment, and journaling. From six to nine prisoners will be involved in the pilot.

"The participants will get the support and encouragement of a trained spiritual director through written correspondence," he said.

"One of the biggest problems for men isolated in prison is the need to feel they are a part of the Body of Christ," Rundell added. "This is one way to reach them to help them understand that God is there with them, that they are part of a community."

He said he designed the program to "draw from their hearts, rather than from their minds, so that they might experience the real presence of God in their lives right where they are."

Rundell added that as the prisoners progress through a module they will compose a "spiritual letter" and a "spiritual reflection" that they are required to mail to their spiritual director through Rundell. Participants will work through about 10 modules in a year.

We volunteers moving from cell-to-cell through an administrative segregation unit are a bit like the old door-to-door salespeople. We cannot stick our toe in the door physically to keep the customer interested, but we can look for ways to connect with each inmate in those cells on a human level. It can be amazing how God finds ways to make those connections.

Can a Tree Grow in Concrete?

Long-term solitary confinement in Florida does not strike anyone as a place for things to grow. Each of the wings is composed of three-story atriums that house almost one hundred inmates in individual six-foot by nine-foot cells behind a solid steel door. The noise is constant and unpleasant, the ambiance oppressive and despairing. It would be less of a miracle for a tree to take root in concrete than for a spirit to sprout in solitary. So, do miracles ever happen there?

From a cell in the middle of the corridor on the lowest level of a solitary wing, the man inside greets me with a mile of a smile. "Man, I've been waiting for you. Why didn't you tell me?"

We have been talking and praying together for four years. He is a big guy, and he is black. Unless you are a football player, those characteristics can get you a lot of negative attention at an early age. Some men handle that negativity better than others. This man responded in kind to the taunts of others.

Four years ago, I told him he was the angriest person I had ever met. Not anymore. Our original discussions focused on the immorality of revolutionary violence to achieve social change. Now, his relationship with God has blossomed and his toe is in the water of the deep personal issues.

"Why didn't I tell you what?" I ask. I peer through the small Plexiglas window into his cell. He blocks my vision by fanning a holy card I have not seen before.

"Why didn't you tell me about him?" he laughs, waiving the picture of a black man who is a canonized saint. "Why didn't you tell me that there is a black saint in the Catholic Church?"

"I didn't think of it as anything special. There are a lot of black saints in the Catholic Church."

"You're kidding! How many?"

"A whole bunch, especially from the early years of Christianity and from the mission fields."

"Man! And you don't think that's anything special?" His words are punctuated with hand slaps against both knees. He is laughing so hard the words can barely come out: "That's because you're white, Bro Dale. If you wasn't white, you'd know it's really something."

Two wings later, I am standing on the mezzanine level at the cell of a young white man who is studying the Catholic faith. RCIA in solitary confinement is a do-it-yourself course. The materials are provided by the Knights of Columbus. I'm here to answer the questions that arise as a man from a fundamentalist background comes to grips with the teachings of the Catholic Church. After we have finished the questions, he shares why he wants to become Catholic.

"When I was living in central Florida, they built this beautiful Catholic church near Disney World. It's named after Our Lady. I think it is the most beautiful thing I've ever seen. Catholics aren't afraid of beauty. Catholics make beauty a part of their faith. I need a beautiful faith.

"Also, I like the intimacy. Catholics talk about the Father and the Holy Spirit like they are real, just like Jesus. And the angels and saints are real. And everybody is helping each other with prayers and love. It's like a big family. I want that intimacy in my faith.

"And I love the Rosary. The Rosary is one of the best things that ever happened to me. I never let mine away from me."

"Most of all," his voice softens, "I love that I'll be able to give this faith to my kids. After all the mistakes I've made, this is something precious that I can do for them, something that will make their lives better. I want to give them a faith that matters."

I am convinced. A tree can grow in concrete.

So much of what we read and hear in the press and electronic media concerning prisons is focused upon men. But with the advent of mandatory minimum sentences for non-violent drug offenses and the use of conspiracy charges to snare wives and girlfriends for the crimes of the man in their life, our female prison population is soaring.

What are the special needs of women in prison, especially those with children? That is the subject of the next chapter.

"When it comes to setting women free from every kind of exploitation and domination, the Gospel contains an ever relevant message which goes back to the attitude of Jesus Christ himself. Transcending the established norms of his own culture, Jesus treated women with openness, respect, acceptance, and tenderness. In this way he honored the dignity which women have always possessed according to God's plan and in God's love. As we look to Christ at the end of this Second Millennium, it is natural to ask ourselves: how much of his message has been heard and acted upon?"

Pope John Paul II [1]

CHAPTER 13

Special Pastoral Needs of Women in Prison and of Inmates with Children

What kind of women end up in prison and jail in America today? Are they all serial killers? Are they all dangerous? Or are some of them women who, out of love for a man, stumbled or were duped into their partner's felonious activities? Are they women who fell into addiction first and, after that, into the criminal activity necessary to support the addiction? Do they have children? Do they have minor children? Are they pregnant when they arrive in prison? What happens to the children when mom goes to prison? Are some of the women in prison primary caretakers for elderly parents? What happens to these elderly parents when their daughter goes to prison?

In *Responsibility, Rehabilitation and Restoration*, the U.S. Conference of Catholic Bishops calls our attention to the disproportionate increase in the number of women in prison as of the year 2000:

While the vast majority of inmates in the United States are men, the number of women being incarcerated has increased 600 percent since 1980, largely as a result of tougher drug laws. This rate of increase is higher than the rate of increase for men. Seventy percent of female inmates are non-violent offenders, and an equal number have left children behind, often in foster care, as they enter prison.[2]

This remarkable state of affairs, especially in a society that claims to hold the nuclear family in such high regard, is less surprising when we look at the history of women in prison in western society over the last four centuries. That history is torrid and marked by sexually abusive policies and practices.[3]

Based upon the then admired workhouse approach in 1645 Amsterdam, houses of prison labor were established to reform women all over Europe. The abuses that evolved included mandatory service in prostitution, as work, for the pecuniary and other benefits of the men in charge. Even when staffing brothels was not part of the prison work detail, the female prisoners, who were considered little better than trash and having no virtue worth protection, were frequently housed along with the male prisoners without supervision. The predictable consequences were commonplace. This intermingling obtained in the colonies before the American Revolutionary War as well.

Women convicted in England of worse than petty crimes were shipped to the colonies on convict ships without protection, totally at the mercy of the sexual appetites of the crew members and the male convicts. Again, if a woman was assumed to already have lost her virginity, there was nothing to protect. Those that survived the crossing were basically assigned to factories and to "husbands" unless they arrived pregnant, in which case they were considered worthless as mates or laborers and were pretty much left to die. The general societal attitude was that the plight of such women prisoners was really their own fault; that it was due to their lack of virtue that they were abused. In fact, some male overseers defended the men who abused

WHEN WE VISIT JESUS IN PRISON

the women, arguing that the presence of women corrupted the otherwise redeemable male convicts and compromised the morals of the men who were in charge of them.

In 1820, Elizabeth Fry successfully mounted a major reform campaign to protect women on the convict ships. Women could no longer be shackled on ship, children were allowed to stay with their mothers, and women who were still nursing were not to be shipped until after the baby was weaned. And by the middle 1800s, separate prisons for women were starting to be commissioned in Europe and the U.S., although the motivations were not altogether healthy:

> The view that "females are, as a class, even more morally degraded than men" meant that protecting men from the corrupting influences of female prisoners was considered as important as saving women from sexual assault.[4]

The 1800s saw the invention of prison nurseries and passage of laws that prohibited male staff or supervisors at prisons for women. The chaplain, at that time inevitably male, had to be accompanied by female staff whenever he was in the presence of female inmates. By the 1900s, significant reform was underway in both Europe and the U.S. Europe was moving toward a psychological approach; reformers in the U.S. were anteing up on their victories in reforming the incarceration of children. This effort included identifying women whose presence in prison was more attributable to limited mental or reasoning ability than to incorrigibility. Generally, growth in female prison populations in Europe and the U.S stagnated from the 1930s through the 1960s.

The situation in the modern U.S. is drastically different from the 1960s. The trends noted by the U.S. bishops from 1980 through 2000 have continued. In its 2007 report *The Sentencing Project* summarized the more recent statistics:[5]

+ More than one million women are currently under the supervision of the criminal justice system in the U.S.

+ More than 200,000 of these women are confined in state and federal prisons or local jails.
+ Expanding at 4.6% annually between 1995 and 2005, women now account for 7% of the population in state and federal prisons.
+ The number of women in prison has increased at nearly double the rate of men since 1985, 404% vs. 209%.
+ Women in state prisons in 2003 were more likely than men to be incarcerated for a drug offense (29% vs. 19%), or property offense (30% vs. 20%), and less likely than men to be incarcerated for a violent offense (35% vs. 53%).

The most recent update of those statistics is reported in *The Changing Racial Dynamics of Women's Incarceration.*[6]

Since that time, the rate of growth of women in prison has exceeded the rate of increase for men, rising 646% from 1980 to 2010, compared to a 419% increase for men. As a result, in 2010 there were 112,000 women in state and federal prison and 205,000 women overall in prison or jail; women now constitute 7% of the prison population....
   As of 2009, 25.7% of women in prison were serving time for drug offenses, as were 17.2% of men.

Other trends noted by the U.S. bishops in 2000 that continue to hold sway are as follows:[7]

+ The "war on drugs" has been most influential in the nationwide expansion of the prison population, having a particularly devastating impact on women over the past 25 years.
+ Women are now more likely than men to serve time for drug offenses.
+ Women are subject to increasingly punitive law enforcement and sentencing practices, despite the fact that women are less likely than men to play a central role in the drug trade.

WHEN WE VISIT JESUS IN PRISON

+ Women's higher proportion of incarceration for property crimes than men's reflects the extreme economic disadvantages that many women face prior to incarceration.

The numbers at the level of state law enforcement and incarceration are equally devastating:[8]

+ Women incarcerated in state prisons were less likely than men to have been convicted of a violent offense (35% vs. 53%).
+ Women incarcerated in state prisons were more likely than men to have been convicted of a property or drug crime (59% vs. 40%).
+ One in three female offenders in state prisons is incarcerated for a violent offense.
+ From 1986 to 1996, despite the fact that the rate at which women used drugs actually declined substantially, the number of women incarcerated in state facilities for drug offenses increased by 888%, compared to a rise of 129% for non-drug offenses.
+ Overall, drug offenses constituted half (49%) of the increased number of women in state prisons between 1986 and 1996.

The report reveals a devastating picture of the impact of female incarceration on families:[9]

The likelihood that children will have parents who are incarcerated is disproportionately linked to race. In 1999, one of every 14 black children had a parent in prison, compared with one in every 125 white children. Black children are almost nine times more likely than white children to have a parent in prison, and Hispanic children are three times more likely.

In absolute number that means:[10]

+ Over 1.5 million children have a parent in prison.
+ More than one in five of these children is under five years old.
+ Among female state prisoners, two-thirds are mothers of a minor child.
+ For many women, incarceration may last for a significant part of their child's formative years, and in some cases it may lead to a loss of parental rights.

The inevitable question in the face of such statistics is, "who is taking care of the children?"[11]

+ 28% of mothers report that their children live with their fathers while they are incarcerated.
+ Nine out of ten mothers (90%) report that their children live with a grandparent, other relative, or a friend of the mother (this could include the children's fathers).
+ 10% of women have children living in a foster home or agency.
+ Women in prison are five times more likely than men to report having children removed from their immediate families and placed in a foster home or other agency.
+ A 1997 survey found that only 6 out of 38 (16%) responding state child welfare agencies had enacted policies or created programs to address the needs of children with incarcerated parents.
+ A majority of parents in state and federal prisons are held over 100 miles from their prior residence.
+ In federal prisons, 43% of parents are held over 500 miles away from their last home.
+ Over half of female prisoners have never had a visit from their children.
+ One in three mothers has never spoken with her children by phone while incarcerated.

The Sentencing Project report concludes that "The growing rate of women's incarceration calls for a critical evaluation of the social impact of our nation's increasing reliance on correctional facilities to deal with women's involvement in crime.... There is an increasing need for further consideration of the nature of women's involvement in crime in order to respond appropriately to the personal and structural causes of their criminal behavior rather than relying solely on punitive responses."[12]

The persistence of the statistical evidence about the effects of incarceration on women in the U.S. makes the recommendations of the Catholic Bishops of the South all the more relevant and timely. In *Women in Prison*, the seventh letter in their series of pastoral letters on the subject of crime and punishment in the southern part of the country, they instruct us as follows:[13]

+ The population of women in prison in the U.S. is escalating faster than that of men in prison.
+ The U.S. now has 10 times more women in prison than the combined nations of Western Europe, with approximately the same number of women in the population.
+ The majority are single parents of minor children.
+ They tend to be depressed rather than angry.
+ They are pregnant; they are mothers and grandmothers.
+ They are undereducated and underemployed.
+ Most should be in treatment programs, not in jail.
+ While women are in prison, they are subject to more sexual misconduct, both from other prisoners and the correctional staff. [14]
+ Nine out of ten women in prison are substance abusers.
+ Many are clinically depressed or are diagnosed with bipolar disorder.
+ Incarcerated women are generally mothers of minor children and suffer deeply as a result of separation from their families.
+ The overwhelming number of women in prison belong

in treatment, classrooms leading to a General Education Diploma, and/or vocational training, rather than in prison.

+ Statistics indicate that more than 57% of the women incarcerated in our nation's prisons have suffered severe and prolonged physical and/or sexual abuse.

+ Most women in our correctional system are poor, and many were accomplices to crimes committed by their boyfriends or husbands.

This last item referenced by the Catholic Bishops of the South is so prevalent that it has a nickname: *the girlfriend problem:*[15]

> In the criminal justice system, the slang term for one aspect of this is called *the girlfriend problem*:
> The advent of mandatory sentencing policies for many drug offenses at times imposed a particularly harsh burden on women offenders, with one aspect of this sometimes described as the "girlfriend" problem. That is, since the only means of avoiding a mandatory penalty is generally to cooperate with the prosecution by providing information on higher-ups in the drug trade, women who have a partner who is a drug seller may be aiding that seller but have relatively little information to trade in exchange for a more lenient sentence. In contrast, the "boyfriend" drug seller is likely to be in a better position to offer information, and so may receive less prison time for his offense than does the less culpable woman.

Thus, the recommendations of the Catholic bishops of the South continue to be valid and applicable.

+ Overwhelming numbers of women in prison belong in treatment, rather than in prison.
+ Greater advocacy for using probation rather than incarceration.
+ Educational opportunities are desperately needed.

WHEN WE VISIT JESUS IN PRISON

+ Vocational training must be greatly expanded.

The U.S. criminal justice system is a far cry from meeting those proposals:[16]

+ With respect to substance abuse treatment:
  • 60% of women in state prison have a history of drug dependence.
  • During incarceration only 1 in 5 women in state prisons with a history of substance abuse, and 1 in 8 women in federal prisons, receives treatment for substance abuse.

+ With respect to mental health care:
  • Nearly 1 in 4 women in prison are diagnosed with a mental illness.
  • 12% of women in jails have severe psychiatric disorders.
  • Fewer than 25% of them receive mental health services.

+ With respect to education:
  • 44% of women in state prison have neither graduated from high school nor received a GED.
  • 14% of women in state prisons have had some college-level education.
  • Half of women in prison participate in educational or vocational programming—only one of every five women takes high school or GED classes.
  • Only half of women's correctional facilities offer post-secondary education.

And, as regards even basic medical care, the situation can be deplorable. In the largest women's prison in the nation, Lowell Correctional Institution for women near Ocala, Florida, there is nothing natural about dying from natural causes.

State investigations seem to focus only on whether or not death was attributable to abuse or physical injury. The fact that women are dying from lack of medical care or from incompetent medical care is not a concern. The state simply notes "death by natural causes" and closes the file.

As a 2015 article in *The Miami Herald* by Julie K. Brown titled "Rats, bugs and 'natural' deaths at Florida women's prison, the nation's largest" documents: "Of the 57 deaths at Lowell over the past decade, only one—a disputed suicide in 2008 in which the inmate allegedly hanged herself while handcuffed—has been categorized as anything other than "natural."[17]

Other peoples' daughters, mothers, grandmothers, and granddaughters are dying in prison from routine conditions that would respond positively to the most basic medical treatment. All in the name of saving money for the taxpayers or increasing dividends for the shareholders of private service prison providers. As Kat Jones, a female inmate at Lowell told *The Miami Herald* investigator:

> When she went to prison she thought it was the other inmates, especially the killers and other violent offenders, she was going to have to worry about.
>
> "You don't have to worry about the inmates; you have to be worried about the people who are supposed to be there to protect you and take care of you."[18]

Perhaps, when it comes to caring for vulnerable women in institutions, our society is not as different from those of the 16th and 17th centuries as we would like to think.

Another major issue faced by women in prison is the specter of completely losing parental rights to their children. Sometimes, a law passed with good intentions can have horrendous consequences on the people it affects, as *The Sentencing Project* report points out:[19]

+ The Adoption and Safe Families Act of 1997 (+ASFA) was passed "to reduce long-term stays in foster care by facilitating quick termination of parental rights and speedy adoption."

+ States are authorized to initiate termination of parental rights when a child has been living under foster care for 15 of the last 22 months.
+ More than 60% of mothers in prison are expected to serve more than 24 months on their current sentence.

It is clear that the incarceration of either parent has a detrimental effect on the children, however, as pointed out in the report *Incarcerated Parents and Their Children*, which summarizes a section of a scholarly article published in *Family Relations: An Interdisciplinary Journal of Applied Family Studies*:

> There is some evidence that maternal incarceration can be more damaging to a child than paternal incarceration, which results in more children now suffering negative consequences.
>
> The number of incarcerated mothers has more than doubled (122%) from 29,500 in 1991 to 65,600 in 2007. The effect of parents' incarceration on children is related to a number of factors, including whether the child was living with the parent, whether the family unit was a one-parent or two-parent household, whether the parent was the sole earner, the age of the child, and the surrounding support network. While the effects can differ among children, the consequences of incarceration of a parent on a child are long-lasting and need to be considered when analyzing the ramifications of an expanding prison population.[20]

Finally, a sad and extremely gruesome reality of modern day incarceration of women is the fact of sexual abuse in prisons and jails. In *Women Behind Bars: The Crisis of Women in the U.S. Prison System*, investigative journalist Silva J.A. Talvi reveals the plight of incarcerated women in gripping detail. After documenting the actual cases of rape and sexual abuse by staff, a horror that had become part of the culture at Federal Correctional Institution, the federal women's prison in Tallahassee, Florida, she notes that:

None of these men went to prison for their crimes. In fact, until 2006, prison rape had not even been classified as a felony within the BOP [Federal Bureau of Prisons]....

Today, one in four women reports having been sexually abused while in jail or prison.... In 2005, more than six thousand inmates filed reports of sexual violence, another figure that is actually likely to be much higher because of the common fear of retaliation within prisons.[21]

The literature dealing with the harsh realities of sexual abuse of women inside prisons and jails is almost too distressing to read. In the pastoral letter *Women in Prison*, the Catholic Bishops of the South cite the investigative report *A World Apart: Women, Prison, and Life Behind Bars* by Cristina Rathbone. The facts recounted by Ms. Rathbone are both gut-wrenching and infuriating. Even so, Ms. Rathbone had to wage two lawsuits against the Massachusetts Department of Corrections in order to get access to the female inmates at MCI-Framingham who wanted to tell their experiences to the outside world. She informs us that state secrecy and lack of public accountability is the order of the day for the island-police states we call prisons and jails:

Almost every major periodical in the country has had to shelve prison stories because access was denied. Despite attempts by press organizations to rally against such restrictions, the trend to exclude media from prisons continues to grow apace with the system itself.[22]

Our federal, state, and local corrections systems for women are screaming for correction themselves. With the realities detailed above firmly in mind, we volunteers in Catholic prison ministry prepare to meet the women at the prison or jail served by our local church. It can be helpful in our preparation for encountering the pastoral needs of women in prisons and jails to visualize ourselves in the place of a woman in the grips of the corrections system.

Imagine a young mother in her late-twenties who has recently been incarcerated in a medium security prison in a two-person cell. She is attractive enough, not ugly and not really beauty queen material. She has left a three-year-old daughter behind to be cared for by her elderly grandmother. It is not surprising that this woman has come to prison on drug charges as a co-conspirator with her boyfriend, who was trafficking. She has the classic girlfriend problem. She did use drugs before coming to prison, but she did not sell them. She has never been violent, never even held or owned a gun, never participated in her boyfriend's drug dealings. As this young woman lies down on her bunk to try and sleep at night in her cell, what might be some of the fears and angers that keep her awake?

+ **Fear for well-being of children:** What will happen to my daughter if grandma dies or gets seriously ill? Will grandma be able to take care of my baby?
+ **Fear for personal privacy:** Will the male guards on the wing be looking through the glass window in the cell door while I sleep? Will the male guards on the wing be looking through the glass window in the cell door when I use the cell toilet? Who will be watching when I use the shower just outside the guard station?
+ **Fear for personal survival:** Will I need to trade sexual favors in order to get phone time to talk to my daughter? Will I need to give in to sexual advances in order to stay out of the hole?
+ **Fear of rape:** Will any of the male guards try to rape me in my cell? Will any of the male guards try to rape me at my work in the kitchen? Will any of the male guards try to rape me after putting me in the hole?
+ **Fear of disappearing:** Will anyone try to kill me if I refuse to give-in or refuse to keep quiet about being raped and abused?
+ **Anger at the boyfriend:** That worthless, no good, poor excuse of a man sold me down the river and cut a deal by

rolling over on his friends. He was the one dealing drugs and he is not in prison as long as I am.
+ **Anger at self:** Why did I get myself into this situation? I deserve whatever happens to me. If anything happens to my child because I am not there, it is my fault.

Imagine that same young women who came to prison in her late-twenties is now about to be released. She has completed her mandatory minimum sentence which, with time off for good behavior and credit for her days in jail pending trial, has come down to six years of hard time. Her daughter is now nine-years old. Her grandmother passed away three years ago and the daughter has been living on the other side of the country with an aunt ever since. They have spoken on the phone about once a month but have had no visits since the grandmother died. It is the night before she will be released. What might be her fears and angers as she lies down on her bunk to try and sleep?

+ **Fear of the unknown:** What will life be like now on the outside? What kind of a neighborhood will I live in?
+ **Fear for personal survival:** Will I be able to get a job and an apartment?
+ **Fear of losing her child:** Will I be able to get my daughter back?
+ **Fear of losing relationship with her child:** Will my daughter even want to live with me?
+ **Fear of being alone:** What kind of people will be willing to be my friends?
+ **Fear of inadequacy:** Will I be able to adapt to life outside prison or have I become "institutionalized" without realizing it?
+ **Fear of revealing her abuse:** Will any man want me as his partner? If there is a man in my future, how can I make sure he never finds out the things I had to do for the guards in order to survive in here?

WHEN WE VISIT JESUS IN PRISON

✦ **Anger at self:** Why did I get myself in this situation? How do I prevent it from happening again?

We volunteers in Catholic prison ministry will recognize that many of these angers and fears are the same or similar to those mentioned in Chapter 11, with respect to inmates newly arrived to prison and jail. Our response will be similar as well. With respect to the anger, we *receive* it without *absorbing* it. We listen, love, and pray. With respect to the fear, we stand with the inmate and say, "Do not be afraid." We are always prayerfully attentive for openings where there may be receptivity to truth, to conviction of sin, to repentance and conversion, and to introduction to the Eucharistic life. These steps cannot be forced or imposed upon anyone. Instead they must be carefully discerned.

The element that is new in the case of some women in prison or leaving prison is their sense of self-loathing and responsibility for the things that have happened to them in prison. No woman should live in prison or leave prison feeling responsible for being raped or for acts she was forced to perform under duress or threats of violence. We cannot allow her to blame herself or side with her abusers. She is the victim. For the woman whose self-image has been buffeted by incarceration or been destroyed by violence and sexual abuse during incarceration, we have to bring the healing words of the Church by recognizing both her human dignity and her special dignity as a woman. As the Catholic Bishops of the South put it:

> Pope Paul VI once wrote: "Within Christianity, more than in any other religion, and since its very beginning, women have had a special dignity, of which the New Testament shows us many important aspects." We do not tolerate sin or crime. But we bishops of the southern US call our people to recognize the dignity of those women who suffer from incarceration in our prison system and to help them toward responsibility, reconciliation and restoration. [23]

This dual dignity which is inherent in each woman is clearly delineated by Pope John Paul II in his Apostolic Exhortation *On the Role of the Christian Family in the Modern World (Familiaris Consortio)*:

> In creating the human race "male and female," God gives man and woman an equal personal dignity, endowing them with the inalienable rights and responsibilities proper to the human person. God then manifests the dignity of women in the highest form possible, by assuming human flesh from the Virgin Mary, whom the Church honors as the Mother of God, calling her the new Eve and presenting her as the model of redeemed woman. The sensitive respect of Jesus towards the women that he called to his following and his friendship, his appearing on Easter morning to a woman before the other disciples, the mission entrusted to women to carry the good news of the Resurrection to the apostles—these are all signs that confirm the special esteem of the Lord Jesus for women. The Apostle Paul will say: "In Christ Jesus you are all children of God through faith.... There is neither Jew nor Greek, there is neither slave nor free, there is neither male nor female; for you are all one in Christ Jesus."[24]

A woman who has experienced violence and sexual abuse before or during incarceration, as Cristina Rathbone describes in her book *A World Apart: Women, Prison, and Life Behind Bars*, has been violated in both her human dignity and her special dignity as a woman. That is addressed clearly by Pope Pope John Paul II in *Familiaris Consortio*:

> Unfortunately the Christian message about the dignity of women is contradicted by that persistent mentality which considers the human being not as a person but as a thing, as an object of trade, at the service of selfish interest and mere pleasure: the first victims of this mentality are women.[25]

We Catholic volunteers come against this violation of dignity with the hope and healing of the Gospel message as expressed by Pope

WHEN WE VISIT JESUS IN PRISON

John Paul II in his *Letter to the Women of the World*:

> When it comes to setting women free from every kind of exploitation and domination, the Gospel contains an ever relevant message which goes back to the *attitude of Jesus Christ himself*. Transcending the established norms of his own culture, Jesus treated women with openness, respect, acceptance, and tenderness. In this way he honored the dignity which women have always possessed according to God's plan and in his love.[26]

That summary crystallizes what Pope John Paul II had already elaborated in detail years before in his Apostolic Letter *On the Dignity and Vocation of Women on the Occasion of the Marian Year (Mulieris Dignitatem)*:

> In the person and mission of Jesus Christ...we also recognize *what the reality of the Redemption means* for the dignity and the vocation of *women*. This meaning becomes clearer for us from Christ's words and from his whole attitude towards women, an attitude which is extremely simple, and for this very reason extraordinary, if seen against the background of his time. It is an attitude marked by great clarity and depth....
>
> It is universally admitted—even by people with a critical attitude towards the Christian message—that i*n the eyes of his contemporaries Christ became a promoter of women's true dignity* and of the *vocation* corresponding to this dignity. At times this caused wonder, surprise, often to the point of scandal: "They marveled that he was talking with a woman" (John 4:27), because this behavior differed from that of his contemporaries. Even Christ's own disciples "marveled...."
>
> In all of Jesus' teaching, as well as in his behavior, one can find nothing which reflects the discrimination against women prevalent in his day. On the contrary, *his words and works always express the respect and honor due to women*. The woman with a stoop is called a "daughter of Abraham" (Luke 13:16),

while in the whole Bible the title "son of Abraham" is used only of men. Walking the *Via Dolorosa* to Golgotha, Jesus will say to the women: "Daughters of Jerusalem, do not weep for me" (Luke 23:28). This way of speaking to and about women, as well as his manner of treating them, clearly constitutes an "innovation" with respect to the prevailing custom at that time.

This becomes even more explicit in regard to women whom popular opinion contemptuously labeled sinners, public sinners, and adulteresses. There is the Samaritan woman, to whom Jesus himself says, "For you have had five husbands, and he whom you now have is not your husband." And she, realizing that he knows the secrets of her life, recognizes him as the Messiah and runs to tell her neighbors. The conversation leading up to this realization is one of the most beautiful in the Gospel (cf. John 4:7-27).

Then there is the public sinner who, in spite of her condemnation by common opinion, enters into the house of the Pharisee to anoint the feet of Jesus with perfumed oil. To his host, who is scandalized by this, he will say: "Her sins, which are many, are forgiven, for she loved much" (cf. Luke 7:37-47).

Finally, there is a situation which is perhaps the most eloquent: *a woman caught in adultery* is brought to Jesus. To the leading question "In the law Moses commanded us to stone such. What do you say about her?" Jesus replies: "Let him who is without sin among you be the first to throw a stone at her." The power of truth contained in this answer is so great that "they went away, one by one, beginning with the eldest." Only Jesus and the woman remain. "Woman, where are they? Has no one condemned you?" "No one, Lord." "Neither do I condemn you; go, and do not sin again" (cf. John 8:3-11).[27]

The failure by anyone to treat a woman as Jesus would treat her is a denial of her dignity, an offense for which the perpetrator is accountable to God and, when society does its job, is accountable to humanity. Jesus would not commit violence against her and would not sexually abuse her. We volunteers in Catholic prison ministry reflect back to each woman in prison or jail the accurate picture of her dignity before God, as a human being and as a woman. We also call her to the conversion and courage of living out that dignity in her choices for herself and her children.

Women in prison have a pastoral need to be reminded and restored in their dignity as a human being and in their special dignity as a woman. This need provides an added dimension of meaning to the Catholic understanding of prison chaplaincy services, the pastoral ministry of the priests and bishops in which we Catholic volunteers are honored to participate:

> *In this regard, the activity that prison chaplains are called to undertake is important, not only in the specifically religious dimension of this activity but also in defense of the dignity of those detained.* Unfortunately, the conditions under which prisoners serve their time do not always foster respect for their dignity; and often prisons become places where new crimes are committed. Nonetheless, the environment of penal institutions offers a privileged forum for bearing witness once more to Christian concern for social issues: "I was…in prison and you came to me" (Matthew 25:35-36). (Emphasis in original.)[28]

Where Every Day Is Mothers' Day

My wife, Susan, finishes her hair and straightens her collar. It is early Sunday morning. Time for us to head for the church.

Morning mist hugs the stucco white walls of St. Mary's of Macclenny, embracing the sanctuary with a transcendent shadow against the sunrise. A three-story stain glass window looms behind the altar. Our Blessed Mother Mary is holding the Child, while the serpent is securely underfoot. As mist and sunbeams dance around the church, the colored-glass image of Mary the protective Mother seems alive, pulsing from brilliance to darkness and back to radiance. We kneel in prayer.

At that very moment, mothers throughout the five counties of our rural parish are calling their children to breakfast and ordering them to put on their Sunday clothes. But Susan and I are praying for the women who are dressing just five minutes away, the mothers who are donning makeup and brushing their hair in the federal cells at the local jail.

We never asked to do a Eucharistic service at the jail. It all started because a young woman from up north found herself doing federal time in the rural south, a thousand miles from home. That is not unusual. Many small counties contract to hold prisoners until beds open up in federal prisons. For the government, it is cheaper to pay the daily charges to the local sheriffs than it is to build more federal prisons. But inmates can end up half a country away from their families.

God bless the non-Catholic ministers at our local jail. The poor fellows had not banked on the tenacity of the Yankee cradle-Catholic who demanded worship services in her own faith. She told us that for six months she had written letters through the jail chaplains to our local church and to our bishop. No one ever received them.

Finally, she met a Southern Baptist Pastor who knew Susan and me personally. He called and gave us the inmate's name, saying, "That girl want a Catholic service and nutin' else 'll do her."

That is how it began. It is time. Susan and I are inside the visiting room to greet the five ladies as they file in. Hair primped. Make-up perfect. Jail inmate uniforms as clean as they can get them. This is their Sunday church. Only one thing is missing: their children.

At the end of the service, we join hands in prayer. The women offer their deepest heartfelt needs. The prayers are for their children. One has three children being raised by her elderly mother in the rural Midwest. If only the inmate could look after them, know what they are doing, who they are with. She prays they won't fall into the ways that brought her to prison. Another has two children being raised by an aunt in Florida. Her three-year-old daughter is sick. The family has decided not to tell the girl that her mom is in prison. She holds Susan's hand as they pray for Jesus to protect the little girl's heart from spirits of fear and abandonment. A third woman has children liv-

WHEN WE VISIT JESUS IN PRISON

ing with a family member in a large urban inner city. She can't even vocalize her prayer. All that will come out is tears.

It is time for us to leave.

Susan and I sit quietly in the jail parking lot for a minute before returning the Blessed Sacrament to the parish church. Susan has ministered to women in prison on Mothers' Day. But today isn't officially Mothers' Day.

"I thought the pain of separation from their children was especially bad on that day," she sighs deeply. "I didn't realize that for a mother in prison, the pain is there every single day. Every day is Mothers' Day."

What can we Catholic volunteers do to be responsive to the needs of families with a mother in prison? Most prisons and jails will not allow the religious volunteers who actually come into the prison to be involved with the family or children on the outside. That means the work of the volunteers in Catholic prison ministry is one of educating the members of their parish about the needs outside the prison and about the teaching of our Church on responding to those needs. As mentioned in Chapter 10, the Church is telling us that our intact families have a Gospel duty to intervene in service and attention to the suffering of those who are impoverished, orphaned, in mourning, in doubt, in loneliness, and abandoned. The Church calls our attention to the activities of guardianship and adoption. Through the words of Pope John Paul II in his Apostolic Exhortation *On the Role of the Christian Family in the Modern World (Familiaris Consortio)*, Holy Mother Church specifically challenges us to be responsive to the needs of the *children of the incarcerated*:

> An even more generous, intelligent and prudent pastoral commitment, modeled on the Good Shepherd, is called for in the case of families who, often independently of their own wishes and through pressures of various other kinds, find themselves faced by situations which are objectively difficult.
>
> In this regard it is necessary to call special attention to certain particular groups which are more in need not only of assis-

tance but also of more incisive action upon public opinion and especially upon cultural, economic, and juridical structures, in order that the profound causes of their needs may be eliminated as far as possible.

Such for example are the families...of those in prison.[29]

This can mean working with the incarcerated parents and the legal community to protect parental rights from premature and unnecessary termination under the Adoption and Safe Families Act of 1997. It can also mean intervening on a temporary basis to assure the safety and health of young children and newborns while their mother is in jail or prison.

Any Catholic parish in the U.S. with retired mothers and retirees with social work or medical backgrounds could work to provide such services. The goal would be to make sure that children with incarcerated parents have their basic needs being met and are surrounded by a community of love and respect. This activity would also frequently involve re-entry services for the mother upon her release. Such an outreach would involve licensing and training of volunteers and extensive networking with social service agencies for wrap-around care. Surely, any parish group that has the talent to organize and handle the logistics for a pilgrimage to Eastern Europe would have the talent to pull together a parish team to create an outreach in their local community for young children and newborns while their mother is in jail or prison. This would be an excellent way for Catholic families to live out the challenge presented us by the *Compendium of the Social Doctrine of the Church* and by Pope John Paul II in *On the Role of the Christian Family in the Modern World (Familiaris Consortio)*.

Another way of assisting with incarcerated mothers and newborn children is through establishing and operating prison nurseries and community-based residential programs. Here is the suggestion of the Institute on Women & Criminal Justice in the report, *Mothers, Infants and Imprisonment: A National Look at Prison Nurseries and Community-Based Alternatives*:

WHEN WE VISIT JESUS IN PRISON

There is no national policy that dictates what happens to children born to mothers who are under correctional supervision. The overwhelming majority of children born to incarcerated mothers are separated from their mothers immediately after birth and placed with relatives or into foster care. In a handful of states, women have other options: prison nurseries and community-based residential parenting programs.

Prison nursery programs allow a mother to parent her infant for a finite period of time within a special housing unit at the prison. Community-based residential parenting programs allow mothers to keep their infants with them while they fulfill their sentences in residential programs in the community.

The profile of women accepted into these two types of programs is nearly identical. They have committed low-level non-violent offenses, face relatively short sentences and will continue as their child(ren)'s primary caregiver upon release.[30]

A federal program available through the Bureau of Prisons that goes by the acronym "MINT," meaning Mothers and Infants Nurturing Together, is a community residential program for women who are pregnant at the time of commitment:

The MINT program is based in a residential reentry center and promotes bonding and enhanced parenting skills for low-risk female inmates who are pregnant. Women are eligible to enter the program if they are in their last three months of pregnancy, have less than five years remaining to serve on their sentence, and are eligible for furlough. Prior to the birth, the mother must make arrangements for a custodian to take care of the child. Institution and MINT staff and community social service agencies may aid the inmate in finding an appropriate placement for the child. The inmate or a guardian must assume financial responsibility for the child's medical care while residing at MINT.

The mother has three months to bond with the newborn

child before returning to an institution to complete her sentence. In select MINT programs, the inmate may stay for an additional period of bonding with the child. The decision to refer an inmate to the MINT program is at the discretion of the inmate's unit team.

Inmates in this program participate in pre-natal and post-natal classes on such topics as childbirth, parenting, and coping skills. In addition to services specifically related to parenting, MINT sites also offer chemical dependency treatment, physical and sexual abuse counseling, budgeting classes, and vocational and educational programs.[31]

Another important aspect of holding together the families of incarcerated parents and their children outside is to ensure that the prisons to which they are assigned are not unreasonably distant from the family home. That is not always easy to do because decisions about inmate transfers can be made bureaucratically for budgetary or other reasons. The needs of the inmate's family rarely register on the ledger of concerns for the decision makers. For example, the Federal Bureau of Prisons (BOP) decided to reassign an entire prison of women from Danbury, Connecticut, to Aliceville, Alabama, simply because the BOP needed more male prison cells in the Northeast. As reported by *The Hartford Courant*, it took a grassroots movement to percolate the crisis to the level of the U.S. Senate: "These women clearly did something wrong in order to get to federal prison, but their kids didn't," said U.S. Sen. Chris Murphy.... "The best way to bring any inmate back into society is to make sure that while they are incarcerated they keep their connections with their families."[32]

The new location in Alabama would be over 1,000 miles away from the homes of these female inmates in Danbury, Hartford, New York, and Boston, which are all within an hour or two drive of the current prison. The U.S. Senators signature to the letter, which included Charles Schumer (New York), Patrick Leahy and Bernard Sanders (Vermont), Jeanne Shaheen (New Hampshire), Robert P. Casey (Pennsylvania), Angus King (Maine) and Elizabeth Warren and

WHEN WE VISIT JESUS IN PRISON

Edward Markey (Massachusetts), pointed out, ironically, that BOP and the U.S. Justice Department claim to "encourage inmates to stay connected with their families."

And what happens when the female inmate is released? How will the fears of release be answered? Who will be there to receive and assist the woman returning from the isolation of prison to the complexities of society?

A model program to bridge that gap for released women is *Catherine's Center*, a Restorative Justice Program of the Society of St. Vincent de Paul of San Mateo (San Mateo County, California) in alliance with the Sisters of Mercy West Midwest Community. This is the stated purpose of *Catherine's Center*:

> The obstacles faced by women upon release from incarceration are so overwhelming that a productive life seems impossible to achieve.
>
> During twelve months of residency at Catherine's Center, women recently released from jail or prison work intensely to understand the root causes of their incarceration, develop new coping skills, and reconnect with family. The women participate in emotional counseling, substance abuse rehabilitation, as well as vocational, educational and spiritual programs.[33]

As recounted by Suzi Desmond, at that time the Program Director for *Catherine's Center*, in the organization's September Report:

> At Catherine's Center, our residents generally have co-occurring disorders (COD). Individuals with co-occurring disorders have one or more disorders relating to the use of alcohol and/or other drugs of abuse, as well as one or more mental disorders.
>
> Quite commonly, the Catherine's Center resident has experienced significant abandonment, neglect and/or abuse. She has then turned to drugs and/or alcohol in her effort to suppress her emotional pain. Often in the midst of her alcohol/

drug usage/addiction, impulsive behavior and resulting incarceration occurs.[34]

Catholic parishioners who are not able to minister inside prisons might well consider becoming involved in the creation and operation of such centers of care to help ensure that women being released from their community's prisons and jails will be empowered and equipped to stay free and never return to prison.

Another aspect of the pastoral needs of parent's inside prison is the need of inmates who are men. In addition to having the need to stay connected and involved with their children and with their extended families, male inmates can hold a need long-recognized in female prisoners: the need to heal from abortion.

Rachel's Vineyard Ministries is well known in Catholic Respect Life circles as a tremendous resource for retreats on post-abortion healing and reconciliation.[35] Thanks to the innovative collaborative efforts of the Palm Beach Diocese's (Florida) Catholic Charities' Prison Ministry and Respect Life Office, *Rachel's Vineyard Ministries* is being made available to men in prison.

As reported in *The Florida Catholic*, the results are significant and inspiring:

The new prison pilot program is a little different from the traditional Rachel's Vineyard retreats. The healing seminars consist of weekly, two-hour, Bible study format sessions.

During the inaugural session that ran ten weeks and began last June at the Martin Correctional Institution, seven men completed the program. The kickoff program was so successful that two weeks after it ended, another session began with the approval of officials. The second session drew more inmates than the first, and additional sessions followed....

"This program is all about talking about feelings. The men are living in their own prisons—emotionally and spiritually," [Donna Garner, M.S., Coordinator] said. "Many of the men in the program are not going to get out. Their acceptance of where they are and how they are going to live life out is so beautiful. That is the best thing about this ministry."

[Tom Lawlor, then Director of Prison Ministry] agrees with Gardner. "To see the men unburden themselves of a great sorrow that they have carried so long and to see them reconcile with the Lord is the best part of this ministry," Lawlor said. "It is the work of God."

One of the men who went through the program and is now a facilitator described his Rachel's Vineyard experience as "a lifesaving grace."

"I was able to accept God's grace to heal and come to know my precious daughter in heaven, Angela Grace," he said. "My life is no longer measured on a before abortion/after abortion timeline. Through the Rachel's Vineyard seminar and God's grace, I am now alive in Jesus through Mary."

Another prisoner also went through the program and signed up to help the ministry as a facilitator. He said the sessions helped him realize the dramatic influence abortion had on his life. "I now know just how much God loves me, even to the point of forgiving me for aborting my children who I now know and have a real relationship with. I know how to talk to God about how I feel and how much I wish I could go back and do it over again differently. I know I can't go back, but through Rachel's Vineyard, I am walking in healing by faith."[36]

Where Have All the Fathers Gone

A French proverb says that the more things change, the more they stay the same. That certainly seems to be true as I work my way from one new face to another in the solitary cells of the wings at Florida State Prison. The recent rounds of transfers have brought in men from all over the state. The flock has rolled over. It is time to start from scratch.

While the faces may be different, the habits are familiar. Peering through the small window into a cell with a new occupant, I cannot help but notice the photographs adorning his wall. He is about my age. Two daughters appear repeatedly in the photo sheen, moving from infants, to toddlers, to braces, to prom dresses and boyfriends. It is time to introduce myself to him and the family.

"Man, where'd you get those pictures," I chide him abruptly. "Don't you know it's against the rules to be putting up pictures of another con's stock?"

"What you talking about, crazy man?" his ricochet response fires without even asking who I am. "This may be FSP, but you got no call challenging me my babies."

"No. Those can't be *your* babies. Fess up. Where'd you buy the pictures?"

"What you mean?" every proud fatherly fiber of his being is bristling. "What are you talking about?"

"Those girls—why they're downright beautiful. Not a whiff of ugly on them. They are beautiful as babies, and gorgeous as young women. Right?"

"Yeah, that's right," he seems a bit confused at agreeing with a compliment from the man he was just wanting to stretch. "So what's your point?"

"Well, you ain't beautiful at all. There ain't any beautiful no place on you. Matter of fact, you're as ugly as sin. Those can't be your babies. They don't have a single ugly gene in their bodies!"

Before he can shake his shock, my second volley is headed his way. "I figured it out. They're adopted ain't they. Do you love 'em just like your own, even though they're adopted?"

"Man, you some kind a whacko or something? They are mine. And I love 'em to pieces." He holds a picture of each child up against the glass and tells me their names. "You blind or something? Can't you see the resemblance? I never stop thinking about 'em. They are always with me."

"No kidding? They're really yours? Wow. Your wife must be a movie star or a model or something," a hearty laugh punctuates my words. "Good thing for those girls that your ugly gene isn't dominant."

After a precious moment of awkward disbelief, the man inside the cell busts out laughing. "You mean all that was just putting me on. You were just stringing me?"

"Yeah mostly, but not completely. They really are beautiful. And, no offense brother, but you ain't."

WHEN WE VISIT JESUS IN PRISON

"Well, I'm glad you don't think I'm beautiful," he's laughing and slapping his side. "I wouldn't be talking to you if you did."

"I bet those girls love you a lot," the mood eases from the hard laughs of macho to the soft center of a father's heart in a breath. "Do they write or send you cards?"

By the end of thirty more minutes, I have listened to poems, letters, diary entries; viewed refrigerator art and Father's day cards; and enjoyed a dozen more pictures. We have become friends and will soon be like brothers.

It is harder to deal with the men who have sons. Everyone involved with prisons knows that the best statistical predictor of whether a young man will end up in prison is whether his father is or was in prison. We all know it. No one wants to talk about it. So we talk about the pictures of track, hoops, football, and prom instead.

There are over 100,000 adults in Florida's state-run prisons. Most are men. Most of them are fathers. That makes for a lot of pictures.

Other than juveniles, no one is more vulnerable in the hands of the criminal justice system than those who suffer with mental illness. The needs of the incarcerated mentally ill and of other inmates with special needs is the subject of the next chapter.

> "*Access to better legal counsel and resources often allow the rich and better educated offenders to defer or avoid prison. The incarcerated tend to be the ill-educated, the mentally ill, drug addicts, or the poor. And, because of ill-considered tougher sentencing laws and tougher parole laws that seek more to punish than to rehabilitate, our prison populations continue to grow.*"

Miami Archbishop Thomas Wenski,
then Bishop of Orlando, Florida[1]

CHAPTER 14

Special Pastoral Needs of Inmates Dealing with Mental Illness

Albert Einstein is credited with the quote: "Insanity is doing the same thing over and over again and expecting different results." Certainly this maxim applies to the corrections systems and mass incarceration of non-violent offenders, such as the mentally ill and those struggling with alcohol and drug dependency. In Florida, election season guarantees wheeling out the platitudes of "billions for punishment, not a penny for treatment," as reported in the *Miami Herald* article, "Florida considers reopening prisons":[2]

> A year after Florida closed several prisons to save money, the state says it must re-open some of them because of projections of a growing inmate population....
>
> The new request is based on a July forecast from the state Criminal Justice Estimating Conference showing that even as the crime rate continues to drop, new admissions to the pris-

on system are rising...requiring more than 1,000 new prison beds....

The sudden shift is reviving the debate over whether Florida locks up too many nonviolent drug offenders who should get treatment, not just punishment.

Archbishop Thomas Wenski succinctly targets this issue with the sharp message of Catholic teaching in his column on prisons:

Our Judeo-Christian tradition has always called for the humane treatment of prisoners and has emphasized that imprisonment should lead to the rehabilitation of prisoners so they can return to society and resume their place as productive citizens. The reality of prisons today is far from this ideal. While society needs to be protected from the worse among us, there is little effort to rehabilitate the nonviolent and the misguided. And while our constitution prohibits cruel and unusual punishment, what we see happening in our prisons is cruel and inhuman.[3]

Why would it be politically vulnerable to advocate treatment instead of punishment for the mentally ill? Why would it be politically risky to advocate drug and alcohol rehabilitation programs instead of incarceration for those with chemical dependency? Why do the press and the media label rehabilitation as coddling criminals? Where does all this misguided vengeance come from?

Western civilization has long wrestled with the problem of mental illness and incarceration.[4] The struggle is in our collective history, going back to the pre-civilization era. Near the middle of the nineteenth century, the western world entered the time known as the Reform Era. As Risdon N. Slate and W. Wesley Johnson explain in their book *Criminalization of Mental Illness: Crisis and Opportunity for the Justice System*:

Dorothy Dix (1802-1887), a socially active nurse practitioner

during the mid-1800s, after visiting jails and prisons throughout the United States, protested the criminalization of persons
with mental illness.... Many state-supported hospitals were
built and thousands of criminals who were mentally ill were
diverted from prisons and jails to state mental hospitals. The
rationale for this move was that punishment would be replaced
with healing that focused on the root cause of the deviant
behavior.... The era of hospital confinement for the mentally
ill had begun. It would last for 150 years. (Citations omitted.)[5]

Now the pendulum has swung back the other way. In addition to
the complex issues of treatment and costs, the mentally ill who end
up in prisons and jails today present a quandary of ethical and moral
challenges. Regardless of where we stand on these moral and ethical
issues, the facts are not in dispute: The number of mentally ill persons
in America's prisons and jails is exploding out of sight, just as the
number of mentally ill in civil mental hospitals is plummeting like a
rock. From 1960 to 2001, the number of mental health patients held
in civil mental hospitals dropped from over 600 per 100,000 adults in
the population down to about 25 per 100,000 adults. Meanwhile, over
the same period, the number of mentally ill persons held in prisons
skyrocketed from under 200 to over 600 per 100,000 adults.[6] It is no
secret how this happened.[7]

In the 1960s and early 1970s, this country was swept by an
enlightened and benign view that the best treatment of the mentally ill is deinstitutionalization. The mentally ill should be dispatched
from mental hospitals and sent home to their communities where
they would be supported by community mental health centers. The
community mental health centers, funded by the money saved from
downsizing mental hospitals, would enable America's mentally ill to
live a quality life outside institutions. To make a long story short, the
easiest part of the plan was completed: hospital beds for the mentally
ill were drastically reduced to a mere fraction of their former numbers, and the mentally ill were dumped back into their home communities. That is about as far as America progressed on the plan.

"Fifty years ago…half a million mentally ill Americans lived in public mental health hospitals…. Today fewer than eighty thousand people live in mental hospitals and that number is likely to fall still further. (Citations omitted.)[8]

By the time we should have been funding the community mental health centers, the Arab oil embargo and its legacy had pushed the prime interest rate into the stratosphere. The economy was on life support; Iran had seized our embassy; the USSR was invading Afghanistan; and the cold war was perilously close to becoming hot. Money was tight, and whatever funds were available were needed for defense and economic stimulation. The deinstitutionalized mentally ill poured into our city centers, surviving day-to-day on the streets and in the alleys of the most violent neighborhoods in the country.

The federal government did not provide ongoing funding for community services and while states cut their budgets for mental hospitals, they did not make commensurate increases in their budgets for community-based mental health services.[9]

During the late-1980s and early-1990s I was a volunteer handling trust funds for the mentally ill on the streets in Tallahassee, Florida's state capital. Aside from being robbed, raped and constantly in fear for their lives, a primary concern of the mentally ill that I served was their frequent visits to the county jail. Not by design, but by pure default, the criminal justice system has become the treatment plan for our severely mentally ill. That means they end up behind bars because there is no place else for them to go…. The numbers of incarcerated mentally ill are astounding:

According to the American Psychiatric Association, over 700,000 mentally ill Americans are processed through either jail or prison each year. In 1999, the National Alliance on Mental Illness (NAMI)…reported that the number of Americans with serious mental illnesses in prison was three times greater

WHEN WE VISIT JESUS IN PRISON

than the number hospitalized with such illnesses. (Citations omitted.)[10]

Florida, where I do my prison work, is no better or worse than the rest of the country. We are also imprisoning our severely mentally ill; turning them over to a massive state agency whose mission is punishment—not treatment. "At least one in nine state prisoners in Florida suffers from *severe* mental illness."[11]

Based on the number of adults incarcerated in state prisons in Florida, that translates to about 11,000 severely mentally ill persons housed in Florida prisons. And when the severely mentally ill cannot make it in prison, when they decompensate from what is being done to them and act out, they are moved to solitary confinement, locked for years at a time in a six-by-ten-foot steel-and-concrete cage, behind a steel door, without air-conditioning. They are fed through a hole in the door.... Such is the fate of the mentally ill in America today.

Recently, Dr. Dean Aufderheide, Director of Mental Health for the Florida Department of Corrections, summarized the national picture presented by the Bureaus of Justice Statistics in Washington, DC:[12]

+ about 20% of prison inmates have a serious mental illness, and
+ 30 to 60% have substance abuse problems.

He also noted that when including broad-based mental illnesses, the percentages increase significantly. In any given year, the portion of inmates that will experience a mental health problem requiring mental health services is astounding:

+ 50% of males and 75% of female inmates in state prisons, and
+ 75% of females and 63% of male inmates in jails.

In fact, according to the American Psychiatric Association, on any given day, between 2.3 and 3.9% of inmates in state prisons are estimated to have schizophrenia or other psychotic disorder; between 13.1 and 18.6% have major depression; and between 2.1 and 4.3% suffer from bipolar disorder.

As volunteers in Catholic prison ministry, we are highly likely to encounter mentally ill persons in the prisons and jails we serve. It is also very likely that, especially in rural areas of the country, we will encounter extremely primitive notions about mental illness and aberrant behavior. For example, I have repeatedly experienced the erroneous understandings of good Christian people when it comes to mental illness. Some honestly believe that mental illness is a result of moral failing. Consequently, for inmates who struggle with actual psychosis, schizophrenia, or fixed delusions, the answer of some is simply: *If they just get their heart right with Jesus, all that will clear up.*

We Catholics volunteers should immediately recognize that this attitude is a denial of the existence of mental illness itself. No one would dream of saying to inmates with a broken leg or a fractured hip: *If they just get their heart right with Jesus, all that will clear up.* In short, this lack of understanding of mental illness is a carry forward of the attitude in the 1500s, before the work of Dr. Johann Weyer used science to disprove the medieval claims of solely spiritual sources for mental illness. This primitive lack of understanding of the scientific basis for mental illness has drastic consequences for handling the needs of the incarcerated mentally ill. It also affects the public attitude toward the funding of mental health services. The latter frequently impacts the extent to which mentally ill citizens will end up incarcerated.

Even in parts of the country where the reality of mental illness is accepted, there is a great deal of misunderstanding concerning what mental illness means. I have experienced many good people who describe mental illness as a kind of slowness in reasoning or inability to make the right choices. For many people who have never dealt up close with mental illness, the concept of a fixed delusion is not something they can imagine. Sooner or later, we volunteers in Catholic prison ministry will deal up close with mental illness. So it is very important that we comprehend the reality of psychosis.

It is difficult to imagine what it must be like to be stricken with mental illness. Try to imagine a young man in his late-twenties who has come to county jail after a psychotic break. To all those around him, it seems quite clear that the young man is in jail because of criminal behavior. But in that young man's inner thoughts, nothing of the kind might be involved. He may well believe that he is sitting in jail for thirty days because he cut a hole in the exterior back wall of a convenience store so he could get to the food after an asteroid hits. That is the asteroid that he saw on television, on a cable show, the one that is going to bring about disaster and mayhem. Perhaps he broke the window of the house next door to let himself in because the neighbors had physically taken his house and put it on their lot. Or he may have set fire to the tree on the playground of a local private school because the tree was trying to demonize the children. The young man may have damaged the skirting under a mobile home in town when he crawled behind it to hide from the CIA. These things are as real to him as we know they are not real.

What is most difficult for a sane person to comprehend is that the young man is not fabricating his tale. In the illness of his mind, that story is what is real. Everything that contradicts that set of facts is not real. Consequently, it is worse than useless to respond to him, as some do: "If his momma had taken a switch to him when he lied as a young'un he wouldn't still be lying" or "Take away his clothes and give him a bucket for a toilet for three days and he'll come around." The essential ingredient of true mental illness is that it is not volitional.

Imagine that young man is in a full psychotic break sitting in a county jail cell serving a thirty day sentence for *trespass with property damage*. He is surrounded by steel and concrete and sights and sounds and smells that are eerie and unfamiliar. As the uniformed officers pass regularly outside his cell and peek in the window, what might his illness be telling him is his situation?

Could it be that the asteroid has hit, the world is under martial law, and he is being held in a walk-in cooler to be used as food for the privileged survivors? Or that his neighbors are furious that he discovered they had moved his house to their property and they have turned him over to the aliens who used their ship to lift the houses? Perhaps his mind is saying that before he could destroy the tree that was demonizing the children, the tree's soul jumped into the police and the judge, who now must be destroyed to save the city. Or maybe that the CIA knows he is here in the jail and if he steps outside the county jail cell for any reason he will be kidnapped and renditioned to a foreign country to be tortured and killed.

Any of those false beliefs would make it terrifying to step out of his cell, even for a shower. When an inmate refuses the order to come out of his cell, however, the prison or jail officers' response is to forcibly extract him from his cell.

Imagine that this young man in full psychotic break—who is sitting in the county jail cell serving his thirty day sentence for trespass with property damage —has refused to come out of his cell, even for showers. He has smeared his feces all over the walls of his cell to hide his real scent, in order to disguise his presence from those who are seeking to kill him. By the twentieth day of his thirty day jail sentence, the stench from his cell is a severe source of distress to all the jailmates and officers. Assume the sheriff of the county gets the judge to knock the sentence down to twenty days so they can get this young man out of the jail and back on the streets immediately.

Based on this young man's delusions, we can expect that he will refuse to come out of his cell. A forcible cell extraction may be ordered, meaning the young man is to be removed from the cell against his will by six officers in full riot gear with electric cattle prods and pepper spray. What might be the psychotic young man's understanding of this event? Does he now know for sure that the privileged survivors from the asteroid hit have decided it is time to marinate and cook him for dinner? Does he believe that the extraction team is really a squad of aliens in black rubber suits with masks and strange stick devices, using force fields and poison gas to subdue him so he can be taken to a laboratory where they will dissect him and study his organs? Or that the police and judge have been inhabited by the evil soul of the demonizing tree and are mutating into creatures that are half-tree, half-human and have come to destroy him so he cannot foil their evil plan. Perhaps he now knows for sure that the CIA has sent a team of black operatives to kidnap him so he can be taken far away and never seen by anyone ever again. Imagine the terror of this young man, who in his broken mind, "knows for sure" that if the extraction team removes him from his jail cell he will be killed or tortured by the CIA.

It would be reasonable to anticipate that a young man believing such things would fight the cell extraction by the jail officers so ferociously that two of them could end up in the hospital, perhaps even in critical condition. That would mean that the young man now faces *big time* for battery on a LEO (law enforcement officer). Soon, he is sitting in a state supermax prison in solitary confinement with a twenty-year sentence.

Now, different officers with different uniforms appear regularly at his door to peer in. Huge ventilator fans in the wing ceiling make constant swishing sounds and the lights keep blinking on and off. As he looks out the little window in his cell door into the open atrium three-story tier of 100 solitary cells that make up his wing, what might be his delusional understanding of his situation?

Do the privileged survivors of the asteroid hit have more food than they need right now, so the people to be eaten are being stored in this huge warehouse? Or, have the aliens moved him to their ship? Is he in a special processing facility where they will try to implant the evil of the demonizing tree into him? Or has the CIA succeeded in renditioning him to a foreign country and it is just a matter of time until they torture and kill him?

Whether the young man's delusions are any of those listed or are some others, the sure fire way to make things worse, over and over again, is for those dealing with him to refuse to believe that he really believes his delusions. Any insistence that he must be taught a lesson and be punished out of his psychosis will escalate and exacerbate the situation. Any system that cannot treat but can only punish will inevitably result in a fatal confrontation between that young man and staff. The core and critical difference between bad choices and delusions is that bad choices can be corrected, but delusions must be treated.

In order to competently approach the issues presented by the incarcerated mentally ill, it is important to be familiar with the basic vocabulary of mental illness in the criminal justice system:

+ **Anxiety disorders:** a group of mental illnesses characterized by excessive fear, distress, or uneasiness.
+ **Bipolar disorder:** a mental illness characterized by oscillating imbalances in mood, energy, and concentration, accompanied by experiences of mania and depression.
+ **Bus therapy:** a practice of some local communities to "solve" the problem of having mentally ill persons on their streets by giving them a one-way bus ticket someplace else.
+ **CIT:** an acronym for "Crisis Intervention Team" which is a police unit of specially trained officers who respond to disturbances involving mentally ill or emotionally disturbed persons. Also can refer to Crisis Intervention Training for such officers.
+ **Clinical depression:** a mental illness characterized by prolonged and recurring mood states of extreme sadness, possibly accompanied by lack of concentration, insomnia, fatigue, and suicidal thoughts.
+ **CMHCs:** the Community Mental Health Centers, local centers of support services for the deinstitutionalized mentally ill, launched under a construction initiative by President John F. Kennedy in 1963.
+ **Cost shifting:** the process of shifting the cost burden of mental health care from the federal government to the state governments and to local communities.
+ **Criminalization of mental illness:** the process of the criminal justice system absorbing the deinstitutionalized mentally ill.
+ **Deinstitutionalization of the mentally ill:** the process of emptying out state mental hospitals by releasing patients to the community outside.
+ **Delusions:** fixed false beliefs.

+ **Hallucinations:** someone's experience of sensory perceptions—visual or auditory events—that are not real.
+ **Jail diversion:** the programs that redirect the severely mentally ill away from the criminal justice system by connecting them with community services.
+ **Mental health courts:** specialized courts based upon therapeutic jurisprudence with the intent to divert the mentally ill into treatment and away from the criminal justice system.
+ **Mental illness:** a medical condition that disrupts thinking, feeling, relating, and/or functioning.
+ **MST:** an acronym for "Military Sexual Trauma," a specific kind of trauma experienced by women in the military through sexual assault or repeated threats of acts of sexual harassment.
+ **NIMBY:** an acronym for the "not in my backyard" opposition of local communities to construction of CMHCs and other social service institutions.
+ **Panic disorder:** an anxiety disorder characterized by the onset of sudden feelings of terror, with both emotional and physiological symptoms.
+ **Pill rolling:** circular movement of the opposed tips of the thumb and index finger, frequently associated with side effects of certain psychotropic medications.
+ **Post-booking diversion:** jail diversion programs that utilize components of the criminal justice system, usually mental health courts, to redirect the severely mentally ill out of the criminal justice system and into treatment after charges are filed but before incarceration.
+ **Pre-booking diversion:** jail diversion programs that utilize law enforcement, usually CITs, to redirect the severely mentally ill out of the criminal justice system and into treatment before charges are filed.

- **Privatization of mental health services:** the process of outsourcing mental health services to for-profit organizations and allocation mechanisms, such as managed care approaches to Medicaid-funded mental health services.
- **PTSD:** an acronym for "Post Traumatic Stress Disorder," which is an anxiety disorder connected with specific traumatic experiences and characterized by nightmares, flashbacks, numbness, anger, irritability, and/or lack of concentration.
- **Re-entry services:** the preventive diversion programs that intervene with severely mentally ill persons at the point of discharge from incarceration, in order to connect them with local treatment and services and thereby reduce recidivism.
- **Schizoaffective disorder:** a mental illness that evidences both the symptoms of schizophrenia and depression.
- **Schizophrenia:** a mental illness characterized by disorganized thoughts and loss of contact with reality, which can include hallucinations and delusions.
- **Snake Pit:** the title of a book (1946) and a movie (1948) which revealed the horrendous conditions inside state mental hospitals; in both cases the title refers to the ancient practice of throwing mentally ill persons into a pit of snakes, based on the theory that such an experience would make a normal person insane, therefore, it should make an insane person normal.
- **Thorazine:** a popular name of an anti-psychotic drug discovered in 1952 and which made deinstitutionalization of the mentally ill possible.
- **Thorazine shuffle:** a minimalist walking movement, with feet barely lifted and legs stiff, frequently associated with side effects of certain psychotropic medications.
- **Transcarceration:** the process of shifting the mentally ill from civil mental hospitals to jails and prisons; also called "transinstitutionalization."

When It Comes to Crime and Mental Illness, Florida's System is Badly Broken

In the heat of a controversy over privatization of one of Florida's last two state-owned and operated civil mental hospitals, State Representative Janet Adkins of Fernandina Beach published a letter in *The Florida Times Union* (Jacksonville). She included some alarming statistics.

Florida has 125,000 mentally ill persons arrested each year. Of this number, 17,000 are incarcerated in state prisons, 15,000 in local jails, and another 40,000 are under probation and parole.

The Department of Corrections spends $68 million annually for mental health care. According to the Department of Corrections, of the 1,300 discharges from state mental health treatment facilities each year an average 782 of these individuals were reported to be living in a correctional facility, hospital, nursing home, homeless shelter, or unknown location a year after discharge.

That is a pretty potent peak under the rug. What is presented as savings from rapid release of the severely mentally ill back into society and out of civil mental hospitals merely transfers them from the *caring* department of government to the *punishing* department of government.

What shows up in the budget as "civil mental health care" and is castigated by pundits as 'nanny government' for trying to take care of our vulnerable citizens is transferred in the budget to a costlier solution—incarceration—and inaccurately used to demonstrate that we are getting tough on crime. This is cost shifting at its most false. We all know it is more expensive to treat the mentally ill in prison than it is to treat them in a civil mental hospital. But the politics of punishment are easier to sell than the politics of mercy.

Representative Adkins did not even get to the issue of Florida wasting over $50 million per year on the death penalty, the extra amount the death penalty costs Florida per year above and beyond the cost of life in prison without possibility of parole.

The math is pretty simply: $68 million plus $50 million equals $118 million. What could Florida do in civil mental health services with $118 million per year?

Now there's a question worth calling a special session for!

The stance of we volunteers in Catholic prison ministry regarding the mentally ill must be cast by the directions of our Church. It is the teaching and instructions of the popes and bishops that should shape our attitude and our outreach to the suffering of the mentally ill. There is no ambiguity in the call by Mother Church for us to make a compassionate response and, when possible, to relieve suffering. Pope John Paul II could not have been more clear as he addressed all our brothers and sisters struggling with disabilities, including the mentally ill, on the occasion of the Year of the Jubilee in 2000:

> In your bodies and in your lives, dear brothers and sisters, you express an intense hope of redemption. In all this is there not an implicit expectation of the "redemption" that Christ won for us by his death and resurrection? Indeed, every person marked by a physical or mental difficulty lives a sort of existential "advent," waiting for a "redemption" that will be fully manifest, for [him or her] as for everyone, only at the end of time. Without faith, this waiting can be tinged with disappointment and discouragement; supported by Christ's word, it becomes a living and active hope....
>
> If your *civil, social, and spiritual rights* must be protected, it is nevertheless even more important to safeguard *human relations*: relations of aid, friendship, and sharing. That is why it is necessary to encourage forms of treatment and rehabilitation that take into account a complete vision of the human person. (Emphasis in original.)[13]

Pope Benedict XVI did not hesitate to add his voice to that of his predecessor when it comes to the Catholic response to the disabled, including those with mental disabilities. In his *Message for the Fourteenth World Day of the Sick* (2006), he reminded us:

> On this occasion, the Church intends to bow down over those who suffer with special concern, calling the attention of public opinion to the problems connected with mental disturbance

that now afflicts one-fifth of humanity and is a real social-health care emergency.

Recalling the attention that my venerable Predecessor John Paul II devoted to this annual event, I too, dear brothers and sisters, would like to be spiritually present on the World Day of the Sick, to pause in order to reflect, in harmony with those taking part, on the situation of the mentally ill in the world and to call for the commitment of Ecclesial Communities to bear witness to the tender mercy of God towards them....

I therefore encourage the efforts of those who strive to ensure that all mentally ill people are given access to necessary forms of care and treatment. Unfortunately, in many parts of the world, services for these sick people are lacking, inadequate, or in a state of decay.

The social context does not always accept the mentally ill with their limitations, and this is another reason difficulties are encountered in securing the human and financial resources that are needed.

One perceives the need to better integrate the two approaches: appropriate therapy and new sensitivity towards disturbance, so as to enable workers in the sector to deal more effectively with these sick people and their families, who would be unable on their own to care adequately for their relatives in difficulty....

I commend pastoral workers and voluntary associations and organizations to support in practical ways and through concrete initiatives those families who have mentally ill people dependent upon them. I hope that the culture of acceptance and sharing will grow and spread to them, thanks also to suitable laws and health-care programs which provide sufficient resources for their practical application.[14]

In the United States, a fruit of the *Pastoral Statement of U.S. Catholic Bishops on People with Disabilities* (1978)[15] has been the creation of the *National Catholic Partnership on Disability* (NCPD).[16] The NCPD office is located in the McCormick Pavilion of the Theological College of Catholic University of America, across the street from The Basilica of the National Shrine of the Immaculate Conception, and its website is a goldmine of information and resources for Catholics who are involved in pastoral care of the mentally ill, including how-to guides for sacramental observances and a Mental Illness Resource Manual.[17] The following teachings are from the NCPD web page, *Theological Framework on Mental Illness*:[18]

Human Life Is Sacred. Every Person Is Created in God's Image. "One of the fundamental truths of Christian belief is that each human being is created in the image and likeness of God (Genesis 1:26-27). The Catholic Church unconditionally embraces and faithfully proclaims this truth. It is the foundation for human dignity. Our commitment to this truth is measured through actions on behalf of the vulnerable and alienated in society, especially the poor and suffering." *Affirming the Dignity of the Mentally Ill, Nebraska Bishop's Conference*, January 2005.[19]

Since All People Are Created in the Image of God, their Dignity and Worth Cannot Be Diminished by Any Condition including Mental Illness. "Whoever suffers from mental illness 'always' bears God's image and likeness in themselves, as does every human being. In addition, they 'always' have the inalienable right not only to be considered as an image of God and therefore as a person, but also to be treated as such." Pope John Paul II, *International Conference for Health Care Workers on Illnesses of the Human Mind*, November 30, 1996.[20]

Suffering Is Redemptive When United to Christ. "Those who share in the sufferings of Christ are also called, through their own sufferings, to share in (eschatological) glory." Pope John Paul II, *On the Christian Meaning of Suffering: Salvifici Doloris*.[21]

The take-home message for us volunteers in Catholic prison ministry is that the upshot of the Church's teaching is diametrically opposed to both the primitive and neo-Calvinistic notions that mental illness is either a moral failing or proof of God's predestination to hell. Pope John Paul II could not be more clear on this:

> It is everyone's duty to make an active response; our actions must show that mental illness does not create insurmountable distances [from] nor prevent relations of true Christian charity with those who are its victims. Indeed it should inspire a particularly attentive attitude towards these people, who are fully entitled to belong to the category of the poor to whom the kingdom of heaven belongs. (Citations omitted.)
>
> The Church looks on these persons with special concern, as she looks on any other human being affected by illness. Instructed by the divine Teacher's words, she believes that "[humans], made in the image of the Creator, redeemed by the blood of Christ, and made holy by the presence of the Holy Spirit, [have] as the ultimate purpose of [their] life to live "for the praise of God's glory" (cf. Ephesians 1:12), striving to make each of their actions reflect the splendor of that glory" (citations omitted.)[22]
>
> The Church is deeply convinced of this truth, even when a [human being's] mental faculties—the noblest, because they testify to [our] spiritual nature—seem severely limited and even impeded by a pathological process. [The Church] therefore reminds the political community of its duty to recognize and celebrate the divine image in all [men and women] with actions that support and serve all those who find themselves in a condition of serious mental illness.[23]

Though armed with the teaching and direction of our popes and bishops, we volunteers in Catholic prison ministry will soon discover that mental illness in our society is like a mountainous iceberg: barely visible to those going about normal life in the mainstream, yet looming beneath the surface is a massive social crisis. The most prominent source of information and resources for addressing the crisis of mental illness in American society is the National Alliance on Mental Illness (NAMI). [24] The numbers, from NAMI's Fact Sheet are sobering:[25]

+ One in four adults—approximately 61.5 million Americans—experiences mental illness in a given year. One in seventeen—about 13.6 million—live with a serious mental illness such as schizophrenia, major depression or bipolar disorder.[26]
+ Approximately 1.1% of American adults—about 2.6 million people—live with schizophrenia.[27]
+ Approximately 2.6% of American adults—6.1 million people–live with bipolar disorder.[28]
+ Approximately 6.7% of American adults—about 14.8 million people—live with major depression.[29]
+ About 9.2 million adults have co-occurring mental health and addiction disorders.[30]
+ Approximately 26% of homeless adults staying in shelters live with serious mental illness and an estimated 46% live with severe mental illness and/or substance use disorders.[31]
+ Approximately 24% of state prisoners and 21% of local jail prisoners have "a recent history" of a mental health condition.[32]

The displacement, or "transcarceration," of the mentally ill from civil facilities to criminal justice facilities is abundantly clear when one looks at the numbers:[33]

+ More than 450,000 Americans with a recent history of mental illnesses are incarcerated in US jails and prisons. This includes 24% of state prison inmates, and 21% of local jail inmates.[34]
+ Of these, about 72% have a co-occurring substance abuse disorder.[35]

WHEN WE VISIT JESUS IN PRISON

+ By comparison, about 6% of the general population has a serious mental illness.[36]
+ Of probationers, 16%, or more than 500,000 people, reported having a mental disorder.[37]
+ In one study, approximately 28% of people with serious mental illness were arrested in a 10-year period. The majority of these arrests were for non-violent charges like crimes against the public order or property offenses. Many experienced repeat arrests.[38]
+ Once arrested, individuals with mental illness and substance abuse disorders spend on average seventeen more days in jail than people without these disorders who were charged with similar crimes.[39] At Riker's Island, New York City's largest jail, inmates with serious mental illness serve on average almost six months more than inmates without serious mental illness.[40]
+ People with mental illness who are incarcerated tend to have higher rates of homelessness and co-occurring substance abuse disorders.[41]
+ People who are incarcerated who have a mental illness have experienced, prior to their incarceration, higher rates of sexual and physical abuse victimization and unemployment than other inmates.[42]
+ When they are incarcerated, people with mental illness often lose access to Medicare, Medicaid, and Social Security benefits. Even when benefits should be restored upon release, reapplying for benefits can be time-consuming and complex. Without case management assistance to restore benefits, prisoners re-entering after prison are at risk of recidivating or requiring costly emergency medical services.[43]

Perhaps, one of the ways that we Catholics can carry out the teaching of our Church in this area is by seeking innovative means to protect the mentally ill from falling through the cracks into the criminal justice system. Part of that effort would be procedural mechanisms that divert the mentally ill away from the prison conveyor belts. These are called *jail diversion programs*. NAMI recommends the following as strategies that work:[44]

+ **Pre-Booking Jail Diversion:** Studies show that police-based jail diversion, especially crisis intervention teams (CIT), significantly reduce arrests of people with serious mental illnesses,[45] while better identifying individuals who need psychiatric care.[46] Individuals diverted through CIT and other pre-booking diversion programs receive more counseling, medication, and other forms of treatment than individuals who are not diverted.[47]

+ **Post-Booking Jail Diversion:** Mental health courts and other post-booking diversion programs have proven effective in reducing incarceration and improving treatment outcomes. A study of the Allegheny County (Pennsylvania) Mental Health Court revealed that the court reduced the amount of time offenders with serious mental illness spent in jail, increased the amount of mental health treatment they received, and did so at no additional cost[48]

+ **Supportive Housing:** Placing individuals who are homeless and who have serious mental illnesses in supportive housing with social services reduces time spent in jail, and reduces financial burdens on the criminal justice system. In one study, the reduced costs to the criminal justice system, shelters and emergency rooms made up for 94% of the cost of supportive housing.[49]

+ **Forensic Assertive Community Treatment:** Forensic Assertive Community Treatment (FACT) treats individuals with serious mental illness who have been involved with the criminal justice system by providing intensive round-the-clock services in the community. In one study, FACT reduced jail days by 83%.[50]

Another critical form of jail diversion program that is preventative in nature is structured re-entry. *Florida Partners in Crisis* is an independent education and advocacy organization that "promotes state and community collaboration across the mental health, substance abuse and criminal justice systems to reduce the contact of people with mental illnesses and addictions with the justice system and to actively promote the cost-effective use of tax dollars to increase public safety and improve lives."[51]

In addition to Pre-Booking and Post-Booking Jail Diversion, *Florida Partners in Crisis* advocates for well-structured re-entry for mentally ill and chemically-dependent inmates so that with community care they will be more likely to avoid the criminal justice system:

> It is estimated that approximately 97% of those individuals serving time in prisons will eventually be released back into the community. Without treatment for pre-existing mental health or substance use disorders and assistance in transitioning back into the community, these individuals are at risk of re-offending and recycling back into the criminal justice system. Florida has a number of re-entry programs under way to assist people with mental illnesses and substance use disorders to make a successful transition.[52]

Another procedural mechanism that can be implemented is specialized courts, such as mental health courts, whose focus is *therapeutic jurisprudence*:

> In mental health courts, all the courtroom personnel, such as the judge, prosecutor, defense counsel, and other relevant professionals have experience in mental health issues and are familiar with relevant community resources. Mental health courts hear cases involving defendants with mental illness in a non-adversarial proceeding. They work with the local mental health system to identify and order appropriate treatment and they monitor the defendant's compliance with its orders. Non-compliance may involve sanctions by the court, although with many courts these sanctions include jail only as a last resort....

Underlying the concept of mental health courts is the principal of therapeutic jurisprudence, which emphasizes that the law should be used, whenever possible, to promote the mental and physical well-being of the people it affects. It assumes that the application of the law can have therapeutic consequences. It should be emphasized that therapeutic jurisprudence does not diminish the importance of public safety, which is fully taken into account by the court. (Citations omitted.)[53]

But without adequate funding, diversion programs can become an interminable purgatory, instead of a therapeutic mechanism:

South Dakota courts routinely jail mentally ill defendants... for half a year or more without trial because of a backlog of court-ordered mental health exams, aggravated by a cap on evaluations at the state's mental health hospital.[54]

The problem is so acute in some communities that courts have ordered the mentally ill to be released without testing. A federal judge in Seattle wrote: "Jails are not suitable places for the mentally ill to be warehoused while they wait for services. Jails are not hospitals."[55]

Specialty courts can also be focused upon drug addiction or the specific needs of Veterans of the U.S. Armed Forces, especially those dealing with PTSD or MST. Once again, the purpose of such a court is to achieve therapeutic justice and divert the offender from the criminal justice system.

In some cases, however, diversion is not possible and compassionate justice must be addressed in terms of the punishment assessed for the crime. Such is the case with respect to U.S. Veterans who have severe PTSD and have killed people after returning home from the battlefield. An almost unknown and virtually undiscussed fact about U.S. death rows is that 10% of the people on death row in the U.S. are American Military Service Veterans.[56]

I have served as spiritual advisor to men in death row with PTSD from horrific battlefield experiences. In some cases their badges for heroic bravery under fire were used against them by the prosecution in the sentencing phase of their trial in order to obtain a death sentence:

> As such facts are finally coming to light, Brig. Gen. (Ret.) James P. Cullen, USA, (a former judge for the U.S. Army Court of Criminal Appeals), Brig. Gen. (Ret.) David R. Irvine, USA (former Deputy Commander of the 96th U.S. Army Reserve Command), and Brig. Gen. (Ret.) Stephen N. Xenakis, USA, M.D (now an adjunct clinical professor at the Uniformed Services University of Health Sciences) published an op-ed column in *USA Today* calling for a drastic and in-depth evaluation of this situation. They were not calling for exemption from punishment but noted: "Such information is a valid reason to spare a defendant from capital punishment. There are alternatives, such as life in prison without parole."[57]

In its *Public Policy Platform*,[58] NAMI spells out a coherent agenda for retooling our civil and criminal justice systems to care for our mentally ill. In addition to the procedural mechanisms available through diversion programs and specialized courts, NAMI also recommends substantive changes to the criminal laws themselves. The first proposal is for wraparound community care without involving the criminal justice system:

> **10.1 Ultimate Responsibility of Mental Health Systems.** Mental health systems have ultimate responsibility for treating all people with severe mental illness. A substantial number of people with severe mental illness require twenty-four hour, seven days per week structured care, either for long or short periods of time. It is never appropriate to allow the care of such persons to be shifted to the criminal justice system.

The second proposal is for creative and constructive use of therapeutic courts in order to access that care before the mentally ill tumble into the maws of the criminal justice system:

10.2 Therapeutic Jurisprudence. NAMI endorses the principal of therapeutic jurisprudence, which emphasizes that the law should be used, whenever possible, to promote the mental and physical well-being of the people it affects. For example, in a system characterized by therapeutic jurisprudence, people with serious mental illnesses charged with non-violent crimes are diverted into programs designed to address their treatment and service needs rather than incarcerated. Individuals with serious mental illnesses convicted of serious crimes are provided with humane and appropriate treatment while incarcerated. And, these individuals are provided with appropriate linkages to needed services and supports upon discharge to enable them to successfully reenter their communities.

The entire community of services will need to work together in order for compassionate care of the mentally ill to become a reality:

10.3 Collaboration. NAMI believes that state and local mental health authorities must work closely in conjunction with state and local correctional and law enforcement agencies to develop strategies and programs for compassionate intervention by law enforcement, jail diversion, treatment of individuals with serious mental illnesses who are incarcerated, and discharge planning and community reintegration services for individuals with serious mental illnesses released from correctional facilities.

(10.3.1) NAMI believes that at least 25% of law enforcement first responders in each jurisdiction should be trained for a minimum of 40 hours consistent with model standards for police crisis intervention training in order to better assure safety, appropriate de-escalation, less lethal consequences, and opportunities for treatment.

After delineating a prohibition on "boot camps" for mentally ill youth (10.4), NAMI proposes that states pass legislation providing a right to mental health treatment for all mentally ill citizens, whether in the criminal justice system or out in the community (10.5). After noting that mentally ill inmates are at heightened risk for sexual assault during incarceration, NAMI calls for aggressive enforcement of laws geared to prevent and punish such abuse (10.6). Next, the policy advocates for jail diversion programs:

10.7 Jail Diversion.

(**10.7.1**) NAMI believes that persons who have committed offenses due to states of mind or behavior caused by a serious mental illness do not belong in penal or correctional institutions. Such persons require treatment, not punishment. A prison or jail is never an optimal therapeutic setting.

(**10.7.2**) NAMI supports a variety of approaches to diverting individuals from unnecessary incarceration into appropriate treatment, including pre-booking (police-based) diversion, post-booking (court-based) diversion, alternative sentencing programs, and post-adjudication diversion (conditional release).

Realizing that the public is focused on fear of violence, especially homicidal violence, from criminal behavior and that there is a gross misperception that mental illness goes hand-in-hand with sociopathic violence, NAMI's proposal next addresses violence and the death penalty:

10.8 Violence and Guns.

(**10.8.1**) NAMI recognizes that when dangerous or violent acts are committed by persons with serious mental illnesses, it is too often the result of neglect or ineffective treatment. Mental health authorities must implement and sustain policies, practices, and programs that provide access to early diagnosis, crisis intervention, appropriate treatment (including integrated treatment when there is co-occurring substance abuse), and support that saves lives. NAMI strongly advocates that people with mental illnesses not be stigmatized and subjected to discrimination by being labeled "criminal" or "violent." There is very rarely correlation between mental illness and violent behavior and mental illness must not be confused with sociopathic behavior.

(10.8.2) NAMI recognizes that epidemic gun violence is a public health crisis that extenuates risks of lethal harm by others, self-harm, and harm to others for people with mental illnesses. Gun violence is overwhelmingly committed by people without mental illness. NAMI believes that firearms and ammunition should not be easier to obtain than mental health care. NAMI supports reasonable, effective, consistently and fairly applied firearms regulation and safety, as well as widespread availability of mental health crisis intervention, assistance, and appropriate treatment. In the absence of demonstrated risk, people should not be treated differently with respect to firearms regulation because of their lived experience with mental illness.

10.9 Death Penalty. NAMI opposes the death penalty for persons with serious mental illnesses.

(10.9.1) NAMI urges jurisdictions that impose capital punishment not to execute persons with mental disabilities under the following circumstances:

(10.9.1.1) Defendants shall not be sentenced to death or executed if they have a persistent mental disability, with onset before the offense, characterized by significant limitations in both intellectual functioning and adaptive behavior as expressed in their conceptual, social, and practical adaptive skills.

(10.9.1.2) Defendants shall not be sentenced to death or executed if, at the time of their offense, they had a severe mental disorder or disability that significantly impaired their capacity (a) to appreciate the nature, consequences or wrongfulness of their conduct, (b) to exercise rational judgment in relation to conduct, or (c) to conform their conduct to the requirements of the law. A disorder manifested primarily by repeated criminal conduct or attributable solely to the acute effects of alcohol or other drugs does not, standing alone, constitute a mental disorder or disability for purposes of this provision.

(10.9.1.3) Sentences of death shall be reduced to lesser punishment if prisoners under such sentences are found at any time subsequent to sentencing to have a mental disorder or disability that significantly impairs their ability (a) to understand and appreciate the nature of the punishment or its purpose, (b) to understand and communicate information relating the death sentence and any proceedings brought to set it aside, or (c) to make rational choices about such proceedings.

With respect to substantive guilt and the balancing of treatment vs. punishment, the NAMI policy proposes:

10.10 Insanity Defense. NAMI supports the retention of the "insanity defense" and favors the two-prong ("ALI") test that includes the volitional as well as the cognitive standard.

(10.10.1) "Guilty but Mentally Ill". NAMI opposes "guilty but mentally ill" statutes as presently applied because they are used to punish rather than to treat persons with serious mental illnesses who have committed crimes as a consequence of their serious mental illnesses.

(10.10.2) "Guilty except for insanity" and other alternative terminology for the insanity defense. NAMI supports systems that provide comprehensive, long-term care and supervision to individuals who are found "not guilty by reason of insanity," "guilty except for insanity," and any other similar terminology used in state statutes.

The position paper explains that:

The "ALI test" refers to the rule for insanity adopted in Section 4.01(1) of the American Law Institute" Model Penal Code. The Code states that "a person is not responsible for criminal conduct if at the time of such conduct as a result of mental disease or defect he or she lacks substantial capacity either to appreciate the criminality (or alternatively, wrongfulness) of his or her conduct (cognitive standard) or to conform their conduct to the requirements of law (volitional standard)."

States currently apply three different terms to verdicts incorporating a formal finding or acknowledgement of mental illness.

"Not guilty by reason of insanity" is the traditional term used when a person is determined as not criminally responsible due to mental illness. Individuals found "not guilty by reason of insanity" are typically sentenced to secure psychiatric treatment facilities instead of prison.

"Guilty but mentally ill" (GBMI) statutes have been adopted in the criminal codes of a number of states. These statutes currently function very similarly to "guilty" verdicts. An individual found GBMI could be sentenced to life in prison or even to death. Additionally, a verdict of GBMI does not guarantee psychiatric treatment.

"Guilty except for insanity" statutes have been adopted in several states such as Oregon and Arizona as substitutes for "not guilty by reason of insanity." These states have developed effective systems for providing long-term treatment and supervision to individuals who are found "guilty except for insanity."

Finally, NAMI recommends:

(10.10.3) "Informing Juries about the Consequences of Insanity Verdicts" NAMI believes that juries in cases where the insanity defense is at issue should be informed about the likely consequences of an insanity verdict to enable them to make a fair decision.

With respect to the handling of the mentally ill, the goal of renovation of the mental health system and the criminal justice system is to provide compassionate and competent care for our mentally ill brother and sisters in the communities where they live. In this day and age, such a notion can seem radical. Yet in reality, it is a concept that is so old, it seems new. The website of the *National Catholic Partnership on Disability*, mentioned earlier in this chapter, also familiarizes the reader with the story of St. Dymphna of Gheel, the patroness of people struggling with mental illness.[59]

There are various legends surrounding the story of Dymphna, but the core narrative is this: She was the daughter of a pagan chieftain in Ireland in the seventh century. Her mother, who had been a Christian and had baptized Dymphna, died when her daughter was 14.

Her father was devastated and had a long period of protracted grief. After a fruitless search for a second wife, his attention fell on Dymphna. Her resemblance to his beloved dead wife, coupled with his emotional and mental struggle after his wife's death, drove him to entreat her to marry him herself. Horrified, Dymphna fled with her confessor, an elderly priest by the name of Gerebran, to the city of Gheel in Belgium.

Her father pursued her and found her. His men murdered Gerebran and then, when Dymphna refused to go with him, he beheaded her.

Dymphna's refusal to participate in this incestuous relationship led to her martyrdom. She has been named patroness of people with mental and emotional difficulties—not only because of the toll that her father's mental illness took on her family but because of her own emotional and mental anguish.

Dymphna was buried in Gheel. When her body was discovered in the thirteenth century, cures and miracles were attributed to her, especially for people with epilepsy and people with mental illness.

But the most outstanding miracle is one that began centuries ago and still continues to this day. In the thirteenth century, an institution was built in Gheel where people with mental illness are admitted for a short time. Following the initial treatment, these patients are then placed with families in the village with whom they live and work side by side. The patients receive treatment without formality and gain greatly by the normal lifestyle offered to them by the villagers. The villagers see them as a part of their lives and have for centuries.

In the context of institutionalization, deinstitutionalization, and reinstitutionalization (in prisons) in our country, this truly is miraculous. All of this is attributed to a simple young princess who lost her life in defense of doing the right thing. St. Dymphna is a legend and a model and has left a legacy for care and treatment of people with mental illness that defies the "wisdom" and sophistication of our own time.

The legend of St. Dymphna is for real, as attested to by secular sources, including J. Goldstein of Samford University in Birmingham, Alabama:[60]

Geel (Gheel): Belgian city of 35,000 located in the province of Antwerp; internationally known for centuries old tradition of foster family care for mentally ill; associated with the legend of St. Dymphna (Dimphna, Dimpna).

During the Middle Ages, the church was the primary source of "treatment" for those besieged with various forms of what today we would call "mental illness." Many sought such treatment by making their way to Geel, Belgium, for intervention, through the church, by St. Dymphna, the patron saint of the mentally ill.

In 1249, this legendary Celtic princess had gained sainthood based on reported miracles and a belief that centuries earlier, in the region of Geel, she chose martyrdom rather than succumbing to her father's mad incestuous demands.

As those seeking treatment filled the church and city, there

WHEN WE VISIT JESUS IN PRISON

developed a lack of housing for the visitors, whereupon church canons instructed townspeople to open their homes to the pilgrims. Thus was planted the seed of what would become an enduring system of foster family care for the mentally ill. Geel's legendary foster family care system continued to evolve over the centuries and even today in the twenty-first century functions as one part of a modern comprehensive system of mental health services, located in Geel and serving the entire region.

Dr. Goldstein proposes the community recovery approach for the mentally ill, a *recovery model* of treatment for mental illness, wherein the individual strives to live a successful, meaningful life within their limitations (in contrast to the *medical model* which has the sole goal of symptom reduction and/or cure of symptoms):

> For the individual with mental illness striving to live a meaningful life in the context of the recovery model of treatment, opportunities for community integration serve that model and are critical to its success. Successful recovery for individuals, in turn, allows them greater ability to function as members of their community. Thus, it is logical to encourage a concept of "community recovery" in which communities strive to live with, rather than fear, the realities of mental illness. In the context of this definition, Geel can be viewed as a "recovered community."

So there is much to be done in the area of the mentally ill and the criminal justice system. That can all seem pretty academic, however, as we volunteers in Catholic prison ministry realize that a troubled inmate is approaching us from across the prison yard. We note that the inmate appears unusually agitated or depressed, or is speaking aloud to no one in particular, or is nervously pill-rolling as he walks. We can never know for sure whether an approaching inmate has slipped into the grips of a psychotic episode or is riding an emotional tsunami launched by mental illness. How do we respond to the looming encounter?

There are no hard and fast rules, but here are some approaches that are geared to minimize the risk of an adverse interaction:

+ **Drive Defensively.** Most of us prison ministry volunteers learned in driver education courses as a teenager that we should be proactive in our driving. In other words, we should not wait for a crisis to evaluate our options. Instead, on a constant basis, as we drive, we should be checking our mirrors and our environment to determine avenues of escape for a sudden emergency. Driving instructors taught us that by the time a child or a dog lurches in front of the vehicle, it is too late to look for an opening to veer off the road. If we have not already assessed an emergency option, there might not be one. This was called *driving defensively.*

  This principle applies in prison. We volunteers are always assessing our changing environment to make mental notes of our emergency options. Is there a squad of officers one hundred feet to the right? The best answer to the approach of an inmate with questionable demeanor may be to suddenly change course toward that group of uniforms.

  Is there a guard tower in the center of the yard? That could be a great place to move toward under the guise of asking directions.

  If there is no one in sight, except the inmate, and no place to move toward except exterior doors and walls of prison buildings, the center of the open space in plain sight is better than any spot shielded from view.

+ **Never Be Assertive.** The "free world" places great value on an energetic approach, a quickly extended hand, a firm handshake, and strong sustained eye-contact. In an encounter with an inmate in the grips of a paranoid psychosis, any or all of those gestures by a volunteer could confirm the inmate's worst paranoid fears and, in his or her mind, justify the inmate taking the volunteer down. The rule of survival in prison is the same

　　　　　WHEN WE VISIT JESUS IN PRISON

as on the street, if someone could be a threat to you, you take them out before they can take you out. This operating principle is not unique to prison or the streets.

In dealing with a possibly psychotic inmate, we volunteers must make sure to totally disarm ourselves of all assertive and aggressive energy, even in body language, stance, and gait. Our staring into the inmate's eyes could be misconstrued as trying to read the inmate's mind or exert control over it. We need to look at the inmate's entire face but not into the inmate's eyes.

We should not extend our hands in any way. Even a gesture intended as friendly could be easily misconstrued. I once encountered a mentally ill inmate who was terrified that people waving "hello" were trying to put curses on him to make him kill himself.

In another example, moving our hands into our pockets could be misunderstood as going for a weapon. Even though reason would tell you and me that there is no way to get a weapon inside the secure prison fence, reason is not working for the mentally ill inmate. We need to keep our hands limply at our sides, fully visible and non-threatening.

✦ **Do Not Escalate Tensions.** Most of us volunteers do not understand how easy it is to escalate tensions with a mentally ill inmate who is in the grips of a paranoid delusion. The situation is reminiscent of an experience I had in grade school. A friend's dog was growling at me. I asked my friend why this was happening, even though I kept smiling at the dog. The friend explained that I was thinking like a person and not like a dog. He explained that dogs only show their teeth to each other when they are going to attack. So, every time I smiled, my friend's dog saw a stranger who was baring his teeth. The dog was getting ready for the fight.

In an encounter with a mentally ill inmate who may be in the grips of a paranoid delusion, we volunteers must think like an inmate. So, for example, we should never ask a "yes" or "no" question. Inmates are not allowed to say "no" to anyone who is not another inmate. The question "would you like to talk?" can be extremely anxiety provoking because the inmate does not want to talk and, for years, has consistently been punished for saying "no" to anyone who is not an inmate. In order to avoid escalating tension, the question must be phrased: "Would you like to talk or *are you fine*?"

+ **Trust Your Gut.** I was at the podium in front of a chapel after leading a Bible study and discipleship course for about 200 inmates. A fellow who was new to the course and had sat in the last row made his way to the front as everyone else was leaving. I immediately noticed that the inmate had his head cocked just a bit, as though he was listening to someone only he could hear. My gut said, "oh-oh."

"Welcome to the Sunday group," I said softly, keeping my hands on the podium. "Would you like to ask me a question, or are you fine?"

"Well, now," he rolled his eyes a bit as he talked with a twinge of *I have got your number* arrogance. "I heard that they sent you here to kill me, so, I thought I'd check it out."

If I was dealing with a rational person, I might have asked "who did you hear that from?" or "who are they?" But reason was obviously not in play.

"Man alive," I chuckled softly. "If they sent me to take you out, they must be really dumb. You are half my age and four times as strong as me. You could whip me blindfolded with one hand tied behind your back."

After an awkward moment, the inmate smirked back, "Yeah. That's right. You ain't nothing." He left and I never saw him again.

+ **Do Not Challenge Fixed Delusions.** The reason that delusions are called "fixed" is because they will not respond to new factual information. When I was in street ministry to the mentally ill, who were living on the streets of downtown Tallahassee, I learned the hard way that challenging a fixed delusion is like repeatedly banging one's head against the wall. The delusion always wins. Delusion may respond to psychotropic medication, but it will not respond to logic or heartfelt pleas.

This is rarely an issue in an unscheduled encounter with a psychotic inmate, but it could be. If the inmate defends his or her actions based on delusional claims, we volunteers really need to avoid falling into the drama by challenging the delusion. Instead we must walk around it.

Usually, this issue presents itself in a long-term relationship with an inmate suffering from mental illness. The answer is the same. We volunteers must keep a mental list of the inmate's delusions, not to challenge them but in order to walk around them. The dynamic is very similar to games where the players must mentally keep track of buried bombs in a minefield. For us volunteers, it is a matter of creatively finding ways to present the Good News while walking carefully around the inmate's minefield of delusions.

All volunteers in Catholic prison ministry know that the Church is emphatic in her desire to bring the Good News to those who are suffering with mental illness, even in prison:

Persons with disabilities must also be considered active participants for the realization of the project of salvation entrusted by the Lord to the Church. This calls for the full inclusion of people with disabilities in ecclesial life as responsible subjects, with the same rights and duties and the same fundamental mission common to all the baptized and also with a personal vocation to fulfill.

"They are called to celebrate in the sacraments their life of faith, according to the gifts received from God and the state in which they find themselves. In this way, by taking part in catechesis, liturgy, and Church life, they may make their journey of faith and become active subjects of evangelization, able, with their own gifts and charisma, to enrich the Christian community" (Citation omitted.)[61]

But what about the mentally ill inmates that seem really dangerous? The ones that are in solitary because they are so good at hurting people no one feels safe around them—even in riot gear. What about them? Can we volunteers really hope to see faith make a difference in the life of a seriously mentally-ill person? The answer is: yes we can.

To Light a Candle

During my middle school years at St. Michael's of Livonia (Michigan), I frequently rose early while the family slept. My morning place was a basement corner near the laundry chute. There, in the shelves of a knotty pine case, my favorite books stood ready to yield their wisdom.

As morning noises of my dad's preparations for work and the drone of the news on WJR radio cascaded down the chute from the second floor bathroom, I would curl in the warm glow of a solitary bulb and consume my treasures. My favorite was a book by The Christopher's: *Three Minutes a Day*.

Each morning's offering was a brief account of real people faced with real problems. In every case, their faith had shown the way, an answer, a power to overcome. It was a reality show, in written form, where the key to winning, the key to staying on the island of hope and perseverance, was faith. Again and again, in those inspiring tales, the phrase returned, "Better to light one candle than to curse the darkness."

In a strange quirk of memory, that phrase and the glow of those mornings come flooding back on me as the bishop and I step into a solitary cell in T Dorm. This dorm is not a pretty place. Here are housed the men whose struggle with mental illness, and possibly a host of other problems, has led them on a path to the most severe restrictions.

The solitary cells in this unit all have Plexiglas doors instead of steel. The man inside is fully visible. One corridor houses those who have repeatedly

WHEN WE VISIT JESUS IN PRISON

attempted to take their own lives in prison. Everything and anything in their hands could become a weapon of self-destruction. They wear only their skivvies and a tear away blanket.

The corridor we are on today holds the men who are functioning at a level above that—some just barely. The ones who do well here will graduate back to S Dorm where the restrictions are a bit milder and the supervision a bit less intense, but the psychotropic medications are still very heavy here.

This place is too stark, too dangerous, and too real for any TV show. This is the reality of the plight of the mentally ill in an affluent society that refuses to pay for their care.

This is the end of the road for many of those who are truly sick in mind and have fended for themselves on the streets, often for years, without community services. This is the last stop on a train to hell in an affluent state that has closed down thousands of civil mental hospital beds, leaving the care of the mentally ill to the criminal justice system. If there is darkness, this is it.

And yet, the man we are here to see is lighting a candle. For four years, despite the ravages of his illness, he has worked steadily to understand the Catholic faith. This morning, his efforts are to be rewarded. The bishop is here to baptize and confirm him and offer his First Communion.

Six officers accompany us to his cell. The door opens. We enter. He is in shackles and waist chains, wearing black-box handcuffs, a helmet and spit shield. The officers remove the helmet and shield and fall back, flanking us with a semi-circle of observant protection. The bishop dons his stole and begins the rite of Baptism. As the words of exorcism fall from the bishop's lips, the man begins to tremble. By the time the water is poured upon his head, he is flowing with tears, whispering over and over, "Thank you, Jesus. Thank you, Jesus."

Finally, I break the quiet pause after his First Communion. "You have become a part of our family of faith. A cloud of witnesses surrounds you. You are not alone anymore."

To myself I think, "I thank God that you have chosen to light a candle instead of cursing the darkness."

PART III: SPECIFIC PASTORAL NEEDS   443

Using Catholic teaching about crime and punishment and the common good as the measure, our criminal justice system falls far short.

What are the pitfalls and obstacles that impede changing the system? That is the focus of the fourth and final portion of this book.

PART IV

CONSTRAINTS
THAT AFFECT
RESTORATIVE JUSTICE

"When the media speaks about the Church, they believe the Church is made up of priests, sisters, bishops, cardinals and the pope. But we are all the Church, as I said. And we all must strip ourselves of this worldliness: the spirit opposing the spirit of the Beatitudes, the spirit opposing the spirit of Jesus. Worldliness hurts us. It is so very sad to find worldly Christians, sure—according to them—of that security that the faith gives and of the security that the world provides. You cannot be on both sides. The Church—all of us—must strip herself of the worldliness that leads to vanity, to pride, that is idolatry."

Pope Francis[1]

CHAPTER 15

Economic Constraints that Affect Prison Ministry and Restorative Justice

When I taught graduate and undergraduate classes in Rome, Italy, on the subjects of law and ethics for international business and cross-cultural negotiations during the years 1996 and 1997, the following maxim was frequently referenced in the classroom case studies: "When the facts on the table do not make sense, look under the table for the money changing hands."

That maxim certainly can be put to good use in assessing why improvements to our criminal justice system fail to be made, even though the changes make sense, even though the changes would result in a more moral and more effective system, and the changes would advance hitting the goals we claim to seek as a society. An example of this phenomenon was provided in Chapter 10 with respect to inmate calling services. Why do positive changes to the system fail to be implemented? Look under the table for the money changing hands.

For the volunteer in Catholic prison ministry, this amounts to nothing less than choosing which kingdom one lives to serve: the kingdom of the powers of this world or the Kingdom of God. Our dear Pope Francis, who unflinchingly calls upon Catholics and all people of Christian faith to make the courageous moral choices for the Kingdom of God, as revealed in Scripture and enfleshed in the words and deeds of Jesus Christ, spoke on October 4, 2013, the feast of St. Francis, in the very room where St. Francis of Assisi "shed himself of his rich clothes and embraced a life of poverty."[2] Pope Francis put the issue to the world quite bluntly:

> Jesus himself told us: "You cannot serve two masters: either you serve God or you serve mammon" (cf. Matthew 6:24). In mammon itself there is this worldly spirit; money, vanity, pride, that path...we cannot take it...it is sad to erase with one hand what we write with the other. The Gospel is the Gospel! God is One! And Jesus made himself a servant for our sake, and the spirit of the world has nothing to do with this. Today I am here with you.
>
> Many of you have been stripped by this callous world that offers no work, no help. To this world it doesn't matter that there are children dying of hunger; it doesn't matter if many families have nothing to eat, do not have the dignity of bringing bread home; it doesn't matter that many people are forced to flee slavery and hunger and flee in search of freedom. With how much pain, how often don't we see that they meet death...?
>
> The spirit of the world causes these things. It is unthinkable that a Christian—a true Christian—be it a priest, a sister, a bishop, a cardinal or a pope, would want to go down this path of worldliness, which is a homicidal attitude. Spiritual worldliness kills! It kills the soul! It kills the person! It kills the Church![3]

There is a great deal of money to be made from the incarceration in prisons and jails of multitudes of human beings. Part of the profit potential exists even with respect to government operated prisons and jails. This was shown in Chapter 10 with respect to the huge profits made by Wall Street tycoons by charging exorbitant rates for

WHEN WE VISIT JESUS IN PRISON

inmate telephone calls. Similar profit potential exists for contracts to provide commissary items, also called canteen items—the personal hygiene, clothing, and miscellaneous items that inmates can purchase inside prison with money from their account. The prices for such items when sold to inmates can be marked up well above their price on the outside. As reported in *Prison Legal News*:

> While the economic downturn has caused the price of goods and commodities to decrease in the free world, the cost of items in Florida's prison canteens has skyrocketed under a new contract....
>
> The trick to making the contract extremely profitable for [the vendor] was to raise the prices for the most commonly purchased canteen items.[4]

This is not just an issue in Florida. A quick visit to the website of the American Jail Association, a trade organization for private sector suppliers to prisons and jails, reveals that their annual expo features products and services for every facet of incarceration, including, computer hardware and software technology, communications systems, security surveillance, building and remodeling facilities, identification and detection systems, food service equipment, and a vast array of restraints and medical services products. Locking up Americans is good for business.

The highly lucrative contracts for such business are frequently the subject of political patronage and can be connected with graft and corruption. For example, a press release from the U.S. Attorney's Office in Jacksonville, Florida, in 2012 reported:

> United States Attorney Robert E. O'Neill announces that Friday, January 13, 2012, United States District Judge Timothy J. Corrigan sentenced Edward Lee Dugger (65, Gainesville) to 26 months in federal prison and Joseph Arthur Deese (38, Gainesville) to 14 months in federal prison for their respective roles in a conspiracy to pay approximately $130,000.00 in kickbacks

to the former Secretary of the Florida Department of Correc-tions (FDOC), James Vernon Crosby, Jr., and another former high-ranking FDOC official, Allen Wayne Clark. Dugger and Deese previously pled guilty to conspiring to pay kickbacks. The Court also ordered Dugger and Deese to jointly forfeit $232,019.11.

According to court documents, Crosby and Clark assisted Dugger and Dugger's business associate, Deese, with obtain-ing a contract with Keefe Commissary Network—a St. Louis, Missouri, corporation. The contract involved having Keefe Commissary operate the canteen grocery stores inside the visiting parks of all prisons within the state of Florida prison system. These canteen stores are areas within the Florida pris-ons stocked with foodstuffs and other items that visitors could purchase while visiting inmates during prison visiting hours. FDOC made millions of dollars each year from the sale of such items to inmates and inmate visitors.

In 2003, FDOC negotiated a contract to privatize FDOC's institutional canteens with Keefe Commissary, which gave Keefe Commissary the right to run both the inmate canteens inside the prisons and the visiting park canteens open to vis-itors, also situated inside the prisons. As part of this contract, Keefe Commissary agreed to pay FDOC a certain fee per day per inmate, which was anticipated to provide FDOC with rev-enues in excess of $20 million per year. As Secretary of FDOC, Crosby had the direct authority to enter into the contract, to implement contractual amendments and to renew their con-tract. Crosby also had to approve the use of any subcontractors.

In June 2004, Crosby and Clark introduced Dugger and Deese to representatives of Keefe Commissary for the purpose of encouraging Keefe Commissary to utilize Dugger and Deese in opening and operating visiting park canteens throughout the prisons in Florida. Dugger and Deese agreed that if Keefe Commissary utilized Dugger as a subcontractor on the Keefe Commissary contract, then Dugger and Deese would kickback a portion of the proceeds to Crosby and Clark.

The full amount of the kickbacks, which were paid over several months spanning 2004 until early 2006, was approximately $130,000.00. The kickbacks were paid monthly and gradually increased over time from approximately $1,000.00 per month up to as much as $14,000.00 per month. Dugger and Deese withheld certain amounts of cash from canteen revenues, out of which Deese delivered the kickback payments to Clark, who, in turn, delivered the kickback payments to Crosby.

In 2007, Crosby and Clark were convicted of corruptly receiving these bribes. Crosby was sentenced to 96 months in federal prison. Clark was sentenced to 31 months in federal prison, and has since been released.[5]

The potential for profit-motivated misuse of power over captive human beings who are held out of sight inside massive prison facilities affects every facet of prison operations. For example, huge contracts for tens of millions of dollars are let to private companies for food services. A recent article by Paul Egan in the *Detroit Free Press*, "Michigan's new prison food contractor accused of skimping on size and quality of meals to boost profits," shows a case of alleged improprieties in privatized prison food services in order to hike profits.[6]

As recently reported by *The Huffington Post*, the potential for profit-motivated abuse exists with services as fundamental as healthcare. Allegedly, the Florida Department of Corrections "awarded two massive contracts to a pair of private health care providers to serve the state's prisoners. Both companies have been besieged by medical malpractice lawsuits, according to a report in the Broward Bulldog," which is a non-profit newsite.[7]

Although a Florida Department of Corrections spokesperson defended the selection of the two companies as a transparent process, the concern is more basic than the methodology of choosing a private company. The concern is whether profit-motivated enterprises should be trusted with the care of vulnerable populations:

David Fathi, Director of the American Civil Liberties Union's National Prison Project, told HuffPost that private companies have no business providing health care to prisoners.

"The claim a private corporation can do the same job as state employees more cheaply and create profits for its shareholders sounds too good on its face and the evidence suggests that it's false," Fathi said.

Companies that care for prisoners have few incentives to provide quality service, according to Fathi.

"Prisoners are a uniquely powerless, politically unpopular, and literally captive market so with private prisons or private prison health care providers the usual rules of market discipline, the idea that bad businesses that injure or kill people will eventually go out of business, doesn't apply," Fathi said. "If [prisoners] are injured, their ability to recover compensation has been dramatically restricted by federal legislation."

"Allowing private health care providers in prisons can be dangerous, Fathi said. "Unlike governments, private companies exist first and foremost to generate profits; if they say they can do it more cheaply than government, it's because they're cutting something. When you combine the profit motive with limited oversight and a uniquely powerless population, you get bad and sometimes lethal results."[8]

Prison privatization is subject to the same potential for criminal wrongdoing as are the other privatized services mentioned above. For example, in Florida the prison privatization system ran amok badly. *The St. Petersburg Times* reported extensively on how the system had run off the rails:

Two companies had been paid hundreds of millions of dollars to run state prisons for six years, and it was time to find out whether taxpayers could get a better deal, a state board decided in 2002.

But the decision would prove to be the undoing of the

Correctional Privatization Commission, an obscure body created by the Legislature to safeguard tax dollars spent on privately run prisons.

Two years later, the commission's executive director stands accused of bad management, poor judgment and impropriety.

The two private companies that run five state prisons still have their contracts, worth a total of $90-million annually, even though audits have found the contracts aren't as efficient as state law requires.[9]

Within weeks the head of the Correctional Privatization Commission had resigned while lamenting the failure of his best efforts to serve the interests of the public. In fact, he suggested that the failure of the commission was partly because he had done his job too well:

The executive director of Florida's private prison commission has resigned his post, weeks after the legislature voted to strip the governor-appointed board of its authority.

In an internal memo written to commissioners last week, Alan Duffee lamented the group's demise as it tried to force the first rebidding of five contracts in Florida's eight-year experiment with private prisons.

Duffee also acknowledged his own actions played a role in the demise....

"It was always my intention to serve the best interest of the taxpayer and this commission, not special interests," wrote Duffee, whose resignation takes effect at the end of May. "I feel that I have certainly done that and unfortunately that was a factor into this commission's demise."[10]

It took a few years for the other shoe to drop. When it did, the facts were far at variance from the former commission head having done his job too well:

A former Florida prison official has pleaded guilty to stealing nearly $225,000 in state money nearly three years after he used the cash to help buy houses for him and his girlfriend.

Alan Brown Duffee, the former executive director of a defunct board that oversaw Florida's private prison contracts, admitted Thursday in Tallahassee to one count each of mail fraud, wire fraud, and money laundering.

Duffee, 40, faces up to twenty years in prison and a $250,000 fine. He is to be sentenced in April.[11]

The former prison privatization commissioner was sentenced "to 33 months in federal prison after admitting he stole $225,000 in state money to help buy houses for him and his girlfriend."[12]

There will always be criminal abuses of any system. The critical question for us volunteers in Catholic prison ministry is whether prison privatization poses a moral and intellectual quandary even when it is done in compliance with all criminal laws. That is the subject of two articles I published on this controversial topic. Here is the first.

If Money Is the Only Thing That Matters

We continue to address the six pastoral letters on the criminal justice system issued by our Catholic Bishops in the South. The second letter, *Wardens from Wall Street: Prison Privatization*, deals with the delicate issue of mixing profit motives with the incarceration of American citizens. If this were just a political or an economic issue, the bishops might do better to avoid such a thorny question. But it is a moral issue, as well.

I made a presentation on the problem of mixing prisons with profits in 1997, when I was teaching international law for multinational business at the graduate school of St. John's University's Vatican Campus in Rome. The textbook discussed the fair trade problems created by convict labor. The major culprit was China.

It all became less of an issue, however, when the U.S. decided to get into the business of convict labor. Paying inmates one or two-bits an hour to manufacture products, while the taxpayers pay for the workers' housing and food, can be too good to refuse. That is one of the problems of mixing profits with the police power of the state.

Yet, technically speaking, that is not privatization. Prison privatization puts a prison's very operations in the hands of outside business. The officers and staff work for a shareholder-owned corporation. The inmates in a privatized prison are subject to the police power of government, but it is exercised by corporate managers with an eye on quarterly profits and personal bonus projections. Many of us have had a taste of this profit-motivated decision-making in the context of HMOs.

Why would anyone who has experienced the fierce dividend and profitability-based pressure that Wall Street's analysts can exert on the culture and management values of any publicly-held company agree to such a situation for prisons? There seems to be one major reason: Money.

There is usually a great deal of money to be made when a private enterprise can take over an essential activity of government, especially when government has traditionally exercised a monopoly on it. In modern times, our country is witnessing this phenomenon with the privatization of warfare, of social services, and now of prisons.

The potential for such great profits can only be realized by successfully obtaining the award of the contract to provide such services. That means politics and political contributions, big political contributions. It also means that profitability, the return on the corporate investment in personnel, facilities, and politics, is directly related to keeping the private prisons full. That could mean keeping American citizens locked up as long as possible, even when that may be much longer than is necessary for public safety.

A strange process of adverse selection exacerbates this possibility. Businesses running prisons usually negotiate contracts to cherry-pick the inmates that are assigned to the corporate prisons. They want the ones that are not violent and do not cause problems. Those are also the inmates who would most likely qualify for early release. These cross-purposes start to look like a conflict of interest.

Two additional facts make it worse. America incarcerates a higher percentage of its people than any other country in the world. And corporations that profit from prisons can be intensely involved in lobbying for and against laws that determine how many Americans are locked up and for how long. This is a severe conflict of interest. The conflict is between the profit-making motive of corporations and proper use of the state's power to take away our freedom. Fallen human nature does not have a good track record for making tough choices against our financial self-interest in the vise of such pressures. That is why we have always left such things as operating prisons in the hands of government.

Every American Catholic should analyze the Southern bishops' pastoral letter against prison privatization and address what is happening in America, especially in the South, as profits are generated by keeping people behind bars.

Prison privatization is on the rise in the United States. As reported by The Sentencing Project in "Too Good to be True: Private Prisons in America":

> In 2010, private prisons held 128,195 of the 1.6 million state and federal, prisoners in the United States, representing eight percent of the total population. For the period 1999-2010, the number of individuals held in private prisons grew by eighty percent, compared to eighteen percent for the overall prison population.
>
> While both federal and state governments increasingly relied on privatization, the federal prison system's commitment to privatization grew much more dramatically. The number of federal prisoners held in private prisons rose from 3,828 to 33,830, an increase of 784 percent, while the number of state prisoners incarcerated privately grew by forty percent, from 67,380 to 94,365.
>
> Today, thirty states maintain some level of privatization, with seven states housing more than a quarter of their prison populations privately.[13]

This rapidly growing encroachment by profit-seeking investors into the relationship between citizens and their governments is filled with conflicts of interest and dangerous possibilities. The practice of contracting for prison services with politically connected-companies that have proven inept and ineffective can also be dangerous for those who are not yet citizens. In the fall of 2015, U.S. Immigration and Customs Enforcement, commonly referred to as "ICE," let a lucrative incarceration contract to the very same company that had been the focus of a major investigation by the U.S. Commission on Civil Rights.[14]

WASHINGTON—The U.S. Commission on Civil Rights (USCCR) today released its annual report to the President and Congress examining the civil rights and due process conditions at immigration detention facilities, as well as the conditions of family detainees... The commission found that some detention centers and contracted facilities are not fully complying with detention standards regarding medical care, legal information and other basic standards of treatment. The commission recommends the Department of Homeland Security (DHS) should release all family detainees, reduce the use of detention, ensure humane treatment of detainees, increase the use of alternatives to detention, allow legal and pastoral access to detention facilities, and strengthen due process protections....

With the full, historic moral authority of this commission, we identified many serious conditions at detention centers," said Martin R. Castro, the USCCR chair. "All people, no matter whether they are immigrants or asylum-seekers, deserve to be treated as humans. The commission stands strongly behind our recommendation to release unaccompanied minors and families from detention, and encourages DHS to find alternatives to the detention centers.[15]

And so it goes. Here is my second article on this topic.

No Strings Attached

In the preceding article, we looked at the inherent problem of mixing profit motives with management and care of vulnerable, voiceless people. Now it is time to address the current American privatization myth, i.e., that everything is better when it is done by the private sector. Says who?

Perhaps not the good people of the State of Indiana, who sold a major state-owned toll road to foreign investors for 3.8 billion dollars and are paying greatly increased toll rates to use it.[16] Texas is also reported to be contracting a toll road to a foreign consortium.[17] Little-by-little, America's essential civil infrastructure is being placed under the control of foreign investors. Do we have any votes of control in the foreign companies running American infrastructure? How could this be any good for us? And how could it do us any good for American-based multinational corporations who report to their shareholders, not the American public, to be running government institutions like prisons? All this activity is under the air cover of ballyhooing about the promised land of privatization. Much of this smoke screen is fanned by media that shares profit interests with some of the companies profiting from the privatization of government activities.

A recent investigative report by a major Florida newspaper into Florida's attempts at privatization of essential government functions leaned hard against the facts in order to name the results at least "mixed." The company that took over the state's employee personnel functions and the officials that supported the move were mystified at how thousands of state employee personnel files were transferred overseas, outside security protection and outside control.[18] How could it happen?

No one has to be a genius to know why and how such things happen. Those events happen because middle-managers can increase their bonus and career potential by cutting corporate expenses now. Any negative ramifications are far down the road, after they will already have collected their bonus and leveraged up into a higher paying job at another company. So, they transfer the files to an unsecured overseas subcontractor to be handled at lower cost. How could anyone be surprised? But why would anyone in government think that taking such risks is a good idea?

Well, one possible answer is that politicians do not raise large political contributions from state employees who are just doing their jobs competently. But politicians sure do roll in the green of political contributions from corporations that want to profit off the backs of the taxpayers and the state's vulnerable populations.

A few years ago, we all were allowed a peak at this cesspool of influence by the study *A Contributing Influence: The Private-Prison Industry and Political Giving in the South*.[19] This study of the year-2000 state-level election cycle found that private-prison industries contributed to 156 candidates in Texas, 107 candidates in North Carolina, and 122 candidates in Florida. According to the report, more than ninety percent of the contributions went to candidates who would vote on government decisions that directly affected the corporate bottom line. All indications are that the corporate brass spent their money well.[20]

In May of 2004, a *St. Petersburg Times* editorial[21] castigated Florida's legislature and the governor for disbanding the state commission that was established to monitor the privatized prison companies in Florida and keep them honest. "The commission's attempt to explore whether other companies could do the job cheaper was met with legal challenges and a full-scale lobbyist assault," said the *Times*. "Lawmakers simply want to make sure, especially in an election year, that they continue to receive the fruits of their generosity to [the private prison companies]."

Such is the landscape of prison privatization.

A few years ago, I made a tour of a privatized prison in Florida. The warden of the particular facility is well-known to me and has impeccable credentials. In addition to holding a doctorate in social work, with specialties in mental health and offender treatment, she was the first female Deputy Secretary of the Florida Department of Corrections. As expected, her facility was absolutely top-drawer and the answer to my queries directed to inmates, staff, professional staff, and officers all confirmed that the facility was indeed exemplary in its balancing of monetary constraints and inmate welfare. So my answer to the question, "can a privatized prison be run in an ethical, humane and moral fashion?" is "yes."

The problem is that the drive for optimization of profit (resulting in increases to shareholder dividends and bigger bonuses for corporate executive management) constantly exert pressure to cut costs, including the cost of competent prison level administration and staff. How many privatized prisons would have a warden with the skills and expertise of the one I toured? Probably, not many. And what else is involved in relentless profit-seeking through the incarceration of human beings?

An article in *Communities Digital News* highlighted the inherent dangers of shareholder prisons wielding the power of the state against the vulnerable freedom of citizens:

> The more prisoners a facility holds, the more profitable the corporation is. That is good for stockholders, but not for the rest of the citizens of America.
>
> In their 2010 annual report, [a privatized prison company] wrote, "Historically, we have been successful in substantially filling our inventory of available beds and the beds that we have constructed. Filling these available beds would provide substantial growth in revenues, cash flow, and earnings per share."
>
> One company was so desperate to keep their prison populations high that it was willing to bribe two Pennsylvania judges to do so. Mark Ciavarella, Jr., and Michael Conahan were sentencing children without proper representation to harsh penalties for petty crimes while receiving kick-backs from the prison corporation for their efforts....
>
> The true tragedy is the cost to the prisoners. These are actual human beings, most often not white, who are being preyed on by people in the more affluent sectors of American society. Lives are ruined every day so that stockholders can enjoy a better return on their investment.[22]

That horrible kickback scheme known as "kids for cash" resulted in a twenty-eight-year prison sentence for Ciavarella, a seventeen-year-sentence for Conahan, and millions of dollars in damages for the victims and their families. But not all the damage can be repaired, for example, the agony of the family whose son committed suicide after being caught up in the "kids for cash" scheme.[23] Truly, lives are ruined every day when government gives its power to shareholder and profit-driven enterprises.

Given the realities already presented in this chapter, a compelling question looms: *Is Prison Privatization a New Form of Economic Servitude?* Subsumed in the blanket issue posed by this question is an equally disturbing one: the connection between private prison profits and the incarceration of African-American citizens, a perspective brought into relief by comparison of historical data from the post-Civil War period to our current time. Dr. Michael Hallett, Chair and Professor of Criminal Justice and Director of the Center for Criminal Justice Policy Research at the University of North Florida, has been honored for his research on the criminal justice system in exactly this area. His book, *Private Prisons in America: A Critical Race Perspective*,[24] presents his historical findings and compares them to the statistics today.

As Catholics, we should not accept Dr. Hallett's personal views on class conflict. After setting those views aside, however, a reader of the historical and current statistics and studies presented in his book finds data-based evidence of the concerns expressed by our bishops of the South, especially with respect to race, poverty, and prison privatization.

Many readers of this book are already aware of the historical connections between the death penalty of slavery and the modern American death penalty.[25] It should not be a surprise that similar historical connections exist with respect to the criminal justice system at large. In addressing the history of "for-profit imprisonment" in America, Dr. Hallett focuses squarely upon the Thirteenth Amendment to the U.S. Constitution, which abolished involuntary servitude (slavery) except as punishment for crime. He documents that immediately after the Civil War the South faced a massive labor shortage. Meanwhile, vast numbers of African-American men were to be found still living on the plantations where they had been enslaved and not yet sure where to go. The solution, he says, was crafted in the shadow of the Thirteenth Amendment's approval of economic servitude as punishment.

First, the laws were changed to redefine "previously petty crimes as felonies after the Civil War, thus elevating the penalties for vagrancy, loitering, and petty theft." Long prison terms replaced small fines and short stints in jail. Then, the Convict Lease System was deployed. Many freed blacks were imprisoned and subjected to the Convict Lease system and sent to work the very same plantations where they had previously been slaves. Dr. Hallett quotes the famous African-American leader W.E.B. Du Bois:

> Throughout the South, laws were immediately passed authorizing public officials to lease the labor of convicts to the highest bidder. The lessee then took charge of the convicts—worked them as he wished under the nominal control of the state. Thus a new slavery and slave trade was established.[26]

Dr. Hallett points out that these changes in laws created an artificial "black crime problem." Whereas before emancipation, almost all prisoners in southern penitentiaries were white, after emancipation, almost all the prisoners were black. In Alabama, for example, the prisons went from 99% white to over 97% black. This was not atypical of the Southern post-Civil War experience. It was in this environment that the prospect of private profit from the misery of incarceration became socially acceptable.

Dr. Hallett shows that the practice of private profit from prisons suddenly rose to the fore again with the advent of the new "black crime problem" of the 1980s. Private prisons, if considered as a group, would now comprise the fourth largest prison system in the U.S. He finds the parallels between the post-Civil War experience and the resurgence of private profit from prisons due to the new "black crime problem" precipitated by the 1980s "war on drugs" both stark and disturbing:

WHEN WE VISIT JESUS IN PRISON

In both cases, the majority of crimes for which blacks were suddenly imprisoned in disproportionately high numbers were nonviolent petty crimes only recently made "serious" by changes in law.

He notes that prior to the 1980s, drug abuse was primarily dealt with as a public health issue: treatment and rehabilitation. With the advent of the 1980s' drug war, however:

Punishment of impoverished black citizen's drug use far outpaced that of whites. By the end of the 1990s, almost 1 of 3 (32.2 percent) African-American men in the age group 20-29 were either in prison, jail, probation, or parole on any given day.

We have already dealt in previous chapters with the disparity in treatment of drug offenses involving cocaine (the more expensive white drug) and crack (the cheaper black drug). That disparity has a vital relationship to the explosion in the number of black men in the criminal justice system and the concurrent revitalization of prisons-for-profit. Dr. Hallett expounds on the connections:

By the late 1990s, when official unemployment rates were at all-time lows, incarceration rates for the same period were at record highs. Not coincidentally, both the highest concentrations of unemployment and incarceration for the period are found among urban African American men.... Imprisonment had replaced welfare as one of society's primary means for regulating the poor.

In short, the war on drugs and its local concentration on relatively low-level, nonviolent offenders artificially precipitated a massive increase in the number of black inmates. This created financial strains on state and local governments, setting the stage for imprisonment for profit.

According to the July 2007 report of *The Sentencing Project*, *Uneven Justice: State Rates of Incarceration by Race and Ethnicity*, that trend continues unabated. African Americans constitute 900,000 of the total 2.2 million incarcerated in America. The incarceration rate for blacks, 2,290 per 100,000, is more than five and a half times higher than the rate of 412 per 100,000 for whites. The report identifies the same source of racial disparity as Dr. Hallett and makes the following statement its first recommendation:

> Both federal and state policymakers should revisit the domestic drug control strategy, taking into account the wealth of empirical evidence demonstrating the efficacy of investing in prevention and treatment rather than a law enforcement-centered approach.

The upshot for our purposes is that the prison population has exploded with African-Americans, just as it did after the Civil War. This creates a fiscal crisis which the private sector stands ready to solve for a profit. In his book *Merchandizing Prisoners: Who Really Pays for Prison Privatization?*[27] Byron Eugene Price debunks the myth that private prisons are more cost effective and better run. He cites numerous studies and cases which show that profit maximization results in understaffing and poorer quality and conditions. After all, every dollar *not* spent on staff, public safety, or inmate care and rehabilitation goes into the pockets of Wall Street investors. Who could be surprised?

Not everyone believes this all just happened by coincidence. We have looked at the role of lobbyists and campaign contributions from private prison companies in passing laws that increase and extend sentences. If one is making money off prisons, then locking people up for smaller offenses and keeping them in prison longer is good for business and great for shareholders. From the standpoint of our Catholic faith, however, that conflict of interest between the justice for and rights of the citizen versus the motives driven by profit is the core of the problem.

The *Catechism of the Catholic Church*[28] is clear that punishment must be proportionate to the gravity of the offense. Primarily, it should redress the disorder introduced by the offense and, in addition to protecting public order and people's safety, contribute to the rehabilitation of the guilty party. *The Compendium of the Social Doctrine of the Church* elaborates:

> There is a two-fold purpose here. On the one-hand, *encouraging the reinsertion of the condemned person into society* and on the other *fostering a justice that reconciles*, a justice capable of restoring harmony in social relationships disrupted by the criminal act committed. (Italics in original.)[29]

Expanded sentencing laws sponsored by prison companies to enhance shareholder returns on investment hardly serve such purposes. And where is the incentive to rehabilitate inmates and successfully reintegrate them into society when management bonuses will be bigger if inmates stay locked-up longer and return to prison sooner?

Our penal system cannot truly serve the purposes of restorative justice when the criminal laws and prison practices are being written with Wall Street in mind. As our bishops of the South have stated:

> We believe that private prisons confront us with serious moral issues, demanding a gospel response. [The activities involved in running prisons] are the most serious of acts. To delegate such acts to institutions whose success depends on the amount of profit they generate is to invite abuse and to abdicate our responsibility to care for our brothers and sisters.[30]

In short, prisons for-profit do not square with our Catholic faith. This is not a small matter, given the current trends and prevalence of privatized mass incarceration in the United States. As *The Sentencing Project* points out:

> In 2010, one in every thirteen prisoners in the U.S. was held

by for-profit companies, despite evidence that private prisons often provide inadequate levels of service and are no more cost-effective than publicly-run facilities. In addition, private prisons operate on a business model that emphasizes profits over the public good, and benefit from policies that maintain America's high incarceration rate. [31] (Citations omitted.)

Not all of the economic barriers to reformation of the criminal justice system reside in the methods of incarceration. Some of the economic barriers have to do with the conditions in society. Poverty does not cause crime, but it certainly can make it more difficult for a person to choose the right things.

Prison Policy Initiative,[32] a non-profit, non-partisan organization that produces cutting edge research to expose the broader harm of mass criminalization, recently released a comprehensive study of how a person's wealth or lack of it contributes to their risk of incarceration:

The findings are as predictable as they are disturbing. The American prison system is bursting at the seams with people who have been shut out of the economy and who had neither a quality education nor access to good jobs. We found that, in 2014 dollars, incarcerated people had a median annual income of $19,185 prior to their incarceration, which is 41% less than non-incarcerated people of similar ages.

The gap in income is not solely the product of the well-documented disproportionate incarceration of Blacks and Hispanics, who generally earn less than Whites. We found that incarcerated people in all gender, race, and ethnicity groups earned substantially less prior to their incarceration than their non-incarcerated counterparts of similar ages.[33]

This aspect of the economic conditions in society is referred to in Catholic social teaching as *the common good*. So, it is not surprising that our Catholic Bishops in the South have tackled the issue of poverty in their first pastoral letter on the criminal justice system,

Challenges for the Criminal Justice Process in the South. The connection between poverty and crime in modern western society has been enunciated since at least the time of Charles Dickens' *Tale of Two Cities.* The most predictable companion to American poverty is poor educational systems. Some attribute this to property tax based funding of school districts, others to the inability to attract premium human resource capital to urban high crime areas or rural communities stricken by extreme poverty. Regardless of the preferred analysis, all agree that the cycle perpetuates itself and is multigenerational. Our Southern bishops focus upon the role of poverty in the criminal justice system, both as a contributing factor to crime and as an impairment of justice:

> Poor education is clearly part of the problem. Two out of every three state prison inmates had not completed high school....
> Public defender attorneys for poor people charged with crimes are usually overworked and underfunded. They are all too frequently unable to provide adequate legal representation. In rural areas, public defenders are often completely absent.[34]

This latter truth is captured in the much quoted punch line, "a person will get all the justice he can afford." But justice is no laughing matter. It has a major role in our understanding of God's order for society and the world. As people of faith, we are not at liberty to allow justice to be reduced to a market commodity. What are our instructions from our Church?

In *Responsibility, Rehabilitation and Restoration: A Catholic Perspective on Crime and Criminal Justice,* the U.S. Catholic Bishops have said:

> Sometimes people who lack adequate resources from early in life...turn to lives of crime in desperation or out of anger or confusion. Unaddressed needs...can be steppingstones on a path towards crime. Our role as Church is to continually work to address these needs through pastoral care, charity, and advocacy.[35]

Okay. Now we are getting uncomfortable. Is there an implication here that we who live above the level of need are supposed to do something about our neighbor's poverty from our excess resources? The excess we have above the level of need is called "riches." The Church does not dabble with mere implications about our duty. She is quite specific. *The Compendium of the Social Doctrine of the Church* quotes Saint Gregory the Great:

> The rich [person] is only an administrator of what he possesses; giving what is required to the needy is a task that is to be performed with humility because the goods do not belong to the one who distributes them. [Those] who retains riches only for [themselves] are not innocent; giving to those in need means paying a debt.[36]

What would St. Gregory the Great say in response to the recent census reports that the gap between rich and poor in the U.S. is continuing to widen? That the poverty rate in America has not seen a statistically significant decline since before the year 2000?" I believe he would stand with our Southern bishops, who say: "We must seek new restorative approaches...must continue to find new ways to respond to crime that are consistent with the love and truth of Jesus Christ."

The good news is that there is hope on the horizon. During the summer of 2015, President Obama toured a male, medium-security prison, *El Reno Federal Correctional Institution* near Oklahoma City. This is apparently the first time a sitting U.S. President went inside an occupied prison. I believe this historic event was made politically possible by the advance announcements of an even more historic event scheduled for just a few weeks later: a papal visit by Pope Francis to *Curran-Fromhold Correctional Facility* in Philadelphia as described by Emma Green in *The Atlantic* magazine:

> The man often called the Holy Father said his sins are equal to those of inmates in a medium-security correctional facility.... Francis really seemed to mean what he said, looking each indi-

WHEN WE VISIT JESUS IN PRISON

vidual in the eye: God has laid a table, and all of you are invited to join. For so public a moment, it felt strangely intimate.[37]

As our leaders and the media penetrate the hidden sites of America's mass incarceration debacle, the first thing that changes is peoples' perceptions of inmates. The invisible monsters suddenly look very human indeed. And then, the questions are asked: Why are they in prison? How long are they in prison? Why are they in prison for so long?

The over-sentencing of nonviolent drug offenders has been a financial boon for prison-related industries, including for-profit prisons. But what about the actual human beings subjected to this practice? And what about their families?

Once the focus shifts to those questions, changes are inevitable. In the fall of 2015, it was announced that the U.S. Sentencing Commission reduced the sentences for certain non-violent drug offenses and made it retroactive. It is estimated that almost half of the 100,000 federal inmates incarcerated for drug convictions will be up for early release. The number already going home is about 6,000 with almost 10,000 more scheduled to be released by the fall of 2016.[38]

These moves by the federal system were paralleled by similar efforts at the state level. For example, in the summer of 2014, *Florida TaxWatch*, an independent, nonpartisan, nonprofit public policy research institute and government watchdog serving Florida taxpayers since 1979, issued a major policy initiative to reduce over-criminalization in Florida:

"Over-criminalization" is the new buzzword among criminologists and legislators looking for ways to reform federal and state criminal justice systems and reduce the cost of corrections. Headline stories once monopolized by tough on crime terminology and prison building and expansion plans, now ask whether over-criminalization is making us a nation of felons.[39]

Reinvigorated by the actual steps being taken in the federal system, in the summer of 2015 Dominic M. Calabro, President and CEO of Florida TaxWatch, referred to the eleven Floridians included in the first federal release and called for Florida to stop wasting taxpayer money on excessive incarceration that serves no public purpose:

> These lengthy prison sentences for low-level offenders were unnecessarily harsh—not only for the offenders but also for the taxpayers. At the end of their prison sentences, which are scheduled for November 10, 2015, the Florida offenders will have served anywhere from 10 to 25 years for nonviolent offenses. Over-incarceration of nonviolent drug offenders... such as these inmates, provides little to no public benefit to community safety, but results in astronomical costs.[40]

In politics, however, even saving taxpayers from wasteful, unproductive use of their money is not always the highest priority. With the mass incarceration binge of the 1980s and 1990s, prisons became overwhelming located in rural areas instead of city centers. The two most dramatic impacts on these rural areas were economic and political. Suddenly, state jobs with benefits became available in impoverished and jobless communities. And with the arrival of thousands of inmates the communities benefitted with increased political clout. The reason is that even though inmates cannot vote they are counted in the population numbers of the host community for purposes of political representation and state and federal elections. "As a result, prison towns get more political representation and more local funding. Meanwhile, predominantly non-white urban communities lose both."[41] This means that:

> While many states are exploring ways to reduce their prison populations because of budget problems and questions about the effectiveness of sentencing, rural legislators representing districts that contain prisons are more likely to oppose such changes."[42]

Another aspect of the economic barriers to reformation of our

WHEN WE VISIT JESUS IN PRISON

criminal justice system has to do with what happens to a person who is released from jail or prison. Have they been prepared to make it in society or are they destined to return to prison? Part of the answer to that question is the process of rehabilitation of the offender that should be attempted during their incarceration.

In the earlier chapters of this book, we inquired into the moral nature of punishment in our first world American society by addressing several critical issues in light of the words of Jesus Christ and the explicit teachings of Popes Paul VI, John Paul II, Benedict XVI, and Francis.

We explored *The Catechism of the Catholic Church*, where paragraph 2266 tells us that government has the right and duty to inflict appropriate punishment. However, such punishment must be proportionate to the offense committed, with the primary purpose of setting things right.

Also paragraph 2302 of the *Catechism* warns: To desire vengeance in order to do evil to someone who should be punished is illicit," but it is praiseworthy to impose restitution" to correct vices and maintain justice."

Hence, the Catholic Church's teaching stands solidly behind restorative justice, punishment that seeks not revenge but rather to redress the disorder through restitution and healing of the community, the victims, and the offenders.

Paragraph 2266 of the *Catechism* goes even further: "Punishment then, in addition to defending public order and protecting people's safety, has a medicinal purpose: as far as possible, it must contribute to the correction of the guilty party."

So used, the word *correction* means to "reform" or "improve." It is almost a synonym for rehabilitation, except, strictly speaking, the latter requires that one was functioning in a proper way to begin with, before falling into error. In our culture, many young people are raised without any moral compass at all; hence, there is no prior proper behavior to return to. Such "correction" in this case necessitates total reform to new ways of conducting oneself. However, the word *rehabilitation* as generally used includes such reformation of the perpetually wayward to conformity with God's and society's laws.

Do we Americans indeed strive for punishment that rehabilitates the offender? We have in the past.[43]

For example, in the State of Florida, Leonard Chapman, the icon in Florida's penal history who ran the State Prison Farm at Raiford for a quarter-century, believed in rehabilitation. Education and job training were priorities. Under Chapman, the word *convict* was forbidden, replaced by *inmate*.

Paul J. Eubanks, Superintendent of the Apalachee Correctional Institution in Florida in the mid-fifties, believed in rehabilitation. In fact, that was the purpose of his facility, opened for youthful offenders in 1949.

L.W. Griffith, Director of the State Road Department's Prison System in Florida before the era of Eisenhower's interstates, stressed to his personnel that: "The prisoners welfare needs are [your] personal responsibility and that wherever possible [you] must work toward the eventual rehabilitation of the men in [your] charge.... Prisoners are sent to prison *as* punishment and not *for* punishment." [Emphasis in original.]

Among other things, Griffith banned the use of sweatboxes, six-by-three-foot metal boxes in which one or two prisoners were locked and left in the sun for minor infractions.

After H.G. Cochran, Jr. was appointed Director of the Division of Corrections of Florida in July 1959, he implemented Transition Officers to assist inmates with placement upon release.

Rehabilitation appeared to be working in Florida. Then the social upheaval of the 1970s saw a 127% jump in Florida's state prison population. Crack cocaine became pervasive in the 1980s, fueling another 93% increase. In just twenty-two years Florida's state prison population skyrocketed from 8,400 to over 42,000. Since then, it has increased more than two and a half times to over 110,000.

When we flesh out the history of the last forty years with the horrible prison riots, hostage takings, violent assaults on staff, and murderous escape attempts—especially in the seventies and eighties—rehabilitation may be a difficult word to enunciate. But if we are

Catholic, *rehabilitation* is a word we must defend. As a matter of our faith, it is part and parcel of proper punishment.

Also critical are the economic barriers to reform that arise in the context of post-release services, known as re-entry services. These issues can arise in regard to employment, training, education, community support, and even victim-offender dialogue. Because the resistance to providing such re-entry services is heavily interwoven with religious barriers to reform of the system, those aspects will be discussed in the next and final chapter of this book.

For me, the most intractable element of criminal justice in the United States due to hidden economic interests is the death penalty. Capital punishment is a cottage industry in the South. I stumbled upon that fact inadvertently, and I have coined it the *invisible death penalty industry*. And so I end this chapter with a true story and a bishop's reflection on this evil.

You Can Fool All of the People Some of the Time

As soon as I step into the main conference room of the hotel in Orlando, I know this is big business.

At least 130 people are seated at three dozen rows of tables. To the rear, stacks of high tech equipment are clicking and chirping in preparation for teleconferencing. Front row center, alternating images of distant participants fade in and out on eight-foot jumbotron screens that tower over each side of the podium.

At the head table, a state supreme court justice and a state senator are scribbling notes for their introductory remarks. Peppered throughout the satellite-connected rooms around the state are familiar faces of prominent jurists, elected officials, and attorneys. The opening speaker mounts the stage: "This is the largest intrastate teleconference ever done in Florida. In addition to Orlando, we are teleconferencing with nine other locations for a total of over 400 participants."

With a few quickly penciled sums, I rough cut the total dollar amount in state salaries that will be consumed today in an eight-hour conference attended by over 400 of Florida's best and brightest talents. What other matter of such moment could gather so many highly visible, well-paid legal professionals and politicians from all across Florida? A brainstorming session on treating and processing Florida's burgeoning wastewater? A statewide panel on better care for our elderly or our children? A planning conference on the energy future of our state? A bold initiative to eliminate poverty housing in Florida in our time? A consensus building session on education, on better equipping our teachers and training our young? A public safety consortium on full deployment of community policing throughout every neighborhood in Florida? An economic platform to image community based job-creation that would raise every head-of-household's earnings to a living wage?

No. Apparently nothing is so important as the topic today. I briefly wonder why, and then I realize that I know the answer: the death penalty in Florida is big business. This is the yearly gathering of one of Florida's most pervasive, but invisible, professional industries. For eight hours, all this talent and time, all these resources and potential will be squarely focused on the legal minutia of sentencing hearings in the miniscule percentage of criminal cases where the death penalty is constitutionally allowed. And this conference is exclusively for the lawyers on the state's side of the cases. It does not include those who handle the defense!

I am amazed. So long as Florida has a death penalty, we want all these people working hard to assure the constitutional systems are solidly in place. Yet, the sheer number of participants brings to mind a survey I read a few years ago.

A 1995 survey of hundreds of randomly selected police chiefs across the nation asked, "What, in your opinion, works in the battle against crime?"[44] The death penalty was mentioned by fewer than two percent of the chiefs and followed twenty-five other areas of concern. They ranked the death penalty last as a way of reducing violent crime, behind curbing drug abuse, behind placing more police officers on the streets, behind longer sentences, and behind a better economy with more jobs. Strengthening families and neighborhoods, punishing criminals swiftly and surely, controlling illegal drugs, and gun control were all considered much more important than the death penalty in fighting crime. The study acknowledged that politicians love the

WHEN WE VISIT JESUS IN PRISON

death penalty, which police chiefs consider a distraction from real crime fighting issues.

As the teleconference winds on, I cannot help but wonder if the public has any idea of the truth. By mid-afternoon, a judicial guest speaker relates that Florida jurors almost always believe that execution is cheaper than life imprisonment without possibility of parole. Laughter peals through the crowd.

Everybody in this conference knows that the truth is just the opposite. Execution can be at least two to three times more expensive than life imprisonment without possibility of parole.

I look around to see if anybody else besides me is not laughing. There are a few who look very concerned.

Bishop Felipe Estévez oversees the diocese with jurisdiction over Florida's death row and death house. As he says so clearly in his January 16, 2016 letter to the editor of the St. Augustine Record (after a U.S. Supreme Court decision held Florida's death sentencing scheme unconstitutional): "The Catholic Bishops of Florida have long [held] our position that life imprisonment without parole is an alternative that keeps society safe and renders the death penalty unnecessary. ... I hope and pray that [recent U.S. Supreme Court decisions] will bring about a much-needed reevaluation of the purpose and futility of Florida's use of capital punishment."

"Reading the Scriptures also makes it clear that the Gospel is not merely about our personal relationship with God. Nor should our loving response to God be seen simply as an accumulation of small personal gestures to individuals in need, a kind of 'charity à la carte,' or a series of acts aimed solely at easing our conscience. The Gospel is about the kingdom of God (cf. Lk 4:43); it is about loving God who reigns in our world. To the extent that he reigns within us, the life of society will be a setting for universal fraternity, justice, peace and dignity. Both Christian preaching and life, then, are meant to have an impact on society."

Pope Francis[1]

CHAPTER 16

Religious Constraints that Affect Prison Ministry and Restorative Justice

The "me and Jesus" culture of pop-American Christianity hardly comports with the Catholic understanding of how one is called to live out the responsibilities of their Baptism, including the duty of evangelization. For us Catholic volunteers in prison ministry, it will be obvious that the rugged frontier individualism of America's history has tilted mainstream media-evangelism's understanding of the leaven of the Gospel away from concern for the temporal needs of our brothers and sisters. The focus of such pop-Christianity can be sharply attuned to "getting saved" for the next world, with little or no energy directed into improving the conditions of life in this world. As so clearly and eloquently stated by Pope Francis in his first *Apostolic Exhortation, the Joy of the Gospel (Evangelii Gaudium)*, Catholic Christianity is extensively concerned with evidencing our faith for the next world especially through our compassion and concern for redeeming the societies and structures of this world, here and now:

Consequently, no one can demand that religion should be relegated to the inner sanctum of personal life, without influence on societal and national life, without concern for the soundness of civil institutions, without a right to offer an opinion on events affecting society. Who would claim to lock up in a church and silence the message of Saint Francis of Assisi or Blessed Teresa of Calcutta? They themselves would have found this unacceptable. An authentic faith—which is never comfortable or completely personal—always involves a deep desire to change the world, to transmit values, to leave this earth somehow better that we found it....

"The Church, guided by the Gospel of mercy and by love for [humankind], hears the cry for justice and intends to respond to it with all her might". In this context we can understand Jesus' command to his disciples: "You yourselves give them something to eat!" (Mark 6:37). [It] means working to eliminate the structural causes of poverty and to promote the integral development of the poor, as well as small daily acts of solidarity in meeting the real needs that we encounter. The word "solidarity" is a little worn and at times poorly understood, but it refers to something more than a few sporadic acts of generosity. It presumes the creation of a new mindset which thinks in terms of community and the priority of the life of all over the appropriation of goods by a few. (Citations omitted.)[2]

The depth at which such words cut against the grain of American pop-Christianity at large can hardly be overstated. Even so, the clash between such faith views in the specific context of criminal justice and punishment is akin to mixing matter and anti-matter.

Why Not Me?

The story is told of a rabbi who was coming home from synagogue and suddenly realized that smoke was pouring from somewhere in the direction of his side of town. Even from a distance, the rabbi knew that somebody's house was on fire. "Lord," prayed the rabbi, "don't let the fire be in our neighborhood." It seemed a holy and godly prayer.

As he walked closer, it became clear that the fire was from his neighborhood. "Lord," prayed the rabbi, "don't let the fire be on our street." It seemed a holy and godly prayer.

As he walked closer, it became clear that the fire was from his street. "Lord," prayed the rabbi, "don't let the fire be from our end of the street." It seemed a holy and godly prayer.

Then, as he turned the corner onto his street, he saw that the fire was from the far end of the street—his end of the street. He saw the familiar faces and familiar outlines of his neighbors and his family in the street. He knew it was either his house or his neighbor's house that was on fire. He started to pray, "Lord, don't let the fire be at my house." But the rabbi suddenly stopped dead in his tracks. To pray that the fire not be at his house was the same as praying that the fire be at his neighbor's house! What a horrendous and ungodly prayer!

He dropped to his knees and prayed, "Lord forgive me for my self-centeredness. If the fire must be, then let it be my house and spare my neighbor."

God answered his prayer, and the rabbi gave thanks.

How rare is such a prayer. That is the stuff of saints. Yet, here on death row the man before me is saying exactly that. He was a very wealthy man who raced horses with the Queen of England. He has lost all his money and many fair-weather friends.

"Everything that is important, I still have," he assures me. "I've been here over 5,000 days, Brother Dale. I was framed. The judge was corrupt. He was charged with taking bribes in other cases and removed from the bench in handcuffs in the middle of my trial. The state's attorney was corrupt. I told everyone that she asked me for a bribe for the judge. No one believed me. Then, after thirteen years, a memorandum was found. The state attorney's office had investigated and found that their lawyer had asked me for a $50,000 bribe. No charges were filed. No grievances with the Florida Bar. She was simply allowed to quit.

"We took my case back in front of the Florida Supreme Court and they were outraged. One judge was so incensed he came out of his chair. A year later that same court refused to give me a new trial. They gave me a new sentencing hearing. Why would an innocent man who was framed want a new sentence? I need a fair trial.

"When I first came to death row I used to say, 'Why me, God? Why is this happening to me?' If I had continued to ask that question I probably would have gone berserk. Instead I realized the real question is: 'Why not me?' Am I so arrogant as to think that only the poor should be victimized by Florida's corrupt justice system? Maybe if more of us well-to-do are put here erroneously, just like the poor have been all along, maybe that is how God will cause things to change.[3]

"That is how I keep my sanity, Brother Dale. By accepting whatever purpose God has in my being here. And by saying, 'Why not me?'"

One might say, in a very broad-brush summary, that the modern American penal system has been shaped by American Protestantism. More narrowly, it has been argued with persuasive force, that it is the *Protestant Ethic* that has shaped American cultural attitudes towards crime and punishment...in much the same way that it has shaped American attitudes toward capitalism and wealth. This has been well noted by both Catholic and Protestant scholars.

In his classic work *The Protestant Ethic and the Spirit of Capitalism*, sociologist Max Weber reveals a deep relationship between the Calvinistic roots of American Protestantism and the American economic system that developed over time. *In Religion and the Development of the American Penal System,*[4] Catholic religious studies professor Andrew Skotnicki reconstructs and analyzes the profound American religious movements that have shaped the country's criminal justice system, especially its penology. This impressive work by Skotnicki plumbs depths beyond the scope of this present book, but it is seminal to an in-depth understanding of how America's penology has been forged by belief. He gives a nod to Max Weber's analysis:

WHEN WE VISIT JESUS IN PRISON

Weber's noted thesis concerning Protestantism and the development of capitalism argues that economic rationalization in the West was immeasurably aided by its affinity to the type of asceticism necessary to Protestantism, especially Calvinism....

Following Weber's scholarship, one can connect the development and increasing complexity of capitalist society to the religious anxiety of the believer, who must seek salvation ethically and yet within the context of economic success. This will prove to be a significant insight with regard to the development of the penal system,...as rehabilitation could not be envisioned without concrete evidence of economic vitality within the institutions.[5]

Skotnicki believes that the Calvinistic roots of American Protestant religion had profound influence upon the conceptualization of the role of government in punishing criminals:

The state, in recognition of its divine purpose, and given the sinful inclinations of its citizens, was to be no less than an established order of repression. For the number of the elect is small and "therefore it is necessary that the rest of the crowd be restrained by a forcible curb. For the sons of God are intermingled with great, savage beasts, or with wolves and false men." (Citing John Calvin's *Institutes of the Christian Religion*.)[6]

It is important that we do not overlook the reference to John Calvin's concept of *the elect*. As noted earlier in this book, the notion of double predestination—that God predestines some for heaven and predestines others for hell—is crucial to the legacy of Calvinism and to the resultant understanding of how the state is to deal with offenders. That understanding is not just historical. It is with us in twenty-first century America.

T. Richard Snyder, a dean and professor of theology and ethics at New York Theological Seminary never thought much about prisons or about the people that live in them. Then, the president of the seminary for which he was on faculty initiated a master's degree program inside New York's Sing Sing prison in 1983.[7] Suddenly, our nation's approach to punishment was right in Rev. Snyder's face. He puts it bluntly: "Getting even feels good.… We'd rather turn the knife than turn the other cheek."[8]

After acknowledging that God's word literally prohibits believers from taking vengeance, Rev. Snyder shares with us the development of his thoughts and his horror through the personal experiences of prison and of what passes for Christian-based punishment in response to criminal offenders:

> Perhaps, I thought, the problem is that we lack more humane alternatives. If we had something better to put in place of the current system, maybe people would support reforms. But my research has uncovered myriads of alternatives that have been around for centuries—alternatives that are more rehabilitative, more humane, and more beneficial to victims, perpetrators, and the larger society. The basic problem [is] that our culture is captive to a spirit of punishment. Until we address this spirit, all calls to reform will fall upon ears that cannot hear and hearts that cannot feel.[9]

Rev. Snyder then summarizes the results of his search for understanding as to the roots of this cultural spirit of punishment by saying that there is a connection between "the punitive ethos in our society and Christian theology as it is popularly understood."[10] He singles out two crucial failings of popular Christian theology in this regard, the first being the issue of depravity of creation: "Because of the strong emphasis upon the fall, original sin, and total depravity, it is difficult to find within Protestantism an affirmation of the beauty, goodness, and worth in all creation."

For me, Rev. Snyder's identification of the theological notion of the depravity of creation as a fundamental flaw that leads to a spirit of punishment is particularly poignant. Back in my early years of volunteer prison ministry at a Florida panhandle prison, I had become a bit overwhelmed by the onslaught of vitriol from fundamentalist and evangelical inmates, and even some volunteers, directed toward my Catholic faith. While lunching with a rural Catholic pastor from South Georgia, I asked, "Father, in ten words or less, what is the essential difference between the Catholic worldview and the Protestant worldview?"

"That's very simple," he responded without a second of pause. "It is the difference of a vowel, the difference between an "a" and an "i." The Protestant worldview is that through the Fall of Adam and Eve all creation is *depraved* and needs to be destroyed. The Catholic worldview is that through the Fall of Adam and Eve grace left the world and all creation is *deprived*—deprived of grace. Our job is to participate with Christ in restoring grace to creation."

"Actually," the priest smiled after a break to sip his iced tea, "the ultimate meaning of that difference is very significant. Catholics are working as partners with Christ in bringing his redemption to the whole world, so that finally he may present it fully redeemed to his Father. Protestants are waiting for the world and the rest of us to be destroyed—right after they get out of Dodge in the Rapture."

I want to make it clear that many Protestant ministers in prison ministry do *not* fall into this category,[11] but that lunch was a beachhead in my personal efforts to understand the slogans and attitudes of many fundamentalist and evangelical Protestants with respect to the Catholic Church's social teaching. It crystalized for me the fundamental difference between the faith handed down to me by my parents as opposed to the understanding of the Christian faith by some of my colleagues in prison ministry.

If someone believes that God has condemned the world irredeemably for destruction, declared the world depraved and incapable of benefiting from the grace of Redemption, then of course they would consider *solidarity* and *working for the common good* to be as worthless as rearranging the furniture on the deck of the Titanic.

Returning to Rev. Snyder's identification of the two crucial failings of popular Christian theology that support and foster an ethos of punishment, he identifies the second as follows:

In the process of redemption, grace is understood almost exclusively in individualistic, internalized, non-historical terms....
The contemporary penal response to crime represents an individualized notion of redemption.

Once again, I find in the words of Rev. Snyder a profound insight
into the rejection by some fundamentalists and evangelicals of the
Catholic understanding of the vocation of the laity to evangelize the
workplace, to evangelize the marketplace, to evangelize the town
square and the courthouse, to evangelize the prisons—not just the
people who work in such places but the actual systems that function
there as well. The difference in Rev. Snyder's outlook and that of some
of the Protestant ministers I have encountered in Florida prisons is
akin to the difference between matter and anti-matter.

But even when it comes to human individuals, the shadow of Calvinistic predestination encroaches upon the generosity of redemptive
grace. Rev. Snyder notes the following results in the penal system
attributable to the theological misunderstandings of grace: "If I am
correct that the spirit of punishment in our society today is fed by and
related to a basic Christian (largely Protestant) misunderstanding of
grace, then it is incumbent upon us to discover other ways of thinking about God and God's grace that might provide a foundation for a
more humane response to crime or deviance from the norm."

Rev. Snyder offers another critical element that adds to the discussion of this book concerning the religious barriers to prison ministry
and restorative justice. This spirit of punishment is a religious cultural phenomenon that is not necessarily obvious, except through the
results of its application: *the highest incarceration rates in the entire
world*. People do not talk about it or analyze it. It has become part of
the culture, part of the air we breathe.[12]

My experience is that with respect to prison ministry and restorative justice, the Calvinistic understanding of election and predestination, as put into practice by some modern Christians, stands against
the very actions our Catholic Church is calling us to take. Because
of their belief that redemption is merely individual, our efforts to

change unjust social structures in prisons is opposed by some modern Calvinists, often called "Neo-Calvinists." Because of their belief in predestination, our efforts to improve the lot of the imprisoned and the mentally ill and the poor and the marginalized is opposed by some modern Neo-Calvinists. For those modern Neo-Calvinists (even if they do not identify themselves as such), any attempt to rescue those who are suffering is an attempt to snatch such people from God's will for their life. And any suggestion that those who have much should use their excess to relive the suffering of those who do not have enough is considered an attempt to take away from the well-heeled their outward sign of God's election—the sign to the world of their predestination for heaven. This is not consistent with the Gospel preached by Pope Francis and our Church, but I am here to testify that it exists in American society and is seen most clearly in our approach to crime and punishment.

If we research Calvinism to find where it literally teaches such things in the context of a modern, affluent First World society, we will be disappointed. That is not how it is recorded. But it can be the result of the theology *in praxis*. It is unfortunate that many American Catholics have absorbed the cultural Calvinism of American society into their understanding of Catholic teaching without analysis or critical evaluation.

So every volunteer in Catholic prison ministry should have a basic knowledge of the actual tenets of Calvinism. An excellent source is the article "Calvinism" available online in the *Catholic Encyclopedia*. [13] But the reader should be prepared to be somewhat puzzled as to how one navigates from the raw theology of John Calvin in theory to the theology of some of his influential followers in prison ministry today.

Rest assured that any effort by us Catholic volunteers to familiarize ourselves with the tenets of Calvinism, in theory and *in praxis*, will be put to use in our work in prisons. The resurgence of Calvinism in America today, frequently called Neo-Calvinism, is a hot topic in both the evangelical and the secular press. Even *Time Magazine* has taken note of the restoration to prominence of Calvinism in America:

Calvinism is back...Evangelicalism's latest success story, complete with an utterly sovereign and micromanaging deity, sinful and puny humanity, and the combination's logical consequence, predestination: the belief that before time's dawn, God decided whom he would save (or not), unaffected by any subsequent human action or decision.[14]

The article goes on to mention the modern stalwarts of the movement: John Piper of Minneapolis, Mark Driscoll of Seattle and, most importantly, Dr. Albert Mohler, President of Southern Baptist Theological seminary in Louisville. The re-emergence of American Calvinism has not been without its problems at the highest levels of evangelical circles, including in the largest evangelical denomination, the Southern Baptist Convention (SBC). *Christianity Today* has reported that:

Starting in 1993, the largest Protestant denomination's flagship seminary quickly lost at least 96 percent of its faculty. SBC inerrantists had tapped 33-year-old Al Mohler to head the Southern Baptist Theological Seminary, which until then had remained open to moderate and liberal professors. Mohler addressed the faculty and re-enforced the school's confession of faith, derived from the landmark Reformed document, the Westminster Confession....

Mohler is an unabashed Calvinist. His seminary now attracts and turns out a steady flow of young Reformed pastors.[15]

As reported in *The Christian Science Monitor*, the trend of American evangelicalism to embrace Calvinism is clear, especially among younger adults:

Twenty-something followers in the Presbyterian, Anglican, and independent evangelical churches are rallying around Calvinist, or Reformed, teaching. In the Southern Baptist Convention, America's largest Protestant body, at least 10 percent of its pastors identify as Calvinist, while more than one-third of recent seminary graduates do.

Now come the New [Neo-]Calvinists with their return to inviolable doctrines and talk of damnation—In essence, the Puritans, minus the breeches and powdered wigs. Is this just a moment of nostalgia or the beginning of a deeper revolt against the popular Jesus-is-our-friend approach of modern evangelicalism?

Where, in other words, is Christianity going?[16]

Where indeed? The reporter from *The Christian Science Monitor* might have done better to ask where *non-Catholic Christianity* is going? Catholic Christianity is on the same trajectory it has been on for 2,000 years. But with the religious phenomenon of the rebirth of American Calvinism spreading through the heartlands and rural lands of America, the locus of most American prisons, we volunteers in Catholic prison ministry need to know the difference between the faith and teaching of the Catholic Church and the beliefs of American cultural Christianity—which today is dominated by Neo-Calvinism.

This is especially true in learning to discern whether advocates who claim to be Catholic are in fact wolves in sheep's clothing: Calvinists wrapped in a thin veneer of claimed Catholic identity. When dealing with secular liberals, the litmus test for authentic Catholicism is the Church's teaching on the dignity and protection of human life, from the moment of conception to death by natural causes. When dealing with secular conservatives, the litmus test for authentic Catholicism is the Church's social teaching which inevitably flows from her Eucharistic consciousness and evangelizing mission.

We volunteers in Catholic prison ministry will be questioned, quizzed, and challenged by inmates, staff, and non-Catholic religious service providers. We had better know what the Church teaches and how it is different from the latest fad of cultural Christianity. Then, with full knowledge of the landscape of religious impediments to prison ministry and restorative justice, we must endeavor to put into practice the teachings and instructions of our Church, which have nothing to do with what John Calvin taught.

Forgiveness: The Forgotten Piece of Justice

I have received many questions in the halls of death row since September 11, 2001. Questions about Catholic beliefs on the supposedly God-sanctioned killing of war and capital punishment.

As the New Year begins, I have been provided with words of answer. Words eloquent and Scriptural as well as consistent with the *magisterium* of the Catholic Church. The words are those of my shepherd and pope, John Paul II in his message for World Peace Day, January 1, 2002:[17]

> Recent events, including the terrible killings [of September 11, 2001], move me to return to a theme which often stirs in the depths of my heart when I remember the events of history which have marked my life.... I have often paused to reflect on the persistent question: *how do we restore the moral and social order subjected to such horrific violence?* My reasoned conviction, confirmed in turn by biblical revelation, is that the shattered order cannot be fully restored except by a response that combines justice with forgiveness. *The pillars of true peace are justice and that form of love which is forgiveness....*
>
> How can we speak of justice and forgiveness as the source and condition of peace? *We can and we must,* no matter how difficult this may be; a difficulty which often comes from thinking that justice and forgiveness are irreconcilable. But forgiveness is the opposite of resentment and revenge, not of justice....
>
> Because human justice is always fragile and imperfect, subject as it is to the limitations and egoism of individuals and groups, it must include and, as it were, be completed by the *forgiveness which heals and rebuilds troubled human relations from their foundations.* This is true in circumstances great and small, at the personal level or on a wider, even international scale. Forgiveness is in no way

WHEN WE VISIT JESUS IN PRISON

opposed to justice, as if to forgive meant to overlook the need to right the wrong done. It is rather the fullness of justice....

Respect for a person's conscience, where the image of God himself is reflected (cf. Genesis 1:26-27), means that we can only propose the truth to others, who are then responsible for accepting it. To try to impose on others by violent means what we consider to be the truth is an offence against human dignity and ultimately an offence against God whose image that person bears....

Following the teaching and example of Jesus, Christians hold that to show mercy is to live out the truth of our lives: we can and must be merciful because mercy has been shown us by a God who is Love (cf. 1 John 4:7-12)....

But what does forgiveness actually mean? And why should we forgive?... Forgiveness is above all a personal choice, a decision of the heart to go against the natural instinct to pay back evil with evil. The measure of such a decision is the love of God who draws us to himself in spite of our sin. It has its perfect exemplar in the forgiveness of Christ, who on the Cross prayed: "Father, forgive them; for they know not what they do" (Luke 23:34)....

Forgiveness is not a proposal that can be immediately understood or easily accepted; in many ways it is a paradoxical message. Forgiveness in fact always involves an *apparent* short-term loss for a *real* long-term gain. Violence is the exact opposite; opting as it does for an apparent short term gain, it involves a real and permanent loss.

Forgiveness may seem like weakness, but it demands great spiritual strength and moral courage, both in granting it and in accepting it. It may seem in some way to diminish us, but in fact it leads us to a fuller and richer humanity, more radiant with the splendor of the Creator. [Emphasis in original.]

Thank you, dear Shepherd, for speaking God's truth to my raging and weeping heart.

Pope Francis echoes the words of our dear Pope John Paul II in defining what is necessary to bring God's peace to a society:

Peace in society cannot be understood as pacification or the mere absence of violence resulting from the domination of one part of society over others. Nor does true peace act as a pretext for justifying a social structure which silences or appeases the poor, so that the more affluent can placidly support their lifestyle while others have to make do as they can. Demands involving the distribution of wealth, concern for the poor and human rights cannot be suppressed under the guise of creating a consensus on paper or a transient peace for a contented minority. The dignity of the human person and the common good rank higher than the comfort of those who refuse to renounce their privileges. When these values are threatened, a prophetic voice must be raised.[18]

That is the peace in society that is the aim of Catholic restorative justice. In *Restorative Justice in the South*, the fourth in a series of pastoral statements by the Catholic Bishops of the South on the criminal justice process and a gospel response, the bishops describe for us the process of restorative justice, incorporating the concepts expressed by the United States Conference of Catholic Bishops (USCCB) in *Responsibility, Rehabilitation, and Restoration*:

Restorative justice focuses first on the victim and the community harmed by the crime. In this way it is different than the state versus criminal model. This shift in focus affirms the hurt and loss of the victim, as well as the harm and fear of the community, and insists that offenders come to grips with the consequences of their actions. These approaches are not "soft on crime" because they specifically call the offender to face victims and the communities. This experience offers victims a much greater sense of peace and accountability. Offenders who are willing to face the human consequences of their actions, are more ready to accept responsibility, make reparations, and rebuild their lives.[19]

The bishops remind us that this does not purport to replace the court system; rather, it can be an alternative process that functions under the guidance of the court with voluntary participation by the victim and the offender.

Another aspect of restorative justice is the effort to find alternatives to incarceration. The Bishops of the South, again incorporating the concepts expressed by the USCCB in *Responsibility, Rehabilitation, and Restoration*, remind us that:

+ A Catholic approach never gives up on those who violate laws.
+ We believe that both victims and offenders are children of God.
+ Despite their very different claims on society, their lives and dignity should be protected and respected.
+ We seek justice, not vengeance.
+ We believe punishment must have clear purposes: protecting society and rehabilitating those who violate the law.
+ We believe a Catholic vision of crime and criminal justice can offer some alternatives. A Catholic approach leads us to encourage models of restorative justice that seek to address crime in terms of the harm done to victims and communities, not simply as a violation of law.[20]

As noted in recent *Florida Bar News* articles, such alternative approaches that take into account the particular and special needs of an offender can include: Drug addicts. Alcoholics. People with serious mental illnesses. Homeless veterans. They wind up in Florida's courts and are behind bars, not for being a danger to society but because there is nowhere else for them to go.[21]

Alternative approaches for the mentally ill can include legislation to provide a broad array of court-ordered treatment options other than just institutionalization. A drastic revisiting of mental health services could also be in order. Florida is not alone among the states in needing to provide care rather than punishment for its mentally ill citizens. Steven Leifman, associate administrative judge of the Miami-Dade County Court Criminal Division calls himself the gatekeeper for the largest psychiatric facility in Florida, the Dade County Jail. He testified before the Florida Senate Appropriations Subcommittee on Criminal and Civil Justice about the plight of the severely mentally ill trapped in the cogs of the criminal justice system:

> On any given day, we have 18,000 prisoners, 10,000 local detainees, and between 25,000 and 40,000 on probation and community control with a serious mental illness in Florida. And this year we are expecting 7,000 inmates with serious mental illness to be released from the prison system.
>
> The consequences of untreated mental illness are overwhelming. As a result, we've seen homelessness increase; we've seen police injuries increase; we've seen police shootings with people with mental illness increase.
>
> We are wasting critical, critical tax dollars in the way we do things. And in some ways, we've made mental illness a crime. Last year, the police in Florida actually initiated more Baker Act cases [involuntary commitment of dangerous mentally ill persons] than the total number of arrests they made for robbery, burglary, and grand theft auto combined.[22]

And, as reported in *The Florida Bar News*, after the longest period of hot-war in American history, our cities are full of mentally ill and disabled veterans:

> More U.S. veterans of Afghanistan and Iraq have committed suicide than actually died from wounds in those wars.
>
> About 460,000 veterans coming out of those wars have been diagnosed with post-traumatic stress disorder, and half of them are at risk of ending up in the criminal justice system.
>
> "I started noticing defendants whose bad behavior could be attributed to their combat experience...," Judge Maney testified [before a Florida Senate Committee]. "These cases are real.

These wounded warriors are in our communities. They are in our jails. Their families feel helpless. Our police deal with them daily. Our counties jail them."

Judge Leifman reported, "In the United States there are approximately 130,000 veterans who are homeless every night. Almost 45% of those homeless individuals, many with co-occurring disorders, have mental illnesses. Half of the 130,000 vets that are homeless in the United States live in four states, and Florida is one of them. And half of them end up in jail."[23]

Catholic social justice teaching and restorative justice would certainly seek to establish humane alternatives to the criminal justice system for such people. Solutions can be fashioned as: Mental Health Courts; Drug Courts; Veterans Courts; etc.

For those who have no such mitigating factors and who are criminally responsible for harm to others, the Bishops of the South recognize a need for prisons. They incorporate the concepts expressed by the USCCB in *Responsibility, Rehabilitation, and Restoration* in defining the Catholic understanding of the role of incarceration:

+ Our criminal justice system should punish offenders and, when necessary, imprison them to protect society.
+ Their incarceration, however, should be about more than punishment.
+ Nearly all inmates will return to society, so prisons must be places where offenders are challenged, encouraged and rewarded for efforts to change their behaviors and attitudes. And where they learn the skills needed for employment and life in community.
+ Programs in jails and prisons that offer offenders education, life skills, religious expression, and recovery from substance abuse greatly reduce recidivism, benefit society, and help the offenders when they reintegrate into the community. These programs need to be made available at correctional institutions regardless of the level of security. And be

offered, to the extent possible, in the language of prisoners.
+ Those in jail could also participate in reentry group conferences with victims and community representatives and mentors to help guide and support their re-entry into society.

Re-entry of inmates into society is a classic flashpoint for the clash between Catholic social teaching and the neo-Calvinistic approach to criminal justice. Catholic social teaching seeks to restore the offender to a productive and meaningful life in society. The punitive neo-Calvinistic approach argues that the offender does not deserve assistance and should not be "rewarded" for having done wrong.

Restorative justice has nothing to do with rewarding someone for crime or with anyone meriting the common good or the assistance of their brothers and sisters in faith to find a foothold in making a life outside prison. In *Post Release from Prison*, the sixth in a series of pastoral statements by the Catholic Bishops of the South on the Criminal Justice process and a gospel response,[24] the bishops begin with the words of St. John Paul II in his *Jubilee for Prisoners*:

> We are still a long way from the time when our conscience can be certain of having done everything possible to prevent crime and to control it effectively so that it no longer does harm and, at the same time, *to offer to those who commit crimes a way of redeeming themselves and making a positive return to society.* [Emphasis in original.]

Then the Bishops adopt the approach of the USCCB in *Responsibility, Rehabilitation, and Restoration* by using the Parable of the Prodigal Son as the model of God's desire for our response to the released offender:

+ The father celebrates the prodigal son because the son has repented and changed his life. Jesus tells us that the lost who have been found are to be welcomed and celebrated.
+ Human dignity, the cornerstone of Catholic social teaching, is not earned by good behavior; it is something we all possess as people who are created in the image and likeness of God.
+ Solidarity also is a core principle of Catholic social teaching. This principle calls us to see the face of Christ in everyone and to see each other as brothers and sisters—common members of the human family.
+ Solidarity demands that we work for justice for all.
+ Our faith calls us to hold people accountable for their actions, but also to forgive and work for healing for those who are troubled. Individual and community acceptance of ex-offenders with love and understanding is necessary for their integration into normal community living.
+ Greater emphasis is needed on practical job training and post-release employment opportunities. Work release and work training programs for prisoners who are approaching release from prison should be as extensive as possible. Career counseling, testing, and guidance should be provided to all who are preparing to be released.

The Bishops identify a special role in this process for Catholic institutions:

+ Catholic institutions, including parishes, schools, and agencies should help provide rehabilitative services for former inmates.
+ Parishes could consider making church property available for transition houses or providing other services that can address the spiritual, material, and emotional assistance that elude the resources of many parole and probation systems.

- Our parishes can train volunteers to help nourish the faith life of ex-offenders.
- Parishes can develop mentoring programs to help with the difficult transition back to a normal life.
- All of these services will provide love and support for ex-offenders while offering the opportunity to educate parishioners about Catholic social teaching and restorative justice.

Finally, after asking all people of good will to cooperate in restoring to released offenders the right to vote and eliminating unnecessary obstacles to their obtaining education, the Bishops of the South have made an eighth and final statement, *Call for Action*, in which they summarize Catholic teaching on this crucial issue:

> Our Catholic belief in the inherent dignity of every human person, even a convicted felon, compels us to declare that virtually no non-violent offender should be incarcerated. The Catholic principle of promoting the common good also suggests that public funds can be more effectively spent on rehabilitation programs, rather than penal facilities. In the event that incarceration has occurred, we urge dioceses to encourage parishes to engage in restorative assistance to prisoners who have completed their sentences, helping them to make the difficult transition from cell to community.[25]

Restorative justice seeks to restore what has been taken or destroyed through crime, in the life of the victim and the offender, and in the community as well. That means that we Catholics must be willing to undertake a great deal in order to be an instrument of God's hand for healing, even as Pope John Paul II has told us, to the point of adopting a child orphaned by a crime:

> Christian families will be able to show greater readiness to adopt and foster children who have lost their parents or have been abandoned by them. Rediscovering the warmth of affec-

tion of a family, these children will be able to experience God's loving and provident fatherhood witnessed to by Christian parents, and they will thus be able to grow up with serenity and confidence in life. At the same time the whole family will be enriched with the spiritual values of a wider fraternity. Family fecundity must have an unceasing "creativity," a marvelous fruit of the Spirit of God, who opens the eyes of the heart to discover the new needs and sufferings of our society and gives courage for accepting them and responding to them. A vast field of activity lies open to families today, even more preoccupying than child abandonment is the phenomenon of social and cultural exclusion, which seriously affects the elderly, the sick, the disabled, drug addicts, ex-prisoners, etc.[26]

A special form of restorative justice recommended by the Bishops of the South and the USCCB is called "victim-offender dialogue." This dialogue is intended to be a therapeutic event that is mediated by a trained professional and is aimed at restoration of relationship between the offender, the victim, and the community. The possibility of such a dialogue usually requires specific authorizing legislation or an enabling executive order in the state where the offender is incarcerated. There has been a great deal of progress and study of this technique in the last decade.

For example, *Prison Fellowship International: Center for Justice and Reconciliation* offers a web page called Victim-Offender Dialogue, which inventories articles on meetings of prisoners with their actual victims while they are in prison: http://restorativejustice.org/restorative-justice/about-restorative-justice/tutorial-intro-to-restorative-justice/lesson-3-programs/victim-offender-mediation/. They can be contacted at Centre for Justice and Reconciliation, Prison Fellowship International, PO Box 17434, Washington, DC 20041 Tel: 1 703 481 0000 Email: rjonline@pfi.org web page: http://restorativejustice.org/contact/

Insight Prison Project offers Victim Offender Dialogue Mediator Training. The non-profit organization can be reached at P.O. Box

151642, San Rafael, CA 94915 Tel. (415) 459-9800/ Info@InsightPrisonProject.org. The relevant web page is: http://www.insightprisonproject.org/victim-offender-dialogue-mediator-training.html.

For the most part, however, such programs are administered through agencies of the states that allow for the practice. A forerunner in this area has been the State of Vermont. Georgia, Texas, and several other states offer such programs, as well. For example:

✦ State of Vermont: The Victim Offender Dialogue (VOD) Program is a service provided by the Victim Services Program to victims who are interested in meeting with the offender in their case. Participation in this program is victim-initiated, victim-centered and voluntary on the part of the victim and offender. Frequently Asked Questions: http://www.doc.state.vt.us/victim-services/the-victim-services-program-of-the-vermont-department-of-corrections/vodp.

✦ State of Georgia: The Office of Victim Services launched Victim Offender Dialogue (VOD) in the fall of 2012. VOD will provide an opportunity for victims of violent crimes to have a structured, safe, one-on-one meeting with their offender. Victims will be able to confront offenders with the full range of emotions they have experienced related to the crime including anger, shame, confusion, and sometimes even compassion. VOD can only be initiated by the victim and the offender must voluntarily agree to participate and must acknowledge his or her role in the crime. The offender must be incarcerated in order to participate in VOD. VOD is not simply a conversation. It requires a lengthy preparation process with both the victim and the offender. A trained facilitator meets with the victim and offender separately during the preparation process over a period of several months. The fundamental role of the facilitator is to build a relationship of trust and honesty with the victim and offender, which allows both participants to feel comfortable enough to share the truth of their pain and shame.

Frequently Asked Questions: http://pap.georgia.gov/frequently-asked-questions and http://pap.georgia.gov/victim-offender-dialogue.

This book, including this final chapter, has dealt with a myriad of variations and permutations of the suffering of God's people. For those toiling daily in the face of such anguish, the burden can become great indeed. Our dear Pope Francis knows this and has offered us a perspective that will help us to stay strong in the work of true justice, which is always God's restorative justice. I offer his perspective in the Closing Thoughts section that follows. But before ending, however, I want to thank each and every one of you readers for your work, whatever it is, to help bring that justice to this troubled world, especially in our prisons and jails.

> "*When I was assigned to be bishop of the Diocese of Pensacola-Tallahassee, which contains about 40% of the incarcerated population in Florida... I was surprised at who I found in the prisons. In the midst of buildings built to isolate and hold those that society has forgotten, I found great faith and the presence of God even in the most unlikely of places.*"
>
> Bishop Gregory L. Parkes,
> Diocese of Pensacola-Tallahassee, Florida[1]

CLOSING THOUGHTS

Our dear Pope Francis encourages us volunteers in Catholic prison ministry to transcend the limitations of our particular kingdom of God effort (including our work in prisons and jails) by keeping a consciousness of God's perspective across time:

> Here we see a first principle for progress in building a people: time is greater than space.
>
> This principle enables us to work slowly but surely, without being obsessed with immediate results. It helps us patiently to endure difficult and adverse situations, or inevitable changes in our plans. It invites us to accept the tension between fullness and limitation, and to give a priority to time. One of the faults which we occasionally observe in sociopolitical activity is that spaces and power are preferred to time and processes.
>
> Giving priority to space means madly attempting to keep everything together in the present, trying to possess all the spaces of power and of self-assertion; it is to crystallize pro-

cesses and presume to hold them back.

Giving priority to time means being concerned about initiating processes rather than possessing spaces. Time governs spaces, illumines them and makes them links in a constantly expanding chain, with no possibility of return. What we need, then, is to give priority to actions which generate new processes in society and engage other persons and groups who can develop them to the point where they bear fruit in significant historical events. Without anxiety, but with clear convictions and tenacity.[2]

Yet, even as we volunteers work diligently to maintain the consciousness of God's time, the suffering of those we serve is always in the forefront. The temptation to retreat from the pain and hide behind the sterile is always there; so, too, is the temptation to resort to criticism and back-biting, to pass on our pain to others rather than clutch it to our bosom before the Cross.

Here too, our beloved Pope Francis, offers us words of solace and encouragement:

Sometimes we are tempted to be that kind of Christian who keeps the Lord's wounds at arm's length. Yet Jesus wants us to touch human misery, to touch the suffering flesh of others. He hopes that we will stop looking for those personal or communal niches which shelter us from the maelstrom of human misfortune and instead enter into the reality of other people's lives and know the power of tenderness. Whenever we do so, our lives become wonderfully complicated and we experience intensely what it is to be a people, to be part of a people.

It is true that in our dealings with the world, we are told to give reasons for our hope, but not as an enemy who critiques and condemns. We are told quite clearly: "do so with gentleness and reverence" (1 Peter 3:15) and "if possible, so far as it depends upon you, live peaceably with all" (Romans 12:18). We are also told to overcome "evil with good" (Romans 12:21) and

WHEN WE VISIT JESUS IN PRISON

to "work for the good of all" (Galatians 6:10).

Far from trying to appear better than others, we should "in humility count others better" than ourselves (Phillippians 2:3). The Lord's apostles themselves enjoyed "favor with all the people" (Acts 2:47; 4:21, 33; 5:13). Clearly Jesus does not want us to be grandees who look down upon others, but men and women of the people.

This is not an idea of the pope, or one pastoral option among others; they are injunctions contained in the word of God that are so clear, direct, and convincing they need no interpretations which might diminish their power to challenge us. Let us live them *sine glossa*, without commentaries. By so doing we will know the missionary joy of sharing life with God's faithful people as we strive to light a fire in the heart of the world.[3]

Those words of our Pope Francis bring to mind a prayer composed by the Most Reverend Ken Untener, former Bishop of Saginaw, Michigan. His prayer has come to be known as the "Prayer of Oscar Romero,"[4] even though the words were never explicitly uttered by Romero. Yet, the thoughts express a view of our labor in the kingdom of God that is totally consistent with Romero's life and his work, even unto martyrdom.

Archbishop Oscar Romero Prayer: A Step along the Way

It helps, now and then, to step back and take a long view. The kingdom is not only beyond our efforts, it is even beyond our vision.

We accomplish in our lifetime only a tiny fraction of the magnificent enterprise that is God's work. Nothing we do is complete, which is a way of saying that the Kingdom always lies beyond us.

No statement says all that could be said.
No prayer fully expresses our faith.
No confession brings perfection.
No pastoral visit brings wholeness.
No program accomplishes the Church's mission.
No set of goals and objectives includes everything.
This is what we are about.

We plant the seeds that one day will grow.
We water seeds already planted,
　　knowing that they hold future promise.
We lay foundations that will need further development.
We provide yeast that produces far beyond our capabilities.
We cannot do everything, and there is a sense of liberation
　　in realizing that.

This enables us to do something, and to do it very well. It may be
incomplete, but it is a beginning, a step along the way,
　　an opportunity for the Lord's grace to enter and do the rest.

We may never see the end results, but that is the difference
between the master builder and the worker.

We are workers, not master builders; ministers, not messiahs.

We are prophets of a future not our own.

ABBREVIATIONS AND NOTES ON CITATIONS

URLs and Websites
Unless otherwise indicated in the note, the last date visited for all
URLs is January 15, 2016.

Abbreviations
In citing certain works in the notes, short titles have been used.
Works frequently cited have been identified by the flowing
abbreviations.

Citations to Scripture
Scripture texts in this work are taken from the *New American Bible,
Revised Edition.* ©2010, 1991, 1986, 1970 Confraternity of Christian
Doctrine, Washington, DC. (The specific URL for each quoted
Scripture text is provided in the related note.)

Citations to Official Sources from the Roman Catholic Church

✦ **The Catechism of the Catholic Church:** *The Catechism
  of the Catholic Church*, 2nd ed. (Washington, DC: United
  States Catholic Conference, 1997).

✦ **Social Doctrine of the Church:** Pontifical Council for
  Justice and Peace, *Compendium of the Social Doctrine of the
  Church* (Washington, DC: United State Catholic Confer-
  ence of Bishops, 2005).

✦ **Documents of the Second Vatican Ecumenical Council**
  • **Apostolicam Actuositatem:** *Decree on the Apostolate of
    the Laity, Apostolicam Actuositatem* (November 18, 1965).
  • **Gaudium et Spes:** *Pastoral Constitution on the Church in
    the Modern World, Gaudium et Spes* (December 7, 1965).
  • **Lumen Gentium:** *Dogmatic Constitution on the Church,
    Lumen Gentium* (November 21, 1964).

- **Nostra Aetate:** *Declaration on the Relation of the Church to Non-Christian Religions, Nostra Aetate* (October 28, 1965).
- **Unitatis Redintegratio:** *Decree on Ecumenism, Unitatis Redintegratio* (November 21, 1964).

+ **Encyclicals**
  - **Pope Benedict XVI**
    > **Spe Salvi:** *On Christian Hope, Spe Salvi* (November 30, 2007).
    > **Caritas in Veritate:** *On Integral Human Development in Charity and Truth, Caritas in Veritate* (June 29, 2009).

  - **Pope John Paul II**
    > **Dives in Misericordia:** *Rich in Mercy, Dives in Misericordia* (November 13, 1980).
    > **Redemptoris Missio:** *On the permanent validity of the Church's missionary mandate, Redemptoris Missio* (December 7, 1990).
    > **Fides et Ratio:** *On the Relationship between Faith and Reason, Fides et Ratio* (September 14, 1998).
    > **Ecclesia de Eucharistia:** *On the Eucharist in Its Relationship to the Church, Ecclesia de Eucharistia* (April 17, 2003).

+ **Apostolic Exhortations and Letters**
  - **Pope Francis**
    > **Evangelii Gaudium:** *Apostolic Exhortation the Joy of the Gospel, Evangelii Gaudium* (November 24, 2013).

- **Pope Benedict XVI**
  - ➤ **Sacramentum Caritatis:** *Post-Synodal Apostolic Exhortation On the Eucharist as the Source and Summit of the Church's Life and Mission, Sacramentus Caritatis* (February 27, 2007).
  - ➤ **Ubicumque et Semper:** *Apostolic Letter in the form of Motu Proprio, Ubicumque et Semper, Establishing the Pontifical Council for Promoting the New Evangelization* (September 21, 2010).

- **Pope John Paul II**
  - ➤ **Familiaris Consortio:** *Apostolic Exhortation, On the Role of the Christian Family in the Modern Word, Familiaris Consortio* (November 22, 1981).
  - ➤ **Salvifici Doloris:** *Apostolic Letter, On the Christian Meaning of Suffering, Salvifici Doloris* (February 11, 1984).
  - ➤ **Mulieris Dignitatem:** *Apostolic Letter, On the Dignity and Vocation of Women on the Occasion of the Marian Year, Mulieris Dignitatem* (August 15, 1988).
  - ➤ **Christifideles Laici:** *Post-Synodal Apostolic Exhortation, On the Vocation and the Mission of the Lay Faithful in the Church and in the World, Christifideles Laici* (December 30, 1988).
  - ➤ **Tertio Millennio Adveniente:** *Apostolic Letter for the Jubilee Year 2000 As the Third Millennium Draws Near, Tertio Millennio Adveniente* (November 10, 1994).
  - ➤ **Ecclesia in America:** *Post-Synodal Apostolic Exhortation, On the Encounter with the Living Jesus Christ: the Way to Conversion, Communion and Solidarity, Ecclesia in America* (January 22, 1999).
  - ➤ **Novo Millennio Ineunte:** *Apostolic Letter, At the Close of the Great Jubilee of the Year 2000, Novo Millennio Ineunte* (January 6, 2001).

- **Pope Paul VI**
  - › **Paenitemini:** *Apostolic Constitution on Fast and Abstinence, Paenitemini* (February 17, 1966).
  - › **Evangelii Nuntiandi:** *Apostolic Exhortation, Evangelization in the Modern World, Evangelii Nuntiandi* (December 8, 1975).

+ **Instructions, Bulls and Moto Proprios**
  - **Pope John Paul II**
    - › **Ecclesiae de Mysterio:** *Instructions on Certain Questions Regarding the Collaboration of the Non-Ordained Faithful in the Sacred Ministry of Priests, Ecclesiae de Mysterio* (August 15, 1997). (Boston: Pauline Books & Media, 1998).
    - › **Incarnationis Mysterium:** *Papal Bull of Indiction of the Great Jubilee of the Year 2000, Incarnationis Mysterium* (November 29, 1998).

+ **Speeches, Homilies, Messages, Audiences, etc.**
  - **Pope Francis**
    - › **Address to Meeting with the Poor:** *Address to Meeting with the Poor Assisted by CARITAS, Room of Renunciation of the Archbishop's Residence, Assisi, Italy* (October 4, 2013).
    - › **Address to Prison Chaplains:** *Audience Address to Participants in the National Meeting of Prison Chaplains, Discorso del Santo Padre Francesco al Partecipanti al Convegno Nazionale dei Cappellani delle Carceri Italiane* (October 23, 2013).

WHEN WE VISIT JESUS IN PRISON

- **Pope Benedict XVI**
  - ❯ **Message for the Sick:** *Message for the 14th World Day of the Sick* (February 11, 2006).
  - ❯ **Beatification of Newman:** *Homily of His Holiness Benedict XVI Mass with the Beatification of Venerable Cardinal John Henry Newman* (Cofton Park of Rednal – Birmingham, UK: Sunday September 19, 2010).

- **Pope John Paul II**
  - ❯ **Letter to Women:** *Letter to Women* (June 29, 1995).
  - ❯ **Illnesses of the Human Mind:** *Pope John Paul II, Speech to the International Conference for Health Care Workers on Illnesses of the Human Mind, Discorso di Giovanni Paolo II Ai Partecipanti alla XI Conferenza Internazionale Organizzata dal Pontificio Consiglio della Pastorale per gli Operatori Sanitari* (November 30, 1996). [Official version available only in Italian]; English translation available at: Eternal Word Television Network, 5817 Old Leeds Road, Irondale, AL 35210 www.ewtn.com.
  - ❯ **Homily, St. Louis, Missouri, USA:** *Homily, Mass in St. Louis, Missouri, U.S.A.* (January 27, 1999).
  - ❯ **Message for the Jubilee in Prisons:** *Message for the Jubilee in Prisons* (June 24, 2000).
  - ❯ **Jubilee of the Disabled:** *Homily, Jubilee of the Disabled* (December 3, 2000).
  - ❯ **No Peace without Justice:** *Message for Celebration of the World Day of Peace: No Peace Without Justice; No Justice Without Forgiveness* (January 1, 2002).

✦ **Congregation for the Doctrine of the Faith**
  - **Aspects of Evangelization:** *Doctrinal Note on Some Aspects of Evangelization, Nota Doctrinalis de quibusdam rationibus evangelizationis* (December 3, 2007).

+ **Pontifical Council for the Laity**
  - **Dignity of Older People:** James Francis Cardinal Stafford, President, Pontifical Council for the Laity, *The Dignity of Older People and their Mission in the Church and in the World* (October 1, 1998).

+ **Committee for the Jubilee Day of the Community with Persons with Disabilities**
  - **Preparation for the Jubilee Day 3 December 2000:** *Part Four The Person with Disabilities: Subject – Receiver of Evangelization and Catechesis* (May 17, 2000).

Citations to Sources from the U.S. Conference of Catholic Bishops (USCCB)

+ **Co-Workers: Co-Workers in the Vineyard of the Lord:** *A Resource for Guiding the Development of Lay Ecclesial Ministry* (Washington, DC: USCCB, 2005).
+ **National Directory for Catechesis:** *National Directory for Catechesis* (Washington, DC: USCCB, 2005)
+ **People with Disabilities:** *Pastoral Statement of U.S. Catholic Bishops on People with Disabilities* (Washington, DC: USCCB, 1978).
+ **Putting Children and Families First:** *Putting Children and Families First: A Challenge for Our Church, Nation and World* (Washington, DC: USCCB, November 1992): Publication No. 469-4 (reported in Origins, November 28, 1991, Vol. 21; No. 25).
+ **Responsibility, Rehabilitation, and Restoration:** *Responsibility, Rehabilitation, and Restoration: A Catholic Perspective On Crime and Criminal Justice: A Statement of The Catholic Bishops Of The United States* (Washington, DC: USCCB, 2000).

+ **Archbishop Oscar Romero Prayer:** *A Step Along the Way:* USCCB: Prayer & Worship page.

Citations to Series of Pastoral Letters by the Catholic Bishops of the South (U.S.A.)

+ **Challenges for Criminal Justice:** *Challenges for the Criminal Justice Process in the South – 1st Letter in Pastoral Series by the Catholic Bishops of the South.*
+ **Wardens from Wall Street:** *Wardens from Wall Street – 2nd Letter in Pastoral Series by the Catholic Bishops of the South.*
+ **Restorative Justice:** *Restorative Justice in the South – 4th Letter in Pastoral Series by the Catholic Bishops of the South.*
+ **Prison Conditions:** *Prison Conditions – 5th Letter in Pastoral Series by the Catholic Bishops of the South.*
+ **Post-Release from Prison:** *Post-Release from Prison – 6th Letter in Pastoral Series by the Catholic Bishops of the South.*
+ **Women in Prison:** *Women in Prison – 7th Letter in Pastoral Series by the Catholic Bishops of the South.*
+ **Call for Action:** *Call for Action – 8th Letter in Pastoral Series by the Catholic Bishops of the South.*

Citations to Statistics and Reports of the BJS

The Bureau of Justice Statistics (BJS) is a component of the Office of Justice Programs in the U.S. Department of Justice and was established to collect, analyze, publish, and disseminate information on crime, criminal offenders, victims of crime, and the operation of justice systems at all levels of government. These data are critical to federal, state, and local policymakers in combating crime and ensuring that justice is both efficient and evenhanded. BJS is the United States' primary source for criminal justice statistics. All BJS quoted statistics and reports, with current updates, are available online. http://www.bjs.gov/.

Citations to Reports, Position Papers, and Statistics of the National Alliance for the Mentally Ill

The National Alliance for the Mentally Ill (NAMI) is the nation's largest grassroots mental health organization and is dedicated to building better lives for the millions of Americans affected by mental illness. NAMI is an association of hundreds of local affiliates, state organizations and volunteers who work in communities to raise awareness and provide support and education that was not previously available to those in need. All of the NAMI reports, position papers, and statistics quoted in this work are available, with current updates, online. https://www.nami.org/. NAMI, 3803 N. Fairfax Drive, Suite 100 Arlington, VA 22203; Phone: (703) 524-7600; Toll free: (800) 950-NAMI (6264); Fax: (703) 524-9094.

Citations to Reports, Analyses and Statistics of The Sentencing Project

The Sentencing Project is a nonprofit organization, established in 1986, to work for a fair and effective U.S. criminal justice system by promoting reforms in sentencing policy, addressing unjust racial disparities and practices, and advocating for alternatives to incarceration. As a result of The Sentencing Project's research, publications, and advocacy, many people know that this country is the world's leader in incarceration; that racial disparities pervade the criminal justice system; that nearly six million Americans can't vote because of felony convictions; and that thousands of women and children have lost food stamps and cash assistance as the result of convictions for drug offenses. The Sentencing Project is dedicated to changing the way Americans think about crime and punishment. All of The Sentencing

Project reports, analyses, and statistics quoted in this work are available, with current updates, on line. http://www.sentencingproject. org/template/index.cfm. The Sentencing Project, 1705 DeSales Street, NW – 8th Floor, Washington, DC 20036; Phone: (202) 628-0871; Fax: (202) 628-1091.

NOTES

INTRODUCTION

1. "Pope Francis Washes Feet of Male, Female Prison Inmates," *CBC World News* (AP) updated: March 28, 2013 4:14 PM ET http://www.cbc.ca/news/world/story/2013/03/28/pope-prison-visit.html.
2. Andrew Skotnicki, *Criminal Justice and the Catholic Church* (New York: Rowman & Littlefield, 2008), 28.

CHAPTER 1
The Social Justice Framework
of Credible and Responsible Prison Ministry

1. *Tzedakah* can be described as the biblical concept of charity as man's God-given duty, not as an option.
2. Jorge Mario Bergoglio and Abraham Skorka, *On Heaven and Earth: Pope Francis on Faith, Family, and the Church in the Twenty-First Century* (New York: Image, 2013), 172.
3. Matthew 25:31-46, http://www.usccb.org/bible/matthew/25.
4. Luke 16: 19-31: http://www.usccb.org/bible/luke/16
5. *On Heaven and Earth*, 168-169.
6. *Responsibility, Rehabilitation, and Restoration.*
7. *Responsibility, Rehabilitation, and Restoration,* 16.
8. Genesis 1:26-27: http://www.usccb.org/bible/genesis/1.
9. "Justice Needed for Peace, Pope Tells Boys' Town," *The Star-News*, Wilmington, NC, January 2, 1972, 3-A: http://news.google.com/newspapers?nid+1454&dat=19720102&id=87osAAAAIBAJ&sjid=vgkEAAAAIBAJ&pg=2612,223932.
10. Pope Paul VI, Homily, Mass at Boys' Town, Rome, Italy [available only in Italian: *V Giornata Mondiale Della Pace*), January 1, 1972: http://www.vatican.va/holy_father/paul_vi/homilies/1972/documents/hf_p-vi_hom_19720101_it.html.
11. *Homily, St. Louis, MO, USA*: ¶5.
12. This discussion is based on the work of Ceslaus Spicq, OP, tr. Sister Marie Aquinas McNamara, OP, and Sr. Mary Honoria Richter, OP, *Agape in the New Testament*: Volume One, *Agape in the Synoptic Gospels* (Eugene, OR: Wipf & Stock, 1963); Volume Two, *Agape in the Epistles of St. Paul, the Acts of the Apostles and the Epistles of St. James, St. Peter, and St. Jude* (Eugene, OR: Wipf & Stock, 1965); Volume Three, *Agape in the Gospels, Epistles and Apocalypse of St. John* (Eugene, OR: Wipf & Stock, 1966).

13. It is impossible to define the disciples' *agapē*, since it *is* a love like Christ's own love—it is his own love by which they also live. It is possible to say what *agapē* is not, however. It is not concupiscence, *erōs*, or natural and spontaneous tenderness, *storgē*, or the measured, beautiful benevolence limited to close friends, *philia*.
    Ceslaus Spicq, *Agape in the New Testament*, Volume Three, 54-55.

14. It must be repeated then that [*agapē*] is not a verb of cordial affection but of an active will to do good, full of respect and indulgence, and generous in kind services.... It would be hard to find a clearer way of saying that the agape of Christians is disinterested.... Our Lord told his disciples not to look for anything on this earth in return for their devotion and kindness.... It is absolutely gratuitous and completely self-forgetful, radically opposed to any expectation of repayment.
    Ceslaus Spicq, *Agape in the New Testament*, Volume One, 84-87.

15. This summary broadly includes nominalized forms of the verbs in Greek. See, generally, Ceslaus Spicq, *Agape in the New Testament*, Volume Three, Appendix I, 197; Appendix V, 224.

16. John 13:34-35: http://www.usccb.org/bible/john/13.

17. Christ suppressed the earthly law of retaliation and replaced it with a celestial law. It is not man's to avenge or reward himself; only God has that prerogative.
    Ceslaus Spicq, *Agape in the New Testament*, Volume One, note 2, 86.

18. This summation of *agapē* is generally credited to Noble Peace Prize Nominee Reverend Emmanuel Charles McCarthy, a Byzantine-Melkite Rite Catholic priest whose youngest daughter's (Teresa Benedicta) miraculous cure through the intercession of the Carmelite nun Benedicta of the Cross (Edith Stein), was documented and accepted by the Vatican in the cause of canonization for St. Benedicta of the Cross.

19. *Social Doctrine of the Church.*

20. Paragraph references on pages 32-34 are to the paragraph of *Social Doctrine of the Church* from which the quoted text is taken.

21. *Christifideles Laici*, ¶37.

22. *Responsibility, Rehabilitation, and Restoration*, 21.

23. Romans 12:19: http://www.usccb.org/bible/romans/12.

24. *Responsibility, Rehabilitation, and Restoration*, 20.

25. *The Catechism of the Catholic Church*, ¶1451.

26. *Catechism of the Council of Trent for Parish Priests Issued by Order of Pope Pius V (1566)* (Rockford, IL: TAN, 1982), 426-427.

27. *Responsibility, Rehabilitation, and Restoration*, 24.

28. Pope John Paul II, Audience, November 26, 2004, as reported in: "Prisons Mustn't Be Limited to Punishment, Pope Stresses: Sees Rehabilitation of Inmates as a Goal," Zenit.org (November 26, 2004): http://www.zenit.org/en/articles/prisons-mustn-t-be-limited-to-punishment-pope-stresses.

CHAPTER 2
The Ecclesial Framework and Catechetical Practices
of Credible and Responsible Prison Ministry

1. *Early Christian Fathers* (New York: Touchstone, 1996), 360-362.
2. *The Catechism of the Catholic Church,* ¶1997.
3. *Ecclesiae de Mysterio.* (Page references are to the pages from which the text is taken; citations omitted unless otherwise noted.)
4. Citing *The Catechism of the Catholic Church,* ¶1547.
5. *Co-Workers.* (Page references are to the pages of *Co-Workers* from which the text is taken; citations omitted unless otherwise noted.)
6. Citing *Christifideles Laici.*
7. Citing *Novo Millennio Ineunte,* ¶46.
8. See, for example, Timothy Williams, "Jails Have Become Warehouses for the Poor, Ill and Addicted, a Report Says," *The New York Times,* February 11, 2015, p. A19: available at: http://www.nytimes.com/2015/02/11/us/jails-have-become-warehouses-for-the-poor-ill-and-addicted-a-report-says.html?partner=msft_msn.
9. *Challenges for Criminal Justice.*
10. Ibid., at notes 1 and 2, citing, respectively, *The Sentencing Project,* "New Prison Population Figures: Crisis and Opportunity," August 2002 and "U.S. Correctional population at record high," CNN.com 8-25-2002.
11. Ibid., at note 4, citing BJS Bulletin, PRISONERS IN 2001, Table 6, released July 2002.
12. BJS Bulletin, PRISONERS IN 2013, Table 6, revised September 2014: http://www.bjs.gov/content/pub/pdf/p13.pdf .
13. *The Sentencing Project,* "Prison Population: National Table" http://www.sentencingproject.org/map/statedata.cfm?abbrev=NA&mapdata=true; and "World Prison Populations: Half of the world's prison populations of about nine million is held in the U.S., China or Russia," BBC News in Depth: http://news.bbc.co.uk/2/shared/spl/hi/uk/06/prisons/html/nn2page1.stm.
14. BJS Bulletin, Correctional Populations in the United States, 2013, December 2014: http://www.bjs.gov/content/pub/pdf/cpus13.pdf.
15. *The Sentencing Project,* "Felony Disenfranchisement: A Primer—June 2013, 1: http://www.sentencingproject.org/doc/publications/fd_Felony%20Disenfranchisement%20Primer.pdf.
16. *The Sentencing Project,* Prison Population: 2015: National Table."
17. *The Sentencing Project,* Prison Population: 1980-2011: State Tables," http://www.sentencingproject.org/map/map.cfm#map.
18. *The Sentencing Project,* Schools and Prisons: Fifty Years after Brown vs. Board of Education (2004), 2: http://www.sentencingproject.org/doc/publications/rd_brownvboard.pdf.

19. Dale S. Recinella, *The Biblical Truth about America's Death Penalty* (Boston: Northeastern University Press, 2004).

20. *The Catechism of the Catholic Church*, ¶4.

21. *The Catechism of the Catholic Church*, ¶6.

22. *The National Directory for Catechesis*, 40.

23. Ibid., 132-134.

24. *The Catechism of the Catholic Church*, ¶2065.

CHAPTER 3
The Pastoral Framework of Credible and Responsible Prison Ministry

1. Brother Ugolino, *The Little Flowers of St. Francis of Assisi*, "Chapter XXVI— How St Francis Converted Certain Robbers and Assassins, Who Became Friars; and of a Wonderful Vision Which Appeared to One of Them Who Was a Most Holy Brother"; reproduced in *St. Francis of Assisi Writings and Early Biographies: English Omnibus of the Sources for the Life of St. Francis* (Chicago: Franciscan Herald Press, 1983); 1360-1363; also available (public domain) at http://www.ccel.org/ccel/ugolino/flowers.txt.

2. "We can understand *the custom of Jubilees*, which began in the Old Testament and continues in the history of the Church. Jesus of Nazareth, going back one day to the *synagogue of his home town*, stood up to read (cf. Lk 4:16-30). Taking the book of the Prophet Isaiah, he read this passage: 'The Spirit of the Lord God is upon me, because the Lord has anointed me to bring good tidings to the afflicted; he has sent me to bind up the brokenhearted, to proclaim liberty to the captives, and the opening of the prison to those who are bound; *to proclaim the year of the Lord's favour*' (61:1-2).

    "The Prophet was speaking of the Messiah. 'Today,' Jesus added, 'this scripture has been fulfilled in your hearing' (Lk 4:21), thus indicating that he himself was the Messiah foretold by the Prophet, and that the long-expected 'time' was beginning in him. The day of salvation had come, the 'fullness of time.' *All Jubilees point to this 'time' and refer to the Messianic mission of Christ*, who came as the one 'anointed' by the Holy Spirit, the one 'sent by the Father.' It is he who proclaims the good news to the poor. It is he who brings liberty to those deprived of it, who frees the oppressed and gives back sight to the blind (cf. Mt 11:4-5; Lk 7:22). In this way he ushers in 'a year of the Lord's favour,' which he proclaims not only with his words but above all by his actions. The Jubilee, 'a year of the Lord's favour,' characterizes all the activity of Jesus; it is not merely the recurrence of an anniversary in time" (¶11, italics in original). *Tertio Millennio Adveniente*.

3. *Incarnationis Mysterium*. (Paragraph references are to the paragraph of *Incarnationis Mysterium* from which the text is taken; citations omitted.)

WHEN WE VISIT JESUS IN PRISON

4. *Message for the Jubilee in Prisons.*
5. *Message for the Jubilee in Prisons,* ¶1.
6. *Message for the Jubilee in Prisons,* ¶¶1-2.
7. *Tertio Millennio Adveniente,* ¶10.
8. *Tertio Millennio Adveniente,* ¶10.
9. "Late Saturday morning on July 17, [1999] Death Row inmate Frank Valdez
   threatens an officer and a five-member "extraction team" is dispatched
   to his cell on the X-Wing, the solitary confinement unit that houses the
   most disruptive inmates at Florida State Prison in Starke, Florida. Valdez is
   subdued and taken to the prison clinic for a post use-of-force physical. He
   is subsequently returned to X-Wing. In-house medical staff and paramedics
   are called to Florida State Prison at 3:25 pm Valdez is pronounced dead at
   Shands Hospital in Starke about 4:18 pm. The Florida Department of Law
   Enforcement is notified the same day and begins a criminal investigation in
   conjunction with the Inspector General's Office.
      "Over the months that follow, nine department employees will be charged
   with crimes related to Valdez' death ranging from second degree murder
   to official misconduct. All nine are dismissed by the Department because
   they have violated department rules including excessive and/or unnecessary
   use of force and falsified reports, according to DC spokeswoman Yolanda
   Murphy.
      "Some of the changes implemented by the department as a result of the
   Valdez incident include the development of a policy whereby use of force
   and cell extractions are video recorded, the installation of cameras on
   X-Wing at Florida State Prison, and the review of all Use of Force reports by
   the Inspector General's Office.
      "Valdez was on Death Row for the 1987 murder of Correctional Officer
   Fred Griffis. Valdez shot him when Griffis refused to give Valdez the keys to
   a vehicle housing an inmate Valdez was trying to help escape. (The inmate
   had been taken outside the prison for a doctor's visit.) The inmate did not
   escape and Valdez was found guilty of the officer's murder and put on Death
   Row."
      Florida Department of Corrections, *Florida Corrections Centuries of
   Progress: 1999,* "Death Row Inmate Frank Valdez Dies": http://www.dc.state.
   fl.us/oth/timeline/1999.html.
10. *Message for the Jubilee in Prisons,* ¶3.
11. *Message for the Jubilee in Prisons,* ¶3.
12. *Message for the Jubilee in Prisons,* ¶4.
13. *Message for the Jubilee in Prisons,* ¶4.
14. With gratitude to Francis and Judith MacNutt, Jacksonville, Florida who
    trained me to pray with men in prison in 1990.
15. Exodus 17:11-13 http://www.usccb.org/bible/exodus/17.

CHAPTER 4
Effective Pastoral Prison Ministry in a Pluralistic Setting

1. *Homily, Beatification of Newman,* quoting Blessed John Henry Cardinal Newman (*The Present Position of Catholics in England,* ix, 390): also available at http://www.newmanreader.org/works/england/.
2. Philip Jenkins, *The New Anti-Catholicism: The Last Acceptable Prejudice* (New York: Oxford University Press, 2003), 1-2.
3. For example, as of calendar year 2000, the percentage of the population identified as Catholic in the following states is, respectively: Tennessee 3.2%, Alabama 3.3%, South Carolina 3.4%, North Carolina 3.9%, Mississippi 4%, Arkansas 4.3%, Georgia 4.5%, Oklahoma 4.8%, West Virginia 5.8%, and Virginia 8.5%.
4. "How many Roman Catholics are there in the world?" *BBC NewsWorld,* March14, 2013: http://www.bbc.co.uk/news/world-21443313.
5. World Population Religious Adherence: Christian 33.39% (of which Roman Catholic 16.85%, Protestant 6.15%, Orthodox 3.96%, Anglican 1.26%), Muslim 22.74%, Hindu 13.8%, Buddhist 6.77%, Sikh 0.35%, Jewish 0.22%, Baha'i 0.11%, other religions 10.95%, non-religious 9.66%, atheists 2.01% (2010 est.): *The World Fact Book 2013-14* (Washington, DC: Central Intelligence Agency, 2013): https://www.cia.gov/library/publications/the-world-factbook/index.html: Table "Field Listing: Religions" https://www.cia.gov/library/publications/the-world-factbook//fields/2122.html.
6. *The Statistical Abstract of the United States 2012,* "Table 76 Religious Bodies—Selected Data" (Washington, DC: U.S. Census Bureau, September 2015): https://catalog.data.gov/dataset/statistical-abstract-of-the-united-states.
7. *Gaudium et Spes,* ¶28.
8. *Unitatis Redintegratio.* (Paragraph references are to the paragraphs of *Unitatis Redintegratio;* citations omitted.)
9. Address from His Holiness Pope Francis to the delegation of Salvation Army leaders (Vatican City, Rome: Friday, December 12, 2014): available at: http://www.salvationarmy.org/thegeneral/vatican.
10. *Nostra Aetate.* (Paragraph references are to the paragraphs of *Nostra Aetate;* citations omitted.)
11. "New Alliance Aims to Create Culture of Life Across All Walks of Life," U.S. News Briefs: *Catholic News Service* (January 26, 2015): available at: http://www.catholicnews.com/data/briefs/cns/20150126.htm.

CHAPTER 5
Catholic Prison Ministry as Evangelization

1. Cardinal Donald Wuerl, *New Evangelization: Passing on the Catholic Faith Today* (Huntington, IN: Our Sunday Visitor Publishing, 2013), 43.
2. Ibid.
3. At the Second Vatican Council an English Archbishop submitted an intervention devoted entirely to the Jägerstätter story. He called upon his fellow bishops, assembled from the entire world, "to consider the man and his sacrifice in a spirit of gratitude" and let his example "inspire our deliberations" on the document which would become *The Pastoral Constitution on the Church in the Modern World.* Gordon Zahn, *In Solitary Witness: The Life and Death of Franz Jägerstätter* (Springfield, IL: Templegate Publishers, 1964), 1.
4. *New Evangelization: Passing On the Catholic Faith Today,* 84, citing, *Aspects of Evangelization,* ¶1.
5. *Aspects of Evangelization,* note 2, citing, *Redemptoris Missio,* ¶9.
6. *Redemptoris Missio,* ¶9.
7. Cardinal Theodore E. McCarrick,: "The Call to a New Evangelization," Keynote Address, *Ministry through the Lens of Evangelization: Major Presentations from the North America Institute for Catholic Evangelization* (Washington, DC: Secretariat for Evangelization, USCCB, 2004), 6-7.
8. *Apostolicam Actuositatem.* (Paragraph references are to the paragraphs of *Apostolicam Actuositatem.*)
9. George Weigel, *Evangelical Catholicism: Deep Reform in the 21ˢᵗ-Century Church* (New York: Basic Books, 2013).
10. *Aspects of Evangelization,* ¶2 (citations omitted).
11. *Aspects of Evangelization,* ¶3.
12. *Evangelii Nuntiandi.* (Paragraph references are to paragraphs of *Evangelii Nuntiandi*).
13. Citing, at note 68, 1 Peter 3:1
14. *Ubicumque et Semper,* citing *Christifideles Laici.*
15. *Aspects of Evangelization,* ¶12 (citations omitted).
16. Sean Salai, SJ, *What Would Pope Francis Do? Bringing the Good News to People in Need* (Huntington, IN: Our Sunday Visitor, 2016), citing, Evangelii Gaudium, ¶120.
17. Catholic Home Study Service, PO Box 363, Perryville, MO 63775-0363 http://www.amm.org/chss/chss.asp.
18. Dismas Ministry, PO Box 070363, Milwaukee, WI 53207: http://www.dismasministry.org/.
19. *Responsibility, Rehabilitation, and Restoration,* 20.
20. This author continues to provide one-on-one spiritual counseling for death row inmates and pastoral services for the condemned in the death house during the six-week deathwatch period prior to their execution.

CHAPTER 6
The Spiritual, Communal and Individual Practices
for Catholic Prison Ministers to Avoid Burnout

1. G.K. Chesterton, *Saint Thomas Aquinas – Saint Francis of Assisi* (San Francisco: Ignatius Press, 2002), 196-197.
2. Generally attributed to Charles M. Schultz, cartoonist and author, *Peanuts*.
3. *Ecclesia de Eucharistia*. (Paragraph references are to the paragraph of *Ecclesia de Eucharistia* from which the text is taken; citations omitted unless otherwise indicated.)
4. Archbishop Charles J. Chaput, O.F.M. Cap., *Living the Catholic Faith: Rediscovering the Basics* (Cincinnati: Servant Books, 2001), 64-66.
5. *Sacramentum Caritatis*. (Paragraph references are to the paragraphs of *Sacramentum Caritatis*; citations omitted.)
6. *Lumen Gentium*, ¶¶39-40.
7. Page references are to the pages of *Co-Workers* from which the text is taken; citations omitted unless otherwise indicated.
8. Citing Canon Law Society of America [CLSA], *Code of Canon Law, Latin-English Edition, New English Translation* (Washington, DC: CLSA, 1999), canon 231.
9. Citing *Holy Communion and Worship of the Eucharist Outside Mass* (New York: Catholic Book Publishing, 1976).
10. See *Sunday Celebrations in the Absence of a Priest: Revised Edition* (Washington, DC: USCCB, 2012).
11. *Ecclesia de Eucharistia*, ¶34, citing *The Way of Perfection (Camino de Perfección)*, Chapter 35.
12. *Ecclesia de Eucharistia*, ¶33.
13. "In Christian terms, the family is sacred and holy, a community of life and love which prepares, nurtures, and sustains the youngest members of the church in their task of building up the kingdom of God." *Putting Children and Families First*, at III.B.2.
14. Charles R. Figley, Ph.D., ed., *Treating Compassion Fatigue* (New York: Brunner-Routledge, 2002), 2. For information and resources on compassion fatigue, see, The Figley Institute, 141 Robert E Lee Boulevard, #255, New Orleans, LA 70124: http://www.figleyinstitute.com/indexMain.html.

CHAPTER 7
Current Theories on Why People Commit Crime

1. *St. Augustine – Confessions,* R.S. Pine-Coffin, tr., (New York: Penguin Books, 1961), 47.
2. Ibid.
3. *The Catechism of the Catholic Church,* ¶¶396-397.
4. *The Catechism of the Catholic Church,* ¶¶404-405.
5. *Diagnostic and Statistical Manual of Mental Disorders,* 5th Edition: DSM-5 (Arlington, VA: American Psychiatric Publishing, 2013).
6. Martha Stout, Ph.D., *The Sociopath Next Door: The Ruthless Versus the Rest of Us* (New York: Broadway Books, 2005), cover.
7. Ibid., 25-26.
8. *The Catechism of the Catholic Church,* ¶1778.
9. *Gaudium et Spes,* ¶16 (citations omitted unless otherwise indicated).
10. *Fides et Ratio,* ¶36.
11. *Fides et Ratio,* ¶98.
12. *The Catechism of the Catholic Church,* ¶¶1783-1785.
13. Tess Livingstone, *George Pell: Defender of the Faith Down Under* (San Francisco: Ignatius Press, 2004), 403-405.
14. *Caritas in Veritate,* ¶34 (citations omitted).
15. *Caritas in Veritate,* ¶68.
16. *The Catechism of the Catholic Church,* ¶1782.
17. *The Catechism of the Catholic Church,* ¶388.
18. Robert Hare, Ph.D., *Without Conscience: The Disturbing World of the Psychopaths Among Us* (New York: The Guilford Press, 1993), xi.
19. The Catechism of the Catholic Church, ¶¶1451-1453.
20. *Spe Salvi,* ¶33:
21. *Spe Salvi,* ¶41.
22. Paul Babiak, Ph.D. and Robert D. Hare, Ph.D., *Snakes in Suits: When Psychopaths Go to Work* (New York: Harper, 2006), 55.
23. *Spe Salvi,* ¶34.
24. Rokelle Lerner, *The Object of My Affection Is in My Reflection: Coping with Narcissists* (Deerfield Beach, Florida: Health Communications, 2009), 4.
25. Luke 15:1-7: http://www.usccb.org/bible/luke/15.

CHAPTER 8
Characteristics of Criminal Thinking

1. Bishop Robert J. Baker and Father Benedict J. Groeschel, C.F.R., *When Did We See You, Lord?* (Huntington, IN: Our Sunday Visitor, 2005), 165.
2. Ibid.
3. Pepper gas, similar chemical agents, and electric prods can be legitimately used to subdue an inmate who is out of control and presenting a danger to self or others. They are not to be used as punishment to teach him a lesson after the inmate has been brought under control and placed in a cooling-off or segregation cell.
4. Bill Cotterell, "Human Bones Found in Dig at Notorious Dozier Reform School in Florida," *U.S. News on NBCNews.com* (August 31, 2013): http://usnews.nbcnews.com/_news/2013/08/31/20273510-human-bones-found-in-dig-at-notorious-dozier-reform-school-in-florida?lite; see update: Saundra Amrhein (Reuters), "Remains of Two Bodies Identified at Notorious Florida Boys' School," *MSN News Crime & Justice* (September 26, 2014): http://news.msn.com/crime-justice/remains-of-two-bodies-identified-at-notorious-florida-boys-school.
5. Stanton E. Samenow, Ph.D., *Inside the Criminal Mind: Revised and Updated Edition (New York: Crown Publishers, 2004).*
6. *Paenitemini*, text accompanying note 34.
7. See *Changing Criminal Thinking*, (infra note 9), 93-94.
8. *Ecclesia in America.* (Paragraph references shown; citations omitted.)
9. Boyd D. Sharp MS, LPC, *Changing Criminal Thinking: A Treatment Program* (2nd Edition) (Alexandria, VA: American Correctional Association, 2006). (Unless otherwise indicated, page references through page 237 are to this work.)
10. Stephen T. Hall, "Faith-Based Cognitive Programs in Corrections," *Corrections Today* (December 2003); available on the American Correctional Chaplains Association website: http://www.correctionalchaplains.org/faith-based/page1.html#2a.
11. Samuel Yochelson and Stanton Samenow, *The Criminal Personality: A Profile for Change* (Lanham, MD: Rowman & Littlefield, 1976).
12. Gary F. Cornelius, *The Art of the Con: Avoiding Offender Manipulation* (2nd Edition) (Alexandria, VA: American Correctional Association, 2009), p. 107. (Ensuing page references are to this work.)
13. Peter Finn, *Addressing Correctional Officer Stress: Programs and Strategies* (Washington, DC: The National Institute of Justice of the U.S. Department of Justice, 2000): https://www.ncjrs.gov/pdffiles1/nij/183474.pdf.
14. Father Pierre Raphael, *Inside Rikers Island: A Chaplain's Search for God* (New York: Orbis, 1990), 27.
15. Genesis, chapter 32: http://www.usccb.org/bible/genesis/32.

CHAPTER 9
Pastoral Needs of Inmates

1. Fr. Walter J. Ciszek, SJ, with Fr. Daniel Flaherty, SJ, *He Leadeth Me* (San Francisco: Ignatius Press, 1973), 73.
2. Ibid.
3. Ibid., 39-40.
4. Luke 18:27: http://www.usccb.org/bible/luke/18.
5. Norval Morris and David J. Rothman, editors, *The Oxford History of the Prison: The Practice of Punishment in Western Society* (New York: Oxford University Press, 1998), 20-21.
6. Hebrews 13:3: http://www.usccb.org/bible/hebrews/13.
7. *Sacramentum Caritatis*, ¶59.
8. *Responsibility, Rehabilitation, and Restoration*, pages 1-13: (italicized language is found at the page noted in brackets).
9. *Prison Conditions.*
10. "Six Million People Are Under Correctional Supervision in the U.S.—More Than Were in Stalin's Gulags." Adam Gopnik, "The Caging of America: Why Do We Lock Up So Many People?" *The New Yorker* (January 30, 2012): http://www.newyorker.com/arts/critics/atlarge/2012/01/30/120130crat_atlarge_gopnik.
11. "An Unlikely Alliance of Left and Right: America Is Waking Up to the Cost of Mass Incarceration," *The Economist* (August 17, 2013), pp. 23-24.
12. U.S. Attorney General Eric Holder, Speech to the American Bar Association's Annual Meeting, San Francisco, CA (August 12, 2013).
13. Adam Gopnik, "Mandatory Sentences and Moral Change," *The New Yorker* (August 16, 2013): http://www.newyorker.com/online/blogs/comment/2013/08/eric-holder-mandatory-drug-sentences-and-moral-change.html.
14. "An Unlikely Alliance of Left and Right," *The Economist.*
15. John M. Schneider, Ph.D., *Finding My Way: Healing and Transformation through Loss and Grief* (Colfax, WI: Seasons Press, 1994), 13.
16. Ibid.
17. *Dives in Misericordia.* (Paragraph references shown; citations omitted).
18. *Salvifici Doloris.* (Paragraph references shown; citations omitted).
19. See, for example, Jim Graves, "Bringing the Lord: Catholic Chaplains Offer Hope and Healing to the Imprisoned," *The Catholic World Report* (February 22, 2012): http://www.catholicworldreport.com/Item/1136/bringing_the_lord.aspx#.UiSgrcnD-Uk.
20. The six-DVD set *Healing the Imprisoned: A Retreat* can be ordered from www.CommunityOfTheCross.com, specifically at: http://www.communityofthecross.com/healing-imprisoned-a-retreat.

21. Rev. David M. Schilder, *Inside the Fence: A Handbook for Those in Prison Ministry* (New York: Alba House, 1999), 35.
22. Kerry Weber, "Theology Behind Bars: A Jesuit Chaplain Brings St. Ignatius to San Quentin," *America* (July 2-9, 2012), 13: http://americamagazine. org/issue/5145/article/theology-behind-bars; slideshow of Fr. George Williams describing the program available at: http://www.youtube.com/ watch?v=6NFehmc-8uc&feature=youtu.be.
23. *Public Correctional Policy on Religious and Faith Practice,* American Correctional Association (Alexandria, VA, 2013).

CHAPTER 10
Pastoral Needs of Families of Inmates and of Staff

1. *Putting Children and Families First,* citing *Familiaris Consortio* and *Apostolicam Actuositatem.*
2. Carol Kent, *A New Kind of Normal: Hope-Filled Choices When Life Turns Upside Down* (Nashville: Thomas Nelson, 2007), 18.
3. Ibid., 20-22.
4. Carol Kent, *When I Lay My Isaac Down: Unshakable Faith in Unthinkable Circumstances* (Colorado Springs: NavPress, 2004).
5. Available from NavPress, PO Box 35002, Colorado Springs, CO 80935 www.navpress.com, specifically: http://www.navpress.com/ product/9781576839584/When-I-Lay-My-Isaac-Down-DVD-Carol.
6. Karen Heuberger and Ron Zeilinger, *Keeping Hope – A Resource for Families and Friends of the Incarcerated* (Atlanta: Visual Dynamics, Inc., 2015).
7. *The Sentencing Project,* "Incarcerated Parents and Their Children: Trends 1991-2007" (2009): http://www.sentencingproject.org/doc/publications/ publications/inc_incarceratedparents.pdf.
8. Susan D. Phillips, "Introduction: Children in Harm's Way," *Children in Harm's Way: Criminal Justice, Immigration Enforcement, and Child Welfare* (Washington, DC: Jointly published by The Sentencing Project and First Focus, 2013), 3: http://sentencingproject.org/doc/publications/ cc_Children%20in%20Harm's%20Way-final.pdf (citations omitted).
9. Charles R. Figley, *Helping Traumatized Families* (San Francisco: Jossey-Bass Publishers, 1989), 12-15.
10. Ibid., (as to functional family coping) 27-29; (as to dysfunctional family coping) 29-30.
11. *Compendium of the Social Doctrine of the Church,* ¶246.
12. *Familiaris Consortio,* ¶77.
13. Chesa Boudin, Trevor Stutz, and Aaron Littman, *Prison Visitation Policies: A Fifty State Survey* (November 5, 2012): http://ssrn.com/abstract=2171412 or http://dx.doi.org/10.2139/ssrn.2171412.

14. *Little Children, Big Challenges: Incarceration. A Guide to Support Parents and Caregivers* (New York: Sesame Workshop, 2013): http://www.sesamestreet. org/cms_services/services?action=download&uid=784d4f44-425b-445a-842b-86b5088cbcc5 .

15. Lori Constantino-Brown, "Can you tell me how to get, how to get to Sesame Street?" *Bridges of America Monthly Newsletter* (August 30, 2013); Bridges of America, 2001 Mercy Drive, Orlando, FL 32808 Ph. 407.291.1500: http:// www.bridgesofamerica.com.

16. Michael D. Crews, Secretary, "Florida Department of Corrections Region III Institutions and Sesame Street Help Children of Incarcerated Parents," Press Release of the Florida Department of Corrections, Tallahassee, Florida (August 24, 2013): http://www.dc.state.fl.us/secretary/press/2013/08-21-SesameStreet.html.

17. See, for example, Elizabeth Chuck, "Bizarre report claims that Kim Yong Un's ex-girlfriend has been executed," *NBC News* (August 29, 2013): "The source also reportedly said all of the families of those executed have been sent to prison camps under 'North Korea's barbaric principle of guilt by association,' according to the paper.": http://worldnews.nbcnews. com/_news/2013/08/29/20247358-bizarre-report-claims-kim-jong-uns-ex-girlfriend-executed?lite&lite=obnetwork.

18. Todd Shields, "Prison Phones Prove Captive Market for Private Equity," *Bloomberg News* (October 4, 2012): http://www.bloomberg.com/news/ articles/2012-10-04/prison-phones-prove-captive-market-for-private-equity.

19. Citizens United for Rehabilitation of Errants (CURE) and International CURE, P.O. Box 2310, Washington, DC 20013-2310 Phone: 202.789.2126: http://www.curenational.org/ and http://www.internationalcure.org/.

20. See David Segal, "Phoning from Prison, at Prices through the Roof," *The New York Times* (February 2, 2014), BU3: http://www.nytimes.com/2014/02/02/ your-money/phoning-from-prison-at-prices-through-the-roof.html?_r=2.

21. See Wright Petitioners' Alternative Rulemaking Proposal Talking Points http://apps.fcc.gov/ecfs/document/view?id=7021983331.

22. Federal Communications Commission Workshop on Reforming Inmate Calling Services Rates, July 10, 2013, 9:00 am - 4:30 pm EDT, Commission Meeting Room, 445 12th Street, S.W., Washington, DC: http://www.fcc.gov/ events/workshop-reforming-inmate-calling-services-rates.

23. Mike Ward, "Guards to join convict litigation over hot state prisons," *Austin American-Statesman*, [Statesman.com] August 29, 2013: http://www. statesman.com/news/news/guards-to-join-convict-litigation-over-hot-state-p/nZgSD/.

24. Lauren McCaughy, "Death Row Inmates Sue Angola Prison Over 'Extreme' Temperatures," *The Times Picayune* (June 10, 2013) [No decision yet recorded.] http://www.nola.com/crime/index.ssf/2013/06/death_row_inmates_sue_angola_p.html

25. See, for example, Hans Toch, *Stress in Policing* (Washington, DC: American Psychological Association, 2002), 75.
26. The plastic edges of laminated cards can be sharpened to a razor's edge and used to slit throats or wrists.

CHAPTER 11
Pastoral Needs of Newly Arrived Inmates, Inmates Facing Long or Life Sentences, and Inmates Facing Serious Illness and/or Death.

1. Antonio Spadaro, S.J., "A Big Heart Open to God: The exclusive interview with Pope Francis," *America*, September 30, 2013.
2. "The most commonly repeated phrase in the whole Bible, in both the Old Testament and the New Testament, is 'Have no fear!' or 'Do not be afraid!'" Rev. Felix Just, SJ, Ph.D., Loyola Institute for Spirituality, 480 South Batavia St., Orange, CA 92868-3907 Phone: 714-997-9587 ext. 28.
3. Pope Francis, *Audience Address to Participants in the National Meeting of Prison Chaplains, Discorso del Santo Padre Francesco al Partecipanti al Convegno Nazionale dei Cappellani delle Carceri Italiane* (October 23, 2013) .
4. 1 John 4.
5. Ibid.
6. *Salvifici Doloris*, ¶26.
7. *Christifideles Laici*, ¶48.
8. *Dignity of Older People*, Part III.
9. *Dignity of Older People*, Part IV.
10. Elisabeth Kübler-Ross, *On Death and Dying* (New York: Touchstone, 1969).
11. See *The Five Stages of Grief*, Elisabeth Kübler-Ross and David Kessler.
12. Aging with Dignity, P.O. Box 1661, Tallahassee FL 32302-1661; Ph. (850) 681-2010; Toll free: (888) 5WISHES (594-7437); Fax: (850) 681-2481.
13. Ibid.
14. Prost, S. G. (2015). *The perception gap in prison hospice: Correlates of inter-rater agreement.* (Unpublished doctoral dissertation prospectus). Florida State University, Tallahassee, FL; pp. 4-5.
15. National Hospice and Palliative Care Organization ("NHPCO"), 1731 King Street, Alexandria, Virginia 22314; Ph. 703-837-1500.
16. "End of Life Care in Corrections: The Facts," NHPCO.
17. Prost, S. G, p. 14.
18. Kirk Mitchell, "Colorado Prison Hospice Program Helps Inmates Die with Dignity," The Denver Post (February 17, 2013).
19. Mary Petrosky, F.M.M., "Praise Be My Lord through Sister Death: A Franciscan Spirituality of Dying," *Dying as a Franciscan: Approaching our Transitus to Eternal Life, Accompanying Others on the Way to Theirs* (St. Bonaventure, NY: Franciscan Institute Publications, 2011), 39.

CHAPTER 12
Pastoral Needs of Inmates in Confinement

1. Abraham J. Heschel, *Who Is Man?* (Stanford, CA: Stanford University Press, 1965), 47.
2. William Shakespeare, *Hamlet* (originally titled: *The tragedie of Hamlet, prince of Denmarke*) (1602).
3. *Who Is Man?*, 47.
4. Bureau of Justice Statistics, Special Report, "Suicide and Homicide in State Prisons and Local Jails," released August 5, 2005: http://www.bjs.gov/content/pub/pdf/shsplj.pdf.
5. Margaret E. Noonan and E. Ann Carson, *BJS Statisticians*, BJS, "Prison and Jail Deaths in Custody, 2000-2009 – Statistical Tables," released December 14, 2011 (NCJ 236219), Table 3: Mortality rate per 100,000 local jail inmates, by cause of death, 2000–2009, 6: http://www.bjs.gov/content/pub/pdf/pjdc0009st.pdf.
6. Ibid., Table 15: Mortality rate per 100,000 state prisoners, by cause of death, 2001–2009, 17.
7. Kevin Rector, "Killings in Md. Prisons Defy Efforts to Improve Security: Families of Slain Inmates Say They Want Answers," *The Baltimore Sun*, April 13, 2013: http://articles.baltimoresun.com/2013-04-13/news/bs-md-prison-homicides-20130413_1_prison-gangs-prison-officials-seven-prisoners.
8. Brian Palmer, "Which is Safer: City Streets or Prisons?" *Slate.com*, June 19 2013 2:29 pm: http://www.slate.com/articles/news_and_politics/explainer/2013/06/murder_rate_in_prison_is_it_safer_to_be_jailed_than_free.html.
9. Alan Gomez, "States Work to Curb Prison Violence," *USA Today.com*, August 21, 2008 10:17pm: http://usatoday30.usatoday.com/news/nation/2008-08-21-prisondeaths_N.htm.
10. "Summary of Findings and Recommendations, Confronting Confinement" (Washington, DC: Bipartisan Commission on Safety and Abuse in America's Prisons, 2006), 4: http://www.vera.org/project/commission-safety-and-abuse-americas-prisons.
11. Jenna Scafuri, "Administrative Segregation: Concerns and Recommendations from Corrections Experts," *On The Line* (ACA), vol. 36, no. 3, May 2013: http://www.aca.org/publications/otl/OTL_May2013/index.html.
12. Scafuri, "Administrative Segregation: Concerns and Recommendations."
13. The policy drafted by NAMI is discussed in chapter 14.
14. Scafuri, "Administrative Segregation: Concerns and Recommendations."
15. Jenna Scafuri, "Administrative Segregation: Continuing the Conversation," *On The Line* (ACA), vol. 36, no. 5, September, 2013: http://www.aca.org/publications/otl/current/index.html.
16. Scafuri, "Administrative Segregation: Continuing the Conversation."

17. Justice Fellowship, 44180 Riverside Parkway, Lansdowne, VA 20176 Ph. 1-800-206-9764 https://www.prisonfellowship.org/about/advocacy/.

18. Pat Nolan, President of Justice Fellowship, "Reassessing Solitary Confinement: The Human Rights, Fiscal, and Public Safety Consequences," Testimony before the Senate Judiciary Subcommittee on the Constitution, Civil Rights, and Human Rights, (June 19, 2012): http://www.judiciary.senate.gov/imo/media/doc/CHRG-112shrg87630.pdf.

19. *Responsibility, Rehabilitation, and Restoration*, 9, 41.

20. Editorial, "A Solitary Scandal," *America*, March 18, 2013, 5.

21. CNA, 4825 Mark Center Drive, Alexandria, VA 22311 USA Ph. 703.824.2000: https://www.cna.org/about.

22. The JFA Institute is a non-profit agency that works in partnership with federal, state, and local government agencies, and philanthropic foundations to evaluate criminal justice practices and design research-based policy solutions. JFA Institute, 720 Kearney St., Denver, CO 80220 Ph: (303) 399-3218 Fax: (303) 321-0363 http://www.jfa-associates.com/.

23. Kenneth McGinnis, "CNA Assesses the Management of Administrative Segregation Programs" The Tear Line, December 2012: https://www.cna.org/solution-centers/cnas-institute-public-research/safety-security/sas-newsletter-1.

24. Erica Goode, "Prisons Rethink Isolation, Saving Money, Lives and Sanity," *The New York Times*, March 10, 2012: http://www.nytimes.com/2012/03/11/us/rethinking-solitary-confinement.html?pagewanted=all.

25. Spiritual Formation in Segregation, SFS Ministries, Inc., 8918 W. 21st St. N., Ste. 200, #174, Wichita, KS 67205 Ph. (316) 461-2432.

26. Christopher M. Riggs (Catholic Advance), "Program Works to Make Saints Behind Bars," *Catholic News Agency*, September 7, 2008: http://www.catholicnewsagency.com/news/program_works_to_make_saints_behind_bars/

CHAPTER 13

Special Pastoral Needs of Women in Prison and of Inmates with Children

1. *Letter to Women*, ¶3.

2. *Responsibility, Rehabilitation and Restoration*, 10.

3. The summary in the next four paragraphs is based upon Lucia Zedner, "Wayward Sisters" in *Oxford History of the Prison*, 295-324.

4. *Oxford History of the Prison*, 297.

5. *The Sentencing Project*, "Women in the Criminal Justice System: Briefing Sheets." May 2007, text accompanying notes 1-5, 1: http://www.sentencingproject.org/doc/publications/womenincj_total.pdf.

6. *The Sentencing Project*, "The Changing Racial Dynamics of Women's Incarceration." February 2013, text accompanying note 14, 9: http://sentencingproject.org/doc/publications/rd_Changing%20Racial%20Dynamics%202013.pdf; citing Guerino, P.; Harrison, P.M.; & Sabol, W.J. Prisoners in 2010 (NCJ 236096) (Washington, DC: Bureau of Justice Statistics, 2012).
7. *Women in the Criminal Justice System*, text accompanying notes 2-3, 3.
8. Ibid., text accompanying notes 4-8, 3.
9. Ibid., text accompanying note 8, 2.
10. Ibid., text accompanying notes 1-4, 4.
11. Ibid., text accompanying notes 5-10, 4.
12. Ibid., text accompanying notes 1-3, 3.
13. *Women in Prison*.
14. Citing GAO report "Women in Prison: Sexual Misconduct by Correctional Staff" June 1999, p. 9.
15. *The Changing Racial Dynamics of Women's Incarceration*, 9-10.
16. *Women in the Criminal Justice System*, text accompanying notes 1-9, 5.
17. Julie K. Brown, "Rats, bugs and 'natural' deaths at Florida women's prison, the nation's largest," *The Miami Herald,* December 26, 2015: http://www.msn.com/en-us/news/us/rats-bugs-and-%e2%80%98natural%e2%80%99-deaths-at-florida-women%e2%80%99s-prison-the-nation%e2%80%99s-largest/ar-BBnVFU0?ocid=se
18. Ibid.
19. *Women in the Criminal Justice System*, text accompanying notes 11-12, 4.
20. Incarcerated Parents and Their Children, 1-2, citing Dallaire, D.H. (2007). Incarcerated mothers and fathers: A Comparison of risks for children and families. *Family Relations,* 56(5), 440-453.
21. Silva J.A. Talvi, *Women Behind Bars: The Crisis of Women in the U.S. Prison System* (Emeryville, CA: Seal Press, 2007), 56-58.
22. Cristina Rathbone, *A World Apart: Women, Prison, and Life Behind Bars* (New York: Random House, 2005), xii.
23. *Women in Prison*, p. 2, citing *Mulieris Dignitatem*.
24. *Familiaris Consortio*, ¶22 (citations omitted).
25. *Familiaris Consortio*, ¶24 (citations omitted).
26. *Letter to Women of the World*, ¶3.
27. *Mulieris Dignitatem*, ¶¶12-13.
28. *Social Doctrine of the Church*, ¶403.
29. *Familiaris Consortio*, ¶77.
30. Institute on Women & Criminal Justice, *Mothers, Infants and Imprisonment: A National Look at Prison Nurseries and Community-Based Alternatives*, May 2009, (New York: Women's Prison Association); http://www.wpaonline.org/wpaassets/Mothers_Infants_and_Imprisonment_2009.pdf .
31. The Federal Bureau of Prisons, an agency of the U.S. Department of Justice,

Female Offender Programs: http://www.bop.gov/inmates/custody_and_care/female_offenders.jsp .

32. "Senators Oppose Female Inmate Transfer: 1,100 Women to be Moved out of Danbury," *The Hartford Courant*, August 2, 2013: http://articles.courant.com/2013-08-02/news/hc-danbury-inmates-transfer-0803-20130802_1_female-inmates-women-inmates-danbury.

33. Catherine's Center, Society of St. Vincent de Paul of San Mateo County, 50 North B Street, San Mateo, CA 94401: http://svdp-sanmateoco.org/catherine.html.

34. Suzi Desmond, SVdP's Catherine's Center September Report (2013), http://svdp-sanmateoco.org/SanMateo_NewSite/PDFs/CC%20Report%20September%202013.pdf.

35. Rachel's Vineyard Ministries, 808 N. Henderson Road 2nd Floor, King of Prussia, PA 19406 Ph. (610) 354-0555 http://www.rachelsvineyard.org/. *Rachel's Vineyard* is transdenominational. Project Rachel is a specific ministry of the Catholic Church for those who have been involved in abortion. It is a diocesan-based network of specially trained priests, religious, counselors, and laypersons who provide a team response of care for those suffering in the aftermath of abortion. In addition to referring for Sacramental Reconciliation, the ministry provides an integrated network of services, including pastoral counseling, support groups, retreats, and referrals to licensed mental health professionals.

36. Linda Reeves, "Ministers Heal and Free Prisoners' Souls," *The Florida Catholic*, October 12-25, 2012, 16: http://www.rachelsvineyard.org/PDF/Articles/PrisonerRachelMinistry.pdf.

CHAPTER 14
Special Pastoral Needs of Inmates Dealing with Mental Illness

1. Most Reverend Thomas Wenski, then Bishop of Orlando, now Archbishop of Miami, "Prison," *Catholic News Agency*, July 9, 2009: http://www.catholicnewsagency.com/column.php?n=846.

2. Steve Bousquet, "Florida Considers Reopening Prisons," *Miami Herald*, November 3, 2013: http://www.miamiherald.com/news/state/article1957049.html.

3. Wenski, "Prison."

4. See Risdon N. Slate and W. Wesley Johnson, *Criminalization of Mental Illness: Crisis and Opportunity for the Justice System* (Durham, NC: Carolina Academic Press, 2008), 13-23.

5. Ibid., 19-20.

6. "Locked In: the Costly Criminalization of the Mentally Ill," *The Economist*, August 3, 2013: http://www.economist.com/news/united-states/21582535-costly-criminalisation-mentally-ill-locked.

7. This summary is adapted and updated from Recinella, *The Biblical Truth*, 218-219.

8. Citing Human Rights Watch, *Ill-Equipped: U.S. Prisons and Offenders with Mental Illness*, (New York: Human Rights Watch, 2003), 19.

9. Ibid., 20.

10. Ibid., 18.

11. Adam C. Smith, "Care of Mentally Ill Prisoners Questioned: For the One in Nine Who Is Severely Ill, Prison Can Lead to Violence, Abuse and Even Death, Experts Say," *St. Petersburg Times*, September 28, 1999: http://www.sptimes.com/News/92899/State/Care_of_mentally_ill_.shtml.

12. Dean Aufderheide, Ph.D., "Mental Illness In America's Jails And Prisons: Toward A Public Safety/Public Health Model," Health Affairs Blog (April 1, 2014): http://healthaffairs.org/blog/2014/04/01/mental-illness-in-americas-jails-and-prisons-toward-a-public-safetypublic-health-model/.

13. *Jubilee of the Disabled*, ¶¶2 and 5.

14. *Message for the Sick*.

15. *People with Disabilities*.

16. National Catholic Partnership on Disability (NCPD), 415 Michigan Avenue NE, Suite 95, Washington, DC 20017-4501 Ph. (202) 529-2933, email ncpd@ncpd.org: http://www.ncpd.org/views-news-policy/policy/church/vatican.

17. See http://www.ncpd.org/ministries-programs/specific/mentalillness.

18. http://www.ncpd.org/ministries-programs/specific/mentalillness/framework.

19. *Affirming the Dignity of the Mentally Ill* (Lincoln, NE: Nebraska Bishop's Conference, January 2005): http://www.nebcathcon.org/bishops'_statements.htm#Mental.

20. *Illnesses of the Human Mind*, ¶8.

21. *Salvifici Doloris*, ¶22.

22. *Illnesses of the Human Mind*, ¶8.

23. *Illnesses of the Human Mind*, ¶2.

24. The National Alliance on Mental Illness (NAMI), 3803 N. Fairfax Drive, Suite 100, Arlington, VA 22203, Ph. Main: (703) 524-7600, Toll free: (800) 950-NAMI, Fax: (703) 524-9094, www.nami.org.

25. NAMI, "Mental Illness: FACTS AND NUMBERS," (2013): http://www.nami.org/factsheets/mentalillness_factsheet.pdf.

26. Citing National Institutes of Health, National Institute of Mental Health. (n.d.). Statistics: Any Disorder Among Adults. Retrieved March 5, 2013, from http://www.nimh.nih.gov/statistics/1ANYDIS_ADULT.shtml.

27. Citing National Institutes of Health, National Institute of Mental Health. (n.d.) *The Numbers Count: Mental Disorders in America*. Retrieved March 5, 2013, from http://www.nimh.nih.gov/health/publications/the-numbers-count-mental-disorders-in-america/index.shtml. Prevalence numbers were calculated using NIMH percentages (cited) and 2010 Census data. Census data is available at: United States Census Bureau. (revised 2011). "USA [State

& County QuickFacts]." Retrieved March 5, 2013, from http://quickfacts.
census.gov/qfd/states/00000.html

28. Ibid.
29. Ibid.
30. Citing Substance Abuse and Mental Health Services Administration.
    (2012). *Results from the 2010 National Survey on Drug Use and Health:
    Mental Health Findings* NSDUH Series H-42, HHS Publication No. (SMA)
    11-4667). Rockville, Md.: Substance Abuse and Mental Health Services
    Administration, 2012 (retrieved January 15, 2016 at: http://www.samhsa.gov/
    data/sites/default/files/NSDUHmhfr2012/NSDUHmhfr2012.pdf).
31. Citing U.S. Department of Housing and Urban Development, Office of
    Community Planning and Development. (2011). *The 2010 Annual Homeless
    Assessment Report to Congress* (retrieved January 15, 2016 at: https://www.
    hudexchange.info/resources/documents/2010HomelessAssessmentReport.
    pdf).
32. Citing Glaze, L.E. & James, D.J. (2006, updated December). Mental Health
    Problems of Prison and Jail Inmates. *Bureau of Justice Statistics Special
    Report*. U.S. Department of Justice, Office of Justice Programs Washington,
    DC Retrieved March 5, 2013, from http://bjs.ojp.usdoj.gov/content/pub/pdf/
    mhppji.pdf.
33. NAMI, *Criminalization Facts* (2013): http://www.nami.org/Template.
    cfm?Section=CIT&Template=/ContentManagement/ContentDisplay.
    cfm&ContentID=57465.
34. Citing James, D, and Glaze, L. (2006). "Mental health problems of prison and
    jail inmates. US Department of Justice, Bureau of Justice Statistics." *Bureau of
    Justice Statistics Special Report*.
35. Citing Ditton, P. M. (2006). "Mental Health and Treatment of Inmates
    and Probationers." US Department of Justice, Bureau of Justice Statistics,
    NCJ174463.
36. Citing Kessler RC, Chiu WT, Demler O, Walters EE. (2005). "Prevalence,
    severity, and comorbidity of twelve-month DSM-IV disorders in the
    National Comorbidity Survey Replication (NCS-R)." *Archives of General
    Psychiatry*, 62(6):617-27.
37. Citing Ditton, "Mental Health and Treatment of Inmates and Probationers."
38. Citing Fisher, W., Roy-Bujnowski, K., Grudzinskas, A., Clayfield, J., Banks, S.,
    and Wolff, N. (2006). "Patterns and prevalence of arrest in a statewide cohort
    of mental health care consumers." *Psychiatric Services*, 57, 1623-1628.
39. Citing McNiel, D., Binder, R., and Robinson, J. (2005). "Incarceration
    associated with homelessness, mental disorder, and co-occurring substance
    abuse." *Psychiatric Services*, 56, 840-846.
40. Citing Butterfield, Fox. (1998) "Asylums Behind Bars: A special report:
    Prisons Replace Hospitals for the Nation's Mentally Ill." *New York Times*:
    http://www.nytimes.com/1998/03/05/us/asylums-behind-bars-special-report-

prisons-replace-hospitals-for-nation-s.html.
41. Citing McNiel, "Incarceration associated with homelessness."
42. Citing James, "Mental health problems of prison and jail inmates."
43. Citing Judge David A. Bazelon Center for Mental Health Law. "Finding the Key to successful transition from jail to the community: An Explanation of Federal Medicaid and Disability Program Rules" (November 2009): http://www.bazelon.org/LinkClick.aspx?fileticket=Bd6LW9BVRhQ=&tabid=104.
44. NAMI, *Criminalization Facts* (2013).
45. Citing Borum, R., Deane, M.D., Steadman, H., & Morrissey, J. (1998). "Police perspectives on responding to mentally ill people in crisis: perceptions of program effectiveness." *Behavioral Sciences and the Law*, 16, 393-405; and Sheridan, E., & Teplin, L. (1981). "Police-referred psychiatric emergencies: advantages of community treatment." *Journal of Community Psychology*, 9, 140-147.
46. Citing Naples, M., & Steadman, H. (2003). "Can persons with co-occurring disorders and violent charges be successfully diverted?" *International Journal of Forensic Mental Health*, 2, 137-143.
47. Citing TAPA Center for Jail Diversion. (2004). "What can we say about the effectiveness of jail diversion programs for persons with co-occurring disorders?" The National GAINS Center. Accessed December 19, 2007 at: http://gainscenter.samhsa.gov/pdfs/jail_diversion/WhatCanWeSay.pdf.
48. Citing Ridgely, et al. (2007). "Justice, Treatment, and Cost." Council of State Governments. Accessed Dec 11, 2007 at: http://www.rand.org/news/press/2007/03/01/index.html.
49. Citing Calhane, D., Metraux, S., & Hadley, T. (2001). "The impact of supportive housing for homeless people with severe mental illness on the utilization of the public health, corrections, and emergency shelter systems: the New York-New York initiative." Fannie Mae Foundation.
50. Citing Lamberti, JS, Weisman, R, and Fadin DI. (2004). "Forensic Assertive Community Treatment: preventing incarceration of adults with severe mental illnesses." *Psychiatric Services*, 55 (11), 1285-1293. (Percentages calculated from data presented.)
51. Florida Partners in Crisis, 175 Marlin Drive, Merritt Island, FL 32952 Ph. 321-453-8825 http://flpic.org/.
52. Ibid., Re-Entry: http://flpic.org/re-entry/.
53. NAMI, *Decriminalizing Mental Illness: Background and Recommendations* – A White Paper Prepared by the Forensic Taskforce of the NAMI Board of Directors September 2008: (Executive Summary available at: https://www.namigdm.org/documents/filelibrary/about_us/Decrimializing_Mental_9AE58A23CC568.pdf
54. Mark Walker, "Locked in Limbo: Court delays leave mentally ill waiting behind bars," *Argus Leader*, November 14, 2015: http://www.argusleader.com/story/news/2015/11/14/court-delays-leave-mentally-ill-waiting-behind-

bars/75362910/

55. Eric M. Johnson, Curtis Skinner and Miral Fahmy, "Federal judge in Seattle orders end to long jail holds for mentally ill," Reuters, April 3, 2015: http://www.reuters.com/article/us-usa-washington-inmates-idUSKBN0MU09020150403.

56. Richard Dieter, *Battle Scars: Military Veterans and the Death Penalty* (Death Penalty Information Center: Washington, DC, Veterans Day 2015): http://deathpenaltyinfo.org/files/pdf/BattleScars.pdf

57. James P. Cullen, David R. Irvine, and Stephen N. Xenakis, "Vets suffering from PTSD need our help: Too many veterans are sentenced to death row by judges and juries who don't understand," *USA Today*, November 12, 2015: http://www.usatoday.com/story/opinion/2015/11/11/vets-suffering-ptsd-need-our-help-death-row-column/75520218/.

58. *NAMI Public Policy Platform, Revised, Tenth Edition (National Alliance on Mental Illness)*, Section 10 Criminal Justice and Forensic Issues (September 2014): http://www.nami.org/template.cfm?section=NAMI_Policy_Platform.

59. See, http://www.ncpd.org/ministries-programs/specific/mentalillness/resources/patronsaint.

60. Jackie Goldstein, *Geel, Belgium: A Model of "Community Recovery"* (2009), Samford University Psychology Department, http://faculty.samford.edu/~jlgoldst.

61. *Preparation for the Jubilee Day 3 December 2000: Part Four The Person with Disabilities: Subject – Receiver of Evangelization and Catechesis*, May 17, 2000: http://www.vatican.va/jubilee_2000/jubilevents/jub_disabled_20001203_scheda4_en.htm.

CHAPTER 15
Economic Constraints that Affect
Prison Ministry and Restorative Justice

1. *Address to Meeting with the Poor.*

2. "Pope, in Assisi, calls on church to renounce 'spirit of the world,'" *Catholic News Service*, October 4, 2013: http://www.catholicnews.com/data/stories/cns/1304184.htm.

3. Pope Francis, *Address to Meeting with the Poor.*

4. David M. Reuter, "Florida DOC and Keefe Gouge Prisoners on Commissary Sales," *Prison Legal News*, October 15, 2009 (citing as sources: Contract between FDOC and Keefe Commissary Network, Associated Press): https://www.prisonlegalnews.org/news/2009/oct/15/florida-doc-and-keefe-gouge-prisoners-on-commissary-sales/.

5. Press Release: "Gainesville Businessmen Sentenced to Federal Prison for Roles in Paying Kickbacks to Former Florida Department of Corrections Officials," U.S. Attorney's Office, Middle District of Florida, January 17,

2012: https://www.fbi.gov/jacksonville/press-releases/2012/gainesville-businessmen-sentenced-to-federal-prison-for-roles-in-paying-kickbacks-to-former-florida-department-of-corrections-officials.

6. Paul Egan, "Michigan's new prison food contractor accused of skimping on size and quality of meals to boost profits," *The Detroit Free Press*, May 7, 2013: http://www.freep.com/article/20130507/NEWS06/305080007/.

7. Simon McCormack, "Florida Gives Huge Contracts to Prison Health Care Providers Plagued by Lawsuits," *The Huffington Post*, October 4, 2013: http://www.huffingtonpost.com/2013/10/04/florida-prison-health-care-contracts_n_4045943.html?view=print&comm_ref=false.

8. Ibid.

9. Joni James, "Prisons agency failing the state: The watchdog agency of privately run prisons likely will be disbanded as Gov. Bush admits to bumps in privatization efforts," *St. Petersburg Times*, April 25, 2004: http://www.sptimes.com/2004/04/25/news_pf/State/Prisons_agency_failin.shtml.

10. Joni James, "Head of private prison commission resigns: The independent Correctional Privatization Commission, stripped of authority, may not survive," *St. Petersburg Times*, May 20, 2004: http://www.sptimes.com/2004/05/20/news_pf/State/Head_of_private_priso.shtml.

11. Joni James, "Ex-prisons official admits thefts: While heading a board overseeing private prison contracts, Alan Duffee stole nearly $225,000," *St. Petersburg Times*, February 14, 2006: http://www.sptimes.com/2006/02/14/news_pf/Tampabay/Ex_prisons_official_a.shtml.

12. Jennifer Liberto, "Ex-state prison official sentenced to prison: While director of a board that oversaw the state's private prison contracts, he admits mail fraud, wire fraud and money laundering." *St. Petersburg Times*, April 21, 2006: http://www.sptimes.com/2006/04/21/news_pf/State/Ex_state_prison_offic.shtml.

13. *The Sentencing Project*, "Too Good to be True: Private Prisons in America," January 2012, 1; http://www.sentencingproject.org/doc/publications/inc_Too_Good_to_be_True.pdf; citing Guerino, P.; Harrison, P.M.; & Sabol, P.M. (2011). Prisoners in 2010. Washington, DC: Bureau of Justice Statistics: available online: http://www.bjs.gov/content/pub/pdf/p10.pdf.

14. Michael Barajas, ICE Awards Contract to Private Prison Company That Was Just Slammed in Federal Report, *Houston Press*, September 22, 2015: http://www.houstonpress.com/news/ice-awards-contract-to-private-prison-company-that-was-just-slammed-in-federal-report-7785696.

15. U. S. Commission on Civil Rights Releases Report on Condition in Immigration Detention Centers and Family Detainees, News Release, September 17, 2015: http://www.usccr.gov/press/2015/PR_ReportReleasedCCR_9-17-15.pdf.

16. Carol Wolf, "State Budgets: The Public-Private Indiana Toll Road Is in Trouble," *Bloomberg Businessweek*, July 7, 2011: http://www.businessweek.

com/magazine/the-publicprivate-indiana-toll-road-is-in-trouble-07072011. html; *Private Roads, Public Costs: The Facts About Toll Road Privatization and How to Protect the Public* (Spring 2009), U.S. PIRG Education Fund (US Public Interest Research Group): Main Office: 294 Washington St, Suite 500 • Boston, MA 02108 Ph. (617) 747-4370 Federal Advocacy Office: 218 D Street SE, 1st Fl. • Washington, DC 20003 Ph. (202) 546-9707: http://www.uspirg. org/sites/pirg/files/reports/Private-Roads-Public-Costs-Updated_1.pdf.

17. Michael A. Lindenberger, "Private toll roads get new push in Texas," *The Dallas Morning News*, January 10, 2011: http://www.dallasnews.com/news/ politics/texas-legislature/headlines/20110104-private-toll-roads-get-new- push-in-texas.ece.

18. Update: See, "Convergys Questions and Answers," Attorney General Pam Bondi, Florida Office of the Attorney General: http://myfloridalegal.com/ pages.nsf/Main/01AB6B8F8E36A253852571410071237F.

19. Edwin Bender, *A Contributing Influence: The Private-Prison Industry and Political Giving in the South,* The National Institute on Money in State Politics, April 28, 2002: http://static.prisonpolicy.org/scans/20020430. pdf; updated and further analyzed in Geoffrey McGovern and Michael D. Greenberg, *Shining a Light on State Campaign Finance: An Evaluation of the Impact of the National Institute on Money in State Politics* (RAND Corporation: Santa Monica, CA, 2014), http://www.rand.org/content/dam/ rand/pubs/research_reports/RR700/RR791/RAND_RR791.pdf.

20. Update: See Policy Lock-down: Prison Interests Court Political Players, The National Institute on Money in State Politics, April 2006: http://www. policyarchive.org/handle/10207/5988.

21. Editorial, "Privatization nightmare: The commission created to oversee private contracts for state prisons is being disbanded after questioning the cost of doing business with two big campaign contributors," *St. Petersburg Times*, May 1, 2004: http://www.sptimes.com/2004/05/01/news_pf/Opinion/ Privatization_nightma.shtml.

22. Kevin J Wells, "America's for profit prisons: Greed over Justice," Communities Digital, February 5, 2014: http://www.commdiginews.com/life/americas-for- profit-prisons-greed-over-justice-7187/.

23. Jon Schuppe, "Pennsylvania Seeks to Close Books on 'Kids for Cash' Scandal," *NBC News* (August 12, 2015): http://www.nbcnews.com/news/ us-news/pennsylvania-seeks-close-books-kids-cash-scandal-n408666

24. Michael A. Hallett, *Private Prisons in America: A Critical Race Perspective* (Chicago: University of Illinois Press, 2006).

25. Recinella, *The Biblical Truth.*

26. *Private Prisons in America*, 49.

27. Byron Eugene Price, *Merchandizing Prisoners: Who Really Pays for Prison Privatization?* (London: Praeger, 2006).

28. *The Catechism of the Catholic Church,* ¶2266.

29. *Social Doctrine of the Church,* ¶403.
30. *Wardens from Wall Street.*
31. *The Sentencing Project,* "Dollars and Detainees: The Growth of For-Profit Detention – July 2012, 1: http://sentencingproject.org/doc/publications/inc_Dollars_and_Detainees.pdf.
32. *Prison Policy Initiative,* PO Box 127, Northampton, MA 01061: http://www.prisonpolicy.org/contact.html.
33. Bernadette Rabuy and Daniel Kopf, *Prisons of Poverty: Uncovering the Pre-incarceration Incomes of the Imprisoned* (Prison Policy Initiative: Northampton, MA, July 9, 2015): available at: http://www.prisonpolicy.org/reports/income.html.
34. *Challenges for Criminal Justice.*
35. *Responsibility, Rehabilitation and Restoration,* 25.
36. *Social Doctrine of the Church,* ¶329.
37. Emma Green, "How Should America Deal With the Sinners in Its Prisons?: Pope Francis's visit to the Curran-Fromhold Correctional Facility in Philadelphia represents a different way of thinking about the humans behind bars," *The Atlantic,* September 28, 2015: http://www.theatlantic.com/politics/archive/2015/09/how-should-america-deal-with-the-sinners-in-its-prisons/407623/.
38. Sari Horwitz, "The U.S. is set to release thousands of prisoners early. Here's where they're headed," *The Washington Post,* October 7, 2015: https://www.washingtonpost.com/news/post-nation/wp/2015/10/07/the-u-s-is-set-to-release-thousands-of-prisoners-early-heres-where-theyre-headed/.
39. Over-Criminalization in Florida: An Analysis of Nonviolent Third-degree Felonies (Florida TaxWatch: Tallahassee, FL, April 2014): http://floridataxwatch.org/resources/pdf/ThirdDegreeFINAL.pdf.
40. Dominic M. Calabro, "TaxWatch Calls for Sentencing Review Following Obama's Commutation," Florida TaxWatch, Press Release, July 15, 2015.
41. Rebecca U. Thorpe, Republicans and Democrats support sentencing reform. This is what stands in their way." *The Washington Post – Monkey Cage,* October 5, 2015: http://www.washingtonpost.com/blogs/monkey-cage/wp/2015/10/05/republicans-and-democrats-support-sentencing-reform-this-is-what-stands-in-their-way/.
42. Rebecca U. Thorpe, assistant professor of political science at the University of Washington, in Tim Marema, "The Politics of Prisons: Location Affects Legislators' Voting on Criminal Reform," *The Daily Yonder* (The Center for Rural Strategies), October 14, 2015: http://www.dailyyonder.com/the-politics-of-prisons-location-affects-legislators-voting-on-criminal-reform/2015/10/14/9102/.
43. Historical information is taken from Florida Department of Corrections, *Florida Corrections Centuries of Progress: 1821-2003*: http://www.dc.state.fl.us/oth/timeline/.

44. Law Enforcement Perspectives on Fighting Crime (A National Poll by Hart): available at http://www.deathpenaltyinfo.org/front-line-law-enforcement-views-death-penalty#sxn2; analyzed in depth in *On the Front Line: Law Enforcement Views on the Death Penalty*, by Richard C. Dieter, Esq. Executive Director, Death Penalty Information Center, Washington, DC (February 1995): http://www.deathpenaltyinfo.org/front-line-law-enforcement-views-death-penalty.

CHAPTER 16
Religious Constraints that Affect
Prison Ministry and Restorative Justice.

1. *Evangelii Gaudium*, ¶180.
2. Ibid., ¶¶ 183 and 188.
3. Since 1973, Florida has had 26 people released from death row for innocence, twice the number in Texas and multiples more than any other U.S. death penalty state.
4. Andrew Skotnicki, *Religion and the Development of the American Penal System* (New York: University Press of America, 2000).
5. Ibid, 4.
6. Ibid., 12-13.
7. *Sing Sing* is short for Sing Sing Correctional Facility, a maximum security men's prison in Ossining (Westchester County), New York, run by the New York State Department of Corrections and Supervision and has a capacity of about 1,700 inmates.
8. T. Richard Snyder, *The Protestant Ethic and the Spirit of Punishment* (Grand Rapids, MI: Eerdmans, 2001), 1.
9. Ibid., 3.
10. Ibid., 11-15.
11. For example, see, Rev. Shane Claiborne, *Executing Grace: How the Death Penalty Killed Jesus and Why It's Killing Us* (New York: HarperOne, 2016).
12. *The Protestant Ethic and the Spirit of Punishment*, pp. 17-24.
13. New Advent: Barry, W. (1908). Calvinism. In *The Catholic Encyclopedia*. New York: Robert Appleton Company: http://www.newadvent.org/cathen/03198a.htm.
14. David Van Biema, "The New Calvinism," *Time Magazine*, March 12, 2009: http://content.time.com/time/specials/packages/article/0,28804,1884779_1884782_1884760,00.html.
15. Collin Hansen, "Young, Restless, Reformed: Calvinism Is Making a Comeback—and Shaking Up the Church," *Christianity Today*, September 22, 2006: http://www.christianitytoday.com/ct/2006/september/42.32.html.
16. Josh Burek, "Christian Faith: Calvinism Is Back—In America's Christian Faith, a Surprising Comeback of Rock-ribbed Calvinism Is Challenging the

Jesus-is-your-buddy Gospel of Modern Evangelism," *The Christian Science Monitor*, March 27, 2010: http://www.csmonitor.com/layout/set/print/USA/Society/2010/0327/Christian-faith-Calvinism-is-back.

17. *No Peace Without Justice.*
18. *Evangelii Gaudium*, ¶218.
19. *Restorative Justice.*
20. Ibid.
21. Jan Pudlow, "Are Problem-Solving Courts the Answer?" *The Florida Bar News*, December 1, 2013, 1: https://www.floridabar.org/__85256AA9005B9F25.nsf/0/E94ADA852C91852985257C2E004809AF?OpenDocument; and "Drug Courts: Twice the Bang for Half the Bucks," *The Florida Bar News*, December 1, 2013, 6: https://www.floridabar.org/DIVCOM/JN/JNNews01.nsf/8c9f13012b96736985256aa900624829/64ca61c082391e7e85257c2e004a0c38!OpenDocument.
22. Jan Pudlow, "Stop Treating Mental Illness as a Crime," *The Florida Bar News*, December 1, 2013, 6: https://www.floridabar.org/DIVCOM/JN/jnnews01.nsf/8c9f13012b96736985256aa900624829/c2729bf949577c1b85257c2e0048ea93!OpenDocument.
23. Jan Pudlow, "Our Veterans Need Help," *The Florida Bar News*, December 1, 2013, 7: https://www.floridabar.org/DIVCOM/JN/9/687bc1e8bcbffa8a85257c2e0049f2ca!OpenDocument.
24. *Post-Release from Prison.*
25. *Call for Action.*
26. *Familiaris Consortio*, ¶41.

CLOSING THOUGHTS

1. Bishop Gregory Parkes, "The Presence of Christ in Prison," *The Catholic Compass* (September/October 2014), 4.
2. *Evangelii Gaudium*, ¶¶222-223.
3. *Evangelii Gaudium*, ¶¶270-271.
4. *Archbishop Oscar Romero Prayer: A Step Along the Way.*

ACKNOWLEDGMENTS

Readers will quickly note that I have taken the position of a tour guide, a narrator of sorts, who leads the way into the hidden world inside the prison fences, all the while incorporating the official teachings of the Catholic Church and the myriad of compilations of facts and studies produced by the specialists in this hidden world. There is no shortage of people to thank for their assistance in the four year effort that resulted in this book.

First of all, thank you to the generosity of the ACTA Foundation and Art and Nancy Gase, whose financial assistance made this book possible. My gratitude also goes to all those who reviewed the various drafts of the manuscript as it edged toward completion, including my wife and partner in ministry, Susan, and our dear friends and colleagues in service, Jim and Lois Galbraith, Rick and Kathy Wissel, Roger and Carol Tompkins, Michael Sheedy, Ingrid Delgado, Michael Pearson, Michael Savage, Lee Chotas, Tom Lang, Dr. Don Barnhorst, William Koenig, Bob Fredericks, Peggy Stanton, Robert Mylod, Steven and Marilyn Hammond, Peter Cowdrey, Arnold Leporati, the sisters of the Poor Clare Monastery in Spokane, Washington, and Barb Ries; also our clergy, including Bishop Felipe Estévez, Fr. Slawomir Bielasiewicz, Fr. Dustin Feddon, Deacons David Williams, Jason Roy, Ray Aguado, Edgardo Farias, Larry Geinosky, and Rev. Robert Richter, Region II Lead Chaplain for the Florida Department of Corrections; and also my students, including Jerry Ciesla, Claudio Gaeta, William Conley, Albert Holzschuh, Chandra Hanson, Vega Girodo, and Jeffrey J. Guiffre.

Special thanks to the staff at ACTA Publications, especially my editor and publisher, Greg Pierce, and graphic artist and typesetter, Patricia Lynch, whose cover design and layout capture the spirit of this work in powerful imagery; and to Rachael Kirk who has spent untold hours in proofreading and other administrative tasks essential to completing this book.

So many others have done tremendous work that was necessary to make this effort possible. I hope that my inclusion of their research, investigations, reports, and analyses will serve as my statement of gratitude for their invaluable contributions.

ABOUT THE AUTHOR

For over twenty years, layman Dale Recinella (generally known as "Brother Dale" by the inmates he serves) has been an outside chaplain in prison ministry handling general population and every category of special confinement, including medical and psychiatric units and cell-front ministry in long-term solitary confinement and death row as well as deathwatch spiritual counseling in Florida's death house. He is a certified Catholic Correctional Chaplain serving under the Bishop of St. Augustine and the Pastor of St. Mary's Mother of Mercy Parish in Macclenny, Florida.

Chaplain Recinella is a licensed Florida lawyer and graduate of University of Notre Dame Law School and had a successful career in the financial industry before leaving to do prison ministry full time. He holds a Master's in Theological Studies in Catholic Pastoral Theology from Ave Maria University, Naples, Florida, and has supervised pastoral internships in prison ministry for candidates for Catholic priesthood and the permanent diaconate. Dale has taught the course in "Credible and Effective Ministry in Prison and Detention Settings" for the Pastoral Certification Program at Saint Leo's University, Tampa, Florida. His ministry work has received numerous recognitions, including the Humanitarian Award from the Franciscan Alumni Association and, at the request of the Catholic Bishops of Florida, the 2016 Holy Cross *Pro Ecclesia et Pontifice*, the highest papal honor a lay person can receive in the Catholic Church, for distinguished service to the Church.

After living for seventeen years in Macclenny, Florida, just fifteen miles from death row, Dale and his wife, Susan, now reside in Tallahassee and are members of Good Shepherd Catholic Church. Brother Dale still ministers at death row and in the death house, making the 2.5-hour commute to Starke, Florida, weekly. Susan, who for fourteen years has served as his partner to minister to the families of the condemned (while Dale is witnessing at the execution for the inmate), continues to serve in that role as often as possible. They have five adult children and numerous grandchildren.

ALSO AVAILABLE

....

Life in Christ
A Catholic Catechism for Adults
336 pages, paperback

Spanish Edition: La Vida en Cristo
Catecismo para Adultos
338 pages, paperback

....

The Confirmed Catholic's Companion
Sr. Mary Kathleen Glavich, SND
224 pages, paperback

....

Invitation to Catholicism
Alice Camille
234 pages, paperback

....

Catholics and Fundamentalists
Rev. Martin Pable, OFM Cap
96 pages, paperback

Spanish Edition: Católicos y Fundamentalistas
Rev. Martin Pable, OFM Cap
96 pages, paperback

....

The College Study Bible
2,048 pages, paperback

....

Available from booksellers
or from ACTA Publications
www.actapublications.com • 800-397-2282